BAY OF PIGS DECLASSIFIED

# BAY OF PIGS
# DECLASSIFIED

*THE SECRET CIA REPORT ON THE INVASION OF CUBA*

EDITED BY
PETER KORNBLUH

THE NEW PRESS    NEW YORK
1998

Published in the United States by The New Press, New York
Distributed by W. W. Norton & Company, Inc., New York

Established in 1990 as a major alternative to the large, commercial publishing houses, The New Press
is the first full-scale nonprofit American book publisher operating in the public interest, rather than
for private gain; it is committed to publishing in innovative ways works of educational, cultural , and
community value that, despite their intellectual merits, might not normally be commercially viable.
The New Press's editorial offices are located at the City University of New York.

www.thenewpress.com

PRINTED IN THE UNITED STATES OF AMERICA

9  8  7  6  5  4  3  2  1

This book is dedicated to

*Deborah Hauger*
*and*
*Barry Sklar*

two deeply respected, much loved, and dearly missed members of Washington's Cuba community, who both understood that uncovering the past is fundamental to improving the present, and future, of U.S.-Cuban relations.

# —Contents

Introduction: History Held Hostage: The Bay of Pigs
Report in Context   1
— The Perfect Failure   2
— Who Lost Cuba?: Invasion Historiography   4
— Revisiting the Bay of Pigs   5
— The Kirkpatrick Report   10
— The Bissell Rebuttal   13
— Lessons Not Learned   14

Key Actors and Acronyms   21

Part I.   The Inspector General's Survey of the Cuban
Operation, October 1961   23
— Introduction   23
— History of the Project   24
— Summary of Evaluation   41
— Evaluation of Organization and Command Structure   42
— Evaluation of Staffing   45
— Evaluation of Planning   47
— The Miami Operating Base   58
— The Political Front and the Relation of Cubans to the Project   66
— Clandestine Paramilitary Operations — Air   75
— Clandestine Paramilitary Operations — Maritime   82
— Clandestine Paramilitary Operations — Training
Underground Leaders   90
— Security   95
— Americans in Combat   98
— Conclusions and Recommendations   99

Part II.   An Analysis of the Cuban Operation by the Deputy
Director (Plans) Central Intelligence Agency, 18 January 1962   133
— Introduction and Summary   133
— The Survey's Statements of the Operational Concepts   149
— Why a Military-Type Invasion   151
— The Decision Making Process   153
— The Assessment of the Adequacy of the Plan   167
— Organization and Command Relationships   179

—The Political Front and Relations with the Cubans 215
—Air Maritime Operations 225

Part III.  Associated Documents 235

Part IV.  The Bay of Pigs Revisited: An Interview with
Jacob Esterline and Col. Jack Hawkins 258

Part V.  The Bay of Pigs Invasion: A Comprehensive
Chronology of Events 267

Source Key 331
Acknowledgments 334
About the National Security Archive 336
Index 337

# Introduction
## *History Held Hostage*

*The Bay of Pigs Report in Context*

"How could I have been so stupid as to let them proceed," John Kennedy asked his advisors more than once following the CIA's fiasco at the Bay of Pigs. For more than thirty-seven years, historians, policy analysts, and even former participants of the now infamous invasion of Cuba have pondered that question. Ever since the early hours of April 17, 1961, when a CIA-led, trained, and equipped brigade of some 1400 Cuban exiles hit the beach at Cuba's *Bahía de Los Cochinos* and was quickly defeated by Fidel Castro's superior forces, the failed invasion has reverberated through domestic and international affairs. Few historical episodes carry such an enduring contemporary relevance.

Yet, for all its importance—to the origins of the U.S.-Cuba conflict, the study of foreign policy failures, the genesis of the Cuban missile crisis, theories of the Kennedy assassination, and the ongoing debate over covert operations, among many other issues—the history of the Bay of Pigs has remained shrouded in secrecy. For years, the CIA refused to release any part of its vast archive, estimated at over 30,000 pages, of top secret planning, policy, and action documents on "Operation Zapata." In particular, the Agency maintained that, for national security considerations, it could not declassify the records of its own internal postmortem of the disaster. Written by CIA Inspector General Lyman Kirkpatrick after a six month inquiry, "The Inspector General's Survey of the Cuban Operation" became one of the most closely guarded secrets of the Cold War—the historical Holy Grail of the Bay of Pigs.

It is not difficult to understand why the CIA kept the IG survey secret for so long; the report represents, perhaps, the most brutally honest self-examination ever conducted inside the agency. As scathing as they are revealing, the pages that follow expose, with stark clarity, the operational and political components of the dark side of U.S. foreign policy. Along with the lengthy rebuttal by the architect of the invasion, CIA Deputy Director of Plans Richard Bissell, this document offers a rare and unique window into the inner sanctum of covert warfare, and the CIA's actions and attitudes toward changing the future of Cuba and other nations.

## THE PERFECT FAILURE

The CIA Inspector General's report addresses one of the most dramatic—
and traumatic—foreign policy disasters of the Cold War. The Bay of Pigs
was, as historian Theodore Draper observed at the time, "one of those rare
events in history—a perfect failure."

Militarily, the 1400-man Cuban exile force known as Brigade 2506 was
crushed by Castro's far larger military and militia in less than 72 hours.[1] A
handful of Cuban fighter aircraft which escaped the destruction of a pre-
invasion bombing raid, attacked and sank the Brigade's ammunition ship and
other support craft; and the exile force could neither hold nor break out of the
beachhead at *Playa Girón*. Some 114 brigade members were killed; 1189 captured. "It doesn't take Price Waterhouse to tell you that 1,500 Cubans aren't
as good as 25,000," former secretary of state Dean Acheson told President
Kennedy as the operation collapsed.

As a covert operation which Washington could "plausibly deny" the invasion also failed. When President Eisenhower authorized the Bay of Pigs
project on March 17, 1960, he admonished CIA officials that "the main thing
was not to let the U.S. hand show." In March 1961, President Kennedy ordered key changes in the CIA plan—changing landing sites from the popu-
lated city of Trinidad to a more isolated location, a night deployment instead
of a day-time assault, and a reduction of airstrikes—to make the operation far
"less noisy." But to both enemies and allies alike, the U.S. "hand" was evident well before D-Day.

As early as November 1960, Cuban intelligence sent a report to Moscow
on CIA training of the anti-Castro exiles in Guatemala; and in early April
1961, the CIA intercepted a cable from the Soviet Embassy in Mexico City
accurately stating that the invasion was expected on April 17. On April 9, the
*New York Times* published a front page story—considerably watered down
after a call from the President—titled "Anti-Castro Units Trained to fight at
Florida Bases." Castro "didn't need agents over here," Kennedy exclaimed.
"All he has to do is read our papers."[2]

Even worse, the U.S. role in the preliminary airstrike on April 15 was immediately exposed to the world—before the full invasion took place. The
CIA managed to launch the strike the very week the United Nations was
meeting to address Cuba's charges of U.S. aggression. A cover-story for the
attack concocted by Deputy Director of Plans, Richard Bissell, his deputy
Tracy Barnes and paramilitary specialist Col. Jack Hawkins—a defecting
Cuban pilot, taking his B-26 and dropping bombs on key airfields around

Havana before flying to Florida—fell apart within hours; but not before U.S. Ambassador to the UN, Adlai Stevenson, had presented the false account to the entire General Assembly.[3] The diplomatic embarrassment of being caught baldly lying to the world community led to the White House decision to cancel a second planned airstrike on D-day, which the CIA considered critical for the success of the operation. After the defeat, denial of U.S. responsibility became wholly implausible.

Kennedy called the failed invasion "the worst experience of my life." In office less than twelve weeks, the new president had suffered a major political humiliation. Yet, the decision to give the CIA a green light had been his alone. "There's an old saying that victory has a hundred fathers and defeat is an orphan," he told the press. "I am the responsible officer of the government."

U.S. credibility as a world leader was also dealt a harsh blow. "Acute shock and disillusion" dominated the reaction in Western Europe, as White House aide Arthur Schlesinger reported back to Kennedy. With a seemingly unprovoked attack on Cuba's sovereignty that left over 1800 military and civilian dead and wounded on the island, European hopes for Kennedy's intelligence, vision and "fresh" approach to the Cold war, had been "wiped away" and Washington was perceived to be as "self-righteous, trigger happy and incompetent as it had ever been." It was the decision to invade, not the failure, that bothered Western European political leaders, Schlesinger noted; "Why was Cuba such a threat to you?," they asked. "Why couldn't you live with Cuba, as the USSR lives with Turkey and Finland."[4] U.S. allies, Kennedy would later concede, "think we are a little demented on Cuba."[5]

Intended to overthrow Castro, the invasion succeeded in helping him to strengthen his regime internally, and enhanced his image internationally as a David defeating Goliath. "Castro's position is stronger than before the invasion attempt," the CIA's Office of National Estimates reported on April 28, 1961. His "hard-core supporters are more heavily armed and more enthusiastic in his behalf, and the widespread support which he has received abroad has probably increased his stature among many other Cubans." In a secret meeting in Montevideo, Uruguay, five months later, Che Guevara expressed Cuba's appreciation to White House aide Richard Goodwin for the Bay of Pigs. "He wanted to thank us very much for the invasion," Goodwin reported in an August 22, 1961 memorandum to Kennedy. "It had been a great political victory for them, enabled them to consolidate, and transformed them from an aggrieved little country into an equal."[6]

Finally, although the operation was designed to deny the Soviet Union a revolutionary ally in the Western Hemisphere, it succeeded only in driving Cuba into a concrete alliance with Moscow. On April 16, at the state funerals of those killed during the airstrike the day before, Premier Castro officially declared Cuba a Marxist-Leninist state—a prelude to closer Cuban-Soviet ties. Fearing a second Bay of Pigs in 1962, the Castro government signed a defense pact with the USSR and accepted the installation of Soviet missiles on Cuban soil—a decision that led to the most dangerous moment in history when the world looked down "the gun barrel of nuclear war."[7]

## WHO LOST CUBA?: INVASION HISTORIOGRAPHY

The emotional, and often acrimonious, debate over what went wrong at the Bay of Pigs divides into two distinct camps: those who blame the failure on President Kennedy's decision to cancel the second airstrike and his refusal to salvage the operation through military intervention; and those who hold the CIA responsible for faulty assumptions about overthrowing Castro and for misleading the White House about the likely success of the operation.

For embittered CIA officials, and numerous Brigade 2506 members who felt abandoned and betrayed, the president's decisions were a profile in cowardice, not courage. "The president is to blame," states Grayston Lynch, the CIA man who was the first to set foot on the beach as the deployment began. "The battle was lost before [Brigade 2506] ever saw the Bay of Pigs." In *Recollections of a Cold Warrior,* Richard Bissell characterizes Kennedy's cancellation of the second airstrike as "certainly the gravest contributory factor in the operation's failure." At the "decisive moment of the Bay of Pigs operation," according to former CIA director Allen Dulles, Kennedy lacked "a determination to succeed, a willingness to risk unpleasant political repercussions, and a willingness to provide the basic military necessities."[8]

The major histories written by Kennedy aides Theodore Sorensen and Arthur Schlesinger Jr., as well as Peter Wyden's authoritative 1979 book, *Bay of Pigs: The Untold Story* present a different account. They highlight the deception and self-deception of the Agency, and particularly Richard Bissell, in dealing with the brigade, Castro's Cuba, and the Kennedy White House. White House officials felt deceived by Bissell's arguments that the brigade landing would touch off an uprising against Castro, or, if not, the brigade would "go guerrilla" into the Escambray mountains—an impossible option from the swamp-enclosed Bay of Pigs. "All of us—Kennedy and Bundy and the rest—were hynotized by Dick Bissell to some degree, and assumed that he knew what he was doing," Schlesinger later observed.[9]

In the "Who Lost Cuba?" debate numerous broader issues surrounding the Bay of Pigs have been lost—among them the propriety of U.S. intervention to rollback the Cuban revolution, the parameters of covert operations, the still hidden aspects of the invasion plan, and the oft-forgotten role of Castro's victorious forces in the U.S. defeat. "Castro's armed forces and militia were effective in defeating the invasion," CIA analysts conceded in a secret intelligence assessment, "Consequences for the US of the Abortive Rebellion in Castro's Cuba," written one week after the debacle. "The reality was that Fidel Castro turned out to be a far more formidable foe and in command of a far better organized regime than anyone had supposed," Schlesinger admits in *A Thousand Days*.[10] But in the historiography of the invasion, why it failed is less important than the foreign policy attitudes, assumptions, and actions that contributed to this human, political, and foreign policy tragedy. "I don't think that the failure was because of the want of a nail," Kennedy's National Security Advisor, McGeorge Bundy testified during one post invasion inquiry. "I think that the men who worked on this got into a world of their own."

## REVISITING THE BAY OF PIGS

In an effort to recreate, and recover, the evidence of that world, in 1995 the National Security Archive began a concerted campaign to advance the historical record on the Bay of Pigs invasion. Collaborating with Brown University's Thomas J. Watson Jr. Institute for International Studies, our goal was to uncover still secret documentation, find surviving U.S., Cuban-American, and Cuban participants, and bring them together for a major historical reexamination of this important, and still relevant, episode.[11]

In early 1996, in preparation for a retrospective conference on the 35th anniversary of the invasion, the Archive filed a series of requests under the Freedom of Information Act for the Inspector General's report and all attached documents; and then stepped up public pressure for the release of these and hundreds of other records.[12] Two factors provided leverage for eventual declassification: first, President Clinton's 1995 Executive Order that all secret documents over 25 years old be processed for release; and second, the CIA's own announcement in 1992 that it would begin a historical review of 11 past covert operations as part of a new post-Cold war "openness campaign."

At the request of the Archive, on the 35th anniversary of the invasion, the State Department did release some 400 Pentagon, State and CIA documents—although the Inspector General's report and other key documents remained secret.[13] The newly declassified documents were reviewed at the conference, held on May 31-June 2, 1996 at the Musgrove Conference Center supported by the Arca Foundation. The meeting also provided an opportunity and a venue for the two managers of "Operation Zapata"— veteran CIA operative Jacob Esterline, and Marine Col. Jack Hawkins —to discuss the operation publicly for the first time. Esterline had been head of the Cuba Task Force known as WH/4; Hawkins, his chief paramilitary officer.[14] Both are referred to prominently in the Inspector General's report and rejoinder by their respective CIA designations: C/WH/4 and C/WH/4/PM (Chief/Western Hemisphere 4 Task Force and Chief/Western Hemisphere 4 Task Force/Paramilitary).

A number of important historical facts and interpretations emerged at Musgrove. On U.S. attitudes toward the target of the operation, Fidel Castro, the complex role of the architect of the operation, Richard Bissell, and the little understood role of political assassination in the invasion planning, the discussion provided a more refined sense of the arrogance, incompetence and ignorance that contributed to this imperial disaster.

**ON CASTRO:** What appears to have alarmed U.S. officials initially about Castro was his transcendent personality and leadership capabilities, as much as his revolutionary plans for Cuba, and potential ties to the Soviet Union. One of the earliest CIA assessments—written by a CIA agent who briefed Castro on the "danger of Communism" during his first post-revolution trip to Washington D.C. in April 1959—described Castro, ironically, as "a new spiritual leader of Latin American democratic and anti-dictator forces."† Esterline, then CIA chief of station in Caracas, first witnessed "the power of his charisma," during Castro's first trip abroad to Venezuela in March 1959,

---

† The CIA memorandum of conversation with Castro, dated May 8, 1959, and declassified in June 1998, records an extraordinary exchange. The CIA official, speaking Spanish, explained that "the U.S. appreciates [you are] not pro-Communist," but "Moscow and Peiping are attempting to exploit the Cuban revolution to destroy [the] Cuban-American friendship." Castro responded that the U.S. was "overly concerned" about international communism, but agreed to allow the CIA to "channel" information on communist activities in Cuba to him via intermediaries in Havana. The CIA briefer reported that the meeting was "beneficial and encouraging."

where he was hailed by massive throngs of supporters. Castro was "something different, something more impressive . . . and definitely harder to handle than anyone we had ever seen," according to Esterline:

> It seemed to me that something like a chain reaction was occuring all over Latin America after Castro came to power. I saw—hell, anybody with eyes could see—that a new and powerful force was at work in the hemisphere. It had to be dealt with.[15]

Vice President Richard Nixon's initial perceptions of Castro were almost identical, albeit less hostile. Nixon met Castro only a few weeks later, during his trip to Washington D.C. in April 1959. For years, Nixon's observation that Castro was "either incredibly naive about Communism or under Communist discipline," was his only known impression of the Cuban leader. But the full text of his memorandum of conversation with Castro shows that Nixon was actually impressed:

> The one fact we can be sure of is that Fidel Castro has those indefinable qualities which make him a leader of men. Whatever we may think of him, he is going to be a great factor in the development of Cuba and very possibly in Latin American affairs generally.[16]

According to the recently declassified minutes of the very first meeting of the Bay of Pigs task force, on March 9, 1960, CIA Western Hemisphere Division chief, J.C. King stated clearly that Castro had a "60 to 70 percent" popular approval rating. For this reason, Esterline's original plan for the Bay of Pigs called for infiltrating small, highly trained cadres into Cuba, according to the Kirpatrick report, "to organize, train and lead resistance groups" in the Escambray mountains. By October 1960, however, Richard Bissell, the CIA's Deputy Director of Plans and the driving intellectual force behind the invasion, had abandoned this plan. He then replaced it with an amphibious landing of a brigade of exiles in Cuba which, he expected, would set off a chain reaction of mass defections and support for the counterrevolution, bringing Castro down. This misreading of Cuba's political situation was the first of many willful mistakes that led to the Bay of Pigs disaster.

ON BISSELL: Richard Bissell was considered the best of the brightest in the U.S. government. A former professor of economics at Yale, he won his reputation for brilliance by implementing the Marshall Plan and overseeing the creation of the CIA's U-2 reconnaisance program. In 1954, CIA director Allen Dulles selected Bissell as a special assistant—"an apprentice," as Bissell described it—and he immediately went to work on PBSUCCESS, the

CIA paramilitary operation to overthrow the democratically elected government of Jacobo Arbenz in Guatemala. That operation proved critical to his misassumptions about Cuba.

"PBSUCCESS was a success, through dumb luck more than anything else," veteran CIA operative Richard Drain told CIA historian Jack Pfeiffer. Militarily, the operation failed when the CIA's ragtag rebels refused to engage in active combat. CIA psychological operations, however, intimidated Arbenz's military into forcing his resignation in the face of fears that the U.S. was about to invade. "We won more because of incompetence on the other side than anything else," notes Jake Esterline who helped run PBSUCCESS, and served as the first post-coup CIA station chief in Guatemala City.

Bissell and other Eisenhower officials appeared to believe that Castro's regime was similarly incompetent, and would similarly collapse under the psychological stress of the invasion. Guatemala, Bissell writes in his rebuttal to the Inspector General's report, "was an analogy and a precedent" for the Bay of Pigs.

Bissell was also responsible for agreeing to the changes in landing sites, and the reduction of air strikes ordered by the new president, John F. Kennedy. These decisions significantly undercut the chances of success, as Bissell's own aides explicitly made clear to him. The deputy director of plans, according to Col. Hawkins, "ignored the emphatic advice given him by the Chief WH/4 and the Paramilitary Chief that a landing at the Bay of Pigs would be disastrous and should be cancelled."[17]

On the Sunday morning of April 8, 1961, Hawkins and Esterline went to Bissell's Washington, D.C. home and said they were resigning. "We looked at every aspect and the odds and the percentages of success and we finally decided that we couldn't deliver on them," Esterline recalled in an interview published in this volume for the first time (see pages 258–266). But Bissell assured them their concerns would be met and that the operation would have the necessary support for success. In the aftermath of the disaster, both his deputies determined that he had misled them—and the President. "I don't think he was being honest," Esterline said. "I don't think he was being honest up—I mean with Kennedy and maybe with Dulles, too; and I don't think he was being honest down—in dealing with his two principal aides, Esterline and Hawkins."[18]

**THE ASSASSINATION TRACK:** One explanation for Bissell's recklessness lies in his most controversial, and most secretive, decision—an August 1960 authorization for a CIA-Mafia plot to assassinate Castro. "Assassination was intended to reinforce the plan," Bissell admitted in an interview many years later. "There was the thought that Castro would be dead before the landing." In his posthumously published memoirs, he admits that "as I moved forward with plans for the brigade, I hoped the Mafia would achieve success."

While the CIA's multiple efforts to eliminate the Cuban leader have been well documented for years—including in a 100-page secret CIA history written by Kirkpatrick's successor in 1968—assassination as an explicit component of the Bay of Pigs operation, paid for through the WH/4 Task Force budget, has come to light only recently.

The assassination "track" started during the Eisenhower administration, and continued under Kennedy.[19] At a November 3, 1960 meeting of the "special group" on Cuba, Under Secretary of State Livingston Merchant asked whether the CIA could take "direct positive action against Fidel, Raul and Che Guevara." Without them, he suggested, Cuba would be "leaderless and probably brainless."[20] CIA deputy director General Charles P. Cabell responded that such action was "uncertain of results and highly dangerous" as well as "beyond our capabilities."

In fact, the CIA had already set in motion a major effort to kill Castro—on the theory that the revolution would collapse without him. As early as December 1959, the head of the Agency's Western Hemisphere Division, J.C. King recommended that "thorough consideration be given to the elimination of Fidel Castro," because it "would greatly accelerate the fall of the present government." Indeed, at the first meeting of the Bay of Pigs task force, King predicted that "unless Fidel and Raul Castro and Che Guevara could be eliminated in one package . . . this operation [would] be a long drawn out affair and the present government will only be overthrown by force."

Unbeknownst to most of the invasion managers, Richard Bissell shared King's assessment, and subsequently authorized an assassination plot to go forward. In a briefing memorandum later prepared for Attorney General Robert Kennedy, the CIA's liaison with the crime syndicates, Sheffield Edwards wrote that "In August 1960" he "was approached by Mr. Richard Bissell . . . to explore the possibility of mounting this sensitive operation against Fidel Castro." The CIA's Technical Services Division (TSD) manufactured a number of poison pills—they were tested for potency on laboratory monkeys—which were passed through Mafia capo Johnny Roselli to a Cuban government operative in mid-March 1961. When this attempt on Castro's life failed, a second set of pills was passed to exile leader Anthony de la Varona, who sent them to Cuba in early April. A restaurant worker was supposed to put the pills in Castro's food, but the assassination effort never took place.

Approximately $200,000 for this operation came out of the invasion budget, according to Esterline, the head of WH/4. "All of a sudden I started getting requests to authorize big payments, $60,000, $100,000, and [not knowing what they were for] I refused them," Esterline recalled in our interview. Esterline demanded, and eventually received a briefing—only after it became clear that he would not otherwise authorize the funds. Told of the assassination plot, Esterline adamantly opposed it. "I said, do you realize that this is going to make people take this whole thing less less seriously if somebody thinks there's an easy way out with Castro being killed:

> I thought it was absolutely immoral that we involve ourselves for the record
> in anything of this sort. Number one, I was just having trouble coming
> to grips with that. But number two, I thought it would be the most
> self-defeating thing for the operation which was going to be [difficult] at
> best.[21]

During the post-invasion inquiry of the Taylor Board—President Kennedy's hand-picked committee led by Gen. Maxwell Taylor to investigate the Bay of Pigs disaster—Bissell informed Attorney General Robert Kennedy that the CIA's "associated planning" for the Bay of Pigs included "the use of the underworld against Castro."[22] No record of this briefing, however, has ever been made public. Indeed, despite the end of the Cold War, and the passage of so many years, the full text and supporting papers of the Taylor Committee inquiry—along with thousands of CIA and other government documents on the Bay of Pigs—remain hostage to the dictates of secrecy.

## THE KIRKPATRICK REPORT

The CIA Inspector General's Survey demonstrates how important such secret records can be for understanding this, and other episodes. The IG report was the only contemporary investigation the CIA conducted on itself after the failed invasion. Almost 37 years after it was written, and after more than two years of repeated requests for its declassification, the CIA finally provided the Kirkpatrick report to the National Security Archive on February 19, 1998.

As a contribution to history, the Inspector General's report provides new and specific details about the Bay of Pigs, as well as a rare internal overview of a major clandestine operation. It charts the transformation of "Operation Zapata" — officially codenamed JMATE, the Pentagon aptly called it "Operation Bumpy Road" — from a $4 million covert infiltration project designed to train a cadre of skilled insurgency leaders and drop them into the Escambray mountains into a $46 million overt amphibious assault. It describes, for the first time, the "intelligence net" of 27 agents inside Cuba when the U.S. broke diplomatic relations in January 1961. In chapters on the CIA's Miami base, political fronts, multifaceted paramilitary preparations, and American combatants, the report catalogues the day-to-day realities of running a massive paramilitary operation to overthrow another government.

The author of the report, Lyman Kirkpatrick — "Kirk" as he was known to his colleagues — served as the CIA's inspector general from 1952 to 1963. A twenty-year member of the U.S. intelligence community, he had been in Army intelligence and the OSS before joining the CIA. When Kirkpatrick contracted polio in 1952, his advancement toward the highest echelons of the agency stalled, and he assumed the IG post.[23] The Bay of Pigs became his most controversial assignment.

Almost immediately after the invasion, CIA director Allen Dulles assigned Kirkpatrick to do a "complete review" of the operation. Rather than focus on the decisions made by the White House, the Pentagon or the State Department, as Kirkpatrick noted in the report's introduction, the purpose was "to evaluate selected aspects of the Agency's performance and describe weaknesses and failures . . . and to make recommendations for their correction and avoidance in the future." Between April and October 1961, the Office of the Inspector General conducted some 125 interviews with the CIA personnel involved in "Operation Zapata," and reviewed hundreds of documents. In a cover letter submitting the report to incoming director John McCone, Kirkpatrick identified "a tendency in the Agency to gloss over CIA inadequacies and to attempt to fix all of the blame for the failure of the invasion upon other elements of the Government, rather than to recognize the Agency's weaknesses." He characterized his 150-page assessment as "highly critical but fair."[24]

As the reader will note, the IG inquiry found fault with almost every organizational and operational aspect of the Cuba project. Kirkpatrick cited "bad planning," "poor" staffing, faulty intelligence, "fragmentation of authority," mistreatment of the exile forces, and "failure to advise the President that success had become dubious," as key factors in the failure. Among his conclusions:

- The president's cancellation of the D-Day airstrike was not "the chief cause of failure." That issue was presented to Kennedy under "ill-prepared, inadequately briefed circumstances," which better CIA planning, organization, staffing and management would have avoided.

- The operation was predicated on the belief, held by CIA deputy director of plans Richard Bissell, that "the invasion would, like a *deus ex machina*, produce a shock" inside Cuba and "trigger an uprising" against Castro. Yet, according to the IG, "we can confidently assert that the Agency had no intelligence evidence that Cubans in significant numbers could or would join the invaders or that there was any kind of an effective and cohesive resistance movement under anybody's control, let alone the Agency's, that could have furnished internal leadership for an uprising in support of the invasion."

- Agency handlers treated the Cuban exile political leaders "like puppets" and some agents treated the exile forces "like dirt" engendering animosity and lack of cooperation. The CIA, Kirkpatrick predicted, was "not likely to win many people away from Communism if the Americans treat other nationals with condescension or contempt," or "as incompetent children whom the Americans are going to rescue for reasons of their own."

- What was supposed to be a covert operation became a major overt military project "beyond Agency responsibility as well as Agency capability." Due to "multiple security leaks," invasion planning became known to the Cubans and widely reported in the U.S. press. "Plausible denial was a pathetic illusion."

- CIA officials misled the White House into believing that success was still likely. "At some point in this degenerative cycle," according to the report, "they should have gone to the President and said frankly: 'Here are the facts. The operation should be halted.'"

Cancellation, Kirkpatrick concluded, would have been a major embarrassment for the United States; the embittered exile forces would have spread the word of the lack of U.S. resolve. But aborting the operation would have averted failure, "which brought even more embarrassment, carried death and misery to hundreds . . . and seriously damaged U.S. prestige."

The report finished with a substantive list of recommendations on organizational and procedural changes that would presumably prevent such egregious errors in the future. "Before it takes on another major covert political operation [CIA] will have to improve its organization and management drastically," Kirkpatrick wrote. "It is assumed that the Agency, because of its experience in this Cuban operation, will never again engage in an operation that is essentially an overt military effort."

## THE BISSELL REBUTTAL

The Inspector General's no-holds-barred criticism outraged the senior CIA officials who had been involved in the debacle. As the architect of the operation, Richard Bissell described himself as "wounded by it." Bissell submitted a comprehensive response drafted by his deputy, Tracy Barnes, titled "An Analysis of the Cuban Operation." After it was turned in on January 18, 1962, the new CIA director John McCone ordered that Bissell's rejoinder be permanently attached to the Kirkpatrick report as part of the official record.

Displaying the sophisticated intellect for which he was renowned, Bissell's "Analysis" addressed and rebutted every major argument in the Kirkpatrick survey. Intelligence on Cuba was "essentially accurate;" there was "solid reason" for a chance of at least "initial success;" staffing was "adequate." The operation had remained "technically deniable." The military plan was executed soundly and effectively. The defeat on the ground was due to defeat in the air, and that was not the CIA's responsibility. "It was directly and unambigously attributable to a long series of Washington policy decisions."

Significant portions of the rebuttal addressed the "Agency vs. Government responsibility," as Bissell again and again returned to the issue of Kennedy's "political compromises," made in order to preserve plausible denial. Covert operations created a policy conundrum, he pointed out, "a clear conflict between two goals, a conflict of the sort familiar in recent American history:

> One objective was that, mainly through the various activities comprised in this project, the Castro regime should be overthrown. The other was that the political and moral posture of the United States before the world at large should not be impaired.

Overthrowing Castro "in such a manner that the official responsibility of the U.S. government could be disclaimed" was the chosen solution, but at the cost of "maximum effectiveness," he argued. "If complete deniability had been consistent with maximum effectiveness, there would theoretically have remained no conflict of goals but in fact this could not be (and never is) the case."

In an assessment that remains entirely relevant to the discussion of covert operations today, Bissell posed the question: "What are the lessons for the future to be drawn from this unhappy experience?

Perhaps the main one is that the U.S. should not support an operation such as this involving the use of force without having also made the decision to use whatever force is needed to achieve success. If the political decisions necessary to facilitate the effective use of force on an adequate scale, up to and possibly including the overt commitment of U.S. military forces, are too difficult to make, then the operation should be called off. . . .

## LESSONS NOT LEARNED

In the years following the Bay of Pigs, one president after another has faced the "clear conflict" in U.S. foreign policy that Richard Bissell identified: pursuing a goal of illegitimate aggression without impairing the moral and political standing of the United States—at home and abroad. They all chose to use covert operations—operations that, in numerous cases, consequently came back to do far more harm to the United States than the targeted enemy ever could. The CIA's first, and most egregious, overt failure appears to have had little impact on succeeding events.

For the Kennedy administration, the lessons of the debacle at Girón beach were deemed primarily procedural. In a secret postmortem written on April 24, National Security Advisor McGeorge Bundy identified the top ten "administrative" lessons of "Operation Zapata":

First, the President's advisors must speak up in council. Second, secrecy must never take precedence over careful thought and study. Third, the President and his advisors must second guess even military plans. Fourth, we must estimate the enemy without hope or fear. Fifth, those who are to offer serious advice on major issues must themselves do the necessary work. Sixth, the President's desires must be fully acted on, and he must know the full state of mind of friends whose lives his decisions affect. Seventh, forced choices are seldom as necessary as they seem, and the fire can be much hotter than the frying pan. Eighth, what is and is not implied in any specific partial decision must always be thought through. Ninth: What is large in scale must always be open, with all the consequences of openness. Tenth: Success is what succeeds.

These lessons were, in fact, applied to the internal decision making process of the Kennedy White House.[25] On the use of major covert operations to overthrow and undermine other governments, however, the broader meaning of the Bay of Pigs failed to register with Kennedy or his successors in office.

To be sure, the President made some superficial changes at the CIA. Director of Central Intelligence Allen Dulles was forced to retire, and after a decent interval of a year, his heir apparent Richard Bissell also left.[26] Upon his departure in March 1962, Kennedy awarded Bissell the National Security Medal. "Mr. Bissell's high purpose, unbounded energy, and unswerving devotion to duty are benchmarks of the intelligence service," Kennedy remarked during the ceremony. "He leaves an enduring legacy. . . . "[27]

That legacy included the misuse and abuse of CIA covert operations as a policy tool. The Bay of Pigs might have provided the dramatic opportunity to fundamentally alter the future of such operations. Instead, President Kennedy rejected a State Department proposal to strip the CIA of its covert operations functions—and even rename the Agency.[28] The Department of State position on the agency reflected a significant internal discussion, generated by anger at the conduct of the Cuba invasion, over reforming the CIA. At the same time, the invasion also sparked the first national debate on the propriety of covert operations in a democracy. Had it been disseminated, the Inspector General's Survey on the Bay of Pigs would have contributed significantly to both the internal and public discourse. Instead, it was literally locked away—purposely hidden from public debate, and policy deliberations over the CIA's future.

"Rather than receiving [the report] in the light in which it had been produced, which was to insure that the same mistakes would not be repeated in the future," Kirkpatrick noted in his memoirs, *The Real CIA*, "those that participated in the operation resented it and attacked it bitterly."[29] Memoranda written by Tracy Barnes, Dulles, Bissell and other CIA officials characterized the report as "malicious," "biased," and "useless." At the highest echelons of the agency, the report was seen as a threat to the CIA's very future. The new CIA director, John McCone, ordered the Inspector General to provide him with the distribution list of all 20 copies of the report; most of them were retrieved and burned; the copies that remained were locked away in the director's office. "In unfriendly hands," deputy director Cabell wrote in a December 15, 1961 memorandum, the report "could become a weapon unjustifiably [used] to attack the entire mission, organization, and functioning of the Agency."[30]

In the ensuing decades, the Bay of Pigs became but the first in a succession of scandals involving covert operations to assert America's will over smaller nations. Cuba was a perpetual target. The White House simply ignored Col.

Hawkins firm warnings, made in a comprehensive secret after-action report dated May 5, 1961, that Castro "will not be overthrown by means short of overt . . . military power," and that "further" covert efforts "should not be made."† Instead, the Kennedy brothers turned again to the CIA to wreak U.S. revenge on Castro for his victory at *Playa Girón*. A "solution" to the Cuba problem, Attorney General Robert Kennedy told CIA and Pentagon representatives in January 1962 was now "the top priority in the United States Government—all else is secondary—no time, money, effort, or manpower is to be spared." The president, he said, had indicated that "the final chapter on Cuba has not been written."

The Kennedy White House attempted to write that chapter by authorizing Operation Mongoose—"a more ambitious and more massive paramilitary activity than the Bay of Pigs," as Bissell described Kennedy's 1962 CIA-Pentagon program. The threat of these sabotage and psychological operations, designed to foment civil upheaval inside Cuba, helped prompt Castro to accept Soviet missiles as protection from U.S. aggression. In the aftermath of the missile crisis, the Attorney General oversaw a $10 million CIA program, codenamed "Second Naval Guerrilla," to fund sabotage operations in Cuba conducted by Bay of Pigs veterans from base camps in Central America. And CIA attempts to assassinate Castro continued to the very last day of the Kennedy administration. According to the CIA's own internal history on efforts to kill Castro, "at the very moment President Kennedy was shot a CIA officer was meeting with a Cuban agent in Paris and giving him an assassination device for use against Castro."[31]

The CIA drew on the basic blueprint of the Bay of Pigs—creating political fronts, mounting propaganda campaigns, and organizing, training, arming and directing a proxy force of exiles—again and again over the next 35 years. From Nicaragua to Afghanistan to Iraq, protracted paramilitary warfare brought violence and bloodshed abroad—and damage to U.S. political institutions at home. The list of scandals generated by these operations is a long one: the CIA-backed Contra war against the Sandinistas alone produced the mining of Nicaragua's harbors, the assassination manual, and the Iran-

---

† "Further efforts to develop armed internal resistance, or to organize Cuban exile forces, should not be made except in connection with a planned overt intervention by United States forces," Hawkins wrote in his 48-page postmortem, "Record of Paramilitary Action Against the Castro Government of Cuba." Like Bissell, he concluded that operational effectiveness had been "completely subordinated" to the dictates of plausible denial. "The Government and the people of the United States," he concluded, "are not yet psychologically conditioned to participate in the cold war with resort to the harsh, rigorous, and often dangerous and painful measures which must be taken in order to win." His secret assessment remained classified until June 4, 1998.

Contra scandal which virtually paralyzed the Reagan administration in 1987. The CIA's Iraq operations between 1991-1996, during which the agency spent over $100 million to arm, and organize rebel exiles to overthrow Saddam Hussein only to abandon them to Hussein's military forces, reminded even current policy makers of the analogy to the Cuba operation. "If you encourage and almost incite people to rise up against their government, you incur a moral obligation," as Clinton's national security advisor Sandy Berger explained the difficulties in Iraq.

The Kirkpatrick report assumed that the CIA would never again engage in such paramilitary plots. Yet, the Bissell mindset—a combination of imperial arrogance, ethnocentric ignorance and a false sense of U.S. omnipotence—has dominated the history of covert operations since the Bay of Pigs. Policy makers, as Col. Hawkins recently observed, "continue to harbor unrealistically overblown ideas about what can be accomplished by covert, deniable means." Indeed, the repeated controversies over recent CIA covert operations in Iraq, Guatemala, Libya, Nicaragua and elsewhere demonstrate that the issues raised by the Agency's machinations in Cuba endure in the making of U.S. foreign policy.

"A wise man once said, 'an error doesn't become a mistake until you refuse to correct it,'" President Kennedy told the press after the Bay of Pigs invasion failed. There were, he said, "sobering lessons" to be learned. Now that the CIA's top secret evaluation of this covert failure has finally fallen into the "unfriendly hands" of the public, those lessons can be learned, the mistakes addressed and, in the future, corrected.

# Notes

1. Each brigade member was given a number when they joined. The Brigade derived its name from the number of Carlos Rodríguez Santana, the first casualty of the operation, who died during a training exercise in Guatemala.

2. Quoted in Peter Wyden's *Bay of Pigs: The Untold Story* (New York: Simon & Schuster, 1979), p. 155.

3. CIA officials Joseph Langan and Clark Simmons, who were in charge of implementing the cover operation "came bouncing into the office all laughter and joy and offered to have a couple of ceremonial drinks, [because the operation] had worked," recalls Richard Drain, an operations officer during the Bay of Pigs. "I remember saying to them, 'well, I hope you are as happy about 5 o'clock this afternoon, as you are now . . . because how long this holds up in Miami seems to me very questionable indeed.'" Reporters immediately noticed that the defector's plane had the nosecone of a U.S. B-26, not a Cuban model, that its guns had not been fired and that it had been freshly painted. Drain made his comments during a January 6, 1976 interview with CIA historian Jack Pfeiffer.

4. See Schlesinger's memo, "Reactions to Cuba in Western Europe," May 3, 1961.

5. Kennedy made this remark on October 18, 1962 during a meeting of the Executive Committee meeting on the Cuban Missile crisis.

6. Goodwin to the President, "Conversation with Commandante Ernesto Guevara of Cuba," August 22, 1961.

7. Kennedy speech writer Theodore Sorenson coined this phrase.

8. Quoted in Richard Bissell's *Recollections of a Cold Warrior* (New Haven: Yale University Press, 1996), pp. 191, 197.

9. Schlesinger made these remarks at the Musgrove conference on the Bay of Pigs, June 1, 1996. See James G. Blight and Peter Kornbluh, *Politics of Illusion: The Bay of Pigs Invasion Reexamined*, (Boulder, CO: Lynne Rienner, 1998), p. 65.

10. Schlesinger notes that "too much comment on the Bay of Pigs has fallen into the fallacy of Douglas Southall Freeman, who once wrote a long chapter analyzing the reasons for Lee's defeat at Gettysburg without mentioning the interesting fact that the Union Army was there too." See Arthur Schlesinger Jr., *A Thousand Days: John F. Kennedy in the White House* (New York: Houghton Mifflin Company, 1965), p. 293.

11. The methodology of combining documents, participants and analysts is known as "Critical Oral History," and was designed by Brown University Professor James G. Blight. The concept, as Blight describes it, "requires the simultaneous interaction of documents bearing on the paper trail of decisions for issues and events under reexamination, memories of those who participated in the decisions, and scholars, whose business it is to know the relevant aspects of the written record." The initial plan was to hold a 35th anniversary conference in Cuba, bringing together members of Fidel Castro's government with former CIA and Kennedy White House officials as well as surviving brigade members to discuss the events of April 1961 at *Playa Girón*. When that conference fell victim to the degeneration of U.S.-Cuban relations in 1996, a smaller meeting of former CIA, White House, and anti-Castro rebels was organized at the Arca Foundation's Musgrove con-

ference center on St. Simons Island, Georgia. For the conference proceedings and a fuller description of critical oral history, see Blight and Kornbluh, *Politics of Illusion*.

12. See, for example, a 35th anniversary op-ed piece, "The C.I.A.'s Cuban Cover-up," in the *New York Times*, April 16, 1996.

13. These documents were part of the State Department's Foreign Relations of the United States (FRUS) series. They were released publically on the 35th anniversary — some 18 months before publication of FRUS Volumes X and XI — at the request of the National Security Archive.

14. Hawkins could not physically attend the conference, but was in touch by phone and sent key documents and memos on the questions being discussed.

15. Esterline, as recorded at the Musgrove Conference, May 31, 1996.

16. Rough Draft of Summary of Conversation Between the Vice President and Fidel Castro, April 25, 1959.

17. Hawkins memo to the editor.

18. Esterline made these remarks at the Musgrove conference, June 1, 1996. See Blight and Kornbluh, *Politics of Illusion*, p. 83.

19. Whether the President Eisenhower or Kennedy knew in advance of the assassination plots remains an enduring historical mystery. It is clear that shortly after Kennedy's election, his national security advisor, McGeorge Bundy was briefed by Richard Bissell on ZR Rifle, the CIA's code name for its program to murder Castro and others. Recently declassified documents also show that in May 1961, and again in May 1962, Attorney General Robert Kennedy was briefed on the CIA-Mafia operation. In the first briefing paper, Edwards indicated that "none of the [Mafia's efforts] have materialized to date and that several of the plans still are working and may eventually 'pay off.'" No memoranda records the Attorney General ordering that these operations be halted. See the FBI's debriefing memo on Sheffield Edwards, "Arthur James Balletti, et al." May 22, 1961, and Edwards' memo on briefing the Attorney General, "Arthur James Balletti et al — Unauthorized Publication or Use of Communications," May 14, 1962.

20. Minutes of Special Group Meeting, 3 November 1960.

21. Interview with Peter Kornbluh, October 10, 1996. See pages 258–266.

22. This information comes from Sheffield Edwards, one of only four CIA officials aware of the CIA-Mafia operation. See the FBI's debriefing memo on Edwards, "Arthur James Balletti, et al." May 22, 1961.

23. A number of his colleagues alleged that Kirkpatrick's bitterness at being relegated to the mundane job of Inspector General because of his disease manifested itself in the starkly critical language in his report on the Bay of Pigs. According to Richard Drain, "Kirk was trying to point blame at enough DDP people so that there would be different personnel involved later on;" Drain acknowledged that "that's a dirty thing to say." Jack Pfeiffer interview with Richard Drain, p. 45.

24. The Kirkpatrick report does not name individuals; the rejoinder, however, does include a biographic summary of key officers involved in the operation. A list of personnel and their CIA designations is included for the reader to identify officials discussed in the documents.

25. During the handling of the October 1962 Cuban Missile Crisis, according to Arthur Schlesinger, Kennedy refused to rely on the CIA and Joint Chiefs of Staff; instead he

brought together an executive committee of top advisors to carefully discuss critical options. "No one can doubt," Schlesinger later wrote, "that failure in Cuba in 1961 contributed to success in Cuba in 1962." *A Thousand Days*, p. 297.

26. Kennedy "felt that I could not continue as DDP," Bissell recalled in an interview with CIA historian Jack Pfeiffer on October 17, 1975: "He said if this were a parliamentary government I would have to resign and you, as a Civil Servant, would stay on; but being the present government that it is, a Presidential government, I cannot resign and you . . . will have to resign."

27. Bissell admits that he left CIA with "a legacy that still has not been put to rest historically and perhaps never well be." Quoted in *Recollections of a Cold Warrior*, p. 204.

28. *A Thousand Days*, p. 428.

29. Lyman B. Kirkpatrick Jr., *The Real CIA* (New York: Macmillan, 1968), p. 200.

30. In an April 1, 1998 letter to the author, Col. Jack Hawkins remembered that "the CIA high command of that time seemed to reject the report out of hand, dismissed it as worthless and a threat to the CIA's very existence. Deeply immersed in their arcane world, they were unable to appreciate that one of their own was illuminating realities about themselves and their organization which deserved careful attention and introspection."

31. See the CIA Inspector General's report, "Report on Plots to Assassinate Fidel Castro," May 23, 1967, p. 94. The CIA official, Nestor Sánchez, brought a fake pen with a hypodermic needle for a high-level Cuban military asset to use against Castro. The asset, Colonel Rolando Cubela, balked at using such a device and asked for a sniper rifle. CIA efforts to kill Castro continued through 1965.

# —KEY ACTORS and ACRONYMS

## *Personnel*

| | |
|---|---|
| DCI | Director of Central Intelligence, Allen Dulles |
| DDCI | Deputy Director of Central Intelligence, Gen. C.P. Cabell |
| DD/P | Deputy Director of Plans, Richard Bissell |
| A/DDP/A | Assistant Deputy Director (Plans), Tracy Barnes |
| COPS | Chief of Operations (Plans), Richard Helms |
| C/WH | Chief, Western Hemisphere Division, J.C. King |
| C/WH/4 | Chief, Cuba Task Force, Jacob D. Esterline |
| C/WH/4/PM | Chief Paramilitary, Cuba Task Force, Jack Hawkins |
| D/WH/4 | Deputy Chief, Cuba Task Force, Edward Stanulis |
| COPS/WH/4 | Chief of Operations, Cuba Task Force, Richard Drain |
| C/WH/4/PP | Chief Propaganda, Cuba Task Force, David Atlee Philips |
| AC/DPD | Acting Chief, Development Projects Div. (Air) Stanley Beerli |
| C/PA/WH/4 | Chief, Political Affairs officer, Gerald Droller (aka Frank Bender) |
| C/FI/WH/4 | Chief, Foreign Intelligence, Cuba Task Force, Bernard Reichhardt |
| PP/PM/WH/4 | Propaganda officer, E. Howard Hunt |
| C/SPU/WH/4/PM | Chief, Strikes and Plans Unit, Cuba Task Force, Frank Egan |
| C/Maritime Ops | Chief of Maritime Operations, Capt. Jacob Scapa |
| COB/WH/4 | Chief of Base, Miami, Robert Reynolds |
| C.G. | Commandant General, U.S. Marine Corps, David Shoup |
| I.G. | CIA Inspector General, Lyman Kirkpatrick Jr. |

## *Acronyms*

| | |
|---|---|
| CEF | Cuban Expeditionary Force |
| CI | Counter-Intelligence |
| CINCLANT | Commander-in-Chief, Atlantic Command |
| COB | Chief of Base |
| COMINT | Communications Intelligence |
| CPO | Chief Petty Officer |
| CRC | Consejo Revolucionario Cubano (Cuban Revolutionary Council) |
| CSPO | Clandestine Services Personnel Office |
| CTF | Cuban Task Force |
| DOD | Department of Defense |

| | |
|---|---|
| DPD | Development Projects Division (CIA Air Operations) |
| DSC | Distinguished Service Cross |
| DZ | Drop Zone |
| E.O.D. | Extension of Duty |
| FI | Foreign Intelligence |
| FRD | Frente Democratico Revolucionario (Democratic Revolutionary Front) |
| G-2 | Intelligence officer |
| GOC | Government of Cuba |
| GS-15 | Government Service level 15 |
| IO | Intelligence Officer |
| JCS | Joint Chiefs of Staff |
| LCI | Landing Craft, Infantry |
| LCU | Landing Craft, Utility |
| MSTS | Military Sea Transport Service |
| O/IC | Office of Intelligence Coordination |
| Ops | Operations |
| OSS | Office of Strategic Services |
| P&P | Policy and Plans operations |
| para. | Paragraph |
| PM | Paramilitary |
| PP | Propaganda operations |
| PRC | Project Review Committee |
| SNIE | Special National Intelligence Estimate |
| TDY | Temporary Duty |
| U-2 | U.S. high-altitude reconaissance aircraft |
| USIA | United States Information Agency |
| USIB | United States Intelligence Board |
| USMC | United States Marine Corps |
| USMCR | United States Marine Corps Reserve |
| USUN | United States Mission at the United Nations |
| WH | Western Hemisphere Division |
| WH/3 | Western Hemisphere Task Force 3 |
| WH/4 | Western Hemisphere Task Force 4, (Bay of Pigs Task Force) |

# Inspector General's Survey of the Cuban Operation October 1961

## A. INTRODUCTION

1. This is the Inspector General's report on the Central Intelligence Agency's ill-fated attempt to implement national policy by overthrowing the Fidel Castro regime in Cuba by means of a covert paramilitary operation.

2. The purpose of this report is to evaluate selected aspects of the agency's performance of this task, to describe weaknesses and failures disclosed by the study, and to make recommendations for their correction and avoidance in the future.

3. The report concentrates on the organization, staffing and planning of the project and on the conduct of the covert paramilitary phase of the operation, including comments on intelligence support, training, and security. It does not describe or analyze in detail the purely military phase of the effort.

4. The supporting annexes have been chosen to illustrate the evolution of national policy as outlined in Section F of the body of the report. Annex A is the basic policy paper approved by President Eisenhower on 17 March 1960. Annex B is a paper prepared by the project's operating chiefs for the briefing of President Kennedy in February 1961. Annexes C, D, and E are the planning papers successively prepared during March and April 1961 in the last few weeks before the invasion.

5. The report includes references to the roles played by Agency officials in Presidential conferences and interdepartmental meetings at which policy decisions affecting the course of the operation were taken, but it contains no evaluation of or judgment on any decision or action taken by any official not employed by the Agency.

6. In preparing the survey the Inspector General and his representatives interviewed about 125 Agency employees of all levels and studied a large quantity of documentary material.

## B. HISTORY OF THE PROJECT

1. The history of the Cuban project begins in 1959 and for the purposes of the survey ends with the invasion of Cuba by the Agency-supported Cuban brigade on 17 April 1961 and its defeat and capture by Castro's forces in the next two days.

2. Formal U.S. Government adoption of the project occurred on 17 March 1960, when, after preliminary preparations by the Agency, President Eisenhower approved an Agency paper titled "A Program of Covert Action Against the Castro Regime" (Annex A) and thereby authorized the Agency to undertake this program:

> a. Formation of a Cuban exile organization to attract Cuban loyalties, to direct opposition activities, and to provide cover for Agency operations.
> b. A propaganda offensive in the name of the opposition.
> c. Creation inside Cuba of a clandestine intelligence collection and action apparatus to be responsive to the direction of the exile organization.
> d. Development outside Cuba of a small paramilitary force to be introduced into Cuba to organize, train and lead resistance groups.

3. The budget for this activity was estimated at $4,400,000. The breakdown was: Political action, $950,000; propaganda, $1,700,000; paramilitary, $1,500,000; intelligence collection, $250,000.

4. This document, providing for the nourishment of a powerful internal resistance program through clandestine external assistance, was the basic and indeed the only U.S. Government policy paper issued throughout the life of the project. The concept was classic. The Cuban exile council would serve as cover for action which became publicly known. Agency personnel in contact with Cuban exiles would be documented as representatives of a group of private American businessmen. The hand of the U.S. Government would not appear.

## Preparatory Action

5. Some months of preparation had preceded presentation of this paper to the President. In August 1959 the Chief of the Agency's Paramilitary Group attended a meeting [excised] to discuss the creation of a paramilitary capability to be used in Latin American crisis situations. At this time Cuba was only one of a number of possible targets, all of which appeared equally explosive. The Chief of the Paramilitary Group prepared a series of staff studies for the Western Hemisphere (WH) Division on various aspects of covert lim-

ited warfare and urged the creation of a division paramilitary staff. He also set up a proprietary airline in [excised]for eventual support use.

6. In September 1959 the WH Division assigned an officer to plan potential Agency action for contingencies which might develop in a number of Latin American countries. There was a lack of sufficient readily available operational information on potential target areas, so a requirement, with special emphasis on Cuba, whose Communist control was now becoming more and more apparent, was sent throughout the intelligence community, and resulted in a three-volume operational study.

7. By December 1959 these studies had produced a plan for training a small cadre of Cuban exiles as paramilitary instructors, these in turn to be used for training other Cuban recruits, in a Latin American country, for clandestine infiltration into Cuba to provide leadership for anti-Castro dissidents.

## Organization of Branch

8. On 18 January 1960 the WH Division organized Branch 4 (WH/4) as an expandable task force to run the proposed Cuban operation. The initial Table of Organization totaled 40 persons, with 18 at Headquarters, 20 at Havana Station, and two at Santiago Base.

9. The branch also began negotiations for a Panama training site. Its officers reconnoitered the area of Miami, Florida, in search of suitable installations for office space, warehouses, safe sites, recruiting centers, communications center, and bases for the movement of persons, materiel, and propaganda into or out of Cuba.

10. At the same time Headquarters and the Havana Station were conducting a study of Cuban opposition leaders to prepare for the formation of a unified political front to serve as the cover instrument for clandestine operations and as a rallying point for anti-Castro Cubans. They were also making a map reconnaissance of the Caribbean, seeking a site for a powerful medium-wave and short-wave radio station.

## Preliminary Progress

11. As a result of this intensive activity over a relatively brief period the Agency was able to report considerable preliminary progress and to predict early performance in a number of respects, when it carried its request for policy approval to the President in mid-March of 1960.

12. Among the facts so reported (Annex A) were: That the Agency was in

close touch with leaders of three major and reputable anti- Castro groups of Cubans whose representatives, possibly together with others, would form a unified opposition council within 30 days; that the Agency was already supporting opposition broadcasts from Miami, had arranged for additional radio outlets in Massachusetts, [excised]and [excised], and that a powerful "gray" station, probably on Swan Island, could be made ready in two months; that publication of an exile edition of a confiscated Cuban newspaper had been arranged; that a controlled action group was distributing propaganda outside Cuba, and that anti-Castro lecturers were being sent on Latin American tours.

13. The President was further informed that an effective intelligence and action organization inside Cuba, responsive to direction by the exile opposition, could probably be created within 60 days and that preparations for the development of an adequate paramilitary force would require "a minimum of six months and probably closer to eight."

## Policy Discussions

14. Discussion at high policy levels of the Government had preceded submission of this program to the President. In the last months of 1959 the Special Group, composed of representatives of several departments and agencies and charged by NSC 5412 with responsibility for policy approval of major covert action operations, considered several Agency proposals for exile broadcasts to Cuba. During January and February of 1960, the Director of Central Intelligence informed the Special Group of Agency planning with regard to Cuba, and on 14 March an entire meeting was devoted to discussion of the Agency's program. Concern was expressed over the length of time required to get trained Cuban exiles into action, and there was discussion of U.S. capabilities for immediate overt action if required. The Chairman of the Joint Chiefs of Staff is reported to have said that forces totaling 50,000 men were ready if needed and that the first of them could be airborne within four hours after receipt of orders. Members of the group urged early formation of an exile junta. The Agency announced its intention of requesting funds to pursue the program, and no objections were raised by the group.

15. The project to unseat Castro had thus become a major Agency activity with the highest policy sanction, engaging the full-time activity of the personnel of a rapidly expanding operating branch, requiring a great amount of detailed day-to-day attention in higher Agency echelons and entailing frequent liaison with other agencies and departments of the Government.

16. The activities described to the President continued at an accelerated rate, but the financial approach to the project was relatively cautious in the early weeks.

## Financial Preparations

17. On 24 March 1960 the project was approved by the Director of Central Intelligence in the initial amount of $900,000 for the rest of Fiscal Year 1960. However, only two weeks later, on 7 April, WH/4 Branch reported that 85% of the $900,000 had been obligated. By 30 June an additional $1,000,000 was obligated.

18. In April the Director of Central Intelligence told a meeting of WH/4 personnel that he would recall people from anywhere in the world if they were needed on the project. From January 1960, when it had 40 people, the branch expanded to 588 by 16 April 1961, becoming one of the largest branches in the Clandestine Services, larger than some divisions. Its Table of Organization did not include the large number of air operations personnel who worked on the project and who were administered by their own unit, the Development Projects Division (DPD), nor did it include the many people engaged in support activities or in services of common concern, who, though not assigned to the project, nevertheless devoted many hours to it.

19. In the early months of the project there were intensive efforts to organize an exile front group, to get a broad and varied propaganda program under way, to begin a paramilitary program, and to acquire sites in Florida and elsewhere for training and recruiting activities and for office space.

20. The so-called "Bender Group" composed of project political action officers, was set up as a notional organization of American businessmen to provide cover for dealing with the Cubans. After a series of meetings in New York and Miami a nominally unified *Frente Revolucionario Democratico* (FRD), composed of several Cuban factions, was agreed upon on 11 May 1960.

## Propaganda Activity

21. Radio broadcasts from Miami into Cuba were continued under the sponsorship of a Cuban group. Preparations were made for exile publication of *Avance*, whose Havana plant had been seized by Castro. Anti-Castro propaganda operations were intensified throughout Latin America, and a boat for marine broadcasts was purchased. The Swan Island radio station, on

which the President had been briefed, was completed and on the air with test signals by 17 May.

22. The action-cadre instruction training program was being prepared, and $25,000 worth of sterile arms were being sent to the Panama training base, which was activated 11 May. At the same time Useppa Island, Florida, was acquired as a site for assessment and holding of Cuban paramilitary sites and for training radio operators. Screening of paramilitary recruits had begun in Miami in April, and the training in Panama began in June.

23. The Miami Base was opened on 25 May in the Coral Gables business district under cover of a New York career development and placement firm, backstopped by a Department of Defense contract, and on 15 June a communications site, with Army cover, was opened at the former Richmond Naval Air Station, which was held under lease by the University of Miami. Safe houses were also acquired in the Miami area for various operational uses. The use of other sites for project activities, in the United States and other countries, was acquired for varying periods as time went on.

24. Project officers were engaged in liaison on numerous matters. In April they reached an agreement with the Immigration and Naturalization Service on special entry procedure for Cubans of interest to the operation. They consulted with Voice of America and the United States Information Agency on propaganda operations. There were many discussions with the Federal Communications Commission on the licensing of Radio Swan and with the Defense Department concerning its cover. The State Department was regularly consulted on political matters.

## Uneasy Front

25. Although Cuban leaders had formed a "front" at Agency urging, it was an uneasy one. They were by no means in agreement, either among themselves or with Agency case officers, on politics or on operations.

26. Power struggles developed early in the life of the FRD. The Cuban leaders wanted something to say about the course of paramilitary operations. As early as May 1960 one of the more prominent leaders was urging an invasion on a fairly large scale from a third country.

27. By June the American press was beginning to nibble at the operation, principally at Radio Swan, some of the stories implying that it was not a completely legitimate commercial venture. Another indication that operational security was less than perfect was a statement by a defected Cuban naval attache that it was common knowledge among exiles in Miami that a certain

Cuban leader was backed by the Agency and that "there were entirely too many Americans running around the area waving money."

28. On 22 June the Deputy Director of Central Intelligence briefed the National Security Council on the project. Ultimate objective of the training program, according to the paper prepared for this briefing, was a minimum force of 500 men split into approximately 25 teams skilled in organizing, training and leading indigenous dissident groups, each team to be provided with a radio operator. Preparations were under way for creating an exile Cuban air force, and attempts were being made to develop maritime capabilities for support of paramilitary groups.

29. This briefing contained an expression of doubt that a purely clandestine effort would be able to cope with Castro's increasing military capability, pointing out that implementation of the paramilitary phase of operations would be contingent upon the existence of dissident forces who were willing to resist and that such groups had not as yet emerged in strength.

## *Training in Panama*

30. The air training program began to get under way in July 1960 with the screening of Cuban pilot recruits and negotiations with Defense for AD-5s and the Navy being asked to supply 75 instruction and maintenance personnel.

31. In mid-June 29 Cubans had arrived in Panama to begin training in small-unit infiltration.

32. The FRD was resisting Agency attempts to persuade it to move its headquarters to Mexico and was demanding direct contact with the State Department or with some high government office in order to argue its case. It also showed reluctance to become involved in the recruiting of Cuban pilots. It presented a budget for $500,000 a month, excluding paramilitary costs, but was told it would have to get along on $131,000 and would get this only if it agreed to move to Mexico. It did agree to furnish 500 paramilitary candidates and finally gave in on the issue of moving to Mexico. It remained there only a few weeks because of harassment by the Mexican Government, in spite of prior agreements to the contrary. It appears that one reason why the FRD leaders were so reluctant to be based in a third country is that they desired to establish a direct, official channel to the U.S. Government.

## *Emphasis on Resistance*

33. In August WH/4 Branch prepared papers for use in briefing the President and the Joint Chiefs or Staff, respectively. By about 1 November it was

expected to have 500 paramilitary trainees and 37 radio operators ready for action. It was stated that this group would be available for use as infiltration teams or as an invasion force. The briefing paper for the Joint Chiefs made the point that "obviously the successful implementation of any large-scale paramilitary operations is dependent upon widespread guerrilla resistance throughout the area."

34. The paper prepared for the President's briefing identified 11 groups or individuals with whom the Agency had some sort of contact and who claimed to have assets in Cuba. The paper for the Joint Chiefs spoke of the problems of obtaining support bases and trained man power and warned that an exile invasion force might have to be backed up by a contingency force, augmented by U.S. Army Special Forces personnel.

35. The terms "invasion," "strike," and "assault" were used in these documents although the strike force concept does not seem to have been given any sort of policy sanction until the Special Group meeting which took place toward the end of 1960.

## Plan of Operations

36. The Presidential briefing paper of August 1960 outlined the plan of operations as follows:

"The initial phase of paramilitary operations envisages the development, support and guidance of dissident groups in three areas of Cuba: Pinar del Rio, Escambray and Sierra Maestra. These groups will be organized for concerted guerrilla action against the regime.

"The second phase will be initiated by a combined sea-air assault by FRD forces on the Isle of Pines coordinated with general guerrilla activity on the main island of Cuba. This will establish a close-in staging base for future operations.

"The last phase will be air assault on the Havana area with the guerrilla forces in Cuba moving on the ground from these areas into the Havana area also."

37. Expenditures were rapidly running beyond the original estimates. The WH Division estimated operating costs for four weeks starting 1 July at $1,700,000 and for the fiscal year at approximately $25,000,000. On 19 August an additional $10,000,000 was requested and obtained. About half of this figure was the estimated cost of paramilitary activities, with about another $2,000,000 estimated for propaganda.

## Anti-Castro Broadcasts

38. Propaganda activity had gotten off to an early start and had developed rapidly. After an initial shakedown period Radio Swan had gone on the air first with anti-Trujillo, then with anti-Castro broadcasts. Radio programs were also originating in Miami and [excised]. The newspaper *Avance in Exile* was being published by the end of the summer, and a second paper and a weekly magazine were planned. There had also been some successful black operations. Most such operations had thus far been conducted without participation by the FRD.

39. By the end of August the FRD had a lawyer team set for a Latin American propaganda tour and was ready with its first broadcast on Radio Swan, which was reported to be getting world-wide reception with many listeners in Cuba. An anti-Castro comic book was being reprinted, and a Spanish-language television program was being prepared in Miami.

40. At the end of August WH/4 Branch was reporting that a machine run search had failed to find any bilingual Agency employee suitable as a Radio Swan announcer. (This search went on for some time. On 28 December the branch reported finding a candidate, but on 18 January 1961 that he had backed out.)

41. Late September 1960 saw the almost simultaneous occurrence of the first maritime operation and the first air drop over Cuba. The former was successful. The latter, the first of a series of failures, resulted in the capture and execution of a paramilitary agent on whom the project had set great store.

## Maritime Operations

42. Several successful maritime operations took place during the latter months of 1960 before severe winter weather began to make them almost impossible. But the project had only one boat regularly available during this period, and the process of supplying and building up a resistance movement through clandestine means began to seem intolerably slow, especially since during this same period Castro's army was reported to have been strengthened with 30 to 40 thousand tons of Bloc arms, and Cuban internal security was being tightened.

43. The strike force concept which, as noted, had already begun to be associated with the project as early as July, began to play an ever greater role in WH/4 planning. This role became dominant in September 1960 with the assignment to the project, as chief of its Paramilitary Staff, of a Marine Corps colonel experienced in amphibious operations.

44. In late October the Nicaraguan Government offered the Agency the use of an air strip and docking facilities at Puerto Cabezas, some 250 miles closer to Cuba than the facilities in Guatemala. At about the same time, the Agency requested the Army to supply 38 Special Forces personnel as instructors. Due to prolonged policy negotiations, those trainers did not arrive in Guatemala until 12 January 1961.

## Switch in Concept

45. On 4 November 1960 WH/4 took formal action to change the course of the project by greatly expanding the size of the Cuban paramilitary unit and redirecting its training along more conventional military lines. Appropriate orders were sent to the Guatemala Base, which had 475 air and ground trainees on 10 November, and to Miami where recruiting efforts were increased.

46. By this time Miami Base, through liaison with the FRD military staff, had already recruited and dispatched to Guatemala 101 air and 370 paramilitary trainees, plus six specialists (doctors, dentists, and chaplains). The base had also recruited 124 maritime personnel for manning the invasion fleet that was being acquired.

47. By 28 January 1961 the strike force strength was 644, on 3 February it was 685, by 10 March it had risen to 826, by 22 March to 973. On 6 April 1961 brigade strength was reported at 1,390.

48. On 3 November 1960 WH/4 reported it had only $2,250,000 left for the rest of Fiscal Year 1961, and by 16 December this was almost gone. A supplementary budget estimate was prepared, and an additional $28,200,000 was obtained from the Bureau of the Budget.

## Freedom Fund Campaign

49. There were also financial problems on a smaller scale. To publicize Radio Swan, and perhaps to enhance its cover, the Cuban Freedom Fund Campaign was organized in November to solicit donations through newspaper advertisements. The radio station, which was budgeted at $900,000 for Fiscal Year 1961, received $330 in gifts during the next few weeks.

50. *Bohemia Libre*, a handsome weekly magazine, budgeted at $300,000 but actually costing about $35,000 an issue, had bad luck from the start in seeking advertising and once missed an issue on that account. Additional funds had to be sought for it several times. Yet it developed an audited circulation of 126,000, said to be second only to the *Reader's Digest* in the Spanish-language field.

51. While the project moved forward, acquiring boats, planes and bases, training men, negotiating with foreign governments, seeking policy clarification, training an FRD security service, publishing magazines and newspapers, putting out radio broadcasts, and attempting to move arms, men and propaganda into Cuba by sea or air, the FRD, in whose name most of this activity was being carried on, was making little progress toward unity.

52. Members would resign in a huff and have to be wheedled back. Each faction wanted supplies to be sent only to its own followers in Cuba, while groups inside were reluctant to receive infiltrees sent in the name of the FRD. The FRD coordinator had his own radio boat which made unauthorized broadcasts until halted by the Federal Communications Commission and the Federal Bureau of Investigation.

## Provisional Government Plans

53. Tentative plans for a provisional government were first discussed with FRD leaders in December, and this set off a flurry of intrigue and bickering which delayed the recruiting process and did nothing to advance the cause of unity. In mid-January Miami Base reported that "the over-all problem is simply to maintain the Frente (FRD) as an operational facade until military action intervenes and a provisional government can be established." Until the question of how and by whom such a government was to be selected could be answered, the base reported, "We are at political dead center."

54. This dead center remained until very near the target date and was only resolved by an ultimatum to the FRD Executive Committee directing its members to agree on the chairman for a Revolutionary Council or risk the loss of all further support.

55. However, in selective ways the FRD proved to be a responsive and useful instrument. An example of this was the counterintelligence and security service which, under close project control, developed into an efficient and valuable unit in support of the FRD, Miami Base, and the project program.

56. By mid-March 1961 this security organization comprised 86 employees of whom 37 were trainee case officers, the service having graduated four classes from its own training center, whose chief instructor was a [excised] police officer.

## Security Activities

57. The FRD's service ran operations into Cuba, many of them successful. It built up a voluminous set of card files on Cuban personalities. One of its

most helpful services was reporting on meetings of FDR committees and other anti-Castro groups and on political maneuvering within the FRD hierarchy. It also helped in recruiting for the strike force at a time when the political leaders were sabotaging the effort. Security and counterintelligence teams were also trained for integration with the strike force. These had the primary mission of securing vital records and documents during the invasion and a secondary mission of assisting in establishing and maintaining martial law.

58. The service also carried on radio monitoring and conducted interrogations and debriefings. An indication of its alertness and efficiency is the fact that it supplied Miami Base with its first information on the location of a C-54 plane which was forced down in Jamaica after a mission over Cuba. The chief of the service was largely responsible for personally persuading the crew of the downed plane to return to the training camp.

59. In the first three months of 1961 the problems faced by the project were many and complex. Although the Army Special Forces instructors had finally arrived in Guatemala the brigade trainee quota was still only half fulfilled and a call went to the training camps for special recruiting teams to be sent to Miami. Meanwhile trainees who had been in the camp for several months had had no contact with the political front and were wondering what sort of a Cuban future they were expected to fight for. Disturbances broke out, and the project leaders persuaded three FRD figures to visit the camp and mollify the men.

## Training in the U.S.

60. During this period the Nicaraguan air strip which had been placed at the project's disposal was being made ready for use and two new training sites were activated. Although a definite policy determination on the training of Cubans in the U.S. had never been made, 25 tank operators were successfully trained for the strike force at Fort Knox. Another eleventh-hour training requirement was fulfilled when the project acquired the use of Belle Chase Ammunition Depot near New Orleans. This was used for the training of a company-sized unit hurriedly recruited for a diversion landing and of an underwater demolition team.

61. During the period between the U.S. national elections and the inauguration of President Kennedy the Government's policymaking machinery had slowed down. A number of piecemeal policy decisions were vouchsafed, but not all the specific ones the project chiefs were pressing for, for example,

authority for tactical air strikes and permission to use American contract pilots.

62. President Eisenhower had given a general go-ahead signal on 29 November and had reaffirmed it on 3 January 1961, but the impending change in administration was slowing matters down. For example, a proposed propaganda drop was turned down on 13 January for this reason. On 19 January, at the Special Group's last meeting before the inauguration, it was agreed that a high-level meeting, to include the new Secretaries of State and Defense, should be set up as soon as possible to reaffirm the basic concepts of the project.

## Preparations Endorsed

63. Such a meeting was held 22 January, and the project and current preparations were generally endorsed. At a meeting with the new President on 28 January the Agency was authorized to continue present activities and was instructed to submit the tactical paramilitary plan to the Joint Chiefs of Staff for analysis. Shortly thereafter, in an attempt to get a high-level internal review of the plan, it was briefed to Gen. Cabell, Gen. Bull (consultant) and Adm. Wright (ONE). By 6 February the Joint Chiefs had returned a favorable evaluation of the strike plan, together with a number of suggestions.

64. On 17 February the Agency presented a paper (Annex B) to the President which outlined three possible courses of action against Castro.

65. Noting plans for early formation of a government in exile, the paper described the growing strength of the Castro regime under Bloc support and observed: "Therefore, after some date probably no more than six months away it will become militarily infeasible to overthrow the Castro regime except by the commitment to combat of a sizeable organized military force. The option of action by the Cuban opposition will no longer be open."

66. This paper found the use of small-scale guerrilla groups not feasible and advocated a surprise landing of a military force, concluding that the brigade had a good chance of overthrowing Castro "or at the very least causing a damaging civil war without requiring the U.S. to commit itself to overt action against Cuba."

67. Following presentation of this paper to the President, the project leaders were given to understand that it would be at least two weeks before a decision would be made as to use of the invasion force. They thereupon withheld action to expand the force up to 1,000 for the time being.

## Movement of Agents

68. Although the invasion preparations were absorbing most of the project's energies and funds WH/4 Branch was still attempting to nourish the underground. There were six successful boat operations, carrying men and materials, in February and 13 in March, and two successful air drops in March. Infiltration of agents was continuing. As of 15 February Miami Base reported the following numbers and types of agents in Cuba: Counterintelligence, 20; positive intelligence, 5; propaganda, 2; paramilitary, 4. As of 15 March the base reported that these numbers had risen, respectively, to 21, 11, 9, and 6.

69. By the invasion date the personnel strength of Miami Base had grown to 160. The intensity of activity there during the latter months of the operation is indicated by the record of a day picked at random—it happened to be 9 February—when 21 case officers spent 140 man hours in personal contact with 125 Cubans.

70. Successive changes in the operational plan and postponements of the strike date are discussed later in this report and are documented in Annexes C, D, and E. Detailed policy authorization for some specific actions was either never fully clarified or only resolved at the eleventh hour, and even the central decision as to whether to employ the strike force was still somewhat in doubt up to the very moment of embarkation.

71. During the weeks preceding the invasion the pace of events quickened. In early March the State Department asked the Agency not to announce formation of the Revolutionary Council or to commit any untoward act until after the 5–9 March Mexico City Peace Conference. The Cubans conferring in New York disagreed on various aspects of a post-Castro platform. The Guatemala camp was having counterintelligence problems.

## Sabotage Action

72. On 12 March the LCI "Barbara J" successfully launched and recovered a sabotage team in an action against the Texaco refinery in Santiago.

73. During 13–15 March project chiefs were working intensively to prepare a revised plan which would meet policy objections cited by the State Department. On the 15th the new plan was presented to the President.

74. In mid-March ten members were added to the FRD Executive Committee, the politicians continued their platform talks, and 23 March was set as deadline for choice of a chairman. An intensive defection project was started from Miami Base. A survey was started with the object of determining the

trainees' knowledgeability of U.S. involvement in the strike preparations. Trainees at Guatemala were impatient, and a number had gone AWOL.

75. José *Miro* Cardona was unanimously elected Chairman of the Revolutionary Council.

76. In late March the [excised] ostensible owner of the Swan Island radio station, thanked all the sponsors of political programs and advised them that no more tapes would be required; purpose of this action was to clear the way for a unity program during the action phase of the operation. A Radio Swan listener survey had received 1,659 replies from 20 countries. Ships with strike force equipment were arriving in Nicaragua, and the Guatemala camp was still receiving trainees as late as the week of 4 April.

## Overflights Suspended

77. Cuban overflights were suspended on 28 March. Two reasons have been given for this suspension: (a) that the air-craft were needed to move the strike force from Guatemala to Puerto Cabezas, Nicaragua, for embarkation on the invasion ships; (b) that the Agency wished to avoid any incident, such as a plane being downed over Cuba, which might upset the course of events during the critical pre-invasion period.

78. For a White House meeting on 29 March papers were prepared on these subjects: (a) The status of the defection program; (b) internal Cuban support which could be expected for the landing operation.

79. On 5 April the B-26 "defection" plan was prepared in an effort to knock out some of Castro's air force before D Day in a manner which would satisfy State Department objections. Project chiefs agreed that in event of a policy decision to call off the invasion they would move the troops to sea, tell them that new intelligence made the invasion inadvisable, and divert the force to Vieques Island for demobilization.

80. On 12 April at a meeting with the President it was decided that Mr. Berle world tell Miro Cardona there would be no overt U.S. support of the invasion. The President publicly announced there would be no U.S. support. On 13 April all WH/4 headquarters sections went on 24 hour duty. The Revolutionary Council was assembled in New York and advised that it would be briefed in stages on the military aspects of the project. On 14 April the Council agreed to go into "isolation" during the landing phase of the military operation.

81. The raids on three Cuban airfields were carried out by eight B-26s on 15 April, and destruction of half of Castro's air force was estimated on the

basis of good post-strike photography. Afterward, according to plan, one of the pilots landed in Florida and announced that the raids had been carried out by defectors from Castro's own air force. The Council was briefed on the air strike. The diversionary expedition by the force which had been trained in New Orleans failed to make a landing on two successive nights preceding the strike.

82. Immediately before D Day, Radio Swan and other outlets were broadcasting 18 hours a day on medium-wave and 16 hours on short-wave. Immediately after D Day, these totals were increased to 55 hours and 26 hours, respectively. Fourteen frequencies were used. By the time of the invasion a total of 12,000,000 pounds of leaflets had been dropped on Cuba.

83. Late on 16 April, the eve of D Day, the air strikes designed to knock out the rest of Castro's air force on the following morning were called off. The message reached the field too late to halt the landing operation, as the decision to cancel the air strike was made after the landing force had been committed.

84. The invasion fleet which had assembled off the south coast of Cuba on the night of 16 April included two LCIs owned by the Agency, a U.S. Navy LSD carrying three LCUs and four LCVPs, all of them pre-loaded with supplies, and seven chartered commercial freighters. All these craft participated in the assault phase, except for three freighters which were loaded with follow-up supplies for ground and air forces. These vessels were armed with 50-caliber machine guns. In addition, each LCI mounted two 75-mm. recoilless rifles.

85. In addition to the personal weapons of the Cuban exile soldiers, the armament provided for combat included sufficient numbers of Browning automatic rifles, machine guns, mortars, recoilless rifles, rocket launchers, and flame-throwers. There were also five M-41 tanks, 12 heavy trucks, an aviation fuel tank truck, a tractor crane, a bulldozer, two large water trailers, and numerous small trucks and tractors.

86. The invasion brigade comprised 1,511 men, all of them on the invasion ships excepting one airborne infantry company of 177 men. The brigade included five infantry companies, a heavy weapons company, an intelligence-reconnaissance company, and a tank platoon.

87. These troops had been moved by air on three successive nights from the Guatemala training camp to the staging area in Nicaragua where they embarked on the ships which had been pre-loaded at New Orleans. The ships had moved on separate courses from Nicaragua, under unobtrusive Navy escort, to the rendezvous 40 miles offshore in order to avoid the ap-

pearance of a convoy. From there they had moved in column under cover of darkness to a point 5,000 yards from the landing area, where they met the Navy LSD. Those complicated movements were apparently accomplished in a secure manner and without alerting the enemy.

88. Of the three follow-up ships, one was due to arrive from Nicaragua on the morning of D Day plus 2 and two others were on call at sea south of Cuba. Additional supplies were available for air landing or parachute delivery at airfields in Guatemala, Nicaragua, and Florida. At a Defense base in Anniston, Alabama, there were also supplies ready for 15,000 men. Altogether there were arms and equipment available to furnish 30,000 dissidents expected to rally to the invasion force.

89. The landing was to be carried out at three beaches about 18 miles from each other on the Zapata Peninsula. The left flank of the beachhead was Red Beach at the head of Cochinos Bay; Green Beach was at the right flank, with Blue Beach at the center. The lodgment to be seized was thus a coastal strip about 40 miles long, separated from the interior by an sizeable swamp penetrated only by three roads from the north and flanked by a coastal road from the east.

90. In the early hours of 17 April Cuban underwater demolition teams, each led by an American contract employee, went ashore to mark Red and Blue Beaches. Each of those parties engaged in fire fights with small enemy forces but accomplished their tasks, and the troops began moving ashore in small aluminum boats and LCUs. Before daylight small militia forces were encountered at both beaches. These offered little opposition, and many of the militiamen were quickly captured.

91. Not long after daylight the airborne infantry company was successfully parachuted from C-46 aircraft to four of the five scheduled drop zones where its elements were given the mission of sealing off approach roads.

92. At dawn began the enemy attacks which the project chiefs had aimed to present by the planned dawn strikes with Nicaragua-based aircraft against Castro's fields. Action by Castro's B-26s, Sea Furies, and jet T-33s resulted in the sinking of a supply ship, the beaching of a transport, and damage to an LCI. The plan for a landing at Green Beach was thereupon abandoned and these troops, with their tanks and vehicles were put ashore at Blue Beach. Shipping withdrew to the south under continuous air attack.

93. The air attacks continued throughout the day. The 11 B-26s of the Cuban exile force which were available for close support and interdiction were no match for the T-33 jets. However, at least four of Castro's other air-

craft were shot down by machine gun fire from maritime craft, assisted by friendly air support.

94. The first ground attacks by Castro's forces occurred at Red Beach which was hit by successive waves of militia in the morning, afternoon and evening of 17 April. While ammunition lasted those attacks were beaten off with heavy enemy casualties and several of Castro's tanks were halted or destroyed by ground or friendly air action. On the morning of 18 April, the Red Beach Force, nearly out of ammunition, retired in good order to Blue Beach without being pressed by the enemy.

95. In addition to supporting the ground forces and protecting shipping on 17 April, the friendly B-26s also sank a Castro patrol escort ship and attacked the Cienfuegos airfield. Four of the friendly B-26s were shot down, while three returned safely to Nicaragua, and four landed at other friendly bases.

96. Attempts were made to resupply the brigade with ammunition by air drops. On the night of 17–18 April one C-54 drop was made at Red Beach and three at Blue Beach, and on the following night Blue Beach received two drops. Preparations for resupply by sea had to be canceled due to enemy air action.

97. At Blue Beach the enemy ground attacks, supported by aircraft, began from three directions on the afternoon of 18 April. Six friendly B-26s, two of them flown by Americans, inflicted heavy damage on the Castro column moving up from the west, using napalm, bombs, rockets, and machine gun fire to destroy several tanks and about 20 troop-laden trucks. Air support to the Blue Beach troops was continued on the morning of 19 April, when three friendly B-26s, including two piloted by Americans, were shot down by Castro T-33s. Jet cover from the Navy aircraft carrier "Essex" had been expected to protect the 19 April sorties but a misunderstanding over timing hampered its effectiveness.

98. In spite of this air action, however, and in spite of a reported 1,800 casualties suffered by the Castro forces, the brigade's ability to resist depended in the last resort on resupply of ammunition, which had now become impossible. On the night of 18 April, when failure appeared inevitable, the Cuban brigade commander refused an offer to evacuate his troops. And on the morning of 19 April, with ammunition rapidly running out, the brigade was still able to launch a futile counterattack against the forces relentlessly moving in from the west.

99. In the last hours of resistance the brigade commander sent a series of

terse and desperate messages to the task force command ship pleading for help:

"We are out of ammo and fighting on the beach. Please send help. We cannot hold."

"In water. Out of ammo. Enemy closing in. Help must arrive in next hour."

"When your help will be here and with what?"

"Why your help has not come?"

100. The last message was as follows: "Am destroying all equipment and communications. Tanks are in sight. I have nothing to fight with. Am taking to woods. I cannot repeat cannot wait for you."

101. An evacuation convoy was headed for the beach on the afternoon of 19 April. When it became known that the beachhead had collapsed the convoy reversed course.

102. During the next few days two Americans and a crew of Cuban frogmen succeeded in rescuing 26 survivors from the beach and coastal islands.

## C. SUMMARY OF EVALUATION

1. In evaluating the Agency's performance it is essential to avoid grasping immediately, as many persons have done, at the explanation that the President's order canceling the D-Day airstrikes was the chief cause of failure.

2. Discussion of that one decision would merely raise this underlying question: If the project had been better conceived, better organized, better staffed and better managed, would that precise issue ever have had to be presented for Presidential decision at all? And would it have been presented under the same ill-prepared, inadequately briefed circumstances?

3. Furthermore, it is essential to keep in mind the possibility that the invasion was doomed in advance, that an initially successful landing by 1,500 men would eventually have been crushed by Castro's combined military resources strengthened by Soviet Bloc-supplied military materiel.

4. The fundamental cause of the disaster was the Agency's failure to give the project, notwithstanding its importance and its immense potentiality for damage to the United States, the top-flight handling which it required— appropriate organization, staffing throughout by highly qualified personnel, and full-time direction and control of the highest quality.

5. Insufficiencies in these vital areas resulted in pressures and distortions, which in turn produced numerous serious operational mistakes and omissions, and in lack of awareness of developing dangers, in failure to take action

to counter them, and in grave mistakes of judgment. There was failure at high levels to concentrate informed, unwavering scrutiny on the project and to apply experienced, unbiased judgment to the menacing situations that developed.

## D. EVALUATION OF ORGANIZATION AND COMMAND STRUCTURE

1. The project was organized at the level of an operating branch, the fourth echelon in the organization of the Agency, in the Western Hemisphere Division. Its chief, a GS-15, was not given the independence and the broad, extensive powers of a fast force commander. Instead, he had to apply constantly for the decision of policy questions and important operational problems to the Deputy Director (Plans) (DD/P), who was in fact directing the project, although this was only one of his many responsibilities. The DD/P delegated much of his responsibility to his Deputy for Covert Action, especially the handling of policy matters involving contact with non-Agency officials. The office of the DD/P and the offices of the project were in different buildings. Consideration was given by the DD/P in late 1960 to raising the project out of WH Division and placing it directly under his Deputy for Covert Action, but this was not done.

2. The Chief of WH Division was in the chain of command between the chief of the project and the DD/P but only in a partial sense. He exercised his right to sign the project's outgoing cables until the week of the invasion even though the project's own signal center was activated at the end of December 1960. He supervised the staffing activities and attended same of the meetings of the Special Group. But the DD/P and his deputy dealt directly with the project chief, and gradually the Chief of WH Division began to play only a diminished role.

3. The DD/P, in turn, reported to the Director of Central Intelligence (DCI) and the Deputy Director of Central Intelligence (DDCI) who usually represented the Agency at the meetings of the 5412 Special Group.

4. The Director delegated his responsibility for major project decisions to a considerable extent. He relied on the DDCI, an Air Force general, for policy matters involving air operations. For military advice he relied on the military officers detailed to the project. This reliance deprived the Director of completely objective counsel, since the project's military personnel were

deeply involved in building up the strike force and the DDCI was taking an active role in the conduct of air operations.

## Fragmentation of Authority

5. Thus, the project lacked a single, high-level full-time commander possessing stated broad powers and abilities sufficient for the carrying out of this large, enormously difficult mission. In fact, authority was fragmented among the project chief, the military chief of the project's Paramilitary Staff, and several high-level officials, whose responsibilities elsewhere in the Agency prevented them from giving the project the attention it required. There were too many echelons; the top level had to be briefed by briefers who themselves were not doing the day-to-day work.

6. Three further extraordinary factors must be mentioned:

(1) The Chief of Operations of the Clandestine Services (COPS), who is the DD/P's chief staff advisor on clandestine operations, played only a very minor part in the project. On at least two occasions COPS was given express warning that the project was being perilously mismanaged, but he declined to involve himself with the project.

(2) The three Senior Staffs, the Agency's top-level technical advisors in their respective areas, were not consulted fully, either at the important formative stages of the project or even after grave operational difficulties had begun to develop; instead, they allowed themselves to be more or less ignored by the chief of the project and his principal assistants. This state of affairs is partly attributable to the inadequate managerial skill and the lack of experience in clandestine paramilitary operations of the WH/4 chiefs; it was not corrected by the DD/P or his deputy or by the Chief of WH Division.

(3) There was no review of the project by the Agency's Project Review Committee, which would at least have allowed the views of the most senior review body in the Agency to be heard.

## Independence of DPD

7. Still another important factor in the diffusion of direction and control was the insistence of the Agency's air arm, the Development Projects Division (DPD), on preserving its independence and remaining outside the organizational structure of the project, in which it had a vital, central role, including air drops to the underground, training Cuban pilots, operation of air bases, the immense logistical problems of transporting the Cuban volunteers from Florida to Guatemala, and the procuring and servicing of the mili-

tary planes. The project chief had no command authority over air planning and air operations. The DPD unit established for this purpose was completely independent.

8. The result was a divided command dependent upon mutual cooperation. There was no day-to-day continuing staff relationship, which is essential for properly coordinated operations. Headquarters of the two units were in different buildings far away from each other. The chiefs of air operations in Guatemala and Nicaragua were DPD representatives, independent of the WH/4 chiefs of these bases, and the Headquarters confusion was compounded in the field.

9. In October 1960, shortly after his assignment to the project, the paramilitary chief noted coordination difficulties between WH/4 and DPD. He pointed out that the organizational structure was contrary to military command principles, to accepted management practices, and to the principles enunciated by the DD/P himself in 1959, and recommended that the DPD Unit be integrated into WH/4, under command of its chief.

## Failure of Integration Effort

10. The DD/P rejected this recommendation as not being the most efficient solution for technical reasons. The insufficiently effective relationship between the project and the DPD unit was one of the gravest purely organizational failures of the operation. The DD/P has subsequently confirmed this conclusion and has ascribed this lack of effectiveness to personality frictions and to the "classic service rivalry." (We would note that this does not exist in present-day combined commands.)

11. The organizational confusion was augmented by the existence of a large forward operating base in the Miami area, which in turn had loose control over several sub-bases. The mission of this base was vaguely defined and not well understood. In theory the base had a supporting role; actually it was conducting operations which for the most part paralleled similar operations being conducted by WH/4 from Headquarters. This divided effort was expensive, cumbersome, and difficult to coordinate. In some cases the efforts of the two elements were duplicating or conflicting or even competing with each other.

12. The upshot of this complex and bizarre organizational situation was that in this tremendously difficult task the Agency failed to marshal its forces properly and to apply them effectively.

## E. EVALUATION OF STAFFING

1. In April 1960 the Director of Central Intelligence stated that he would recall from any station in the world personnel whose abilities were required for the success of the project. This recognition of the need for high-quality personnel is nowhere reflected in the history of the project. The DD/P's Deputy for Covert Action advised his subordinates that the Director's words did not mean that the project was to be given *carte blanche* in personnel procurement but that officers could be adequately secured through negotiation.

2. In actual fact, personnel for the project were secured by the customary routine method of negotiation between the project and the employee's office of current assignment; no recourse was had to directed assignment by the Director of Central Intelligence. The traditional independence of the 55 individual division and branch chiefs in the Clandestine Services remained unaffected by the Director's statement. The lists prepared by the project for the purpose of negotiation for personnel naturally reflected the preferences of the chief of the project and the willingness of the person in question to accept the assignment. In many cases, the reason for assigning a given person to the project was merely that he had just returned from abroad and was still without an assignment.

3. The basic mistake was made of filling the key spots early, without realizing how much the project would grow and that it should be staffed for a major effort. In same cases, officers originally selected to supervise five persons ultimately had to supervise 15 or 20 times as many. Of the three GS-16 officers assigned to the project, none was given top-level managerial responsibilities. The result of all these factors was that none of the most experienced, senior operating officers of the Agency participated full time in the project.

## An Indication Of Quality

4. An interesting insight into the quality of the personnel of WH/4 is afforded by the initial "Relative Retention Lists" prepared in April 1961 by the divisions and senior staffs of the Clandestine Services and other Agency units pursuant to the requirements of Regulation 20–701 (Separation of Surplus Personnel). Each such unit was required to group its officers in each grade into ten groups, on the basis of the performance and qualifications of each one. (Under the prescribed procedure, these lists are to be reviewed at several levels before becoming definitive.)

5. Of the 42 officers holding the principal operations jobs in WH/4 in

grade GS-12 through GS-15, 17 officers were placed in the lowest third of their respective grade, and 9, or 21% in the lowest tenth. The ratings of 23 of these 42 were made by WH Division, which placed seven in the lowest third, and 19 were rated by other units, which together placed ten in the lowest third.

6. It is apparent from these ratings that the other units had not detailed their best people to WH/4 but had in some instances given the project their disposal cases.

7. Furthermore, although the project eventually included the large number of 588 personnel, there were long periods in which important slots went unfilled, due to difficulty in procuring suitable officers. For example, the counterintelligence officer of the Miami Base was never supplied with a case officer assistant, there was a long period in which the project professed inability to find a CI officer for the Guatemala Base, and months were spent in search of an announcer for Radio Swan. Few Clandestine Services people were found who were capable of serving as base chiefs; the support services had to supply most of them. All of the paramilitary officers had to be brought from outside WH Division, or even from outside the Agency. (Air operations presented no staffing problem for WH/4, since DPD supplied its own people.)

8. There were in fact insufficient people to do the job during the latter stages of the project. Personnel worked such long hours and so intensively that their efficiency was affected. Personnel shortages were one of the reasons why much of the work of the project was performed on a "crash" basis.

## Scarcity of Linguists

9. Very few project personnel spoke Spanish or had Latin American background knowledge. In a number of instances those senior operating personnel in the field stations that did speak Spanish had to be interrupted in their regular duties merely in order to act as interpreters. This lack occurred in part because of the scarcity of Spanish linguists in the Agency and in part because WH Division did not transfer to the project sufficient numbers of its own Spanish speakers.

10. There were many other examples of improper use of skilled personnel. In many instances, case officers were used merely as "handholders" for agents and technical specialists were used as stevedores. Some of the people who served the project on contract turned out to be incompetent.

11. Staffing of the project was defective because the whole Clandestine Services staffing system, with absolute power being exercised by the division and branch chiefs, is defective. Each division seeks to guard its own assets; scanty recognition is given to the respective priorities of the various projects.

12. In spite of the foregoing, there were a great many excellent people in the project who worked effectively and who developed considerably in the course of their work. It should also be emphasized that, almost without exception, personnel worked extremely long hours for months on end without complaint and otherwise manifested high motivation, together with great perseverance and ingenuity in solving the manifold problems that the project constantly raised. It should be stated that in general the support people sent to the project by the support component were of excellent quality and effective performance.

13. Unfortunately, however, while many persons performed prodigies of effort, these were often directed towards overcoming obstacles which better organization and management would have eliminated. Such efforts were especially necessary (a) in support of the chimera of "non-attributability" of the operation; (b) in negotiating with the Armed Services for equipment, training personnel, etc., which the Agency should have been able to request as of right; and (c) in providing the support for an overt military enterprise that was too large for the Agency's capabilities.

## F. EVALUATION OF PLANNING

1. Before proceeding to an evaluation of the Agency's planning, the overall policy decisions of the United States Government with reference to the Cuban operation will first be stated in summary form. These decisions not only constituted the background against which Agency planning was conducted but also presented numerous important factors that limited or otherwise determined its scope.

2. We will next endeavor to point out the various occasions on which we believe that the Agency officials responsible for the project made serious planning errors, both of commission and of omission, which affected the project in vital respects.

3. Between the plan approved by President Eisenhower on 17 March 1960 (Annex A) and the invasion plan actually carried out on 17 April 1961 (Annex E) there was a radical change in concept. Originally the heart of the plan was a long, slow, clandestine build-up of guerrilla forces, to be trained and devel-

oped in Cuba by a cadre of Cubans whom the Agency would recruit, train and infiltrate into Cuba.

4. But thirteen months later the Agency sponsored an overt assault-type amphibious landing of 1,500 combat-trained and heavily armed soldiers. Most of them were unversed in guerrilla warfare. They were expected to maintain themselves for a period of time (some said a week) sufficient to administer a "shock" and thereby, it was hoped, to trigger an uprising.

## Discard of Original Plan

5. By November 1960 the original planning paper (Annex A) had for practical purposes ceased to exist as a charter for Agency action. By that date the Special Group had come to be unanimously of the opinion that the changed conditions, chiefly Castro's increased military strength through Soviet support and the increased effectiveness of his security forces, had made the original covert activities plan obsolete.

6. The Special Group had, however, not yet agreed on a substitute plan and strong doubt was expressed whether anything less than overt U.S. forces would suffice to obtain Castro's downfall. But there appeared to be agreement that, whatever the ultimate decision, it would be advantageous for the United States to have some trained Cuban refugees available for eventual use, and that CIA should continue to prepare such a force.

7. At the end of November 1960, the Agency presented a revised plan to President Eisenhower and his advisors. This included (a) infiltration into Cuba by air of 80 men in small paramilitary teams, after reception committees had been prepared by men infiltrated by sea; (b) an amphibious landing of a team of 650–700 men with extraordinarily heavy firepower; (c) preliminary air strikes against military targets. CIA stated that it believed it feasible to seize and hold a limited area in Cuba and then to draw dissident elements to the landing force, which would then gradually achieve enough stature to trigger a general uprising. At this stage of the planning, clandestine nourishment of resistance forces was still an important element, though now overshadowed by the overt strike force concept.

8. President Eisenhower orally directed the Agency to go ahead with its preparations with all speed. But this meeting occurred during the U.S. political interregnum and the proposed target date was later than 20 January 1961, so that in effect the President's instructions were merely to proceed and to keep the preparations going until the new Administration should take of-

fice and should make the definitive decisions, especially whether and under what circumstances the landing should take place.

## Search for Policy Decisions

9. As an example of the decision-making process, at the meeting of the Special Group held 8 December 1960 the Agency requested authorization (a) to make propaganda leaflet flights over Cuba; (b) to screen non-official U.S. personnel for use in maritime operations; (c) to resupply Cuban resistance elements from U.S. air bases at the rate of two flights a week. Only the first authorization was given at that time.

10. In mid-January 1961 various major policy questions were, at CIA's request, under discussion by the Special Group. These included: (a) use of American contract pilots for tactical and logistical air operations over Cuba; (b) use of a U.S. air base for logistical flights to Cuba; (c) commencement of air strikes not later than dawn of the day before the amphibious assault and without curtailment of the number of aircraft to be employed from those available; (d) use of Puerto Cabezas, Nicaragua, as an air-strike base and maritime staging area.

11. In the end only one of these policy questions was resolved in the affirmative, that with regard to the use of Puerto Cabezas. It should be especially noted that the project's paramilitary chief had strongly recommended that the operation be abandoned if policy should not allow adequate tactical air support.

## Conflicting Views

12. The raising of those questions and the failure to resolve many of them demonstrates the dangerous conflict between the desire for political acceptability and the need for military effectiveness. It also indicates the fluctuating policy background against which the officers running the project had to do their day-to-day business. This policy uncertainty was, in several respects, never satisfactorily resolved right up to the very hour of action, and many problems arose out of the changing limitations to which authority to do certain things was subjected in the name of political necessity.

13. Thus, during the months immediately preceding the inauguration on 20 January 1961, the Agency was recruiting and training Cuban troops and otherwise proceeding with a changed plan not yet definitely formulated or reduced to writing, with no assurance that the invasion, which was now the essence of the plan, would ultimately be authorized by the new Administra-

tion. The Agency was driving forward without knowing precisely where it was going.

14. The first formal briefing of President Kennedy and his advisors took place on 28 January 1961. (He had received briefings on earlier occasions, even before his election.) At this meeting there was a presentation, largely oral, of the status of preparations, and President Kennedy approved their continuation. But there was still no authorization, express or implied, that military action would in fact eventually be undertaken.

15. In the ensuing weeks, the Director of Central Intelligence and the Deputy Director (Plans), accompanied in some instances by other Agency representatives, attended a number of meetings with the new President and his advisors. (The paper prepared for a 17 February meeting is appended as Annex B.) In the course of these meetings, the Agency presented three informal planning or "concept" papers, dated 11 March 1961, 16 March 1961 and 12 April 1961, each a revision of its predecessor (Annexes C, D and E, respectively). These papers served chiefly as the basis for oral discussions at these meetings.

## Successive Alterations

16. According to our information, the revised concept, as exposed by the paper of 12 April 1961, was apparently acceptable to the President although he indicated he might order a diversion. Before that he had authorized the Agency to proceed with mounting the operation, but had reserved the right to cancel at any time. The President was advised that noon on the 16th was the last hour for a diversion. The DD/P checked with Mr. Bundy shortly after noon on the 16th, and no diversion being ordered, authorized the landing to proceed.

17. These three papers disclose that, starting with the World War II commando-type operation outlined in the 11 March 1961 paper (Annex C), the plan had been swiftly and successively altered to incorporate four characteristics which had been deemed essential in order to ensure that the operation would look like an infiltration of guerrillas in support of an internal revolution and would therefore be politically acceptable.

18. The four characteristics were:

a. an unspectacular night landing;

b. possibility of conducting air operations from a base on seized territory;

c. a build-up period, after the initial landing, to precede offensive action against Castro's forces, and

d. terrain suitable for guerrilla warfare in the event the invasion force could not hold a lodgment.

19. The airfield requirement obliged the planners to shift the invasion site from Trinidad to Zapata. The former area was close to the Escambray Mountains and therefore offered better guerrilla possibilities, but only the latter had a suitable airfield.

20. The third paper also introduced a plan for a guerrilla-type, diversionary landing in Oriente Province two days before the strike and provided that supplies should be landed at night during the initial stages. It also provided for air strikes on military objectives at dawn of D Day as well as on D Day minus 2.

## Guerrilla Role

21. Close reading of the three papers also discloses that the invasion was no longer conceived as an effort to *assist* Cuban guerrilla forces in a coordinated attack. The papers make no claim that significant guerrilla forces existed with whom—after evaluative reports from our own trained agents, confirming their strength, sufficiency of arms and ammunition, and their readiness—we had worked out plans for a coordinated, combined insurrection and attack against Castro. As the 12 April 1961 paper expressly states, the concept was that the operation should have the *appearance* of an internal resistance.

22. With reference to the strength of the resistance in Cuba, the 11 March 1961 paper refers to an estimated 1,200 guerrillas and 1,000 other individuals engaging in acts of conspiracy and sabotage, but it makes no claim of any control exercised by the Agency or even that coordinated plans had been made and firm radio communications established.

23. The 12 April 1961 paper states the estimate at "nearly 7,000 insurgents" (without specifying the number of guerrillas included therein), who were "responsible to some degree of control through agents with whom communications are currently active." It locates these in three widely separate regions of the island and states that the individual groups are small and very inadequately armed and that it was planned to supply them by air drops after D Day, with the objective of *creating* a revolutionary situation.

24. The foregoing language suggests existence of 7,000 insurgents but retrains from claiming any prospect of immediate help from trained guerrilla forces in being. The term "insurgents" seems to have been used in the sense

of "potential" insurgents or mere civilian opponents of Castro. A statement about military and police defectors was similarly vague; the Agency was in touch with 31 such persons whom it hoped to induce to defect after D Day.

## Arrests of Agents

25. These tacit admissions of the non-existence of effective, controlled resistance in Cuba correspond to the intelligence reports which clearly showed the unfavorable situation resulting from the failure of our air supply operations and the success of the Castro security forces in arresting our agents, rolling up the few existing nets, and reducing guerrilla groups to ineffectiveness.

26. It is clear that the invasion operation was based on the hope that the brigade would be able to maintain itself in Cuba long enough to prevail by attracting insurgents and defectors from the Castro armed services, but without having in advance any assurance of assistance from identified, known, controlled, trained, and organized guerrillas. The Agency hoped the invasion would, like a *deus ex machina,* produce a "shock," which would cause these defections. In other words, under the final plan the invasion was to take the place of an organized resistance which did not exist and was to generate organized resistance by providing the focus and acting as a catalyst.

27. The Agency was matching the 1,500-man brigade, after an amphibious landing, against Castro's combined military forces, which the highest-level U.S. intelligence (USIB reports entitled "The Military Buildup in Cuba," dated 30 November 1960 and 9 February 1961, respectively) estimated as follows: The Revolutionary Army—32,000 men; the militia—200,000 men; employing more than 30 to 40 thousand tons of Bloc-furnished arms and heavy materiel of the value of $30,000,000.

28. It is difficult to understand how the decision to proceed with the invasion could have been justified in the latter stage of the operation. Under the Trinidad plan (Annex C), access to the Escambray Mountains for possible guerrilla existence might have constituted some justification for the enormous risks involved. This justification did not apply to the Zapata area which was poor guerrilla terrain and offered little possibility for the break-out of a surrounded invasion force. The lack of contingency planning for either survival or rescue of the brigade has never been satisfactorily explained.

29. The argument has been made that the Agency's theory of an uprising to be set off by a successful invasion and the maintenance of the battalion for a period of a week or so has not been disproved. It was not put to the test, this

argument goes, because the canceled D- Day air strikes were essential to the invasion's success. Such an argument fails in the face of Castro's demonstrated power to arrest tens of thousands of suspected persons immediately after the D-Day- minus-2 air strikes and the effectiveness of the Castro security forces in arresting agents, as demonstrated by unimpeachable intelligence received.

## Views of Joint Chiefs

30. Agency participants in the project have sought to defend the invasion plan by citing the approval given to the plan by the Joint Chiefs of Staff (JCS). To this argument, members of the JCS have replied, in the course of another inquiry, (1) that the final plan was presented to them only orally, which prevented normal staffing; (2) that they regarded the operation as being solely CIA's, with the military called on to furnish various types of support and the chief interest of the JCS being to see to it that every kind of support requested was furnished; (3) that they went on the assumption that full air support would be furnished and control of the air secured and on the Agency's assurances that a great number of insurgents would *immediately* join forces with the invasion forces; and (4) that, in the event the battle went against them, the brigade would at once "go guerrilla" and take to the hills.

31. The Agency committed at least four extremely serious mistakes in planning:

a. Failure to subject the project, especially in its latter frenzied stages, to a cold and objective appraisal by the best operating talent available, particularly by those not involved in the operation, such as the Chief of Operations and the chiefs of the Senior Staff. Had this been done, the two following mistakes (b and c, below) might have been avoided.

b. Failure to advise the President, at an appropriate time, that success had become dubious and to recommend that the operation be therefore canceled and that the problem of unseating Castro be restudied.

c. Failure to recognize that the project had become overt and that the military effort had become too large to be handled by the Agency alone.

d. Failure to reduce successive project plans to formal papers and to leave copies of them with the President and his advisors and to request specific written approval and confirmation thereof.

32. Timely and objective scrutiny of the operation in the months before the invasion, including study of all available intelligence, would have dem-

onstrated to Agency officials that the clandestine paramilitary operations had almost totally failed, that there was no controlled and responsive underground movement ready to rally to the invasion force, and that Castro's ability both to fight back and to roll up the internal opposition must be very considerably upgraded.

33. It would also have raised the question of why the United States should contemplate pitting 1,500 soldiers, however well trained and armed, against an enemy vastly superior in number and armament on a terrain which offered nothing but vague hope of significant local support. It might also have suggested that the Agency's responsibility in the operation should be drastically revised and would certainly have revealed that there was no real plan for the post-invasion period, whether for success or failure.

## Existence of Warnings

34. The latest United States Intelligence Board, Office of National Estimates, and Office of Current Intelligence studies on Cuba available at that time provided clear warning that a calm reappraisal was necessary.

35. But the atmosphere was not conducive to it. The chief of the project and his subordinates had been subjected to such grueling pressures of haste and overwork for so long that their impetus and drive would have been difficult to curb for such a purpose. The strike preparations, under the powerful influence of the project's paramilitary chief, to which there was no effective counterbalance, had gained such momentum that the operation had surged far ahead of policy. The Cuban volunteers were getting seriously restive and threatening to get out of hand before they could be committed. The Guatemalan Government was urging the Agency to take away its Cubans. The rainy season was hard upon the Caribbean. The reappraisal never happened, though these very factors which helped prevent it should have warned the Agency of its necessity.

36. These adverse factors were compounded and exacerbated by policy restrictions that kept coming one upon another throughout a period of weeks and right up until the point of no return. These caused successive planning changes and piled up more confusion. Rapidly accumulating stresses, in our opinion, caused the Agency operators to lose sight of the fact that the margin of error was swiftly narrowing and had even vanished before the force was committed. At some point in this degenerative cycle they should have gone to the President and said frankly: "Here are the facts. The operation should be halted. We request further instructions."

## Consequences of Cancellation

37. Cancellation would have been embarrassing. The brigade could not have been held any longer in a ready status, probably could not have been held at all. Its members would have spread their disappointment far and wide. Because of multiple security leaks in this huge operation, the world already knew about the preparations, and the Government's and the Agency's embarrassment would have been public.

38. However, cancellation would have averted failure, which brought even more embarrassment, carried death and misery to hundreds, destroyed millions of dollars' worth of U.S. property, and seriously damaged U.S. prestige.

39. The other possible outcome—the one the project strove to achieve—was a successful brigade lodgment housing the Revolutionary Council but isolated from the rest of Cuba by swamps and Castro's forces. Arms were held in readiness for 30,000 Cubans who were expected to make their way unarmed through the Castro army and wade the swamps to rally to the liberators. Except for this, we are unaware of any planning by the Agency or by the U.S. Government for this success.

40. It is beyond the scope of this report to suggest what U.S. action might have been taken to consolidate victory, but we can confidently assert that the Agency had no intelligence evidence that Cubans in significant numbers could or would join the invaders or that there was any kind of an effective and cohesive resistance movement under anybody's control, let alone the Agency's, that could have furnished internal leadership for an uprising in support of the invasion. The consequences of a successful lodgment, unless overtly supported by U.S. armed forces, were dubious.

## The Choice

41. The choice was between retreat without honor and a gamble between ignominious defeat and dubious victory. The Agency chose to gamble, at rapidly decreasing odds.

42. The project had lost its covert nature by November 1960. As it continued to grow, operational security became more and more diluted. For more than three months before the invasion the American press was reporting, often with some accuracy, on the recruiting and training of Cubans. Such massive preparations could only be laid to the U.S. The Agency's name was freely linked with these activities. Plausible denial was a pathetic illusion.

43. Insistence on adhering to the formalities imposed by a non-attribut-

ability which no longer existed produced absurdities and created obstacles and delays. For example, the use of obsolete and inadequate B-26 aircraft, instead of the more efficient A-5s originally requested, was a concession to non-attributability which hampered the operation severely. A certain type of surgical tent requested for the landing beach was not supplied because it could be traced to the U.S. A certain modern rifle was not supplied, for the same reason, although several thousand of them had recently been declared surplus. In the end, as could have been foreseen, everything was traced to the U.S.

44. U.S. policy called for a covert operation and assigned it to the agency chartered to handle such things. When the project became blown to every newspaper reader the Agency should have informed higher authority that it was no longer operating within its charter. Had national policy then called for continuation of the overt effort under a joint national task force, vastly greater man-power resources would have been available for the invasion and the Agency could have performed an effective supporting role. The costly delays experienced by the Agency in negotiating for support from the armed services would have been avoided.

## Piecemeal Policy

45. In the hectic weeks before the strike, policy was being formed piecemeal and the imposition of successive restrictions was contracting the margin of error. The last of these restrictive decisions came from the President when the brigade was already in small boats moving toward the Cuban shore. Had it come a few hours earlier the invasion might have been averted and loss of life and prestige avoided.

46. If formal papers outlining the final strike plan in detail and emphasizing the vital necessity of the D-Day air strikes had been prepared and left with the President and his advisors, including the Joint Chiefs, with a request for written confirmation that the plan had received full comprehension and approval, the culminating incident which preceded the loss of the Cuban brigade might never have happened.

47. We are informed that this took place as follows: On the evening of 16 April the President instructed the Secretary of State that the D-Day strikes set far the following morning should be cancelled, unless there were overriding considerations to advise him of. The Secretary then informed the Deputy Director of Central Intelligence, the Director being absent from Washington, and the Deputy Director (Plans) of this decision, offering to let them call the

President at Glen Ora if they wished. They preferred not to do so, and the Secretary concluded from this that they did not believe the strikes to be vital to success.

## A Civilian Decision

48. Earlier that evening the project chief and his paramilitary chief had emphatically warned the DD/P to insist that cancellation of the strikes would produce disaster. Thus the DD/P, a civilian without military experience, and the DDCI, an Air Force general, did not follow the advice of the project's paramilitary chief, a specialist in amphibious operations. And the President made this vital, last-minute decision without direct contact with the military chiefs of the invasion operation.

49. The President may never have been clearly advised of the need for command of the air in an amphibious operation like this one. The DD/P was aware that at least two of the President's military advisors, both members of the Joint Chiefs, did not understand this principle. This might well have served to warn the DD/P that the President needed to be impressed most strongly with this principle, by means of a formal written communication, and also have alerted him to the advisability of accepting the Secretary's invitation to call the President directly.

50. If the project's paramilitary chief, as leader of the overt military effort, had accompanied the DDCI and the DD/P to the meeting with the Secretary he might have brought strong persuasion to bear on the decision.

51. This fateful incident, in our opinion, resulted in part from failure to circulate formal planning papers together with requests for specific confirmation.

## Shifts in Scope

52. The general vagueness of policy and direction permitted a continual shifting of the scope and scale of the project, that is, the type of operation planning commonly referred to as "playing it by ear," and this in turn led to various kinds of difficulties about people, money, supplies and bases.

53. A staffing guide prepared in May 1960 listed a total of 235 personnel required for the foreseeable future (107 being on board). By September, the strength had been built up to 228. In October another staffing guide listed a total of 363 positions. By the end of the project, 588 people were working in WH/4. There were 160 people in the Miami area alone.

54. The original plan contemplated 200 to 300 Cubans as a contingency

force. By mid-July, a force of 500 was being considered. In early November, the plan was to use 1,500 men, and there was talk of as many as 3,000. In early December, a brigade or 750 was agreed upon. Its strength was built up to 664 by the end of January. By 17 March the ground forces in training numbered 973. By 28 March equipment for 1,600 men had been ordered, and the actual brigade strength on 6 April was 1,390. Such changes made it very difficult for the supporting components, particularly the Office of Logistics and Development Projects Division, who were not given much lead time.

55. The original estimate for the project anticipated expenditures to the total of $4,400,000 during the two fiscal years, 1960 and 1961. On 24 March 1960, $900,000 was released for the balance of Fiscal Year 1960. This amount was expended within a month and an additional million dollars released to carry the project to the end of June.

56. In August, a budget was presented for Fiscal Year 1961 which amounted to $13,000,000. By December, $11,300,000 had been obligated and an additional $28,200,000 was requested and authorized. In May 1961, an additional $5,000,000 was requested to meet obligations incurred. The total amount of money for this project for Fiscal Years 1960/61, instead of $4,400,000, was more than $46,000,000.

57. When the project started, it was not realized that bases would be needed at Useppa Island, Key West, Miami, and Opa-locka, Florida; New Orleans, Puerto Rico, Panama, Guatemala, and Nicaragua, as well as innumerable safe houses and other facilities. Consequently the project suffered, because many of these facilities were not ready when needed. The WH Division launched into a large paramilitary project without the bases, the boats, the experienced paramilitary personnel, or a complete and sufficient plan, and never really caught up.

## G. THE MIAMI OPERATING BASE

1. The confused relationships between WH/4 headquarters and the forward operating base in the Miami area were a significant factor in the over-all performance of the project mission. The base was activated in late April 1960 and was put in Miami mainly because it was the chief center of Cuban refugees in the United States.

2. From the beginning, the DD/P and his associates took a firm stand against allowing the base to become more than a small support organization, and until September 1960 the base did little except carry on liaison with the

Cuban exile organizations and U.S. law enforcement agencies. For example, there was only one paramilitary officer at the base during this period.

3. The DD/P's Chief of Operations wrote in June 1960: "I recognize your need for more operational personnel in the Miami area to service and conduct certain activities there. I am firmly opposed, however, to the growth of an organization which would represent a second headquarters or intermediate echelon there." At this same time, the DD/P's Assistant for Covert Action emphasized that the function of the forward operating base should be one of coordination, with command remaining in Headquarters.

4. In August the DD/P wrote that he was worried about Miami and wanted to be sure that "we are not duplicating there any functions that are being performed in Headquarters. For instance, I am not quite clear what are the duties of the PM types there since this component is neither a headquarters nor a training installation nor even a forward command post." And in another memo in November, he again urged that WH/4 be especially careful to avoid any duplication of effort between Miami and Headquarters.

## Duplication of Effort

5. By this time there was plenty of duplication. Headquarters and the Miami Base had become engaged in many parallel or overlapping operations and were even competing with each other. Both components were handling all kinds of agents and in some cases the same ones. The only activity that Miami did not get into was air operations, but even here, it necessarily had a role in many of the clandestine air drops.

6. There was a general feeling at headquarters that the forward base existed solely for support and that Headquarters was in the best position to handle operations because it had ready access to policy guidance and fast radio communications to and from all elements. This view ignored the fact that much of the communication with Cuba was only by secret writing and couriers; that Miami was the main source of information, politicians, agents, and soldiers for the project; that it was the logical location for infiltration and exfiltration; that the base, through the maintenance of effective liaison, had the complete cooperation of the local FBI, the Border Patrol, Immigration, Coast Guard, FCC, Customs, Navy, and police officials.

7. Except for the Director of Central Intelligence, who visited the base, top Agency officials concerned with the project did not have first-hand knowledge of what was being done and what could be done at Miami. The limitations they placed on base activities had serious consequences. For example,

when the resistance organizers being trained in Guatemala were ready to go into Cuba in September, the maritime capability to infiltrate them did not yet exist. By the time the base had built up some capabilities in various lines, valuable months had been lost.

## The Miami View

8. On the other hand, there was a general feeling at the base that it should be a "station," conducting operations just as Havana was able to do (up to the date when diplomatic relations were broken off), with Headquarters providing support, guidance and policy. This view failed to realize that a station with several hundred people would have been very difficult to conceal, that it would have cost a million dollars to move everyone to Miami, and that Headquarters would have gotten into the operations anyhow, due to the easy access to Miami from Washington, especially by telephone.

9. The letter of instructions to the base chief, dated 6 October 1960, was pretty vague. It stated that he would have authority over all project personnel and responsibility for the supervision of any project activities conducted through the Miami area from other areas. It authorized him to use personnel, material, facilities and funds for the accomplishment of the over-all Agency mission. He was made responsible to the chief of the project.

10. The first intelligence (FI) case officer reported to the base in September 1960 and proceeded to acquire, train and direct agents. At the time of the invasion, the Miami Base had 31 FI agents in Cuba, all of whom were reporting and all of whom had been recruited by the base.

## The CI Section

11. The counterintelligence (CI) section began to functioning mid-July 1960. By the time of the strike, this section had 39 carefully selected, highly educated Cubans trained as case officers to form a future Cuban Intelligence Service; also, 100 selected Cubans trained as future CI officials and civil government officials; also, a reserve of 100 older non-political individuals trained as a reserve intelligence corps.

12. The paramilitary (PM) section was opened in late June 1960 with *one* officer. His job was to conduct liaison with the Cuban leaders in order to obtain recruits for the Guatemala camps. A second PM officer reported in August, and at this time there was a beginning of an attempt to infiltrate arms, ammunition and personnel into Cuba clandestinely by boat. (These were the "PM types" whose duties had mystified the DD/P.) There were also two mari-

time "types" who were training the crew of a borrowed small boat for clandestine trips.

13. By 15 November 39 people had been assigned to the Miami base in addition to 44 people from the Agency's Office of Communications. In addition to support elements, there were sections for propaganda, FI, CI, political action, and PM.

14. By 15 April 1961, the base and its sub-base had 160 persons assigned, as follows:

| | |
|---|---|
| 10 | FI |
| 5 | CI |
| 2 | Political Action |
| 7 | Propaganda |
| 25 | Support |
| 26 | PM |
| 14 | Security |
| 68 | Communications |
| 3 | Miscellaneous |

15. While the Havana Station was still operating, Miami Base was in close touch with it by courier and secure communications. When Havana Station was closed, Miami expected to take over the stay-behind assets, such as they were. However, Headquarters took over their control. Miami concentrated on the training and infiltration of agents.

## PM Support Role

16. In PM activities, control was tightly held by Headquarters, and the PM section of the base was limited pretty much to providing support in recruiting soldiers and running small boat operations. This tight control meant that the PM officers at the base looked to Headquarters for guidance rather than to the chief of base. The PM and other sections had their own channels to Headquarters, and this led to uncontrolled action and considerable confusion. PM officers in Key West, a sub-base of Miami, also sometimes communicated directly with Headquarters.

17. There are alleged to have been cases in which a Headquarters decision was conveyed to the Miami Base by three persons simultaneously, each over the telephone. The result of this was that the base had an enormously high phone bill and the base chief often was not informed of events until after they were over, if at all.

18. The Miami case officers retained their agents as long as the agents were

reporting by secret writing. Once the agents reported by radio, they were taken over by Headquarters. This was resented by the Miami case officers, who felt that they were in the best position to know the agents, having recruited and trained them.

19. Case officers in Headquarters, on the other hand, felt that Miami case officers tried to steal their agents when they passed through the Miami area. One agent who visited Headquarters received promises of money and support which went far beyond what the case officer in Miami had offered. The base was not informed of these promises until the agent mentioned them. For the next several months, this particular agent was unmanageable and would not even meet with the Miami case officer. This was naturally viewed as Headquarters meddling.

## Examples of Confusion

20. Case officers in Miami also felt that they were unduly handicapped in that Headquarters was not only competing with them but also reviewing their actions, which was something like playing a game with the umpire on the other team. It is doubtful that a reviewing component can maintain objectivity when it is also competing with the component whose activities it is reviewing.

21. Numerous examples could be cited to illustrate the confusion that existed. The divided control over maritime operations is discussed elsewhere in this paper. There was an expensive fiasco over some special lubricating oil additive intended for sabotage use in Cuba. The organizational arrangement made necessary hundreds of telephone calls and cables which otherwise would not have been sent, and the areas for uncertainty and misunderstanding were still considerable. For example, a Miami cable of 15 February referred to an agent message and asked, "Does Headquarters intend to answer and arrange this operation?"

22. The general situation also led to an extraordinary number of temporary-duty trips back and forth between Washington and Miami. These were not only expensive but added a great many problems in the way of support and security.

23. In December 1960 the base chief pointed out to Headquarters that the base needed "clarification and specification of the requirements it is expected to fulfill and tasks that it is expected to perform, together with the investment of sufficient authority and discretion for the operational action which may be involved." In March 1961 he pointed out that "the base would welcome more

precise requirements for its agents than had been received up to that time in the interests of making efficient use of them."

24. In May 1961 he wrote a memorandum on control of denied-area operations which pointed out that future operations should either be controlled from Headquarters or from a forward operating base, but that the divided control which had existed during the project had resulted in parallel, sometimes duplicative and conflicting efforts and in operational relationships which were competitive, without purpose, and sometimes counterproductive.

25. The inspectors agree that this divided effort represented an ineffective and uneconomical use of time, money, and materiel, and less than maximum utilization of Agency employees, plus unexploited, delayed or poorly coordinated use of Cuban agents and assets.

## H . INTELLIGENCE SUPPORT

1. The WH/4 Branch had not only the responsibility for the Cuban project but also the normal area duties of a geographical unit in the Clandestine Services. Besides being considered a task force with the mission of overturning the Castro government, it also had the Headquarters desk responsibility for Cuba, including support of Havana Station and Santiago Base until the break in diplomatic relations.

2. This arrangement required WH/4's intelligence (FI) section to collect intelligence on Cuba not only for the task force, with its special requirements, but also for the entire U.S. intelligence community, with its diverse and long-range needs.

3. The section was plagued with personnel shortages from the start, but as long as the U.S. Embassy in Havana remained open, thus assuring communications, it received and processed a good yield of intelligence from Cuba, chiefly on political, economic, and Communist Party matters. Late in 1960 the section was directed to place emphasis on military information, but it found that its agents in Cuba lacked access to high-level military sources.

4. The FI section transmitted copies of all the reports it processed to the paramilitary section as well as to the rest of its regular intelligence customers.

### The Net in Havana

5. The section devoted considerable effort to supporting Havana Station in preparing its agents for stay-behind roles in the event of a break in diplo-

matic relations. When the embassy finally closed on 3 January 1961 the station had a single net for possible intelligence. It comprised some 27 persons, 15 of whom were reporting agents and the rest radio operators, cutouts and couriers. The principal agents and one of the radio operators were U.S. citizens and thus had doubtful status after the break in relations.

6. In September 1960 as the military invasion concept was beginning to gain ascendancy in project planning, the chief of the project created a G-2 unit. But instead of placing this unit directly under himself as a project-wide unit and making its chief a member of his immediate staff, he put it in the paramilitary section under the aggressive Marine Corps colonel who became the paramilitary unit chief at about that time.

7. As chief of this low-echelon intelligence unit, whose analyses were to have important influence on an action vitally affecting national security and prestige, WH/4 brought in an officer of undoubted ability but of limited experience in paramilitary and FI operations. It was a grave error to place this G-2 unit in such a subordinate position in the project, and this error produced the serious consequences described below.

## Function of G-2 Unit

8. The paramilitary G-2 unit consisted of four officers and several secretaries. Its principal function was to prepare intelligence annexes to the successive invasion plans. Its sources of information included, in addition to the FI section's reports, photographic intelligence, cartographic intelligence, Special Intelligence, armed services reports, and messages received from the paramilitary section's own agents in Cuba. Reports from the armed services were procured rapidly through direct informal liaison rather than through the usual slower channels.

9. In various ways the functioning of the regular FI section, which was directly under the project chief, was adversely affected by the paramilitary G-2 unit.

10. The PM unit absorbed the available personnel. The chief of the FI section was not invited to attend WH/4 staff meetings, and for security reasons, he never had access to WH/4's war room. During the final weeks the FI section was not permitted to examine the PM section's incoming operational cables for possible positive intelligence content. The FI section chief did not have a clearance for photographic intelligence.

## Lack of Liaison

11. There was no close liaison between the two sections, and this resulted in some duplication in preparation of reports requested by the DD/P, be-

cause neither section would learn of the requests made of the other. Until the end of 1960 the two sections were housed in different buildings.

12. The most serious consequence of the third-echelon position of the G-2 unit was that it concentrated in the hands of the unit chief the dual function of receiving all the information available from Government-wide sources, including that from the agents of his own paramilitary section, and of interpreting all these data for the purpose of supplying intelligence support to the various invasion plans.

13. Interpretation of intelligence affecting the strike force aspect of the operation was thus entrusted to officers who were so deeply engaged in preparations for the invasion that their judgments could not have been expected to be altogether objective. This circumstance undoubtedly had a strong influence on the process by which WH/4 arrived at the conclusion that the landing of the strike force could and would trigger an uprising among the Cuban populace. This conclusion, in turn, became an essential element in the decision to proceed with the operation, as it took the place of the original concept, no longer maintainable, that the invasion was to be undertaken in support of existing and effective guerrilla forces.

14. Irrespective of the validity of that conclusion, it is clear that the interpretative analysis should have been made not by the persons who were working day and night to prepare the invasion but by an objective and disinterested senior interpretation specialist from the Agency's FI Staff or from its Office of Current Intelligence.

## Intelligence Support Vacuum

15. Another serious error in the field of intelligence support was that Miami Base received almost no intelligence support from the Headquarters G-2 section. This may be attributed to the facts that the paramilitary chief was almost completely preoccupied with the strike force preparations and that his subordinate G-2 was not given project-wide responsibilities and to the rigid security restrictions under which the paramilitary section was expected to operate, as well as to the general confusion in the organizational position of the Miami Base.

16. This serious support vacuum at Miami was compounded because the base, in spite of its large size and the fact that it was deeply engaged in its own operations in Cuba, had no intelligence support section. There was no single officer or unit charged with responsibility for interpreting the considerable

amount of intelligence derived directly from base sources and from Special Intelligence.

17. Furthermore no photographic intelligence was available to Miami Base, which had no officer with a clearance entitling him to receive it. There was substantially no intelligence support covering the Cuban beach areas or the political situation inside Cuba. There was no analysis or interpretation of Special Intelligence, and there was no mechanism to call critical material to anyone's attention.

18. The result of this highly protective state of affairs was that individual Miami case officers were forced to rely upon their own interpretation of the separate intelligence reports, instead of having this material interpreted for them by specialists. They were not given a number of other items of operational intelligence which were in existence in the G-2 unit of the paramilitary section at Headquarters.

## I. THE POLITICAL FRONT AND THE RELATION OF CUBANS TO THE PROJECT

1. The Cuban opposition front, as conceived by the Agency in consultation with the State Department, was to have the following characteristics:

a. Full restoration of the 1940 Cuban constitution.

b. Return to the basic principles of the revolution, as enunciated in the 1958 Caracas Declaration.

c. Pro-Western and strongly anti-Communist orientation.

d. Political complexion ranging from a little to the right of center to somewhat left of center.

e. Ability to muster the broadest possible support from the Cuban population.

2. The functions of such a front organization were conceived to be:

a. A cover for covert action against the Castro regime.

b. A catalyst and a rallying point for anti-Castro groups variously reported to number 178, 184, or 211.

c. A possible nucleus for a provisional government of Cuba following Castro's downfall.

3. The terms of reference thus excluded followers of the former dictator, Fulgencio Batista. They also excluded extreme leftists.

4. Exclusion of the Batistianos and other ultra-conservatives caused one kind of problem. Many of the exiles had been Batista followers. Many of them were rich and had assets, such as boats and followers, which could be used. Some had military experience. Some of them had American friends who were influential enough to urge their claims to consideration upon the White House.

## The Leftist Fringe

5. Inclusion or the far-left fringe caused another kind of problem. It was hard to tell how far left some persons were. And some of those whose political acceptability was questionable nevertheless claimed such substantial following inside Cuba that it was difficult to ignore them.

6. In forming the *Frente Revolucionario Democratico* (FRD) the Agency focused its attention principally on personalities and groups who had either participated in Castro's government or supported his revolution but had become disillusioned and gone into opposition.

7. In early 1959 the Havana Station was already assessing a wide variety of anti-Castro personalities with whom it was in contact. In mid-1959 a station agent was exploring the possibility of covert support to the Montecristi Movement of Justo Asencio *Carrillo* Hernandez.

8. In the mid-1950s the Montecristi group had been active against Batista, who exiled Carrillo. He returned after the revolution to take an important banking post but found Castro's Communist tendencies intolerable and went into opposition again. His group is described as liberal and progressive but rejecting any accommodation with Communism.

## The Organizing Committee

9. Carrillo was one of several Cuban figures whom the Agency induced to defect in late 1959 or the early months of 1960. Others were Manuel Francisco *Artime* Buesa, José Ignacio *Rasco* Bermudez, and Manuel Antonio *Varona* Loredo. It was these four who, after long negotiations, formed the organizing committee of the FRD in May 1960.

10. Artime, who is still under 30, joined Castro's movement as an anti-Batista student. Under instructions from the Catholic Church he organized a group of 4,000 Catholic Action students to gain the farmers' help against Batista. The view has been expressed that he ran the Jesuits' penetration of

the 26 July Movement. Castro gave him a high post in National Agrarian Reform Institute (INRA) from which he resigned after ten months to form the Movement to Recover the Revolution (MRR), composed in part of his former Catholic Action followers. This exile opposition group provided a large proportion of the recruits for the strike force.

11. Rasco, a college and university classmate of Castro's, is a lawyer and history professor, described as a nice young intellectual without much talent for action. In the fall of 1959 he became the first president of the Christian Democratic Movement (MDC), an anti-Communist Catholic group which Castro drove underground in April 1960 at which time Rasco fled the country.

12. Varona's career in government and in opposition politics goes back to the 1920s. During the regime of President *Prio* Socarras he held several important posts, including that of prime minister, and was responsible for anti-Communist policies and measures. He collaborated with Castro until the Communist pattern of the new regime became evident, coming to the U.S. in April 1960. Before leaving Havana he had presented a plan for Castro's overthrow, including a unified opposition and U.S. aid for developing propaganda and military capabilities.

## The Political Spectrum

13. Varona was representative of the older opposition parties (Autentico and Ortodoxo) which had survived both Batista and Castro and which were roughly in the middle of the political spectrum. Artime's group also occupied a centrist position, but its membership was drawn from the younger generation on Cubans. Carrillo and Rasco appeared to be a little left and a little right of center, respectively.

14. Thus the original group of organizers represented a fairly broad range of political views. They were joined in June 1960 by Aureliano *Sanchez Arango* who claimed leadership of the AAA group, the initials possibly representing *Asociacíon de Amigos de Aureliano*. Both Sanchez Arango and Varona claimed to have considerable following in the Cuban labor field. Sanchez Arango and his followers appeared to have some general knowledge of the use of clandestine techniques.

15. These five associated themselves in issuing a manifesto at Mexico City on 22 June 1960. This document called upon Cubans, other Latin Americans and the world at large to help the FRD overthrow Castro's dictatorship. The FRD pledged itself to establish a representative democratic government with

full civil liberties under the 1940 Cuban constitution. It pledged free general elections within 18 months of establishment of a provisional government. It proposed to ban the Communist party and institute a program of social and economic progress for all classes of Cubans.

16. Varona's maturity and experience led to his selection as coordinator, in effect, general manager, of the FRD. This immediately precipitated the resignation of Sanchez Arango and in turn led to the beginning of a problem in establishing and maintaining FRD unity which the project never fully solved.

## Change in Policy

17. The FRD had originally been conceived as the channel through which all of the project's aid to the Cuban cause would flow. However, Sanchez Arango's walkout threatened a loss of assets and capabilities which the project wanted to preserve. The result was expressed as follows in a briefing prepared by WH/4 for CINCLANT in November 1960:

> In October we made a change in operational policy. Heretofore we had kept our efforts centered on the FRD; however, we will now consider requests for paramilitary aid from any anti-Castro (and non-Batista) group, inside or outside Cuba, which can show it has a capability for paramilitary action against the Castro regime. We feel that the combination of our controlled paramilitary action under the FRD aegis and the lesser-controlled operations of other Cuban revolutionaries will bring about a considerable acceleration of active anti-Castro expressions within Cuba. We will, in any event, have the lever of support as a mechanism for influencing the ultimate emergence of one individual or group as the primary figure in the anti-Castro community.

18. Because of the gregariousness of Cuban exiles, the project was unable to prevent this change in policy from becoming known to the FRD executive committee. When the Bender Group, now generally understood by Cubans and many others to represent the CIA, began responding to requests from and giving support to defectors from the FRD and to groups which the FRD considered politically unacceptable, the organization which was supposed to be a world-wide symbol of Cuban freedom and which was being groomed as the nucleus of the next government of Cuba naturally felt that its prestige had been undermined.

## Diffusion of Effort

19. This complicated relations between project case officers and the FRD leaders. It also appears to have resulted in some diffusion of effort in the at-

tempts at clandestine infiltration of arms and paramilitary leaders into Cuba. It seriously hampered progress toward FRD unity, sharpened internal FRD antagonisms, and contributed to the decline in strike force recruiting efforts.

20. The composite political complexion of the FRD shifted a little to the right in August 1960 with the joining of Ricardo Rafael *Sardinia*, who headed an organization called the *Movimiento Institutional Democratico* (MID).

21. A source of friction between the FRD and its project sponsors was the effort to induce it to set up its headquarters outside the U.S. The Cuban leaders were finally persuaded by financial leverage to move to Mexico City where the Mexican Government had agreed to be hospitable. Housing and office space were arranged for the executive committee members and their families and for a project case officer and his secretary. [Excised] in Mexico City was reactivated for support duties, such as [excised] and the move was made.

22. However, the Mexican Government appears not to have kept its word, and the Cubans were subjected to surveillance and other harassment. Within a few weeks it became evident that the situation was intolerable, and everybody moved back to Miami, which is where the Cubans wanted to be in the first place.

## The Bender Group

23. The man responsible for laying the groundwork of the FRD, arranging a long series of meetings among the Cubans, and persuading them to merge their differences and issue a joint manifesto, was the chief of the project's political section. He was known to the Cubans and inevitably to the press as "Frank Bender." The Bender Group, for reasons of plausible denial, purported to be composed of U.S. businessmen who wanted to help overthrow Castro. The Cubans do not seem to have cared whether this was true or not, but the guise irritated them because they wanted to be in direct touch with the U.S. Government at the highest level possible.

24. Bender's linguistic accomplishments did not include Spanish and this may have diluted his effectiveness in dealing with Cubans.

25. After the FRD was launched the handling of purely FRD affairs in Mexico City and later in Miami was turned over to a case officer with fluent Spanish and long experience in Latin American affairs.

26. However, Bender continued to be identified with the project. The FRD leaders' antagonism toward the Bender Group was sharpened when, at

the time of the change in operational policy noted above, WH/4 assigned Bender the responsibility of dealing with Cuban individuals and groups outside of the FRD framework.

## The Rubio Padilla Group

27. One of the outside groups the project continued to work with was the Action Movement for Recovery (MAR), headed by Juan *Rubio* Padilla. Use of this conservative group of rich landlords was strongly advocated by William D. Pawley, an influential Miami businessman. A paper prepared by WH/4 for the Director of Central Intelligence's use in briefing Senator Kennedy in July 1960 stated MAR's claims to a widespread resistance organization needing only arms and ammunition and orders to go into action and called the MAR relationship a most encouraging development.

28. However, Rubio was too conservative for the FRD's taste, and the MAR was never incorporated into the FRD.

29. An organization which resisted incorporation in the FRD until March 1961 and which meanwhile had a stormy relationship with the Bender Group was the *Movimiento Revolucionario del Pueblo* (MRP), headed by Manuel Antonio *Ray* Rivero. Ray had been Castro's minister of public works until he lost his job to a Communist. He arrived in this country in November 1960 and agreed to accept assistance from the Bender Group but wished to maintain his freedom of choice. The project's unilateral use of Ray resulted in some successful maritime operations.

30. Bender's efforts to get Ray to join the FRD produced strained relations, but in December Ray agreed to accept military aid through the FRD. Ray's program appeared to be identical with Castro's but without Communism and without hostility to the United States. Ray became less intransigent as time went on and in February and March 1961 was participating in talks with Bender and Varona on the formation of the Revolutionary Council which he ultimately joined. There seems to be no substance to allegations in the press that Ray was ignored. In fact, his unsubstantiated claims to wide underground resources are said to have been received uncritically by some project personnel.

## Contact with Batistianos

31. Another allegation which gained some currency was that the project was supporting and otherwise using former associates and supporters of Batista. At one point WH/4 did have contact with one ex-Batista leader,

*Sanchez* Mosquerra, and gave some support to his group, but this effort was soon called off. There were also attempts by Batistianos to penetrate the project's military effort, but these were resisted. The FRD's own intelligence section was active in attempting to screen out Batistianos. The strike force contained some members of the former Cuban Constitutional Army, which existed under Batista, but these were recruited as soldiers not as politicians.

32. The brigade officers seem to have been clean of the Batista taint. However, the FRD, for whom they were supposedly fighting, justly complained that it had had no hand in their selection.

33. José *Miro* Cardona, a distinguished lawyer who turned to politics late in his career, was the first Cuban prime minister after the Castro revolution, was later ambassador to Spain, and was ambassador-designate to the United States when he broke with Castro, took asylum in the Argentine Embassy, and was eventually granted safe conduct to this country (in October 1960) where he became the FRD's secretary-general for public relations.

34. Under the guidance of Bender he became a strong force for unity in the FRD during its most difficult period, the virtual political interregnum before the inauguration of President Kennedy. Miro was influential in bringing Ray into the Revolutionary Council which was formed on 20 March with Miro as chairman.

## Visit to Training Camp

35. Miro, with other Council members, visited the strike force in Guatemala on 29 March in a much-needed effort to spur troop morale. There had been far too little contact between the FDR and the soldiers being trained in its name. Artime, Varona, and Antonio Jaime *Maceo* Mackle had been there in February in an attempt to calm mutinous spirits. The last previous visit had been made in the fall of 1960 by Col. Eduardo *Martin* Elena, head of the FRD's military staff and a former constitutional Army officer. Martin Elena antagonized the trainees, and with the beginning of straight military training under a U.S. Army officer, who had no interest in Cuban politics, a ban was placed on visits to the camp by Cuban politicians.

36. This was probably a mistake and an unreasonable interference in the Cubans' management of their own affairs. Controlled contact between the FRD and the troops could have done much to improve the morale and motivation of the troops and make the training job easier. There was nobody in the Guatemala camp who could answer the political questions of the trainees, who were all volunteers and deserved to know what kind of a future they were

preparing to fight for. Furthermore, the FRD needed a chance to develop the loyalty of the troops who were presumably to install and protect its leaders on Cuban soil as members of a provisional government.

37. This was one example of a high-handed attitude toward Cubans that became more and more evident as the project progressed. Cubans were the basic ingredient for a successful operation and, although the aim of having the exiles direct activities was probably idealistic and unattainable, nevertheless the Agency should have been able to organize them for maximum participation and to handle them properly to get the job done.

## An American Operation

38. But with the Americans running the military effort, running Radio Swan, and doing unilateral recruiting, the operation became purely an American one in the exile Cuban mind, and in the public mind as well. In by-passing the Cubans the Agency was weakening its own cover.

39. The official attitude which produced this situation is reflected in the project's progress reports. In November a report noted that the Agency had "plenty of flexibility to choose the Cuban group we would eventually sanction as a provisional government." A January report indicated that the Agency, rather than the Cubans, was making the plans and decisions: "We have charted five different lists of proposed assignments for any future provisional government of Cuba and are compiling biographic data on those Cubans who might be utilized by us in forming a future Cuban government."

40. The crowning incident which publicly demonstrated the insignificant role of the Cuban leaders and the contempt in which they were held occurred at the time of the invasion. Isolated in a Miami safe house, "voluntarily" but under strong persuasion, the Revolutionary Council members awaited the outcome of a military operation which they had not planned and knew little about while Agency-written bulletins were issued to the world in their name.

41. They had not been puppets in the early days of the project. Some of the Cubans had drawn up detailed operational plans for resistance in areas of Cuba that they knew intimately; others provided cover and support. One wealthy exile even voluntarily went through the assessment routine at Useppa Island along with the young trainees. They had reason to feel that the project was in the nature of a joint venture, at least.

## The Military Emphasis

42. But when the project began to shift from a clandestine operation to a military operation, Cuban advice and participation no longer seemed neces-

sary. Cubans who up to about November 1960 had been close to some of the plans and operations were cut out. To the military officers on loan to the project, the problem was a military one, and their attitude was "to hell with the Revolutionary Council and the political side."

43. The paramilitary and the political action sections of WH/4 were not in effective touch with each other; in effect, they treated their tasks as unrelated, and this was reflected in the field. The diminished relationships with the Cuban leaders were a measure of the extent to which people in the project became carried away by a military operation.

44. The effective utilization of Cubans and cooperation with them was also hampered to some extent because many of the project officers had never been to Cuba, did not speak Spanish, and made judgments of the Cubans on very slim knowledge. (A notable exception was the propaganda section, which was well qualified in this respect.) They considered the Cubans untrustworthy and difficult to work with. Members of the Revolutionary Council have been described to the inspectors as "idiots" and members of the brigade as "yellow-bellied."

45. However, many staff employees in the project realized that the Cubans would have to be dealt with realistically and allowances made for their differences and weaknesses. In some instances, case officers achieved quite remarkable rapport with the Cubans they were handling. These officers were ones who had had considerable experience in dealing with foreign nationals in various parts of the world, and the results showed it.

## Dealing with Cubans

46. Some military officers on loan to the project were less successful in dealing with Cubans. They simply gave military orders to these foreign nationals and expected to be obeyed.

47. Some of the contract employees, such as ship's officers, treated the Cubans like dirt. This led to revolts, mutinies, and other troubles. Some very able Cubans withdrew from the project because of the way they were treated.

48. The inspecting team has received a definite impression that this operation took on a life of its own, that a number of the people involved became so wrapped up in the operation as such that they lost sight of ultimate goals.

49. There is a substantial question whether any operation can be truly successful when the attitudes toward the other people are so unfavorable. There does not seem to be much excuse for not being able to work with

Cubans. If this nationality is so difficult, how can the Agency possibly succeed with the natives of Black Africa or Southeast Asia?

50. The Agency, and for that matter, the American nation is not likely to win many people away from Communism if the Americans treat other nationals with condescension or contempt, ignore the contributions and the knowledge which they can bring to bear, and generally treat them as incompetent children whom the Americans are going to rescue for reasons of their own.

## J. CLANDESTINE PARAMILITARY OPERATIONS — AIR

1. The first attempt at a clandestine air drop over Cuba took place on 28 September 1960. (By coincidence this was the same night as the first maritime operation.) A 100-man arms pack was dropped for an agent rated as having considerable potential as a resistance leader. The crew missed the drop zone by seven miles and dropped the weapons on a dam. Castro forces scooped them up, ringed the area, caught the agent and later shot him. The airplane got lost on the way back to Guatemala and landed in Mexico. It is still there.

2. This operation might have indicated an unpromising future for air drops. In fact, its failure was influential in persuading the chiefs of the project of the futility of trying to build up an internal resistance organization by clandestine means, and within the next few weeks the operational emphasis was beginning its fateful swing toward the overt strike-force concept. To this extent the portent of failure was heeded, but it did not suffice either to halt the air drops or to ensure arrangements for their success. The attempts went on and on with results that were mostly ludicrous or tragic or both.

3. On 26 December 1960, Headquarters received word that a Cuban agent, who had been given Agency training in this country, wanted an air drop of not more than 1,500 pounds of demolition and sabotage materiel and weapons. He clearly specified the layout and the location of the drop zone, and also the amounts and kinds of materiel desired. WH/4 cabled this requirement to the air base in Guatemala, where all the flights originated. However, the Development Projects Division (DPD) then cabled Guatemala that arms and ammunition would be dropped *with food to make a maximum load*, also 200 pounds or leaflets for a drop elsewhere. This cable was not coordinated with WH/4 which sent a message to the agent the following day, stating

that a cargo drop would take place *as requested* and that the weight would be 1,500 pounds.

## Rice and Beans

4. A drop was made on 31 December. The 15-man reception team received, not only 1,500 pounds of materiel which was different from the original request because the specific items could not be packed in waterproof containers in time, but also 800 pounds of beans, 800 pounds of rice and 160 pounds or lard.

5. This was the only drop to this Cuban agent. He was so vexed with the drop that he came out of Cuba specifically to make a complaint and to cancel a succeeding drop which had been planned. He stated that he would not accept another drop, no matter what the cargo was. He pointed out that the Agency had endangered his safety by dropping cargo which he had not asked for, did not need, and could not handle. Furthermore, the aircraft had stayed in the vicinity too long, had flown with its landing lights on, had circled around and made numerous U-turns and even dropped propaganda leaflets on his property. He decided the Agency lacked the professional competence to made clandestine air drops.

6. This operation was recorded as "successful" by the Agency because cargo was actually delivered to the people it was meant for. There were *four* such "successes" in all, out of *30 missions flown* up to 21 April 1961. (The Fiscal Year 1961 budget called for 105 air drops.) The first of these took place on 30 December after numerous attempts beginning in mid-October. There were 13 unsuccessful attempts during January and February. The third success took place on 3 March, when three agents were dropped (previous attempts to drop them had been made on 7 February and 27 February). The fourth successful drop was on 29 March.

## The Successful Drops

7. Except for the rice-and-beans drop, the successful drops were all to an agent who had been trained in air reception procedures by staff personnel at Headquarters.

8. The three cargo drops known to be successful were all made in the Pinar del Rio Province. In other words, practically all the supplies went to one small area of western Cuba. Small amounts are thought to have been received in Camaguey and Oriente, but none in Matanzas or Havana. Ten missions were flows into the Escambray at the request of an agent who had no training

in air reception. Twice the cargo was not dropped because the drop zone was not located, and once the plane turned back because of bad weather. On the seven occasions cargo was dropped, it was either totally or in large part recovered by the Castro forces. Three times cargo was dropped blind, three times in the wrong place, and once on the drop zone when the reception committee was not there.

9. In all, about 151,000 pounds of arms, ammunition and equipment were transported by air. Not more than 69,000 pounds of this was actually dropped, the rest was returned to base. Of this 69,000 pounds, at least 46,000 pounds were captured by Castro forces, who recovered all or a large part of ten drops, compared with our agents, who recovered three. In other words, out of 75 tons which were air-lifted, paramilitary agents actually got about twelve (about enough to arm 300 men, figuring 7,500 pounds to a hundred-man pack).

10. Except for the one team, there were no clandestine personnel drops made or even attempted during the entire project.

## *Lack of Procedure*

11. The agents on the ground did not have a standard procedure for air reception (most of them had not been trained). The locations of drop zones were variously and insufficiently described by coordinates, sketches, or azimuths. In two operations the requesting agents did not even have maps of their areas. In one of these WH/4 headquarters, DPD and Miami Base each arrived at a different set of coordinates from the reference points given. In another case the coordinates given for a drop zone were in the ocean. Reception parties proposed to mark the drop zone with various bizarre and impractical patterns, such as: two red lights and one white light about 15 feet apart moving clockwise; an arrow 50 meters long with lights at two-meter intervals; lights in the form of a straight line with a sign in the middle lit up with Christmas lights (on this one, the crew at one point mistakenly identified cars on a road as the drop-zone-sign); two crosses side by side; a triangle of three lights with a fourth light in the center. In some areas there were so many small lights in the vicinity that no pattern could be located. For one drop the agents made four proposals in rapid succession: no lights, a nine-man cross, a line of five bonfires, a 60-meter line of colored flash-lights.

12. The standard light patterns taught by paramilitary instructors and generally accepted as best, were (a) an "L" of 4 lights;(b) a "T" of 5 lights; and (c)

a cross of 6 lights. All lights should be 15 to 25 yards apart, with one light different from the others.

13. The Cuban air crews must share the blame for the failures, as must their trainers. Policy did not allow American observers to go along on the missions to correct the errors. Pilot discipline was lacking and instructions were not followed in numerous instances.

14. For example, one air crew, under specific orders to abort the mission if the drop zone was missed on the initial run and not to search for it or circle around, made four passes four miles away, according to the ground report (which added, "Pilots drunk or crazy.").

15. Another crew commander, under orders not to drop unless the T pattern was positively identified, elected to drop without seeing the T because he had a "positive feeling" that he was over the drop zone. Another aircraft remained in the drop zone area 41 minutes before dropping cargo.

## Headquarters Direction

16. The Headquarters direction of these air drops left much to be desired. DPD, which controlled the crews and planes, never had a representative physically assigned to WH/4, and the two activities were operating in a divided command situation on the basis of mutual cooperation rather than generally accepted management practice and military command principles.

17. Daily consultation proved impossible although there was a requirement of it. There was trouble on cover stories, on funding, on security, and on cables, among other things. It was difficult to determine where the responsibilities of one component ended and those of the other began.

18. The WH/4 paramilitary chief recommended that the DPD unit be assigned to the chief of the task force for integration within his staff. But no action was ever taken, and the situation remained as described for the duration of the project.

19. WH/4 and DPD did not even agree on doctrine and techniques. In addition, all flight plans had to be personally reviewed and approved by the Deputy Director of Central Intelligence (DDCI) and by the 5412 Special Group. The requests for air drops came from Cuba by radio, secret writing or telephone to Miami and then were forwarded to WH/4 headquarters, which then put in an operational request to DPD, which in turn directed the Guatemala air base to mount the flight after approval had been given by DDCI. DPD could and did release its own cables, without coordination.

20. This cumbersome system was complicated even more by the scarcity

of agent radio operators inside Cuba. Some of the arrangements had to be made by secret writing, which was not only slow but contributed to misunderstanding. Necessary last-minute changes of plan by the reception groups or air crews could not be communicated to each other.

## Example of Confusion

21. The drop finally accomplished on 30 December is an outstanding example of the confusion that prevailed.

22. WH/4 informed Havana that the drop would be made from 400 feet. DPD told the Guatemala Base that the drop would be at 1,000 feet. Guatemala, on the other hand, felt that 600 feet would be best. WH/4 informed the agents that the aircraft definitely would make only one pass over the drop zone. But DPD authorized one 360° turn in order to make the drop good if the drop zone was not located on the initial run. (Actually, the crew made *three* passes.) This drop then failed (on 5 December) because the reception group understood that the plane would make only one pass, and turned off the lights when the plane came back for a second try. There was also confusion over the time of the drop and the number of bundles. The difficulties in arriving at an understanding among all parties concerned were so great that this operation, first planned for 22 October, was re-scheduled for 13 November, run on 5 December without dropping, then scheduled for 19 December. Then this had to be changed to 25 December and finally to 30 December.

23. For another operation WH/4 told Guatemala that the cargo should weigh 6,000 pounds, but DPD told Guatemala it could not be more than 4,000 or 5,000 pounds. The DPD message was not coordinated with WH/4, as Guatemala then pointed out.

24. Some of the techniques used by DPD were highly questionable. In one instance DPD told Guatemala that in the event the drop-zone lights were not seen by the crew the pilot should nevertheless drop his cargo on the drop zone as determined by dead reckoning. As it turned out, the reception group had dispersed after an encounter with a Cuban army patrol and was unable to be at the drop zone. The Castro forces then picked up at least half of the bundles dropped.

## Supplies for Castro

25. In another case 1,600 pounds of food and materiel were dropped blind (in the dark of the moon) on each of four hilltops to a group which was known to be in such a precarious position that it was not able to stay in place long

enough to lay out a drop zone. Again, the Castro forces got most of the load.

26. In still another, DPD told Guatemala that turns were allowed if the plane was not lined up on the initial run over the drop zone. The agents reported that the plane passed over twice without dropping, and that this alerted the Castro army to attack the resistance group and to disperse it.

27. Once two planes were sent over the drop zone half an hour apart and allowed to make two passes each. Not surprisingly, 200 militia searched the area the next day and seized the cargo. The drop altitude for another operation was set at 4,000 feet. The pilot reported he had hit the drop zone from 3,500 fact, even though unable to recognize the marker, but there is evidence that the enemy got at least half the drop.

28. One aircraft received heavy fire and was damaged. Its crew thus learned the hard way that dropping leaflets first had helped to alert the area and recommended that in the future the cargo be dropped first. Miami Base pointed out to Headquarters that it was a mistake to drop heavy weapons before a group had a known capability of using them or had specifically requested them.

29. For a long time the results of the drops, as reported by the ground elements, were not forwarded to the air crews, who got no critiques but continued to report successes when in fact they were missing the drop zone by many kilometers.

## Handling an Emergency

30. The handling of an emergency also left something to be desired. One of the planes had to land in Jamaica. The commander's phone call to an emergency number in Guatemala produced the reply, "Never heard of you." [Excised] first heard of this landing from [excised] who had assumed (wrongly) that [excised] had been advised by Headquarters.

31. In January 1961 Division D of the Agency's FI Staff made a study which raised pertinent questions about the air drops. The project's paramilitary staff made a study in March and concluded that the Cuban crews did not have sufficient experience or supervised training in clandestine paramilitary air operations to meet the project objectives and that they were too undisciplined to obey instructions or to make correct reports. This study recommended that contract American aircraft commanders be used, but it did not receive the approval of the paramilitary chief and went no further.

32. DPD also made an analysis in March and recommended certain overdue corrective action such as obtaining agent reports of drop results for

prompt dispatch to the air base in Guatemala, critiques for each mission regarding compliance with instructions, elimination of blind drops, and better identification of drop zones. DPD cabled Guatemala on 7 March that an analysis of the mission results to date would be forwarded shortly to be used as a basis for refinement of tactics and improvement of coordination with the reception teams. And at the end of March a check pilot was included for the first time in a mission crew. He noted discrepancies in pilot procedure and crew coordination.

## Tardy Corrective Action

33. These corrective actions came too late. The seeming inability to support resistance elements augmented the growing reliance being placed on the idea of an amphibious strike force to accomplish the objective; then, as the strike idea took over more and more, interest in clandestine drops decreased among officers in charge of the project. On or about 28 March a policy decision was made that there would be no more clandestine drops until after the amphibious assault. Inasmuch as the WH/4 case officers handling these drops were not informed as to the strike plan or the date, this posed a problem for them because 19 drops to specific drop zones were requested between 22 March and 19 April, and it was necessary to stall off the requests with such messages as:

"Don't give up hope. We'll drop as soon as we can."

"Regret unable mount BERTA. Definitely planning support your operation. Beg you understand our problems."

But the agents had their own problems during this time:

"Unjust to delay operation so much...This is not a game."

"How long will I have to wait for the drop. The lives of peasants and students depend on you."

"Dear Allies: Arms urgent. We made a commitment. We have complied. You have not. If you have decided to abandon us, answer."

"We are risking hundreds of peasant families. If you cannot supply us we will have to . . . demobilize. Your responsibility. We thought you were sincere."

"All groups demoralized . . . They consider themselves deceived because of failure of shipment of arms and money according to promise."

Perhaps the situation was best summed up by this agent message:

"Impossible to fight . . . Either the drops increase or we die . . . Men without arms or equipment. God help us."

34. The Inspector General reluctantly concludes that the agent who was showered with rice and beans was entirely correct in his finding that the Agency showed no professional competence in its attempts at clandestine air drops into Cuba. Furthermore these attempts in their over-all effect probably hurt the resistance more than they helped.

## K. CLANDESTINE PARAMILITARY OPERATIONS — MARITIME

1. WH/4 Branch had two separate maritime problems. It needed to transport men and supplies clandestinely to the coast of Cuba by small boats, and it needed ships to transport and support an amphibious landing of a military force, more or less overtly. This section of the report will be mostly concerned with small boat operations.

2. The WH Division had no assets in being there was no Agency element comparable to DPD to call on; and for obscure reasons the Navy was not asked to provide the help it might have. WH/4 had to start with nothing; there seemed to be very little maritime know-how within the Agency.

3. The original operational plan called for building up a substantial resistance organization, which could be done only if supplies and people were delivered to the right places. During the critical period March-December 1960, WH/4 had *one* boat, the "Metusa Time," a 54-foot pleasure cruiser which was lent to the Agency by a friend. Two maritime operations officers, more or less under deep cover, labored from March to October to outfit this boat and train its crew.

4. The boat went on its first mission on 28 September, offloading 300 pounds of cargo and picking up two exfiltrees. By January it had made five additional trips and transported about five tons, but only one infiltree. It had another successful operation in March 1961 and another in April.

### [Excised] Boats

5. In November and December there were six other successful small boat operations conducted with boats owned by various Cubans. The arrangements were made by individual case officers at Miami (there being no maritime section) and mainly in response to requests by the owners. No memoranda of understanding were made and the agreements as to support-

ing, equipping, and funding these Cuban boats were exceedingly loose, thus causing many problems later.

6. A Cuban would say, "Give me a tank of gas and a machine gun, and you can use our boat and we will help run it." After the operation he was likely to come back and say that the boat needed all sorts of equipment which had been damaged by the operation, and many claims were built up in this way.

7. Although more than twenty of these boats were offered to case officers, most of them were too small and too limited in range to be of much use. Furthermore, the bad weather which lasted from December into late March made small boat operations impossible at a time when they were badly needed. In January 1961 there was not a single successful operation.

## *[Excised] Boats*

8. By December the need for some [excised] boats was becoming obvious. The "Sea Gull" (see below) was picked up by Headquarters about that time. It turned out to be a complete "lemon"; one of the most experienced employees in small boats spent most of his time from December to June trying to get it to run, and it never did participate in an infiltration or exfiltration operation. Also, about December a 75-foot yacht, the "Wasp," [excised]. It had a 17-knot speed and a 600-mile range and ran its first successful mission on 15 February.

9. About February the "Tejana" also became operational. This was a 110-foot yacht which became available through a Cuban contact of a case officer. The arrangements made by the case officer with the Cuban owner were so vague that payment of bills incurred was a continuing problem. However, the "Tejana," in four operations in March, infiltrated 19,000 pounds, as compared with 12,700 pounds which had been infiltrated from September up to February by all available boats.

10. The statistics compiled by WH/4 and by Miami Base on the small boat operations are somewhat confused and inconsistent. However, the general picture is clear. The small boat operations succeeded in getting about 76 people into Cuba clandestinely. Most of these were taken in during March. Up to the middle of February only ten had been successfully infiltrated by this means, the first being in mid-November.

11. In the matter of arms, ammunition and other supplies to the resistance, the boat operations were not an outstanding success. From September to the time of the strike about 70,000 pounds were successfully infiltrated. This was about three times as much as was put in by air drops. The total amount of

supplies put into Cuba by air and boat operations amounted to about 93,000 pounds (46.5 tons); this would be about enough to equip 1,250 men.

## Limited Area

12. There was one successful boat operation in September; two in October; three in November; six in December, none in January; six in February; thirteen in March; and two in April. Up to February only six and a half tons were sent in.

13. One should not get the idea that these supplies were uniformly distributed throughout Cuba. Most of them were placed in one small area, the north coast of Cuba close to Havana. The small boats did not have the range to go farther.

14. In almost all cases the supplies were transferred to a Cuban boat or an offshore key rather than deposited on the shores of Cuba itself. In the fall, boat operations were restricted by policy to offshore rendezvous. By January Miami had begun to plan beach landing operations as a means of overcoming the unreliability of Cuban-based boats. At this time Miami Base did not even have aerial photos of the north coast of Cuba.

15. Of the 33 missions rated as successful only 27 could be considered entirely so since the cargo on the other operations was later recovered by the Castro government or the success was only partial. The reception committees did not seem to have had much training in maritime reception procedures.

16. In sum, a small amount of materiel was put into the Havana area in the period September-December by some ill-suited small boats. Then by using the "Wasp" and the "Tejana" a substantially larger amount of supplies was put in during February and March as well as some people, but to a limited area only. At this point the "Barbara J" and the "Blagar" (former LCIs) were used because of their longer range and larger size; however, for various reasons they were also unsuccessful in placing anything on the south coast except at the westernmost part.

## Lack of a Plan

17. Officers who worked on these operations reported that there was no effective project plan for using small boats to deliver men and equipment to forces inside Cuba who were best suited to use them to build up a powerful underground movement against Castro. According to these officers, WH/4 did not plan small boat operations; the case officers simply responded to

requests by individual Cubans and groups. One officer remarked that the Cubans were running the operations.

18. Of all the attempts made to land men and supplies in Cuba clandestinely by water some of the most notable were made by the "Barbara J," a surplus LCI which the Agency bought in October 1960. It was intended that this craft would serve as a mother ship for small boat operations and also provide a long-range lift capability.

19. After a shakedown voyage in December, featured by a mutiny, the ship was scheduled for clandestine maritime infiltration of three paramilitary teams into Cuba. Initially there was some confusion as to who was running the operation since Miami had been handling small boat operations and had made the rendezvous plans for this one, but Headquarters had responsibility for the "Barbara J." WH/4 then sent the chief of its maritime section to Miami to coordinate, to brief the captain, and to dispatch the boat on its mission on 16 January.

20. The "Barbara J" put into Vieques Island on 31 January 1961 after having been unsuccessful in putting anybody ashore in Cuba. The crew's morale continued to deteriorate. Some refused to take direct orders, attempts to discipline the men were ineffective, the engineers refused to stand watch, and all of the crew wanted to return to Miami and resign. Also, nine of the ten agents did not wish to stay on the ship for another mission.

## A Sit-down Strike

21. On 4 February the "Barbara J" sailed from Vieques for a rendezvous on the south coast of Cuba, 24 crew members having been left on a Vieques beach, where they staged a sit-down and a hunger strike. On 9 February the "Barbara J" reported that the contact had not shown up at the rendezvous point.

22. After trying again on 10 February, the captain of the "Barbara J" cabled: "Take a message to Garcia: The reluctant heroes in fishing boat again conspicuous by their absence." On 11 February he sent another odd cable: "Last message to Garcia: Your fishing boat still manifesting extreme shyness. Suggest next operation send in varsity." On 13 February he sent: "Cruised without making contact. Picked up small target on radar, tracked it down, and scared hell out of some fishermen who wanted no part of us."

23. The case officer and the team leaders had a different story. They stated that when the "Barbara J" arrived at the rendezvous point it was approached by a small boat that came at the right time and gave the correct signals, but

that as the boat came alongside the captain of the "Barbara J" ordered two floodlights turned on the boat which apparently scared it away. On 18 February the reception party sent a message that their boat had been at the right place at the right time and that a patrol boat had showed up. The "Barbara J" arrived at [excised] on 14 February without having received arrival instructions. On 15 February Miami sent a message saying that it was setting up facilities at Key West to receive the "Barbara J." Upon landing in Key West the ten paramilitary agents, having been on this trip for a month after spending two months in a safe house, were ready to resign and it took a considerable amount of persuasion to get them to stay with the program. They were then sent to New Orleans for holding.

## Earning a Citation

24. Several officers who were associated with the captain of the "Barbara J," a contract employee acquired from Military Sea Transportation Service (MSTS), have testified to his drinking on duty, his bullying of Cubans, and his disregard for security. Drew Pearson wrote about the drunken American LCI skipper who scared away Cuban underground leaders with his ship's floodlights, and who threatened to abandon a sabotage team. On 21 March the project's paramilitary chief relieved the captain of his command and requested that he be terminated. However, the captain was retained on duty and eventually received full pay and a bonus for a six-month contract period in the amount of $14,698.

25. WH/4 Branch initiated action to get the captain commended by his parent service for outstanding performance. In July 1961 he was cited "for completing an assignment involving extreme hazards in an outstanding manner, and displaying exceptional skill and courage" and given the Navy Superior Civilian Service Award—the highest honorary civilian award within the authority of the MSTS commander.

26. The branch had never taken action either to clear him or to convict him of serious charges, and the high commendation he received casts doubt not only on the validity of other WH/4 recommendations for merit citations but also on the quality of personnel management in the project.

## Peculiar Organization

27. The organization for controlling clandestine maritime operations was peculiar. The forward operating base in Miami had the responsibility for small boat operations but could not run any without Headquarters approval.

It was seldom that Headquarters had any query or refused to give approval.

28. But the Miami Base did not have the equipment and experience that were needed. For a long time the docking facilities were inadequate. The desirability of having a base at Key West was recognized as early as November 1960, but this base was not established until mid-February. It was insufficiently staffed and had a great many cover, security and administrative problems on which it received little assistance. At first it was under the direction of the Miami paramilitary section; eventually it was placed under the chief of the Miami Base.

29. The small staff at Key West not only supported small boat operations; it also had to take whatever action was necessary when disabled black flights came in to the local Naval air station since DPD had no representative in the area. Each unsuccessful maritime operation doubled the work. Boats coming back to a safe haven loaded with arms and explosives, usually crewed by Cubans and sometimes disabled in various ways, had to be unloaded again by whoever was available among paramilitary case officers and security and support people. A few staff employees worked almost around the clock for a month loading and unloading cargo without benefit of even a forklift. Many tons were so handled.

30. It is clear that there was no over-all policy in regard to the small boats. There was no clear directive as to whether to acquire short-range, speedy boats or long-range, slower boats; whether to use fishing craft and crews or special-purpose boats built specifically for our use. There was no policy on the use of a mother craft. There was no control over the amount of money spent on these small boats and their outfitting.

## The Maritime Unit

31. WH/4 Headquarters had a staff employee whose job was small boat coordinator. This meant, in effect, checking proposed operations with the intelligence section, extending approvals and keeping records. WH/4 also had a separate maritime unit which handled the technical side of the small boats, approved funds for them, and arranged for personnel for them, but had nothing to do with their operations.

32. This maritime unit also had the responsibility for acquiring and fitting out the larger ships such as the "Barbara J," the "Blagar," the three LCUs and the ships used in the strike. This unit also had the responsibility for training underwater demolition teams, directing raiding operations, and overseeing the Vieques Base.

33. The lack of equipment, the shortage of experienced personnel, the press of time and the problems of coordination are shown by the experience which the maritime unit had with the acquisition and outfitting of the LCIs and the LCUs. The press of time hardly allowed for advertising for specific types of craft or soliciting competitive bids. The two LCIs (the "Barbara J" and the "Blagar") were purchased from a private corporation in Miami for $70,000. About $253,000 was then spent in modifying, repairing and outfitting them.

34. This work, which extended over a period of several months, was directed by officers from Headquarters during short temporary duty tours in the Miami area. The day-to-day supervision of the work was under several Navy chief petty officers (borrowed from the Agency's Office of Training) who had no contact with Miami Base, no authority to spend money or give orders, and no channel to procure parts and equipment. The technical and training abilities of these Navy chiefs were grossly misused by the project; much of their time was spent as stevedore or deckhand labor.

## Training on LCUs

35. [Excised] three LCUs were bought directly from the Navy in September 1960 at $125,000 each. Supposedly in operating condition, these craft had been stripped and were in such bad shape that they could hardly be moved from the dock. The dozen or so Agency employees who went to Little Creek to get them into operational condition were so busy with repairs that there was little time left for learning how to operate the craft, even though some members of the group were not familiar with LCUs, the engineers did not all know engineering and the skippers did not all know navigation. This group got the LCUs to Vieques Island somehow and proceeded to train the Cuban crews, which, however, were given no training in night landing and very little in navigation.

36. In all, about $1,400,000 was spent on boats and ships, and the total cost of the maritime phases of the project was about $2,679,000. Wages were a considerable item. For example, ship's masters on contract were budgeted at $2,500 a month, cooks at $1,000. There seemed to be a general failure at the top to realize how much boats cost to run and to keep in repair. The arrangement whereby officers in Headquarters tried to control the expenditures being made in Florida to repair and operate boats which were urgently needed was highly impractical. The high cost of boats in this project is well illustrated by the dismal case of the "Sea Gull."

## Case of the "Sea Gull"

37. [Excised] It had previously been used to service offshore oil- drilling rigs and was estimated to have a fair market value of $74,500.

38. The request for approval [excised] was signed for the chief of the project by a special assistant in the FI section (acting for the acting chief!) and approved by the Deputy Chief of WH Division (acting for his chief). It was [excised] christened the "Sea Gull" and transported to Miami, where it broke down 500 yards from the pier on its first trial run. On 6 January 1961 it was estimated that repairs and modifications would cost $10,000; by 30 January, the estimate had grown to $32,000; by 22 February, to $40,000; and on 24 February, the shipyard doing the work submitted a bill for $65,000! In all, the "Sea Gull" cost:

| | |
|---|---|
| [Excised] | $39,500 |
| Repairs (eventually reduced from $5,000) | $58,000 |
| Communications gear, tools, arms, navigation aids | $14,000 |
| | $111,500 |

39. The "Sea Gull" was not ready to be used until the last week of March; at this time it was commandeered (along with the "Wasp") by a headquarters unit which was staging a deception operation in connection with the amphibious strike, over the strong protests of Miami Base, which never got to use the boat on an infiltration operation.

40. The lack of qualified personnel, the confusion of responsibility, the lack of planning, and the skyrocketing costs in the maritime activity led to a high-level request for the assignment of a qualified senior Naval officer to the project. When a captain reported, no one seemed to know what to do with him and, after he briefly visited Miami and Key West bases, he was assigned to the naval side of the strike planning at Headquarters. He is reported to have been not entirely happy with his brief Agency tour. In any event he was another example of poor handling of people in this project, and he was not given a chance to solve the problems of maritime operations.

41. It is apparent that the Agency had very little capability for maritime operations even of a clandestine nature. It lacked trained personnel, boats, bases, doctrine, and organization. The employees who worked in this sadly slighted activity were well aware of this, and morale was not high. As one of them said, "The lowest kind of operations officer is a paramilitary operations officer, and the lowest kind of PM officer is a maritime operations officer."

## L. CLANDESTINE PARAMILITARY
## OPERATIONS — TRAINING
## UNDERGROUND LEADERS

1. Early in the project a carefully selected group of Cubans was trained for infiltration into Cuba to organize resistance. The loose management of the project is illustrated by the confusion between the headquarters elements and the training elements over what these men were being trained for, and by the failure to have their missions, means of entry, and reception ready for them.

2. The trained Cubans put into Cuba were too few and too late to do very much, and the strike planners ignored them. The cost of training and holding these men probably ran well over a million dollars, yet most of them were never used for what they were trained to do, and some were not used at all.

3. This particular endeavor began in December 1959 when the WH Division made a decision to pick a small group of Cubans and train them to train other Cubans for infiltration into Cuba in small paramilitary teams to organize resistance forces. Possible training sites in Panama were surveyed at this time, but no further action was taken. The basic policy paper approved by the President in March 1960 included the above proposal.

4. In April 1960, the Cuban leader Manuel Artime, who was in Miami, offered a number of his followers as recruits for the program. Useppa Island was acquired as an assessment and holding site, and a preliminary screening of the candidates for the training program began.

5. During May and June 1960 complete polygraphs, psychological and psychiatric teats, and evaluations were obtained on 66 individuals. Basic Morse code training was begun at the island. In June 29 trainees were sent from Useppa Island to Panama for basic paramilitary training. In July 32 trainees were sent to Guatemala to be trained as radio operators, and Useppa Island was then closed down.

## The Training Site

6. A worse training site could hardly have been chosen than the one in Guatemala, it being almost inaccessible, with no training facilities and almost no living facilities. The trainees were put to work building the camp, working during the day and studying at night. This went on for several months.

7. The number of Americans at the camp was held to a bare minimum for security reasons. They were represented to be either tourists or adventurers. The camp commander was also the chief of training and the project officer for Guatemala. When he arrived, he had to set up the temporary camp, find an

area for a permanent camp, contract for buildings, supplies and equipment; he also had to find sites for a suitable air base, a maritime base, and a prison and contract for these facilities to be built. He had three assistants: a communications officer and two contract employees.

8. The initial group of paramilitary trainees was transferred to the Guatemala Base from Panama after two months of training. By 23 August there were 78 paramilitary trainees, 34 communications trainees, and nine staff and contract employees.

9. By September the training camp had enough facilities and instructors to begin a four-week basic training course. The trainees were sorted into seven-man teams according to their area knowledge and their aptitudes. Sixty were selected to go into Cuba (either legally or illegally) and to contact resistance groups; 60 were selected for action teams to go in illegally and join the resistance groups that had been contacted by the first teams; the remainder of the trainees would be formed into a small conventional strike force. The training base expected the teams to be ready to go in October and asked Headquarters to provide the infiltration plans.

10. The trainers did not realize that Headquarters had changed the plan. Already in July the FRD, the exile political front, had been asked to provide 500 individuals for a paramilitary action cadre, and the training base was asked if it could accommodate this number. Obviously, it could not. Conditions actually got worse. In September the training camp was plagued by torrential tropical rains, shortages of food and supplies, plus trouble with agitators and hoodlums among their recently arrived trainees, who were not being screened and assessed as the first ones had been. The training base chief got into disfavor with Headquarters apparently because of his blunt cables asking for assistance. ("My men are going hungry and barefoot.")

## Request for Missions

11. In October the infiltration teams that had been selected from among the trainees worked out detailed operational plans for themselves, complete with maps, propaganda handouts, and resistance operations. Then the base announced that about a hundred men were ready to go, Headquarters replied that it was proposing the illegal infiltration of the teams in November by boat. (Actually, the only boat the project had at this time was the 54-foot "Metusa Time.") Headquarters further cabled that it was engaged in preparing a general plan for the employment of the infiltration teams but that *the details were not yet ready*. The base chief was recalled in October, and thereafter the train-

ing base had a new chief each week for five weeks. *One trainee* was put into Cuba legally at the end of October.

12. In November 1960 (12 months after the original decision had been made to train Cuban teams for resistance organization) ten teams were reportedly ready to go. But they were *still awaiting Headquarters plans* for infiltration. In all 178 men (including 23 radio operators) had been trained in security, basic clandestine tradecraft, intelligence collection and reporting, propaganda and agitation, subversive activities, resistance organization, reception operations, explosives and demolitions, guerrilla action, and similar matters.

13. Headquarters approved the use of 60 of these men for the resistance teams; all others were scheduled to begin formal, conventional combat training on 15 November as an element of a strike force of 1,500 men. This drastic change in over-all planning was announced to the training base by a cable on 4 November and led the base to plead for closer coordination in the future between Headquarters planning and the field training. During this month six trainees were moved to a Miami safe house where they stayed for two months, awaiting transportation into Cuba.

## Move to Panama

14. In December 1960 Headquarters advised the training base that it was expecting approval of its operational concept, which included internal resistance stimulated by teams as well as the use of a ground and air assault force. It advised the base that a 750-man brigade (instead of 1,500) was being planned and that 80 men (instead of 60) were approved for infiltration teams. During this month the 80 men were moved to Panama where they were held until somebody could find out what to do with them. An offer from DPD to give them jump training was turned down by the project.

15. By January 1961 the morale of the trainees still in Panama had declined considerably. There was not even an interpreter available for briefing and debriefing them. Headquarters then had 24 of them brought to safe houses in Miami to be made ready for dispatch. Twelve radio operators were moved from Panama to the Agency's training base in the United States for further training.

16. By February 1961 the 32 trainees still in Panama were described as disillusioned and at the breaking point. They were then transferred to a base in New Orleans to be given additional training in sabotage and air-maritime reception. February was actually a red-letter month. Six of the radio opera-

tors were infiltrated legally. On 14 February the first resistance team was put into Cuba, and two more teams went in at the end of the month. However, the two teams which had sat in a Miami safe house from mid-November to mid-January returned to Miami in bad humor in mid-February after a month on the "Barbara J" circumnavigating Cuba without being put ashore.

17. An effective infiltration mechanism never was developed. Not one of the paramilitary teams was ever delivered by air. On 29 March the project was able to put four agents into Cuba through Guantanamo Base. It is not clear why this could not have been done earlier. No infiltration was ever tried by submarine.

## Morale Problems

18. On 10 March 1961 (16 months after the original decision to train resistance teams) the 90 men who had been trained for this were distributed as follows:

32  infiltrated including 14 radio operators
5   at sea on a sabotage mission
6   in New Orleans as members of a raider team
28  in New Orleans still awaiting infiltration
19  detached to Miami for various impending
     operations.

The morale of the remaining trainees was low and their anger high. This caused a great many problems in New Orleans. Some of these men had been *held in five different camps over a ten-month period.* On 30 March, about three weeks before the invasion, the remainder of the group (about 20) were transferred to Miami and turned loose, being described as a collection of spoiled individuals distinguished by bad conduct. At least 30 of the agents who were recruited between May and September 1960 *never got into Cuba at all*; among the 30 were eight who came into the project in the original group in May 1960 and who were in training almost continuously from that time up to April 1961.

19. The time spent in training is no measure of the quality of the training, of course, and there was undoubtedly a great waste of time. One of the Cubans trained for infiltration into Cuba wrote that after he arrived in Panama in December 1960:". . . during almost three weeks, the only thingh I did . . . was cleaning a small dam and the shoting range. after that we just din't do anythingh, just sleep and ate, thats all." When he arrived in Florida on 18 January: "There, the same history, sleep, eat, play card and watch tele-

vision. The only training I receveid during that time was on secret writting, wich was very good but nothing else." The same agent pointed out serious deficiencies in his weapons training and his final briefing.

20. One of the instructors in Guatemala in the early months later claimed that only two instructors knew their business; the others were chosen from the trainee cadre, who had only a background of two months' training themselves. He included himself among the unqualified.

## Training Omission

21. The remoteness of the training site caused additional difficulties. When brigade training started on 29 November there were only two compasses for 405 troops, and these belonged to trainees. Compasses had first been requested on 2 October, but when they were not received the training in their use had to be omitted from the program.

22. More serious, there had never been any definition of training goals, and the base and Headquarters were working at cross-purposes. The chief of the training base in Guatemala never received any letter of instruction.

23. The situation at the New Orleans Base in March 1961 was even more chaotic. The instructors found a training area which was 90% swamp and filled with poisonous snakes. Demolition classes had to be conducted along a footpath leading from a theater to a mess hall, with constant interruptions from passers-by. Nobody seemed able to define the training that was required. A demolitions instructor was assured on arrival that the group he had come to train did not need the instruction; in any case, there were no explosive trainee materials, no adequate range, and no gear to set one up. Another instructor, sent to New Orleans to train a small raider group, found himself expected to train, organize and equip a 90-man guerrilla force. A week later he found himself training a 164-man assault battalion instead. The training requirement was never spelled out, and the training equipment never showed up.

24. Training activity of various sorts was going on continually; there were requirements for everything from counterintelligence to small boat handling. But there was no full-time chief of training in the project to oversee requirements, define responsibilities, set up facilities and provide support. Consequently, what training was done, was done without control, by individual case officers doing the best they could. How effective this training was cannot be determined. Much of it took place in Miami, where personnel from the base were instructing Cubans in intelligence collection, counterintelligence

techniques, psychological warfare activities, or paramilitary subjects, according to need.

25. The training was necessarily conducted in safe houses, and required a considerable expenditure of time on the part of base personnel. Other training was conducted in the Washington area, usually by case officers. One man was trained in a hotel room to make a parachute jump (he made one successfully!). Many requests were levied on the Office of Training for instructors and training materials. But those were uncoordinated and wasteful. Many of the instructors, when made available, were not used in their specialties, ending up in such jobs as stevedoring instead.

26. A well thought-out project would have had a training annex which would have laid specific requirements on the Office of Training, particularly when the training of hundreds of people was an integral part of the venture. Instead, the requirements were met in piecemeal and improvised fashion, under difficult conditions, and with dubious results.

## M. SECURITY

1. The assault on Cuba is generally acknowledged to have been a poorly kept secret. It could hardly have been otherwise, considering the complexity of the operation and the number of people involved, both Cuban and American. The inspection team did not make a detailed study of the security aspects of the operation but came across many weaknesses in the protection of information and activities from those who did not "need to know."

2. In general the Cubans who were in the operation do not seem to have had any real understanding of the need to keep quiet about their activities. Many of them knew much more than they needed to know, and they were not compartmented from each other and from Americans to the extent that was necessary. For example, one wealthy Cuban who was close to the operation was being contacted by at least six different staff employees.

3. Some agents were being handled by two or three different case officers at the same time, with confusing results and lack of control. Many of the agents who were sent into Cuba had known each other during training; for example, a dozen radio operators had been trained as a group. If one was arrested, he would know who the other ones were. One radio operator inside Cuba was aware of almost every paramilitary operation in Cuba from the beginning of the project.

4. Agents who were supposedly well trained disregarded elementary rules

of personal security and were arrested because they needlessly gave away their true identities by visiting relatives who were under surveillance or by carrying identifying documents in their pockets.

## Hazard in Miami

5. The Miami area represented a particular hazard because stories and rumors spread rapidly through the large Cuban community, which included Castro agents. Movements of boats and people soon became known. One agent, who had been infiltrated into Cuba by boat, reported later that within three days his family in Miami knew when and how he had landed, because one of the crew members of the boat had told many people in Miami about it. Letters from the training camp, although censored, managed nevertheless to convey information to the Miami Cubans.

6. The Americans on the project in many cases also failed to observe strict security discipline. One senior case officer holding an operational meeting with Cubans in a Miami motel was overheard by a citizen, who reported to the Federal Bureau of Investigation.

7. It has been testified that the security measures at the training camps in Guatemala and at New Orleans were inadequate. Furthermore, the training camps had no adequate counterintelligence capability. Except for an instructor borrowed from the Office of Training for a few weeks, the Agency was unable to provide a counterintelligence officer to the camps. This lack was serious because, in order to obtain a great many recruits for the strike force in a hurry, there was very little screening of the volunteers, and some who were sent to camp had been inadequately checked.

## Poor Backstopping

8. Instances were noted of poor backstopping of the cover stories of Agency employees, sketchy briefings on cover, weak cover stories, and faulty documentation. Much of this can be ascribed to lack of attention to detail due to the press of time. Many of the early difficulties in Guatemala stemmed from the inadvisability of providing supplies and support to instructors who were posing as "tourists" and "soldiers of fortune." This pretense eventually had to be dropped because of its impracticality. A serious weakness showed up in the poor arrangements for backstopping overflights (for example, the plane that landed in Jamaica).

9. Somewhat curiously, a strict compartmentation was applied in certain areas of the project which actually denied information to people who needed

it. Those who were engaged in running agents into Cuba were never allowed into the War Room or given the plan for the strike.

10. For security reasons, the resistance elements inside Cuba were not advised of the time of the assault, and could hardly have risen up even if there had been 100,000 of them. The entire complement of the Miami Base was likewise uninformed and was unprepared to take action when the strike occurred. Staff employees at the Miami Base, who could have benefited by special clearances, did not get them until much too late.

## Use of Guatemala

11. The use of Guatemala for training bases was, in terms of security, unfortunate. It is obvious now that the training could have been done more securely in the United States (as for example, the tank crew training, which got no publicity at all). The Guatemala camps were not easily hidden and not easily explained. The air base was located on a well-traveled road and in view of a railroad where trainloads of Guatemalans frequently halted on a siding.

12. It is strange that the training of the Cubans was undertaken in a foreign country, where the trainees were necessarily exposed to the natives and reporters could pick up information. Presumably this was done on grounds of security and non-attributability; however, the radio operators who were trained in Guatemala were later brought to the United States for further training. The force for the abortive diversionary expedition was trained in New Orleans rather than being sent outside the country. Other Cubans were trained in both paramilitary and espionage subjects in the outskirts of Miami and Washington, and still others were trained on American soil at Vieques Island. Of all these training locations, only the ones in Guatemala became known to the world.

13. It is acknowledged that many Cubans and Americans observed strict security discipline, that the security officers of the project made an outstanding contribution, and that many arrangements and activities are not open to criticism regarding their security. Unfortunately, this was not good enough for a project of this size and importance, conducted by professional intelligence officers.

14. Because of the operation's magnitude, the errors committed resulted in the exposure of Agency personnel and *modus operandi* to many uncontrolled individuals, both foreign and American.

## N. AMERICANS IN COMBAT

1. During the invasion landing two Agency contract employees, assigned as operations officers aboard the two LCIs, went ashore to mark two of the beaches and exchanged gunfire with Cuban militia. One of these employees had taken part in a sabotage raid on a Cuban oil refinery a month earlier. Both of them engaged in rescue operations along the Cuban shore after the brigade collapsed.

2. In late 1960 the project leaders were becoming doubtful of the motivation of the Cuban pilots they were training and of their ability to perform tactical missions successfully. In January 1961 the Agency requested the Special Group to authorize the use of American contract pilots. The authorization given was limited to the hiring of the pilots and reserved for later decision the question of their actual use. The Special Group also granted authority to recruit and hire American seamen to serve in the invasion fleet.

3. Three American contract pilots with long Agency experience were made available from another project. A number of other pilots and air-crew technicians, members or ex-members of several Air National Guard units, were recruited especially for the project in early 1961 under cover of a notional commercial company.

4. Through the first day of fighting, 17 April, only Cuban air crews were used for combat or drop missions. Of 11 Cuban-manned B-26s which had gone over the beachhead, only three had returned to base, and four of the others had been shot down. That night the available Cuban crews were exhausted and dispirited.

5. On 18 April the hard pressed exile brigade was calling for air support. Two American fliers volunteered to go, and several Cuban crews followed their example. The result was a highly successful attack against a column of Castro forces moving on Blue Beach. Four American-manned aircraft were in combat over the beachhead the following day, and two of them were shot down by Castro's T-33s. Later the same day two American crews returned for another sortie. Four American fliers were either killed in combat or executed by Castro forces after being shot down.

6. In addition to these actions, an American-manned PBY patrolled the waters south of Cuba for a total of 57 hours during five days on air-sea rescue and communications relay duty.

7. The American pilots lost in combat were aware of United States Government sponsorship and probably also of Agency interest, but had been instructed not to inform their families of this. In spite of wide press coverage

of the invasion failure, the story of the American pilots has never gotten into print, although its sensational nature still makes this a possibility. In dealing with the surviving families it has been necessary to conceal connection with the United States Government. This effort has been complicated by the fact that the original cover story was changed and a second notional company substituted.

8. The resolution in a secure manner of the legal and moral claims arising from these four deaths has been costly, complicated and fraught with risk of disclosure of the Government's role. These problems were aggravated by the inclusion in the employment contracts of certain unnecessarily complicated insurance clauses and by the project's failure to prepare in advance an effective plan for dealing with the eventual legal and security problems.

## O. CONCLUSIONS AND RECOMMENDATIONS

Certain basic *conclusions* have been drawn from this survey of the Cuban operation:

1. The Central Intelligence Agency, after starting to build up the resistance and guerrilla forces inside Cuba, drastically converted the project into what rapidly became an overt military operation. The Agency failed to recognize that when the project advanced beyond the stage of plausible denial it was going beyond the area of Agency responsibility as well as Agency capability.

2. The Agency became so wrapped up in the military operation that it failed to appraise the chances of success realistically. Furthermore, it failed to keep the national policy-makers adequately and realistically informed of the conditions considered essential for success, and it did not press sufficiently for prompt policy decisions in a fast moving situation.

3. As the project grew, the Agency reduced the exiled leaders to the status of puppets, thereby losing the advantages of their active participation.

4. The Agency failed to build up and supply a resistance organization under rather favorable conditions. Air and boat operations showed up poorly.

5. The Agency failed to collect adequate information on the strengths of the Castro regime and the extent of the opposition to it; and it failed to evaluate the available information correctly.

6. The project was badly organized. Command lines and management controls were ineffective and unclear. Senior Staffs of the Agency were not

utilized; air support stayed independent of the project; the role of the large forward base was not clear.

7. The project was not staffed throughout with top-quality people, and a number of people were not used to the best advantage.

8. The Agency entered the project without adequate assets in the way of boats, bases, training facilities, agent nets, Spanish-speakers, and similar essential ingredients of a successful operation. Had these been already in being, much time and effort would have been saved.

9. Agency policies and operational plans were never clearly delineated, with the exception of the plan for the brigade landing; but even this provided no disaster plan, no unconventional warfare annex, and only extremely vague plans for action following a successful landing. In general, Agency plans and policies did not precede the various operations in the project but were drawn up in response to operational needs as they arose. Consequently, the scope of the operation itself and of the support required was constantly shifting.

There were some good things in this project. Much of the support provided was outstanding (for example, logistics and communications). A number of individuals did superior jobs. Many people at all grade levels gave their time and effort without stint, working almost unlimited hours over long periods, under difficult and frustrating conditions, without regard to personal considerations. But this was not enough.

It is assumed that the Agency, because of its experience in this Cuban operation, will never again engage in an operation that is essentially an overt military effort. But before it takes on another major covert political operation it will have to improve its organization and management drastically. It must find a way to set up an actual task force, if necessary, and be able to staff it with the best people. It must govern its operation with clearly defined policies and carefully drawn plans, engaging in full coordination with the Departments of State and Defense as appropriate.

Previous surveys and other papers written by the Inspector General have called attention to many of these problems and deficiencies, and have suggested solutions. For example, in June 1958 a recommendation was made, in a survey of the Far East Division, that a high-level Agency study be made of the extent to which the Agency should be engaged in paramilitary operations, "if any"; and that it include an evaluation of the capabilities of other government departments to assume primary responsibility in this field.

In January 1959 the Inspector General pointed out in a memorandum to the Deputy Director (Plans) that: "A basic problem in the PM field is the delineation of responsibility between the Agency and the military services. In our view, the Clandestine Services tends to assume responsibilities beyond its capabilities and does not give sufficient consideration to the ability of other Departments of the Government to conduct or participate in these operations."

A 1955 survey of the then Psychological and Paramilitary Operations Staff warned against the by-passing of this staff by the operating divisions, who were dealing directly with the Deputy Director (Plans) and the Director of Central Intelligence instead. In March 1961 the survey of the Covert Action Staff again warned against ignoring the staff and failing to utilize its services.

The July 1959 survey of the Deputy Director (Plans) organization again stressed the importance of the functional staffs, particularly in relation to the conduct of complex operations, and advocated the use of a task force for covert operations having major international significance.

"These operations," the survey stated, "may be aimed at the overthrow of a hostile regime and may require extensive paramilitary operations, . . . . . . and clandestine logistics and air support of substantial magnitude. Such operations must be coordinated with national policy on a continuing basis, and may require constant high-level liason with the State Department and the White House. To be successful, major covert operations of this nature require the effective mobilization of all the resources of the DD/P, and are clearly beyond the capabilities of any one area division."

The same survey added that the Caribbean task force located in the WH Division was planning at a great rate, but accomplishing little because it was too low-level to act decisively or to obtain effective policy guidance from other departments of the Government; it did not even inspire confidence among many senior DD/P officers. Such task forces within a single division "represent a woefully inadequate response to a problem of major national significance. Command of such a task force must be a full-time job, and the task force commander must be of sufficient stature to deal directly with the Under Secretary of State or with other senior officials of the government as the need arises."

The same survey also discussed the management problem in the DD/P area at length, and made a number of recommendations which are on record. Among other things, it pointed out the confusion as to the relationship and functions of the three top officers.

The study of the Cuban operation shows that these criticisms and many others discussed in previous Inspector General surveys are still valid and worthy of review. But the Cuban operation, in addition to demonstrating old weaknesses again, also showed Agency weaknesses not clearly discerned before.

The Inspector General, as a result of his study of the Cuban operation, makes the following *recommendations* regarding future Agency involvement in covert operations which have major international significance and which may profoundly affect the course of world events:

1. Such an operation should be carried out by a carefully selected task force, under the command of a senior official of stature on a full-time basis, and organizationally outside the DD/P structure but drawing upon all the resources of the Clandestine Services.

2. The Agency should request that such projects should be transferred to the Department of Defense when they show signs of becoming overt or beyond Agency capabilities.

3. The Agency should establish a procedure under which the Board of National Estimates or other body similarly divorced from clandestine operations would be required to evaluate all plans for such major covert operations, drawing on all available intelligence and estimating the chances of success from an intelligence point of view.

4. The Agency should establish a high-level board of senior officers from its operational and support components, plus officers detailed from the Pentagon and the Department of State, to make cold, hard appraisals at recurring intervals of the chances of success of major covert projects from an operational point of view.

5. A mechanism should be established for communicating these intelligence and operational appraisals to the makers of national policy.

6. In return, a mechanism should be established to communicate to the Agency the national policy bearing on such projects, and the Agency should not undertake action until clearly defined policy has been received.

7. The Agency should improve its system for the guided collection of information essential to the planning and carrying out of such projects.

8. The Agency should take immediate stops to eliminate the deficiencies in its clandestine air and maritime operations.

9. The Agency should take steps to improve its employees' competence in foreign languages, knowledge of foreign areas, and capability in dealing with foreign people, when such skills are necessary.

10. The Agency should devise a more orderly system for the assignment of employees within the DD/P area than that currently in use.

Annex A

16 March 1960

## A PROGRAM OF COVERT ACTION AGAINST THE CASTRO REGIME

1. *Objective*: The purpose of the program outlined herein is to bring about the replacement of the Castro regime with one more devoted to the true interests of the Cuban people and more acceptable to the U.S. in such a manner as to avoid any appearance of U.S. intervention. Essentially the method of accomplishing this end will be to induce, support, and so far as possible direct action, both inside and outside of Cuba, by selected groups of Cubans of a sort that they might be expected to and could undertake on their own initiative. Since a crisis inevitably entailing drastic action in or toward Cuba could be provoked by circumstances beyond control of the U.S. before the covert action program has accomplished its objective, every effort will be made to carry it out in such a way as progressively to improve the capability of the U.S. to act in a crisis.

2. *Summary Outline*: The program contemplates four major courses of action:

a. The first requirement is the creation of a responsible, appending and unified Cuban opposition to the Castro regime, publicly declared as such and therefore necessarily located outside of Cuba. It is hoped that within one month a political entity can be formed in the shape or a council or junta, through the merger of three acceptable opposition groups with which the Central Intelligence Agency is already in contact. The council will be encouraged to adopt as its slogan "Restore the Revolution," to develop a political position consistent with that slogan, and to address itself to the Cuban people as an attractive political alternative to Castro. This vocal opposition will: serve as a magnet for the loyalties of the Cubans; in actuality conduct and direct various opposition activities; and provide cover for other compartmented CIA controlled operations.(Tab A)

b. So that the opposition may be heard and Castro's base of popular support undermined, it is necessary to develop the means for mass communication to the Cuban people so that a powerful propaganda offensive can be initiated in the name of the declared opposition. The major tool proposed to be used for this purpose is a long and short wave gray broadcasting facility, probably to be located on Swan Island. The target date for its completion is two months. This will be supplemented by broadcasting from U.S. commercial facilities paid for by private Cuban groups and by the clandestine distribution of written material inside the country. (Tab B)

c. Work is already in progress in the creation of a covert intelligence and action organization within Cuba which will be responsive to the orders and directions of the "exile" opposition. Such a network must have effective communication and be selectively manned to minimize the risk of penetration. An effective organization can probably be created within 60 days. Its role will be to provide hard intelligence, to arrange for the illegal infiltration and exfiltration of individuals, to assist in the internal distribution of illegal propaganda, and to plan and organize for the defection of key individuals and groups as directed.

d. Preparations have already been made for the development of an adequate paramilitary force outside of Cuba, together with mechanisms for the necessary logistic support of covert military operations on the Island. Initially a cadre of leaders will be recruited after careful screening; and trained as paramilitary instructors. In a second phase a number of paramilitary cadres will be trained at secure locations outside of the U.S. so as to be available for immediate deployment into Cuba to organize, train and lead resistance forces recruited there both before and after the establishment of one or more active centers of resistance. The creation of this capability will require a minimum of six months and probably closer to eight. In the meanwhile, a limited air capability for resupply and for infiltration and exfiltration already exists under CIA control and can be rather easily expanded if and when the situation requires. Within two months it is hoped to parallel this with a small air resupply capability under deep cover as a commercial operation in another country.

3. *Leadership*: It is important to avoid distracting and divisive rivalry among the outstanding Cuban opposition leaders for the senior role in the opposition. Accordingly, every effort will be made to have an eminent, non-ambitious, politically uncontentious chairman selected. The emergence of a successor to Castro should follow careful assessment of the various personalities active in the opposition to identity the one who can attract, control, and lead the several forces. As the possibility of an overthrow of Castro be-

comes more imminent, the senior leader must be selected, U.S. support focused upon him, and his build up undertaken.

4. *Cover*: All actions undertaken by CIA in support and on behalf of the opposition council will, of course, be explained as activities of that entity (insofar as the actions become publicly known at all). The CIA will, however, have to have direct contacts with a certain number of Cubans and, to protect these, will make use of a carefully screened group of U.S. businessmen with a stated interest in Cuban affairs and desire to support the opposition. They will act as a [excised] and channel for guidance and support to the directorate of the opposition under controlled conditions. CIA personnel will be documented as representatives or this group. In order to strengthen the cover it is hoped that substantial funds can be raised from private sources to support the opposition. $100,000 has already been pledged from U.S. sources. At an appropriate time a bond issue will be floated by the council (as an obligation on a future Cuban government) to raise an additional $2,000,000.

5. *Budget*: It is anticipated that approximately $4,400,000 of CIA funds will be required for the above program. On the assumption that it will not reach its culmination earlier than 6 to 8 months from now, the estimated requirement for FY-1960 funds is $900,000 with the balance or $3,500,000 required in FY-1961. The distribution of costs between fiscal years could, of course, be greatly altered by policy decisions or unforeseen contingencies which compelled accelerated paramilitary operations. (Tab C)

6. *Recommendations*: That the Central Intelligence Agency be authorized to undertake the above outlined program and to withdraw the funds required for this purpose as set forth in paragraph 5. from the Agency's Reserve for contingencies.

## THE POLITICAL OPPOSITION

1. CIA is already in close touch with three reputable opposition groups (the Montecristi, Autentico Party and the National Democratic Front). These all meet the fundamental criteria conditional to acceptance, i.e. they are for the revolution as originally conceived—many being former 26th of July members—and are not identified with either Batista or Trujillo. They are anti-Castro because of his failure to live up to the original 26th of July platform and his apparent willingness to sell out to Communist domination and possible ultimate enslavement. These groups, therefore, fit perfectly the planned opposition slogan of "Restore the Revolution."

2. An opposition Council or Junta will be formed within 30 days from representatives of these groups augmented possibly by representatives of other groups. It is probably premature to have a fixed platform for the Council but the Caracas Manifesto of 20 July 1958 contains a number of exploitable points. Two of the CIA group leaders were signers of the Manifesto. The following points are suggested as a few possibilities:

a. The Castro regime is the new dictatorship of Cuba subject to strong Sino-Soviet influence.

## PROPAGANDA

1. Articulation and transmission of opposition views has already begun. Private opposition broadcasts (i.e. purchase of commercial time by private individuals) have occurred in Miami (medium wave) and arrangements have been made with Station WRUL for additional broadcasts from Massachusetts (short wave) and Florida (broadcast band). [Excised] and [excised] have also agreed to the use of commercial stations for short wave broadcasts from [excised] and [excised]. CIA has furnished support to these efforts through encouragement, negotiating help and providing some broadcast material.

2. As the major voice of the opposition, it is proposed to establish at least one "gray" U.S.-controlled station. This will probably be on Swan Inland and will employ both high frequency and broadcast band equipment of substantial power. The preparation of scripts will be done in the U.S. and these will be transmitted electronically to the site for broadcasting. After some experience and as the operation progresses, it may be desirable to supplement the Swan Island station with at least one other to ensure fully adequate coverage of all parts of Cuba, most especially the Havana region. Such an additional facility might be installed on a U.S. base in the Bahamas or temporary use might be made of a shipborne station if it is desired to avoid "gray" broadcasting from Florida.

3. Newspapers are also being supported and further support is planned for the future. *Avance*, a leading Cuban daily (Zayas' paper), has been confiscated as has *El Mundo*, another Cuban daily. *Diario de la Marina*, one of the hemisphere's outstanding conservative dailies published in Havana, is having difficulty and may have to close soon. Arrangements have already been made to print *Avance* weekly in the U.S. for introduction into Cuba clandestinely and mailing throughout the hemisphere on a regular basis. As other leading newspapers are expropriated, publication of "exile" editions will be considered.

4. Inside Cuba, a CIA-controlled action group is producing and distributing anti-Castro and anti-Communist publications regularly. CIA is in con-

tact with groups outside Cuba who will be assisted in producing similar materials for clandestine introduction into Cuba.

5. Two prominent Cubans are on lecture tours in Latin America. They will be followed by others of equal calibre. The mission of these men will be to gain hemisphere support for the opposition to Castro. Controlled Western Hemisphere assets (press, radio, television) will support this mission as will selected American journalists who will be briefed prior to Latin American travel.

*Tab C*

# FINANCIAL ANNEX

| | FY-1960 | FY-1961 |
|---|---|---|
| I. *Political Action* | | |
| Support of Opposition Elements and other Group Activities | 150,000 | 800,000 |
| II. *Propaganda* | | |
| Radio Operations and Programming (including establishment of transmitters) | 400,000 | 700,000 |
| Press and Publications | 100,000 | 500,000 |
| III. *Paramilitary* | | |
| In-Exfiltration Maritime and Air Support Material and Training, | 200,000 | 1,300,000 |
| IV *Intelligence* | | 200,000 |
| Collection | 50,000 | |
| Totals | *900,000 | 3,500,000 |

*These figures are based on the assumption that major action will not occur until FY-1961. If by reason of policy decisions or other contingencies over which the Agency cannot exercise control, the action program should be accelerated, additional funds will be required.

CUBA

1. *BACKGROUND*: About a year ago the Agency was directed to set in motion the organization of a broadly based opposition to the Castro regime and the development of propaganda channels, clandestine agent nets within Cuba, and trained paramilitary ground and air forces wherewith that opposition could overthrow the Cuban regime. The concept was that this should be so far as possible a Cuban operation, though it was well understood that support in many forms would have to come from the United States. Great progress has been made in this undertaking. A Government-in-Exile will soon be formed embracing most reputable opposition elements. It will have a left-of-center political orientation and should command the support of liberals both within Cuba and throughout the hemisphere. It will sponsor and increasingly control trained and combat-ready military forces based in Central America. A decision must soon be made as to the support (if any) the United States will render the opposition henceforth.

2. *PROSPECTS FOR THE CASTRO REGIME*: The Castro regime is steadily consolidating its control over Cuba. Assuming that the United States applies political and economic pressures at roughly present levels of severity, it will continue to do so regardless of declining popular support. There is no significant likelihood that the Castro regime will fall of its own weight.

a. The regime is proceeding methodically to solidify its control over all the major institutions of the society and to employ them on the Communist pattern as instruments of repression. The Government now directly controls all radio, television, and the press. It has placed politically dependable leadership in labor unions, student groups, and professional organizations. It has nationalized most productive and financial enterprises and is using a program of so-called land reform to exercise effective control over the peasantry. It has destroyed all political parties except the Communist party. Politically reliable and increasingly effective internal security and military forces are being built up.

b. Cuba is in economic difficulties but the Communist Bloc will almost certainly take whatever steps are necessary to forestall any decisive intensification of these troubles. Economic dislocations will occur but will not lead to the collapse or the significant weakening of the Castro regime.

c. At the present time the regular Cuban military establishment, especially the Navy and Air Force, are of extremely low effectiveness. Within the next few months, however, it is expected that Cuba will begin to take delivery of jet aircraft and will begin to have available trained Cuban pilots of known political reliability. During the same period the effectiveness of ground forces will be increasing and their knowledge of newly acquired Soviet weapons will improve. Therefore, after some date probably no more than six months away it will become militarily infeasible to overthrow the Castro regime except through the commitment to combat of a sizeable organized military force. The option of action by the Cuban opposition will no longer be open.

3. *THE NATURE OF THE THREAT*: Cuba will, or course, never present a direct military threat to the United States and it is unlikely that Cuba would attempt open invasion of any other Latin American country since the U.S. could and almost certainly would enter the conflict on the side of the invaded country. Nevertheless, as Castro further stabilizes his regime, obtains more sophisticated weapons, and further trains the militia, Cuba will provide an effective and solidly defended base for Soviet operations and expansion of influence in the Western Hemisphere. Arms, money, organizational and other support can be provided from Cuba to dissident leaders and groups throughout Latin America in order to create political instability, encourage Communism, weaken the prestige of the U.S. and foster the inevitable popular support that Castro's continuance in power will engender. A National Estimate states: "For the Communist powers, Cuba represents an opportunity of incalculable value. More importantly, the advent of Castro has provided the Communists with a friendly base for propaganda and agitation throughout the rest of Latin America and with a highly exploitable example of revolutionary achievement and successful defiance of the United States."

4. *POSSIBLE COURSES OF ACTION*: For reasons which require no elaboration the overt use of U.S. military forces to mount an invasion of Cuba has been excluded as a practical alternative. Broadly defined the following three possible alternative courses of action remain for consideration:

a. Intensification of economic and political pressures coupled with continued covert support of sabotage and minor guerrilla actions but excluding substantial commitment of the Cuban opposition's paramilitary force.

b. Employment of the paramilitary force but in a manner which would not have the appearance of an invasion of Cuba from the outside.

c. Commitment of the paramilitary force in a surprise landing, the installation under its protection on Cuban soil of the opposition government and either the rapid spread of the revolt or the continuation of large scale guerrilla action in terrain suited for that purpose.

These alternatives are discussed in the following paragraphs.

5. *DIPLOMATIC AND ECONOMIC PRESSURE*: There is little that can be done to impose real political and economic pressure on the Castro regime and no such course of action now under serious consideration seems likely to bring about its overthrow.

a. A true blockade of Cuba enforced by the United States would involve technical acts of war and has now been dismissed as infeasible.

b. Action to halt arms shipments from Cuba into any other part of the hemisphere would be cumbersome and easily evaded if air transport were employed. While undoubtedly of some value it is difficult to see that the institution of such measures would either impose severe pressure on the Castro regime or effectively insulate the rest of the hemisphere from it. Castro's principal tools of subversion are people, ideology, the force of example, and money. The flow of these items cannot be dammed up.

c. Further economic sanctions are theoretically possible but can quite readily be offset by an increase of trade with the Bloc.

d. In any event, it is estimated that the prospects for effective international action are poor.

6. *THE MIDDLE COURSE*: Careful study has been given to the possibility of infiltrating the paramilitary force gradually to an assembly point in suitable terrain, hopefully avoiding major encounters in the process and committing it to extensive guerrilla action. This course of action would have the advantage of rendering unnecessary a single major landing which could be described as an invasion. The infiltration phase would take on the coloration of efforts by small groups of Cubans to join an already existing resistance movement. Unfortunately, it has been found to be infeasible on military grounds. Basically the reasons (explained more fully in the attachment) are:

a. It is considered militarily infeasible to infiltrate in small units a force of this size to a single area where it could assemble, receive supplies, and engage in coordinated military action. Such an operation would have to be done over a period of time and the loss of the element of surprise after initial infiltrations would permit government forces to frustrate further reinforcements to the same area.

b. Military units significantly smaller than the battalion presently undergoing unit training would fall short of the "minimum critical mass" required to give any significant likelihood of success. Smaller scale infiltrations would not produce a psychological effect sufficient to precipitate general uprisings of wide-spread revolt among disaffected elements of Castro's armed forces.

c. Actually, the least costly and most efficient way to infiltrate the force into terrain suitable for protracted and powerful guerrilla operations would be by a single landing of the whole force as currently planned and its retirement from the landing point into the chosen redoubt.

7. *A LANDING IN FORCE*: The Joint Chiefs of Staff have evaluated the military aspects of the plan for a landing by the Cuban opposition. They hare concluded that "this plan has a fair chance of ultimate success" (that is of detonating a major and ultimately successful revolt against Castro) and that, if ultimate success is not achieved there is every likelihood that the landing can be the means of establishing in favorable terrain a powerful guerrilla force which can be sustained almost indefinitely. The latter outcome would not be (and need not appear as) a serious defeat. It would be the means of exerting continuing pressure on the regime and would be a continuing demonstration of inability of the regime to establish order. It could create an opportunity for an OAS intervention to impose a cease-fire and hold elections.

a. Any evaluation of the chances of success of the assault force should be realistic about the fighting qualities of the militia. No definitive conclusions can be advanced but it must be remembered that the majority of the militia are not fighters by instinct or background and are not militiamen by their own choice. Their training has been slight and they have never been exposed to actual fire (particularly any heavy fire power) nor to air attack. Moreover, the instabilities within Cuba are such that if the tide shifts against the regime, the chances are strong that substantial numbers will desert or change sides.

b. There is no doubt that the paramilitary force would be widely assumed to be U.S. supported. Nevertheless, this conclusion would be difficult to prove and the scale of its activity would not be inconsistent with the potentialities for support by private Cuban and American groups rather than by the U.S. Government. It must be emphasized, moreover, that this enterprise would have nothing in common (as would the use of

U.S. military forces) with the Russian suppression of Hungary or the Chinese suppression of the Tibetans. This would be a force of dissident Cubans with Cuban political and military leadership.

c. There could be adverse political repercussions to a landing in force but it is not clear how serious those would be. Most Latin American Governments would at least privately approve of unobtrusive U.S. support for such an opposition move, especially if the political coloration of the opposition were left-of-center. The reaction of the rest of the free world, it is estimated, would be minimal in the case of unobtrusive U.S. support for such an attempt. It might produce a good deal of cynicism throughout the world about the U.S. role but if quickly successful little lasting reaction. Generally speaking it is believed that the political cost would be low in the event of a fairly quick success. The political dangers flowing from long continued large scale guerrilla warfare would be greater but there are diplomatic preparations that could be made to forestall extreme adverse reactions in this contingency.

8. *DISSOLUTION OF THE MILITARY FORCE*: A decision not to use the paramilitary force must consider the problem of dissolution, since its dissolution will surely be the only alternative if it is not used within the next four to six weeks. It is hoped that at least one hundred volunteers could be retained for infiltration in small teams but it is doubtful whether more than this number would be available or useful for this type of activity.

a. There is no doubt that dissolution in and of itself will be a blow to U.S. prestige as it will be interpreted in many Latin American countries and elsewhere as evidence of the U.S. inability to take decisive action with regard to Castro. David will again have defeated Goliath. Anti-U.S. regimes like that of Trujillo would gain strength while pro-U.S. Betancourt would undoubtedly suffer. Surely Ydigoras, who has been an exceedingly strong ally, would also be placed in a very difficult position for his support of a disbanded effort. It must be remembered in this connection that there are sectors of Latin American opinion which criticize the U.S. for not dealing sufficiently forcefully with the Castro regime. In fact, one reason why many Latin American governments are holding back in opposing Castro is because they feel that sooner or later the U.S. will be compelled to take strong measures.

b. The resettlement of the military force will unavoidably cause practical problems. Its members will be angry, disillusioned and aggressive with the inevitable result that they will provide honey for the press bees and the

U.S. will have to face the resulting indignities and embarrassments. Perhaps more important, however, will be the loss of good relations with the opposition Cuban leaders. To date almost all non-Batista, non-Communist political leaders have been encouraged or offered help in fighting Castro. An abandonment of the military force will be considered by them as a withdrawal of all practical support. In view of the breadth of the political spectrum involved, this will cause some difficulties for the future since it is hard to imagine any acceptable post-Castro leadership that will not include some of the exiles dealt with during the past year.

9. *CONCLUSIONS*:

a. Castro's position is daily getting stronger and will soon be consolidated to the point that his overthrow will only be possible by drastic, politically undesirable actions such as an all-out embargo or an overt use of military force.

b. A failure to remove Castro by external action will lead in the near future to the elimination of all internal and external Cuban opposition of any effective nature. Moreover, the continuance of the Castro regime will be a substantial victory for the Sino-Soviet Bloc which will use Cuba as a base for increased activity throughout the Western Hemisphere, thereby accentuating political instability and weakening U.S. prestige and influence.

c. The Cuban paramilitary force, if used, has a good chance of overthrowing Castro or at the very least causing a damaging civil war without requiring the U.S. to commit itself to overt action against Cuba. Whatever embarrassment the alleged (though deniable) U.S. support may cause, it may well be considerably less than that resulting from the continuation of the Castro regime or from the more drastic and more attributable actions necessary to accomplish the result at a later date.

d. Even though the best estimate of likely Soviet reaction to a successful movement against Castro indicates problems to the U.S. arising from the removal or substantial weakening of the Castro regime, Soviet propaganda and political moves will still be much less prejudicial to the long-range interests of the U.S. than would the results of a failure to remove Castro.

## A. CLANDESTINE INFILTRATION BY SEA OF SMALL GROUPS (up to 50 men)

1. The only areas of Cuba with mountainous terrain of sufficient extent and ruggedness for guerrilla operations are the Sierra Escambray of La Villas Province in Central Cuba and the Sierra Maestra of Oriente Province at the eastern extremity of the island. The Sierra de les Organos of Western Cuba, do not encompass sufficient area and are not rugged enough to sustain guerrilla operations against strong opposition. Of the two areas with adequate terrain, only the Sierra Escambray is truly suitable for our purposes, since the mountains in Eastern Cuba are too distant from air bases in Latin America available to CIA for air logistical support operations. Primary reliance would have to be placed on this method of supply for guerrilla forces.

2. The Government of Cuba (GOC) has concentrated large forces of army and militia in both Las Villas and Oriente Provinces. Estimates of troop strength in Las Villas have varied recently from 17,000 to as high as 60,000 men, while up to 12,000 men are believed to be stationed in Oriente.

3. While of dubious efficiency and morale, the militia, by sheer weight of numbers has been able to surround and eliminate small groups of insurgents. A landing by 27 men of the Masferrer Group in Oriente, for example, was pursued and eliminated by 2,000 militia. A similar group of insurgents in Western Cuba, was attacked and destroyed by six battalions of army and militia (about 3,000 men).

4. A build-up of force in a given area by infiltration of small groups would require a series of night landings in the same general vicinity. Discovery of the initial landing by GOC forces would be almost a certainty, since security posts are located at all possible landing areas. Even if the initial landing were successful, the GOC could be expected to move troops and naval patrol craft to the area making further landings difficult if not impossible. Any small force landed, experience has shown, will be rapidly engaged by forces vastly superior in numbers. Therefore it is considered unlikely that small groups landing on successive occasions would succeed in joining forces later. A series of surrounded packets of resistance would be the result.

5. Repeated approaches to the Cuban coast by vessels large enough to land up to 50 men would probably provoke attack by the Cuban Navy and/or Air Force, either of which is capable of destroying any vessels which could be used by CIA for these purposes.

6. In the Sierra Escambray, which is the only area of Cuba in which true guerrilla operations are now being conducted, ill-equipped and untrained groups of up to 200 to 300 men have been hard pressed to survive and have been unable to conduct effective operations. The only worthwhile accomplishment of these bands has been to serve as a symbol of resistance. Smaller groups, even though better trained and equipped, could not be expected to be effective.

7. There are very few sites on the south coast of the Sierra Escambray where small boats can be landed. These are found principally at the mouths of rivers and are all guarded by militia posts armed with machine guns. A small group landing at such a point by shuttling from a larger vessel in small boats would probably receive heavy casualties.

8. Small-scale infiltrations would not produce a psychological effect sufficient to precipitate general uprisings and widespread revolt among disaffected elements of Castro's armed forces. *These conditions must be produced before the Castro Government can be overthrown by any means short of overt intervention by United States armed forces.* As long as the armed forces respond to Castro's orders, he can maintain himself in power indefinitely. The history of all police-type states bears out this conclusion.

9. The CIA Cuban Assault Force, composed entirely of volunteers, has been trained for action as a compact, heavily armed, hard-hitting military unit, and the troops are aware of the combat power which they possess as a unit. They have been indoctrinated in the military principle of mass and instructed that dispersion of force leads to defeat in detail. They will be quick to recognize the disadvantages of the infiltration concept, and it is unlikely that all would volunteer for piecemeal commitment to military action in Cuba. The troops can be used in combat only on a voluntary basis. The Government of the United States exercises no legal command or disciplinary authority over them.

## CONCLUSIONS:

1. This course of action would result in large scale loss of life, both through military action against forces vastly superior in numbers and as a result of drum-head justice and firing squad execution of those captured.

2. This alternative could achieve no effective military or psychological results.

### PROPOSED OPERATION AGAINST CUBA

1. *Status of Preparatory Action*: About a year ago the Agency was directed to set in motion: the organization of a broadly-based opposition to the Castro regime; a major propaganda campaign; support for both peaceful and violent resistance activities in Cuba; and the development of trained paramilitary ground and air forces of Cuban volunteers.

A decision should shortly be made as to the future of these activities and the employment or disposition of assets that have been created. The status of the more important activities is as follows:

a. *Political*: Over a period of nearly a year, the FRD (Frente Revolucíonario Democratico), which was created in the hope that it would become the organizational embodiment of a unified opposition to Castro, has proved to be highly useful as a cover and administrative mechanism but important political elements refused to join it.

Accordingly, a major effort was undertaken three weeks ago to form a more broadly-based revolutionary council which would include the FRD, and which could lead to the setting up of a provisional government. Considerable progress has been made in negotiations with the principal Cuban leaders in which great efforts have been made to permit the Cubans to chart their own course. It is expected that the desired result will be accomplished shortly. What is emerging from these negotiations is a provisional government with a center to left-of-center political orientation, and a political platform embodying most of the originally stated goals of the 26 July Movement. It is believed that this will command the support of a very large majority of anti-Castro Cubans although it will not be altogether acceptable to the more conservative groups.

b. *Military*: The following paramilitary forces have been recruited and trained will shortly be in an advanced state of readiness.

(1) A reinforced battalion with a present strength of 850 which will be brought up to a strength of approximately 1,000 through the addition of

one more infantry company to be used primarily for logistic purposes and as a reserve.

(2) A briefly trained paramilitary force of approximately 160 intended to be used for a diversionary night landing to be undertaken in advance of commitment of the battalion.

(3) An air force of 16 B-26 light bombers, 10 C- 54s and 5 C-46s.

(4) Shipping including 2 100-ton ships, 5 1500- ton ships, 2 LCIs, 3 LCUs and 4 LCVPs.

A JCS team recently inspected the battalion and the air force at their bases in Guatemala. Their findings led them to conclude that those forces could be combat-ready by 1 April. Certain deficiencies were indicated that are in progress of correction partly by further training and partly by the recruitment of the additional infantry company referred to above.

c. *Timing*: It will be infeasible to hold all these forces together beyond early April. They are in large part volunteers, some of whom have been in hard training, quartered in austere facilities for as much as six months. Their motivation for action is high but their morale cannot be maintained if their commitment to action is long delayed. The onset of the rainy season in Guatemala in April would greatly accentuate this problem and the Guatemalan Government is in any event unwilling to have them remain in the country beyond early April. The rainy season in Cuba would also make their landing on the island more difficult.

2. *The Situation in Cuba*: We estimate that time is against us. The Castro regime is steadily consolidating its control over Cuba. In the absence of greatly increased external pressure or action, it will continue to do so regardless of declining popular support as the machinery of authoritarian control becomes increasingly effective.

a. The regime is proceeding methodically to solidify its control over all the major institutions of the society and to employ them on the Communist pattern as instruments of repression. The Government now directly controls all radio, television, and the press. It has placed politically dependable leadership in labor unions, student groups, and professional organizations. It has nationalized most productive and financial enterprises and is using a program of so-called land reform to exercise effective control over the peasantry. It has destroyed all political parties except the Communist party. Politically reliable and increasingly effective internal security and military forces are being built up.

b. There is still much active opposition in Cuba. It is estimated that there are some 1200 active guerrillas and another thousand individuals engaging in various acts of conspiracy and sabotage, the tempo of which has been rising in recent reeks. Nevertheless, the government has shown considerable skill in espionage and counter-espionage. It is making good use of the militia against guerrilla activities and the infiltration of people and hardware. The militia is relatively untrained and there is evidence that its morale is low but the government is able to use very large numbers against small groups of guerrillas and is able to exercise surveillance of suspicious activities throughout the island. Short of some shock that will disorganize or bring about the defection of significant parts of the militia, it must be anticipated that violent opposition of all kinds will gradually be suppressed.

c. At the present time the regular Cuban military establishment, especially the Navy and Air Force, are of extremely low effectiveness. Within the next few months, however, it is expected that Cuba will begin to take delivery of jet aircraft and will begin to have available trained and well indoctrinated Cuban pilots. During the same period the effectiveness of ground forces will be increasing and their knowledge of newly acquired Soviet weapons will improve. Therefore, after some date, probably no more than six months away it will probably become militarily infeasible to overthrow the Castro regime except through the commitment to combat of a more sizeable organized military force than can be recruited from among the Cuban exiles.

3. *Possible Courses of Action*: Four alternative courses of action involving the commitment of the paramilitary force described above are discussed in succeeding paragraphs. They are:

a. Employment of the paramilitary force in a manner which would minimize the appearance of an invasion of Cuba from the outside.

b. Commitment of the paramilitary force in a surprise landing with tactical air support, the installation under its protection on Cuban soil of the opposition government and either the rapid spread of the revolt or the continuation of large scale guerrilla action in terrain suited for that purpose.

c. Commitment of the paramilitary force in two successive operations: first, the landing of one company without air support in a remote area in which it could sustain itself for some days (hopefully indefinitely), and second, the landing of the main force forty-eight hours later in a widely different location in the same manner as in paragraph 3.b. above.

d. Commitment of the whole force in an inaccessible region where it would be expected to keep control of a beachhead for a long period of time to permit installation and recognition of a provisional government and a gradual build-up of military strength.

4. *Covert Landing of the Paramilitary Forces*: Careful study has been given to the possibility of infiltrating the paramilitary forces in a night amphibious landing, using man-portable equipment and weapons and taking ashore only such supplies as can be carried by the troops. The force would move immediately in-land to the mountains and commence operations as a powerful guerrilla force relying entirely upon continuing air logistical support. Shipping would retire from the coast before dawn and no tactical air operations would be conducted. Unfortunately, it is believed that such an operation would involve unacceptable military risks.

a. The paramilitary force would run the risk of becoming completely disorganized and scattered in a night landing. (Such an operation is very difficult for even highly trained forces experienced in amphibious operations.)

b. The force would not have motor transport, heavy mortar, 75 mm recoiling rifles, heavy machine guns, nor tanks. Initial ammunition and food supplies would be limited and it would be wholly dependent on air logistical support. If the rainy season commences in April, overcast conditions could prevent effective support. Casualties could not be evacuated.

c. Since tactical aircraft would not participate, the objective area could not be isolated; enemy forces could move against the beachhead unimpeded. The Castro Air Force would be left intact.

5. *A Landing in Full Force*: This operation would involve an amphibious/airborne assault with concurrent (but no prior) tactical air support, to seize a beachhead contiguous to terrain suitable for guerrilla operations. The provisional government would land as soon as the beachhead had been secured. If initial military operations were successful and especially if there were evidence of spreading disaffection against the Castro regime, the provisional government could be recognized and a legal basis provided for at least non-governmental logistical support.

a. The military plan contemplates the holding of a perimeter around the beachhead area. It is believed that initial attacks by the Castro militia, even if conducted in considerable force, could be repulsed with substantial loss to the attacking forces. The scale of the operation and the display of professional competence and of determination on the part of the assault force would, it is hoped, demoralize the militia and induce defections therefrom, impair the morale of the Castro regime, and induce widespread rebellion. If the initial actions proved to be unsuccessful in thus detonating a major revolt, the assault force would retreat to the contiguous mountain area and continue operations as a powerful guerrilla force.

b. This course of action has a better chance then any other of leading to the prompt overthrow of the Castro regime because it holds the possibility of administering a demoralizing shock.

c. If this operation were not successful in setting off widespread revolt, freedom of action of the U.S. would be preserved because there is an alternative outcome which would neither require U.S. intervention nor constitute a serious defeat; i.e., guerrilla action could be continued on a sizeable scale in favorable terrain. This would be a means of exerting continual pressure on the regime.

6. *A Diversionary Landing*: As a variant of the above plan, it would be feasible to conduct a diversionary landing with a force of about 160 men in an inaccessible area as a prelude to a landing of the main assault force. The initial operation would be conducted at night without tactical air support. At least a part of the provisional government would go in with the diversionary landing and presumably the establishment of the provisional government on Cuban soil would thereupon be announced. The subsequent landing of the main assault force would be carried out as outlined in paragraph 5 preceding.

a. This course of action might have certain political advantages in that the initial action in the campaign could be of a character that could plausibly have been carried out by the Cubans with little outside help.

b. There would be a military advantage in that the diversionary landing would distract attention and possibly divide some enemy forces from the objective area for the main assault. If reports had reached the Castro government that troops trained in Guatemala were on the move, the diversionary landing might well be taken to be the main attack thus enhancing the element of surprise for the main assault force. These advantages would be counterbalanced by the diversion of troops otherwise supporting the main unit.

7. *Landing and Slow Build-up*: Under this fourth alternative the whole paramilitary force could carry out a landing and seize a beachhead in the most

remote and inaccessible terrain on the island with intent to hold indefinitely an area thus protected by geography against prompt or well-supported attacks from the land. This would permit the installation there of the provision government, its recognition by the U.S. after a decent interval, and (if needed) a long period of build-up during which additional volunteers and military supplies would be moved into the beachhead.

a. A major political advantage of this course of action would be that the initial assault might be conducted in such a way as to involve less display of relatively advanced weaponry and of professional military organization than the landing in force discussed above, especially so as there is every likelihood that the initial landing would be virtually unopposed by land forces. Recognition could provide a suitable political and legal basis for a protracted build-up after the initial assault.

b. Such an operation would, however, require tactical air support sufficient to destroy or neutralize the Castro Air Force. If this were not provided concurrently with the landing, it would be needed soon thereafter in order to permit ships to operate into the beachhead and the planned build-up to go forward. If the initial landing could include seizure of an air strip, the necessary air support could fairly soon be provided from within the territory controlled by friendly forces. There is, however, no location which both contains a useable airstrip and is so difficult of access by land as to permit protection of a slow build-up.

c. This type of operation by the very fact of being clandestine in nature and remote geographically would have far less initial impact politically and militarily than courses two or three.

8. *Conclusions*:

a. The Castro regime will not fall of its own weight. In the absence of exterior action against it, the gradual weakening of internal Cuban opposition must be expected.

b. Within a matter of months the capabilities of Castro's military forces will probably increase to such a degree that the overthrow of his regime, from within or without the country, by the Cuban opposition will be most unlikely.

c. The Cuban paramilitary force if effectively used has a good chance of overthrowing Castro, or of causing a damaging civil war, without the necessity for the United States to commit itself to overt action against Cuba.

d. Among the alternative course of action here reviewed, an assault in force preceded by a diversionary landing offers the best chance of achieving the desired result.

DD/P:RNB:djm:bp&gb
1-President & returned—
DD/PChrono
2-Sec. State & returned—
Destroyed
3-V. Pres. & returned—
Destroyed
4-Adolph Berle & returned—
Destroyed
5-Thomas Mann State & returned—
Destroyed
6-Sec. Defense &-returned—
Destroyed
7-Lemnitzer—retained
8-McGeorge Bundy—retained

9-DD/P-RMB retained

10-Wm. Bundy—retained

11-Gen. Gray—retained

12-Mr. Barnes—retained

13-DD/P Subj. file—Cuba

14-Destroyed

15-Destroyed
16-D/DCI—retained
17-Destroyed

(17 of 17)

### REVISED CUBAN OPERATION

1. *Political Requirements*: The plan for a Cuban operation and the variants thereof presented on 11 March were considered to be politically objectionable on the ground that the contemplated operation would not have the appearance of an infiltration of guerrillas in support of an internal revolution but rather that of a small-scale World War II type of amphibious assault. In undertaking to develop alternative plans and judge their political acceptability, it has been necessary to infer from the comments made on the earlier plan the characteristics which a new plan should possess in order to be politically acceptable. They would appear to be the following:

a. *An Unspectacular Landing*: The initial landing should be as unspectacular as possible and should have neither immediately prior nor concurrent tactical air support. It should conform as closely as possible to the typical pattern of the landings of small groups intended to establish themselves or to join others in terrain suited for guerrilla operations. In the absence of air support and in order to fit the pattern, it should probably be at night.

b. *A Base for Tactical Air Operations*: It was emphasized that ultimate success of the operation will require tactical air operations leading to the establishment of the control of the air over Cuba. In order to fit the pattern of revolution, those operations should be conducted from an air base within territory held by opposition forces. Since it is impracticable to undertake construction of an airbase in the rainy season and before any air support is available, the territory seized in the original landing must include an air-strip that can support tactical operations.

c. *Slower Tempo*: The operation should be so designed that there could be an appreciable period of build up after the initial landing before major offensive action was undertaken. This would allow for a minimum decent interval between the establishment and the recognition by the U.S. of a provisional government and would fit more closely the pattern of a typical revolution.

d. *Guerrilla Warfare Alternative*: Ideally, the terrain should not only be protected by geography against prompt or well-supported attack from land but also suitable for guerrilla warfare in the event that an organized perimeter could not be held.

2. *Alternative Areas*: Five different areas, three of them on the mainland of Cuba and two on islands off the coast, were studied carefully to determine whether they would permit an operation fitting the above conditions. One of the areas appears to be eminently suited for the operation. All the others had to be rejected either because of unfavorable geography (notably the absence of a suitable air strip) or heavy concentrations of enemy forces, or both. The area selected is located at the head of a well protected deep water estuary on the south coast of Cuba. It is almost surrounded by swamps impenetrable to infantry in any numbers and entirely impenetrable to vehicles, except along two narrow and easily defended approaches. Although strategically isolated by those terrain features, the area is near the center of the island and the presence of an opposition force there will soon become known to the entire population of Cuba and constitute a serious threat to the regime. The beach-head area contains one and possibly two air strips adequate to handle B-26's. There are several good landing beaches. It is of interest that this area has been the scene of resistance activities and of outright guerrilla warfare for over a hundred years.

3. *Phases of the Operation*:

a. The operation will begin with a night landing. There are no known enemy forces (even police) in the objective area and it is anticipated that the landing can be carried out with few if any casualties and with no serious combat. As many supplies as possible will be unloaded over the beaches but the ships will put to sea in time to be well offshore by dawn. The whole beachhead area including the air strips will be immediately occupied and approach routes defended. No tanks will be brought ashore in the initial landing. It is believed that this operation can be accomplished quite un-obtrusively and that the Castro regime will have little idea of the size of the force involved.

b. The second phase, preferably commencing at dawn following the landing, will involve the movement into the beachhead of tactical aircraft and their prompt commitment for strikes against the Castro Air Force. Concurrently C-46's will move in with gas in drums, minimal mainte-nance equipment, and maintenance personnel. As rapidly as possible, the whole tactical air operation will be based in the beachhead but initially only enough aircraft will be based there plausibly to account for all observable activity over the island.

c. In the third phase, as soon as there is adequate protection for shipping from enemy air attack, ships will move back into the beach to discharge supplies and equipment (including tanks). It must be presumed that counter attacks against the beachhead will be undertaken within 24 to 48 hours of the landing but the perimeter can easily be held against attacks along the most direct approach routes. The terrain may well prevent any sizeable attacks (providing the enemy air force has been rendered ineffective) until the opposition force is ready to attempt to break out of the beachhead.

d. The timing and direction of such offensive action will depend upon the course of events in the island. At least three directions of break out are possible. Because of the canalization of the approaches to the beachhead from the interior, a break out will require close support by tactical air to be successful unless enemy forces are thoroughly disorganized. The opposition force will have the option, however, of undertaking an amphibious assault with tactical air support against a different objective area if it should seem desirable.

4. *Political Action*: The beachhead area proposed to be occupied is both large enough and safe enough so that it should be entirely feasible to install the provisional government there as soon as aircraft can land safely. Once installed, the tempo of the operation will permit the U.S. Government to extend recognition after a decent interval and thus to prepare the way for more open and more extensive logistical support if this should be necessary.

5. *Military Advantages*:

a. This is a safer military operation than the daylight landing in force originally proposed. The landing itself is more likely to be unopposed or very lightly opposed and the beachhead perimeter could be more easily held.

b. There are no known communications facilities in the immediate target area. This circumstance, coupled with the plan for a night landing, increases the chance of achieving surprise.

c. By comparison with any of the known inaccessible parts of the Oriente Province the objective area is closer to rear bases for air and sea logistical support.

d. The plan has the disadvantage that the build up of force can be only gradual since there is virtually no local population from which to recruit additional troops and volunteers from other parts of Cuba will be able to infiltrate into the area only gradually.

6. *Political Acceptability*: The proposal here outlined fits the three conditions stated in paragraph 1 above for the political acceptability of a paramilitary operation. The landing is unspectacular; no tactical air support will be provided until an air base of sorts is active within the beachhead area; the tempo of the operation is as desired; and the terrain is such as to minimize the risk of defeat and maximize the options open to the opposition force.

a. It may be objected that the undertaking of tactical air operations so promptly after the landing is inconsistent with the pattern of a revolution. But most Latin American revolutions in recent years have had aircraft and it is only natural that they would be used in this case as soon as the opposition had secured control of an air strip. Wherever in the island a paramilitary operation is attempted and whatever its tempo, command of the air will sooner or later have to be established, and aircraft will have to be flown into a beachhead to enable this to be done. Sooner or later, then, it is bound to be revealed that the opposition in Cuba has friends outside who are able and willing to supply it with obsolescent combat aircraft. This revelation will be neither surprising nor out of keeping with traditional practice.

b. An alternative way to handle this problem would be to make a few strafing runs against the Castro Air Force some days before the landing and apparently as an opposition act unrelated to any other military moves.

7. *Conclusion*: The operation here outlined, despite the revision of concept to meet the political requirements stated above, will still have a political cost. The study over the past several months of many possible paramilitary operations makes perfectly clear, however, that it is impossible to introduce into Cuba and commit to action military resources that will have a good chance of setting in action the overthrow of the regime without paying some price in terms of accusations by the Communists and possible criticism by others. It is believed that the plan here outlined goes as far as possible in the direction of minimizing the political cost without impairing its soundness and chance of success as a military operation. The alternative would appear to be the demobilization of the paramilitary force and the return of its members to the United States. It is, of course, well understood that this course of action too involves certain risks.

## CUBAN OPERATION

1. *Orientation and Concept*: The present concept of the operation being mounted to overthrow Castro is that it should have the appearance of a growing and increasingly effective internal resistance, helped by the activities of defected Cuban aircraft and by the infiltration (over a period of time and at several places) of weapons and small groups of men. External support should appear to be organized and controlled by the Revolutionary Council under Miro Cardona as the successor to a number of separate groups. To support this picture and to minimize emphasis on invasion, the following steps have been taken:

a. The public statements of Cardona have emphasized that the overthrow of Castro was the responsibility of the Cubans, that it must be performed mainly by the Cubans in Cuba rather than from outside, and that he and his colleagues are organizing this external support free of control by or official help from the U.S. Government.

b. The plans for air operations have been modified to provide for operations on a limited scale on D-2 and again on D-Day itself instead of placing reliance on a larger strike coordinated with the landings on D-Day.

c. Shortly after the first air strikes on D-2 a B-26 with Cuban pilot will land at Miami airport seeking asylum. He will state that he defected with two other B-26 pilots and aircraft and that they strafed aircraft on the ground before departing.

d. A preliminary diversionary landing of true guerrilla type will be made in Oriente Province on D-2. The main D-Day landings will be made by three groups at locations spaced some distance apart on the coast. These will be followed about one week later by a further guerrilla type landing in Pinar Del Rio (at the western end of the island).

e. Ships carrying the main forces leave the staging base at staggered times. (The first one sailed on Tuesday morning.) They will follow independent courses to a rendezvous for the final run-in. Until nearly dusk on

D-1 they would appear to air observation to be pursuing unrelated courses so there will be no appearance of a convoy.

f. All the landings will be at night. At least in the first 24 hours, supply activity over the beaches will be at night. There will be no obtrusive "beachhead" to be seen by aircraft. Most troops will be deployed promptly to positions inland.

2. *The Time Table* of the plan is as follows:

| | |
|---|---|
| D-7: | Commence staging main force—staging completed night of D-5. |
| D-6: | First vessel sails from staging area—last vessel departs early morning D-4. |
| D-2: | B-26 defection operation—limited air strikes. |
| D-2: | Diversionary landing in Oriente (night D-3 to D-2). |
| D-Day: | Main landings (night D-1 to D)—limited air strikes. Two B-26s and liaison plane land at seized air strip. |
| D to D+1: | Vessels return night of D to D+1 to complete discharge of supplies. |
| D+7: | Diversionary landing in Pinar del Rio. |

3. *Diversion or Cancellation*: It would now be infeasible to halt the staging and embarkation of the troops. In the event of a decision to modify the operational plan or to cancel the operation, ships will be diverted at sea, either to Vieques Island or to ports in the U.S. If cancellation is directed, the troops and ships' officers will be told that the reason for the diversion is that all details of the operation, including time and place of intended landings, had been blown to the Castro regime and that under these circumstances the landings would be suicidal. This explanation would be adhered to after the demobilization of the force in the U.S. The U.S. Government could take the position that this enterprise had been undertaken by the Cubans without U.S. Governmental support, that it had failed because of their poor security, and that the U.S. could not refuse to grant asylum to the Cuban volunteers. If

ere committed. Similarly, the decision making process in the Execu-
nch of the Government operated in a manner that left something to be
. Nevertheless, this paper argues: that a large majority of the conclu-
ached in the Survey are misleading or wrong; that the Survey is es-
weak in judging what are the implications of its own allegations and,
e, that its utility is greatly impaired by its failure to point out fully or
ses correctly the lessons to be learned from this experience. This
ed rejection can be made more meaningful by an elaboration at this
nich will at the same time serve the purpose of outlining the structure
per and summarizing certain of its main conclusions.

## A. Organization and Execution

he first set of allegations, there is not too much that can be said short
d discussion which is contained in later sections, except to make the
oint that perfection in organization and execution is never attained
he real question is whether the mistakes that were made were worse
reasonably should have been and justify blanket condemnation.
tly, the conclusions reached here on the main substantive points

hat Agency command and organizational relationships were what
ould have been.
nat any shortcomings in the internal planning process reflected, for
t part, the difficulty of securing clear policy guidance from outside
ncy and prompt, willing, support based on that guidance.
at the failure of most air operations in support of the resistance was
t of circumstances completely beyond the control of the air arm
bably not remediable by any action that the Agency could have

at the intelligence on the Castro regime and on the internal oppo-
ereto was essentially accurate.

test operational weaknesses were in the early phases of maritime
nd, possibly, in the failure to place trained paramilitary agents
nce groups, although it must be recognized that major effort
to accomplish this result and even with hindsight it is not clea
erent operational procedures or any greater effort could hav
ater results.
ate test of any project such as this is, of course, its outcome bu

by reason of either new intelligence or policy considerations it is necessary to effect a major change in the operational plan, it will be necessary to divert to Vieques Island so that officers and ships' captains can be assembled and briefed on the new plan. (The advantages of this location are its security together with the opportunity for the troops to be ashore briefly after a few days on board ship.)

4. *Naval Protection*: The ships carrying the main force will receive unobtrusive naval protection up to the time they enter Cuban territorial waters. If they are attacked they will be protected by U.S. Naval vessels but following such an intervention they would be escorted to a U.S. port and the force would be demobilized.

5. *Defections*: Every effort is being made to induce the defection of individuals of military and political significance. At the present time contact has been established by and through Cuban agents and anti-Castro Cuban groups with some thirty-one specific military and police officers, including [excised] and the [excised] and the [excised]. An approach is being made to [excised]. There are, of course, in addition many others rumored to be disaffected but to whom no channel of approach is available. The objective of these efforts is not to induce immediate defections but to prepare the individuals for appropriate action in place after D-Day.

6. *Internal Resistance Movements*: On the latest estimate there are nearly 7,000 insurgents responsive to some degree of control through agents with whom communications are currently active. About 3,000 of these are in Havana itself, over 2,000 in Oriente, about 700 in Las Villas in central Cuba. For the most part, the individual groups are small and very inadequately armed. Air drops are currently suspended because available aircraft are tied up in the movement of troops from their training area to the staging base. After D-Day when it is hoped that the effectiveness of the Castro air force will be greatly reduced, it is planned to supply these groups by daytime air drops. Every effort will be made to coordinate their operations with those of the landing parties. Efforts will be made also to sabotage or destroy by air attack the microwave links on which Castro's communication system depends. The objective is of course to create a revolutionary situation, initially perhaps in Oriente and Las Villas Provinces, and then spreading to all parts of the island.

7. *Propaganda and Communications:* Currently medium and short wave broadcasting in opposition to Castro is being carried on from seven stations in addition to Radio Swan. Antennae modifications of the latter have increased its effective power in Cuba and it is believed that there is now good medium wave reception of Swan everywhere except in Havana itself where it can still be effectively jammed. The number of hours of broadcasting per day will be increased beginning immediately from about 25 to almost 75 soon after D-Day. The combination of multiple long and short wave stations which will then be in use, supplemented by three boats which carry broadcasting equipment (two short wave and one medium wave) will assure heavy coverage of all parts of the island virtually at all times. Radio programs will avoid any reference to an invasion but will call for up-rising and will of course announce defections and carry news of revolutionary action. Soon after D-Day a small radio transmitter will be put in operation on Cuban soil.

8. *The Political Leadership*: As of the present moment, the six members of Cardona's Revolutionary Council, notably including Ray, have reaffirmed their membership. Although no specific portfolios have been confirmed, the following possibilities are currently under discussion: Varona, Defense; Ray, Gobernacion (Interior); Carrillio, Finance; Hevia, State; Maceo, Public Health. The political leaders have not yet been briefed on the military plan but they will be informed at each phase of military operations. Advance consultation with the political leaders is considered unacceptably dangerous on security grounds and although last minute briefings will be resented, it is believed that the political leaders will want to take credit for and assume control as quickly as possible over these major operations against Castro. The present plan is that one them (Artime) will go into Cuba with the main force, others will follow as soon as possible after D-Day and they will announce the establishment of a Provisional Government on Cuban soil.

9. *Command:* Military command will be exercised in the name of the Revolutionary Council and later of the Provisional Government. In fact, however, the CIA staff constitutes the general staff of the operation and the Agency controls both logistics support and communications. Accordingly, in the early stages at least, the functions of a general headquarters will be exercised from the Agency with the Cuban brigade commander exercising field command over the units that land on D-Day.

*—An ...*
*Cu...*
by the Deputy D...
Central Intelli...
1...

I . INTRODUCTION AN...

The purpose of this paper is to contribute ...
ture of and the reasons for the failure of the Cu...
to suggest what are the correct lessons to...
prompted by and is, for the most part, a com...

That document gives a black picture of the ...
It makes a number of different kinds of allega...

*First*, there are numerous charges of bad ...
execution, including specifically criticisms ...
quality of personnel; the internal operationa...
of maritime and air operations; and the col...
gence. These deficiencies are portrayed as r...
up and supply resistance organizations und...

*Second*, and more serious is the allegati...
notably (a) the decision to convert the pro...
overt military operation beyond the Agenc...
the Cuban exiles as "puppets," (c) the inad...
invasion, and (d) the failure "to appraise th...

*Third*, the Survey is critical of the Agen...
sion making process in the Executive Bra...
Agency, it is alleged, "failed to keep the ...
and realistically informed of the condition...
and it did not press sufficiently for promp...
situation." As a corollary of this judgment ...
incompetence of execution and for err...
Agency alone.

It is almost self-evident that some of ...
part. In any large and rapidly organized ...
errors of organization and of execution.

if a judgment of the effectiveness of organization and execution is to be made, the deficiencies need to be balanced by the accomplishments. As even the Survey remarks, "There were some good things in this project." After a slow start, a sizable number of small boat operations were run efficiently and a large number of persons and volume of cargo were infiltrated successfully into the Island. In the last weeks before the invasion, a political organization was formed which covered a remarkably broad spectrum of political opinion and brought together what was described by a State Department officer at the time as the best group of exile leaders that could be assembled and that left outside no important politically acceptable element. In the military build-up, a force was created that was twice as large as originally envisaged and larger than any paramilitary force ever developed by the Agency. It was brought to a high state of combat effectiveness with a remarkably low percentage of individuals who had to be eliminated for unsuitability and with high morale later proven in combat. This force was airlifted to a staging base, the location of which was never revealed until after the finish of the operation. It was loaded on ships which sailed on dispersed courses and achieved complete surprise five days later. The Brigade then successfully carried out what had been described as the most difficult type of military operation, a landing on a hostile shore, carried out largely at night. Finally, as the battle was joined, adequate supplies of all sorts were available within a few hours of the beaches, had conditions permitted their off-loading. These various results were accomplished in such a way that only a small number of Agency staff officers were ever exposed to the Cuban participants and the true identities of these Americans have never been revealed. Moreover, the entire build-up was accomplished under the limitation that it contemplate no use of Americans in combat and no commitment of American flag shipping. As the event proved (and the Survey remarks), "This was not enough." Nevertheless, a recital of affirmative accomplishments suggests that whatever shortcomings there were in organization, personnel, and execution were not the decisive reasons for failure. It will be necessary to return to this point later.

## B. Errors of Judgment

The second set of criticisms, those described above as allegations of major errors of judgment and the third, relating to the Agency's relationships with the rest of the Executive Branch, are more complex. Their validity is discussed in separate sections below (Section III on Why a Military Type Invasion and IV on The Decision Making Process, Section VIII on The

Relationships with the Cubans, and Section V on The Assessment of the Adequacy of the Plan and on the Appraisal of its Success.) Summarized in flat statements, the conclusions there reached are these:

a. The basic reason for placing increasing emphasis as the build-up progressed upon the planned military operation and decreasing emphasis on the internal resistance is that for a number of reasons the capacity of the resistance to achieve an overthrow without a significant assist from the outside appeared to be diminishing rather than growing despite the best efforts of which the Agency was capable to support it. Moreover, preparation for the military operation was not intended to reduce support of the resistance and the two efforts became truly competitive only in the last week before the invasion was mounted.

b. The decision to deny the Cuban political leadership control of or close contact with the Brigade and to withhold from them knowledge of the impending invasion was based on two considerations. First, it was believed at the time that if the Brigade was to achieve unity and esprit de corps, it must not be split by political rivalries and its officers must be chosen on professional grounds. This clearly precluded control of the Brigade, or even free access to it, by the political leaders. Second, the insecurity of the Cubans was notorious. It was quite inconceivable that they could know the details of times and places without the gravest risk that the essential advantage of surprise would be lost. It was clear at the time that the Agency assumed a significant risk in denying responsibility to the Cubans and inevitably assuming this responsibility itself. No evidence that has come to light during or since the invasion suggests that military effectiveness and security could have been obtained without paying that price.

c. The conclusions of this paper on the adequacy of the military plan are really too complex to be summarized in a sentence or two. All that can be said here is that (1) there was solid reason to believe that it had a good chance of at least initial success; (2) the last minute cancellation of the D-Day air strike significantly reduced the prospects of success; (3) there was never a test of whether internal support for the invasion would materialize on the scale and in the manner anticipated; and (4) the main deficiencies in the plan and in the capabilities of the Cuban force which may have contributed to the defeat have not been touched on in the Survey.

d. The appraisal of the chances of success may well have been faulty. The intelligence was generally good but it may have underestimated the skill with which the Castro forces would be directed, the morale of the militia units he would deploy against the Brigade and the effectiveness of any T-33's that remained in operation. There was some exaggeration of the capabilities of both ground and air forces of the invasion. It is impossible to say how grave was the error of appraisal since the plan that was appraised was modified by elimination of the D-Day air strike. Had the Cuban air been eliminated, all of these estimates might well have been accurate instead of underestimated. Probably, therefore, the primary fault lay in having one factor (i.e., the elimination of Cuban air) achieve so vital a significance to the whole plan. Although the D-Day air strikes were essential to the destruction of the Cuban air, no guaranty of such destruction was possible even had there been authority for the strikes.

The conclusions summarized above bear on the correctness of the Survey's allegations of deficiencies of execution and major errors of judgment but for the purposes either of understanding what happened or of learning how to avoid such a failure in the future, it is far from sufficient to know that certain activities were (or were not) incompetently performed and certain mistakes were (or were not) made. With many of the deficiencies it is essential to understand why they existed. And with all of them it is important to know what part they played in causing the outcome to be what it was. The central weakness of the Survey is that it is often misleading in its implications as to why certain things were done and it is grossly incomplete in its analysis of the consequences of mistakes alleged to have been made. Accordingly, before proceeding to the detailed discussion beginning in Section II of this paper which supports the conclusions summarized here, it has been felt necessary to make good in some degree these errors of omission by commenting on the nature and causes of the failure in a manner which will be in part alternative and in part supplementary to the Survey.

## C. The Decisions That Led To Failure

It has been suggested not only in the Survey but elsewhere that the operation against the Castro regime should never have been allowed to take the form that it did of a military invasion. It ultimately did take this form, however, and it was in this form that it failed. The military failure has been analyzed far more exhaustively and with greater authority by General Taylor and others than this paper can pretend to do. Nevertheless, certain conclusions as to the nature of the military failure must be restated here if its causes are to be understood.

There is unanimous agreement that the proximate cause was a shortage of ammunition on the beachhead and that this shortage was directly traceable, in turn, to the effective interdiction of shipping and air resupply by the Castro Air Force. It has been less emphasized that Castro's command of the air deprived the Brigade of its capability for battlefield reconnaissance, of the equivalent of field artillery, and of close air support against enemy ground forces. It deprived it, too, of the possibility of "strategic" strikes against enemy lines of supply and communications. Finally, reliance had been placed on daytime and virtually unopposed air and sea resupply as a necessary condition for the activation of resistance groups throughout the Island. It is incontrovertible that, without control of the air, and the air crews and aircraft to exploit that control of the air, the whole military operation was doomed. Even with control of the air it might have failed but without it there could not have been any chance of success. If, then, one wishes to learn what actually caused the military operation to fail, rather than what might have done so, the starting point must be an inquiry into why control of the air was lost and never regained. Of equal significance for an understanding of the whole operation is an awareness of the circumstances that did not contribute to the failure in the air.

Fortunately, it is possible to list without much possibility of controversy the circumstances that led to the outcome in the air. First, the nearest real estate that could be used was Puerto Cabezas in Nicaragua a distance of over 800 miles from the target area. The only way to avoid this severe limitation on the capability of any but the most modern aircraft would have been to use a base on U.S. territory. Second, in choosing types of aircraft, no sort of plausible denial could be maintained unless the project limited itself to the kinds of obsolete aircraft that might plausibly be found in the hands of a privately financed Cuban force. There was the further argument that it was desirable to use types of aircraft that could have defected from the Castro Air Force. The choice was thus rapidly narrowed down to B-26's. Third, policy guidance throughout the project was to the effect that no U.S. air crews could be committed to combat or placed where they might be involved in combat. This restriction was not relaxed until the second day of the invasion and then only in desperation. This had implications not only for the quality of the air crews but also for the number that could be assembled, screened for security, and trained within the time period available.

Given these limitations, the only way in which there was the slightest possibility of achieving control and maintaining control of the air was by destruction of the Castro Air Force on the ground before the dawn of D-Day when vulnerable shipping would be exposed to air strikes. The one air strike on D-2 was not expected to be, and in fact was not, sufficient to accomplish this purpose. Only one other strike was planned for this purpose and that was canceled. Moreover, in the interests of making the air strikes appear to have been done by the Castro Air Force, a restriction was placed on the number of aircraft that could be committed to these strikes by the invasion force.

Even after the very considerable damage done on D-Day itself by enemy air, it is possible that a determined and major strike on the night of D/D+1 would have crippled the Castro Air Force, the final destruction of which might have been completed the following night. By the evening of D-Day, however, the Cuban air crews were exhausted and dispirited and the opportunity could not be fully exploited.

Even if things had gone better on D-Day, it is questionable whether the 17 Cuban air crews that constituted the air arm of the strike force would have been adequate to accomplish all of the tasks for which reliance was placed on the air arm. The chance of success would have been greater (with or without the D-Day strike) if it had been possible to assemble and commit to action more trained Cuban or U.S. air crews.

## D. Washington Decision Making

These, then, were the circumstances which together led to defeat in the air and made inevitable a defeat on the ground. Several things are notable about them. In the first place, it should be emphasized that these all trace back to Washington decisions. The defeat in the air cannot be blamed on bad maintenance at Puerto Cabezas, or on a shortage of spare parts or fuel. It cannot be blamed on a shortage of B-26's, inasmuch as it proved possible rapidly to replace losses from the U.S. It cannot be blamed on the cowardice or lack of skill of the Cuban air crews, who by and large gave a good account of themselves. Nor can it be attributed to bad tactical decisions made either at Puerto Cabezas or in the Washington command post. The crucial defeat in the air was to no significant degree the result of bad execution. It was directly and unambiguously attributable to a long series of Washington policy decisions.

Before exploring the touchy question of whose decisions these were and how they were made, the implications of this conclusion deserve emphasis and elaboration. It suggests that the bad organization, improperly drawn lines of command, low quality personnel and operational inadequacies alleged by the Survey were not in the actual event responsible for the military failure. If organization and execution had approached perfection, the invasion would still have failed in the absence of more and larger pre-D-Day air strikes or the use of more modern aircraft from U.S. bases.

To be sure, this conclusion derives from an analysis only of the failure to gain control of the *air*. It is arguable that even if control of the air had been achieved, maintained, and exploited, the beachhead would not have been consolidated nor the Regime ultimately overthrown. Without arguing that point here, however, the evidence strongly suggests that if the Brigade had been defeated by ground action under those more favorable circumstances, it would have been because of errors of planning and conception rather than by errors of execution. The Brigade fought long enough to prove its determination and tactical skill. It appears to have been well handled by its officers. There were ample supplies at hand to support continued ground action. And Castro himself has admitted that the terrain was well chosen. Given control of the air, the Brigade might ultimately have been defeated by a complete failure of any resistance to materialize under conditions which would have encouraged it and permitted air support coupled with continued effectiveness in the face of heavy casualties of the Castro militia. Either of these possible developments would have confirmed the errors of intelligence and assessment that are alleged but would have given no support to the view that errors of organization and execution in the build-up phase were responsible for the military defeat. Despite whatever mistakes of this character there were, the Agency did after all (with the invaluable help of the Department of Defense) build up, train, equip, and deploy a force that proved itself in combat to be of high quality.

## E. Agency vs. Government Responsibility

Another notable feature of the decisions that together were responsible for failure to achieve control of the air (in addition to the fact that they were all Washington policy decisions) is that they were all interdepartmental decisions. Other elements of the Executive Branch were involved along with the Agency in making them. This is not to imply that in all cases they were imposed on the Agency. Regardless, however, of how blame should be assessed between the Agency for accepting restrictions and the policy makers outside the agency for imposing them, it is necessary to have clearly in mind the nature of the decision making process in a project of this sort in order to understand how the ultimate failure came about.

Inherent in this situation was a clear conflict between two goals, a conflict of the sort familiar in recent American history. One objective was that, mainly through the various activities comprised in this project, the Castro regime should be overthrown. The other was that the political and moral posture of the United States before the world at large should not be impaired, The basic method of resolving this conflict of objectives that was resorted to was that of attempting to carry out actions against Castro in such a manner that the official responsibility of the U.S. Government could be disclaimed.

If complete deniability had been consistent with maximum effectiveness, there would theoretically have remained no conflict of goals but in fact this could not be (and never is) the case. The most effective way to have organized operations against the Castro regime, even if they would have been carried out exclusively by Cubans, would have been to do so perfectly openly, on the largest scale and with the best equipment feasible. Practically every departure from this pattern of behavior imposed operational difficulties and reduced effectiveness. Inherent in the concept of deniability was that many of these restrictions would be accepted but at every stage over a period of many months questions had to be answered in which operational effectiveness was weighed against the political requirement of deniability.

As those decisions presented themselves week after week, the Agency as the executive agent for the conduct of the operation was usually and naturally the advocate of effectiveness. The State Department and, with respect to certain matters, the Department of Defense were the guardians of the correctness of the country's political posture and thus the advocates of deniability. There was obviously no way in which a generalized policy could have been laid down which would have furnished guidance as to the way the many successive decisions ought to be made. There was no quantitative measure of either the improvement in the chances of success that would have resulted from say, permission to use American air crews in overflights or of the decrease in deniability that would have resulted therefrom. Each of many such decisions had to be discussed and made on its own merits, and in almost all of them several agencies had to take part.

One of the consequences of this state of affairs was that prompt decisions were hard to obtain. Another was that, like so many interdepartmental decisions, these were subject to differing interpretations by different participants in the process. Delays and differences of interpretation were compounded by the constantly changing situation both of Cuba and the Castro regime on the one side and of the opposition on the other, which would have rendered rigid and entirely orderly planning difficult under the best of circumstances.

The nature of the decision making process had other consequences as well. It explains in large measure the failure to write tidy and comprehensive plans and have them properly approved in writing by competent authority well in advance. It explains why there was a long succession of alternate plans and of modification to plans under consideration. Above all, the constant weighing of costs and benefits in the effort to satisfy the military requirements for success without excessive impairment of the political requirement of deniability explains why the final plan (and most of the variants considered in the last six weeks) was a compromise.

## F. Why An "Overt" Operation

Against the background of these remarks on the way decisions were made and on the nature of policy issues involved, it is worth commenting briefly on one of the major errors of judgment alleged by the Survey: the decision to "convert the project into what rapidly became an overt military operation beyond the Agency's capability." In part this "decision" was compelled by the failure of the internal resistance the reasons for which are discussed in later sections and are not germane to the current context. As for the Agency's capability, enough has already been said to suggest that the operation was not so much beyond the Agency's capability as it was beyond the scope of activities judged to be acceptably deniable. The question that is highly relevant to the policy making process is how and why the project was allowed to become overt and, when this had happened, why it remained the responsibility of the Agency.

That it did become "overt" in the sense that there was extensive public discussion of the preparations for invasion and that the military action was widely attributed to the United States Government, both before and after it took place, there can be no doubt. Nor is there any mystery as to why this happened. It was quite out of the question to infiltrate men and arms by sea and air for months, recruit, train and arm a strike force of some 1800 Cubans, to organize the political fronts, first the FRD then the CRC and run a major propaganda campaign, without at least reports and rumors of those activities becoming widespread. Nor were there any illusions either in the Agency or elsewhere in the Executive Branch as to the degree to which the facts were surmised and accepted as true by journalists and other informed persons. Why, then, would anyone continue to regard the involvement of the United

States as plausibly deniable and why was the undertaking not converted into an overt operation, which presumably would have become the responsibility of the Department of Defense?

The answer to the first part of this question is that up to and through the invasion itself the operation remained to an extraordinary degree *technically* deniable. Funds were disbursed in such a way that their U.S. Government origin could not be proved. No Agency case officer who played an active role was publicly revealed as such by true name. No Americans were captured (although the bodies of an American B-26 crew were probably recovered after its loss on the second day of the invasion). In short, even the best informed correspondents in Miami who published what purported to be detailed, factual reports could substantiate them only by quoting Cubans who themselves were often not well informed.

This limited and purely technical maintenance of deniability was less important to the decisions of the Executive Branch, however, than the fact that no one in the Executive Branch was ready at any point until after the defeat officially to avow U.S. support. Indeed, this alternative was never seriously considered. Even the most inadequate fig leaf was considered more respectably than the absence of any cover whatsoever. Indeed, the final changes in the operational plan made in March, the official announcement in April that the United States would not give support to the rebels, and the cancellation of the D-Day strike were all last minute efforts to shore up the plausible deniability of an enterprise for which Governmental support was bound to be conclusively surmised even if it could not be proved. These decisions were made by the senior policy makers of the Government who were reading the newspapers every day and knew well to what degree the project had in fact become "overt." These men simply were not willing to state officially either that the United States itself was about to make war on Cuba or that the U.S. Government was openly supporting a group of Cubans, not even recognized as a Government in exile, in a military invasion. In the aftermath of failure this decision may have seemed a wrong one. Had the operation succeeded reasonably quickly and without too much bloodshed, the decision would probably have seemed a correct one. Be that as it may, it was not the Agency's decision and, as the above cited actions suggest, the pressure to strengthen deniability in the last few weeks came from outside the Agency and led to decisions which were unwelcome to the Agency. To suggest, as the Survey seems to do, that the Agency was responsible for this clinging to deniability is demonstrably false.

## G. Government vs. Agency Decisions

The same comment applies in some degree to the three other alleged major errors of judgment. (Those have to do respectively with the treatment of the Cuban exiles, the adequacy of the military planning, and the appraisal of the chances of success. They have been touched upon above and are discussed at some length in Section V below.) In the context of the decision making process, the most important conclusion that emerges is that, whether they were wise or unwise, they were Governmental decisions in a very real sense. As to the handling of the Cubans, this was a matter of the most intimate consultation with the State Department, especially in the two months preceding the invasion when the CRC was in process of formation. As to military planning, the record clearly shows that there was detailed consultation with the Joint Chiefs of Staff, that the JCS considered the successive plans both formally and informally, and that these were the subject of review and discussion at the highest levels of Government. The chances of success were assessed favorably by the Joint Chiefs (minus, of course, the last minute cancellation of the D-Day strike) as well as by the Agency. The Agency must accept a sizable share of the blame for whatever mistakes were made in these three areas but no one who studies the record with care can assert (and no one who has done so has asserted) that the responsibility was narrowly focused on any one of the participants in the decision making process.

## H. Conclusions

This introductory and summary section began with a re-statement of the main allegations of error made in the Survey and it followed with a summary of the conclusions reached in this paper (partly in the foregoing discussion but principally in the later more detailed sections) with respect to those allegations. For the most part the allegations are rejected. In concluding this section it may be useful first to list, for comparison and contrast with the Survey, what in the judgment of this paper do appear to have been the strengths and weaknesses of this undertaking and second to suggest some of the lessons to be drawn therefrom. The list is as follows:

1) Small boat infiltration and exfiltration operations were slow to start (but by and large were effective and well run in the last three months). Moreover, due to the existence of the U.S. Embassy in Havana, defectors and legal travel, the need for illegal infiltration was comparatively slight until January 1961.

2) Partly for this reason, the effort to place trained communicators, para-

military types, and other agents with resistance groups inside the Island, and thereby to create a reception capability for air and maritime resupply, never caught up with Castro's improving security measures. This impaired the build-up not only of guerrilla groups but of intelligence nets. It is doubtful, however, whether significantly more could have been accomplished in building up an effective internal resistance particularly in view of the timing of the whole operation and the lead time involved in recruiting and training.

3) Aside from these weaknesses, alleged defects of organization and execution had little to do with the unsuccessful outcome. In particular, the limiting factor on air operations in support of the resistance was not bad management but the limitations of the reception parties and competence of Cuban air crews.

4) The air arm should have been stronger by the time of the invasion in numbers of air crews, type of equipment, availability of U.S. bases, or some combination of all these. If relief could not have been obtained from any of the politically motivated restrictions, and if a larger number of competent Cuban air crews could not have been recruited, the Agency should on its own responsibility have assembled more U.S. nationality air crews in the hope that their commitment would be permitted in an emergency.

5) There should have been more pre-D-Day air strikes and they should have employed the full strength of the air arm. The D-Day strike should not have been canceled.

6) The military plan was a good one (except for the restrictions on, and possible inadequacy of, the air arm). It was properly worked out as between the Agency and the Joint Staff and was a product of highly competent, professional military planning.

7) The appraisal of the chances of success was probably faulty for reasons summarized above (para. d).

8) The important decisions were Governmental not those of one Agency. It was frustrating but of little practical consequence that the decision making process was at times cumbersome and did not promote tidiness. It was inevitable that the whole shape of the operation was determined as a compromise between the conflicting goals of deniability and effectiveness.

## I. Lessons For The Future

What are the lessons for the future to be drawn from this unhappy experience? Perhaps the main one is that the U.S. should not support an operation such as this involving the use of force without having also made the decision to use whatever force is needed to achieve success. If the political decisions necessary to facilitate the effective use of force on an adequate scale, up to and possibly including the overt commitment of U.S. military forces, are too difficult to make, then the operation should be called off unless the odds in favor of success within the politically imposed restrictions are very great.

It is a fact of life that the use of force by the U.S. (or any major Western nation—the Communists seem to be judged by a different standard) in an effort to influence the course of events in another country is deeply unpopular with an important body of opinion. Most of the damage to the political posture of the U.S. that is done by such action occurs when the action is identified, whether on the basis of evidence or of pure surmise, with the U.S. Once this point of identification has been passed, it will almost invariably be true that ultimate failure not only means loss of the original objective but further exaggeration of the political damage. Ultimate success, on the other hand, is the only way partially to retrieve and offset the political damage. It is, therefore, only the part of wisdom to reassess an undertaking of this sort when identification of the U.S. Government with it has begun to occur or appears imminent and to determine at that time either to insure success or to abandon it.

The feeling has been widespread that another major lesson to be learned has to do with respect to the decision making process in the Executive Branch. In any major operation involving the exercise of power by the U.S. Government (as distinguished from the threat to exercise power), some branch of the Government will be responsible for execution, preoccupied with the achievement of success, and therefore generally the advocate of a massive and effective exercise of power. At the same time, the U.S. will always be in pursuit of a variety of essentially political objectives which will impose a requirement to maintain a certain public posture (notably in the UN). This requirement, in turn, will imply limitations on the manner in which and the scale on which power can be exercised. The guardian of the public posture whose primary responsibility it will be to devise and support restrictions on action will typically be the Department of State, or policy makers outside the action organization. In such a situation there is almost bound to be a succession of operational decisions that present (or appear to the participants to present) major issues of policy and, since there is an inevitable, and in a sense legitimate, conflict of interests between departments reflecting the conflict of objectives, there will typically have to be an arbiter who is himself neither the activist operator nor the statesman-like guardian of the country's political posture.

Such issues are continuously brought to top levels for resolution. The result is a very human tendency on the part of the decision makers to decide not only the policy matters which only they can handle but also operational matters in which they have little of the expertise necessary for judgment and can rarely acquire through briefings enough depth of factual detail for a full understanding. Admittedly, expert advisors can be used but under pressure of time compounded by the unavoidable ambiguity of committee consider- ations, decisions are often made by the policy makers without full concur- rence of the experts based on an inadequate understanding of the issues or their implications.

These are of course eternal problems of high level decision making and minor changes in governmental structure will not cause them to disappear. Nor are they in any sense unique to clandestine operations conducted by this Agency. Whenever something like the Cuban situation arises, what seem to the operators to be operational decisions will in fact raise policy issues. The issues will be real because they arise out of a real conflict of objectives. The decision making process could be tidier than it usually is and a meticulous written record would minimize recriminations after the fact, but tidiness and a good written record will have little bearing on the substantive wisdom of the decisions themselves. Whether in important matters of this sort any one other than the President himself can resolve the conflict between the require- ments for effectiveness of action and acceptability of the political conse- quences remains to be seen. Perhaps the most useful lesson about Government decision making to be learned from the Cuban case is that one must be prepared for and philosophical about this process.

A third lesson of lesser generality has to do with the covertness or deni- ability of paramilitary and other large scale operations. An operation can be said to be covert only so long as the knowledge that it is being performed can be restricted to authorized individuals. This is possible if an activity can re- ally be concealed (e.g., photography of a document without the knowledge that the document has been reproduced) or if that part of the activity which is observable by unwitting people can be made to appear to them to be perfectly normal (the black movement of bodies or cargo from place to place through the use of false documentation). Unfortunately, a good many large projects including notably most paramilitary operations cannot be covert in this sense. Journalists and other unwitting people are almost certain to learn that something untoward is afoot. The only aspect in which such operations can be kept clandestine is by successfully concealing the part played by the U.S. Government.

It is a necessary condition for the preservation of such deniability that no unwitting individual acquire hard evidence of Governmental participation but this is by no means a sufficient condition. If it comes to be widely believed even in the absence of hard evidence that the U.S. Government is assisting or participating in an illegal activity, then a considerable part of the benefit that accrues from deniability has already been lost. After all, the effect on public opinion depends on what is believed by that part of the public with which the policy makers are for the moment concerned. There may still remain, however, a benefit to be derived from deniability after the public has decided that the denials are false because the Government can still maintain a formally "correct" posture. The Soviets frequently derive advantage from this limited official deniability. As a rule, however, the advantages that accrue to a Western Government, with a lively and at least partly hostile press and with statesmen who shrink from the utterances of flat untruths, are limited.

The lesson suggested by these remarks is that in future clandestine operations of any size, it behooves all concerned to assess realistically the degree to which the operation is, and is likely to remain, clandestine. If the very scale of the activities makes it impossible to conceal them, can they be made to appear to suspicious journalists and others to be perfectly normal? If it is becoming apparent that something newsworthy is going on, can suspicion of Government involvement be kept to an acceptably low key? Or is the only option that remains open that of firm, repeated, public official disclaimer of a responsibility which will generally be attributed to the Government anyway? A corollary is that the advantages of whatever degree of deniability that remains feasible should not be overestimated. With hindsight, the U.S. did not buy very much political advantage with all the restraints imposed on air activity in the Cuban operation. Had it been decided even ten days before the invasion that responsibility for the operation would be unanimously attributed to the U.S. and that only official deniability could be preserved, consideration might have been given to recognizing the Cuban Revolutionary Council as a government in exile and allowing it to make as many and as powerful air strikes as it could. Another possibility might have been to use U.S. aircraft for a night strike. No one proposed either course of action at the time. They are mentioned here as theoretical possibilities only to illustrate the kind of conclusion that might have flowed from a more realistic assessment of the achievable degree of covertness and of the benefits to be obtained by maintaining only that limited degree of covertness.

There may be a fourth lesson to be drawn with respect to the assessment of the chances of success of any inherently risky operation. As stated above, a conclusion of this paper is that the assessment may have been faulty. Generally, this has been attributed, both in the Survey and elsewhere, to the circumstance that those responsible for conducting the operation were doing the appraising and exhibited a predictable bias. But this diagnosis ignores the role of the JCS who were directed by the President to review the prospects for the operation principally so that there would be an independent and professionally competent judgment. It is also true that in judging the temper of the Cuban people, principal reliance was placed on a National Estimate. Nevertheless, it is probably true that the views of men deeply involved in the operation received too much weight in the assessment of the probable outcome, though it is far from clear where and how additional skeptics could have been introduced into the process of judgment without simply adding to the confusion. The only clear lesson is that policy makers should not make mistakes, which is scarcely helpful.

Finally, there are various lessons to be drawn with respect to Agency organization, procedures, and resources. No attempt will be made here to elaborate them, partly because to do so would require rather detailed exposition and partly because these are not among the really important lessons. It must be repeated still again that errors of execution did not have much to do with the failure and it must be emphasized that ways were found of bringing to bear on the conduct of the operation professional talent of a high order, especially in the military field. The mistakes were mainly those of judgment which a different organization would not have forestalled.

## II. THE SURVEY'S STATEMENTS OF THE OPERATIONAL CONCEPT

The Survey quite accurately refers to changes in the "military" plan which occurred on a number of occasions prior to the adoption of the final plan (i.e., the Zapata plan). The final plan, however, is the only one here considered except that earlier plans will be discussed to the extent that they are relevant to it.

As described by the Survey, the attack involved about 1500 "combat-trained and heavily armed soldiers" in an "overt assault-type amphibious landing" on certain beaches on the Zapata Peninsula on the south coast of Cuba. The troops had been moved by air on three successive nights from a Guatemalan training camp to the staging area in Nicaragua where they embarked on ships which had been pre-loaded at New Orleans.

"The ships had moved on separate courses from Nicaragua, under unobtrusive Navy escort, to the rendezvous 40 miles offshore in order to avoid the appearance of a convoy. From there they had moved in column under cover of darkness to a point 5000 yards from the landing area, where they met the Navy LSD. These complicated movements were apparently accomplished in a secure manner and without alerting the enemy."

The intention was to seize a "coastal strip about 40 miles long, separated from the interior by an impassable swamp penetrated only by three roads from the north and flanked by a coastal road from the east."

The landing which occurred during the night of April 16–17 was substantially unopposed. In addition, shortly after daylight an "airborne infantry company was successfully parachuted from C-46 aircraft to four of the five scheduled drop zones where its elements were given the mission of sealing off approach roads."

Air support prior to the landing was given by raids by eight B-26's on three Cuban airfields on 15 April and "destruction of half of Castro's air force was estimated on the basis of good post-strike photography." Air strikes planned for dawn on 17 April in order to knock out the rest of the Cuban air force were "called off . . . late on 16 April."

Early morning enemy air attacks on 17 April resulted in sinking a supply ship and beaching a transport as well as damage to an LCI. Ground attacks by Cuban militia occurred during the day of 17 April. "While ammunition lasted, these attacks were beaten off with heavy enemy casualties, and several of Castro's tanks were halted or destroyed by ground or friendly air action. On the morning of 18 April, the Red Beach Force, nearly out of ammunition, retired in good order to Blue Beach without being pressed by the evening." [sic].

Adequate resupply (whether by sea or air) became increasingly difficult and finally impossible due to enemy air action with the inevitable collapse resulting. The Survey, referring to air support attempted for the Brigade on 18 and 19 April:

"In spite of this air action, however, and in spite of a reported 1800 casualties suffered by the Castro forces, the Brigade's ability to resist depended in the last resort on resupply of ammunition, which had now become impossible."

/NB: No mention has been made of a separate landing planned for D-2 at a point 30 miles east of Guantanamo. Nino Diaz, who had a following in

Oriente Province, was to land with 170 men with the idea of starting a fairly large scale diversion by drawing to him his followers and the resistance known to exist in Oriente. Although the Diaz group put to sea and reached its Cuban landing area on schedule, it never in fact landed due to a number of factors beyond U.S. control. Since the group played no role, no further discussion seems warranted.

//NB: By letter, dated 22 April 1961, the President charged General Maxwell D. Taylor with the responsibility of investigating among other things the Cuban operation and of reporting the lessons to be learned therefrom. General Taylor, in association with Attorney General Kennedy, Admiral Burke and Mr. Allen Dulles (known as the Cuban Study Group) immediately held continuous hearings receiving testimony from all possible informed witnesses including a number of individuals who had been on the Zapata beachhead. General Taylor filed no written report but gave the President an interim oral report on 16 May 1961 and wrote the President on 13 June 1961 that he was ready to make his final report orally, which he did thereafter. The oral reports were supported by four memoranda which are here referred to as they provide a far more complete review of all aspects of the military portion of the operation than given above or in the Survey. Brief references to certain of these memoranda are made hereafter./

## III. WHY A MILITARY-TYPE INVASION

The answer is based on a number of factors. First, it became clear through the summer of 1960 that Castro was more firmly settled as Chief of State than had originally been hoped. Moreover, it became apparent that he was receiving and would continue to receive significant support from the Soviet Bloc (including the Chinese) economically, in military materiel, and in much needed advisers, e.g., military, internal security, positive intelligence and communications (to name the main fields). Thus, it was recognized that it was becoming more and more difficult to organize and maintain internal opposition, and, moreover, it was daily becoming more apparent that forceful evidence of outside support was needed to cause the internal opposition to show its hand.

During the summer and fall of 1960, some guerrilla resistance continued in the Escambray Mountains and in some of the provinces. Although poorly fed and equipped, this resistance was respected by the militia which despite vast superiorities in number would not engage the resistance in direct combat. Rather, the militia surrounded resistance pockets, staying on the main roads away from the hills; kept food and supplies out of resistance areas, and captured the guerrillas when they came out of the hills singly or in small numbers seeking food or other aid. Nevertheless, until the morale of the militia could be shaken, it seemed clear that, due to its vast superiority in numbers, it could continue at least to contain the resistance. Moreover, it became evident through the fall and early winter that the outside force to be successful needed to be self-sustaining since small bands or elements would, due to numerical inferiority in all likelihood, be cut off, surrounded and overwhelmed or rendered harmless by the militia.

In addition, difficulties of supplying the opposition soon became apparent. Air drops were rarely successful which is not an unusual operational experience. Under much simpler conditions approximately the first 12 or 13 drops in support of Castillo Armas were wholly unsuccessful in Guatemala. Thereafter, slight improvement occurred but mainly due to the fact that the drops were made in daylight and directed to terrain held by the invaders who were in open conflict and not in hiding. Even in France during WW II at a time when experienced pilots were dropping to experienced reception committees in vastly more favorable terrain than available in most of the attempted Cuban drops the rule of thumb was that only 50% success should be expected. At any rate the lack of success by air and the difficulty of distributing within Cuba the substantial amount of materiel landed by boat (plus, of course, the restrictions imposed by the constantly increasing and improving internal security) made it clear that no internal resistance buildup could achieve adequate size to eliminate the regime without substantial outside support.

As early as November, therefore, the Government decided to continue to aid the internal resistance as much as possible but to begin to plan for the introduction into Cuba of a trained force from the outside. Unquestionably, Castillo Armas in Guatemala was an analogy and precedent. Over the period from November until April the possibility—indeed the probability—of a military type invasion was continuously a generally approved part of the concept. In addition, by common consent of all involved, the size of the Brigade was increased bit by bit until the final 1500 total was reached. There was no magic in any particular number. Nevertheless, factors such as features and size of terrain to be attacked desired fire power and logistics were carefully weighed by officers experienced in guerrilla and special force actions with the result that a minimum basic force of 750 was decided in December 1960 to be the proper size for the requirements. Thereafter, the increase was undertaken to provide extra strength on the simple theory that as long as flexibility was retained more men and guns would inevitably be useful.

Although the decisions involving size and use of the Brigade were in general based on its employment as a single force, the possibility of piecemeal use through infiltrations in small groups was seriously studied. Obvious political advantages would have been gained with such use rather than the larger "invasion" type landing. Nevertheless, the considered military judgment (i.e., of both Agency and JCS staff and military officers) was that small groups would not be able to prevent the large numbers of militia from either isolating or gradually eliminating them. Moreover, it was felt that the state of the internal opposition was such that they would not respond aggressively to the undramatic and, at best, slow impact of small bands of this sort. Consequently, such a plan could only result in a wasting of assets and a failure to use effectively the trained manpower of the Brigade. The military-type concept of introducing the entire Brigade into Cuba as a single force, therefore, emerged as the most feasible possibility.

## IV. THE DECISION MAKING PROCESS

In order to place the Agency's role in the proper perspective and to indicate the general participation of the Executive Department, it is essential to examine the planning process that was involved. The Survey is highly critical of this aspect but it should be noted that the Survey is particularly incomplete in the discussions of decision-making and planning.

Regarding the planning process, for example, the Survey comments that in January 1961 "the Agency was driving forward without knowing precisely where it was going." What is meant is unclear, particularly as in the next paragraph the Survey states:

"At this meeting (28 January 1961) there was a presentation, largely oral, of the status of the operation, and President Kennedy approved their continuation."

In the same connection, the Survey states that at the end of November 1960, the Agency presented a revised plan to President Eisenhower and his advisors and "President Eisenhower orally directed the Agency to go ahead with its preparations with all speed."

Some direction, therefore, was visible to two Presidents even though no definitive decisions were made until the very last minute. The fact, however, that the Survey could make such a statement and at the same time include only the barest facts suggests a lack of understanding of the decision-making process.

The Special Group prior to 20 January 1961 (Messrs. Dulles; Gray; Herter until appointed Secretary, then Merchant; Douglas, with Irwin sitting for him on occasion) reviewed the entire situation on numerous occasions and considered special issues on others. Cuban discussion in the Special Group started in 1959 when concerns about the political situation and the undesirability of Castro were aired. Covert actions (e.g., radio broadcasting, economic actions, possible sabotage) were discussed at several meetings in January, February and March 1960 including the examination of a detailed "General Covert Action Plan for Cuba" on 14 March 1960. This plan was approved by the Special Group, then partially rewritten and finally approved by President Eisenhower on 17 March 1960.

Between mid-March and 20 January 1961, the Special Group had discussions of Cuba at 37 meetings, of which at least 8 to 10 in the period during and following November 1960 were detailed discussions. Gordon Gray, as the President's representative on the Special Group, reported to the President regularly on such Special Group activities. Moreover, at a general briefing on the project at the Special Group meeting of 8 December 1960, Assistant Secretary Mann and Mr. Joseph Scott of State also attended as did General Lansdale from Defense. In addition, C/WH regularly held weekly meetings with the Assistant Secretary of State at which Cuba was often discussed; liaison with Mr. Scott's office in State by A/DDP/A and others was almost on a daily basis on Cuba alone; and members of WH/4 also had substantially daily contact (on Cuba) with General Erskine's office in Defense (General Lansdale, the Deputy) regarding Defense support and details of the preparation for the possible "invasion."

President Eisenhower, in addition to the 29 November 1960 meeting referred to in the Survey, held a further detailed meeting on 3 January 1961 so that with those plus the reports which he received from Mr. Gray and others he was personally familiar with the status of the project at the time he left office.

Also as the result of an understanding first worked out with General Bonesteel of the JCS and later adopted by the Secretary of State, the Secretary of Defense and the DCI, a Task Force (or committee) was created chaired by Ambassador Willauer with representatives of State (Assistant Secretary Mann and his deputy, Mr. Coerr); JCS (General Gray and other military members of his staff); and CIA (A/DDP/A and C/WH/4 or when absent, his deputy). Later William Bundy of Assistant Secretary of Defense Nitze's office joined the Task Force. The Task Force was responsible for examining the project with a view to determining what actions should be considered which were either not covered by existing plans or necessary to support existing plans. Ambassador Willauer reported to the Special Group at its meetings of 12 and 19 January 1961. The work of this Task Force resulted in the creation of a special JCS team headed by General Gray (discussed below) to review military planning and a committee to keep track of non-military aspects of planning consisting of Defense (General Gray), State (Mr. Braddock, last Chargé in Havana prior to the break in relations) and CIA (A/DDP/A). This latter committee met regularly from about mid-February and prepared a list of tasks to be discharged by the Agency and each Department. This paper was approved by the Secretary of State, Secretary of Defense and the DCI and was used as a check list. A copy is attached as Annex A. As noted, it contained no reference to the military or Brigade action.

The new Administration was brought into the picture as soon as possible. President Kennedy was given a general briefing by the DCI and the DD/P on 18 November 1960 and Secretary of State Rusk was briefed by the DCI prior to inauguration on 17 January 1961. Rusk was again briefed on 22 January by the DCI and the DD/P in a group including the Secretary of Defense and the Attorney General.

Thereafter, there were a number of meetings with the President at which the Secretary of State, Secretary of Defense, the Chairman of the JCS, the Attorney General, the DCI were present. In addition, Messrs. McGeorge Bundy and Schlesinger from the White House Staff; Berle and Mann from State; Nitze and William Bundy from Defense; General Gray from the JCS; and the DD/P were present. Such meetings were held on:

28 January
17 February
11 March
14 March (smaller meeting)
15 March
4 April
12 April

(Special communications regarding action under the Plan were also held with the President on 14 and 16 April via McGeorge Bundy and the Secretary of State).

In addition to the foregoing, the President on 7 March met with the Ambassador from Guatemala to the U.S. and the Ambassador's brother, a special emissary from President Ydígoras, who presented President Ydígoras' views. Numerous meetings also were held with Messrs. McGeorge Bundy, Berle and Mann, and Mr. Berle met with Miro Cardona, President of the Cuban Revolutionary Council. Also in the second week in April due to attacks in the UN by Foreign Minister Roa of Cuba and stories in the press, mainly the *New York Times*, a substantial amount of time had to be spent with the State Department preparing material for use by the USUN delegation including a briefing of Ambassador Stevenson. It is fair to say, therefore, that the senior members of the Administration were personally and intimately familiar with the status of the project and the issues and problems involved.

On the military side, General Lemnitzer with the approval of the Secretary of Defense designated General Gray of the JCS on 4 January 1961 as the chief military liaison for the project. General Gray, thereafter, became closely associated with the military planning. From 31 January to 6 February a complete, detailed review of the operations plan was made by General Gray and a team of officers. This involved a thorough briefing by Esterline, Chief/WH/4 and Colonel Hawkins, Chief/WH/4/PM, and officers of their staffs plus several days of study by the JCS team. The Trinidad plan was the one reviewed on this occasion. During the review a memorandum was prepared by the team, approved by the JCS, and sent to the Secretary of Defense. (JCS Memo 57–61 of 3 February 1961, to Secretary of Defense, Subject: Military Evaluation of the CIA Para-Military Plan, Cuba).

This memorandum reached a favorable assessment of the plan. It stated, however, that it was unable to evaluate the combat capabilities of the Cuban Brigade and Air Force except on the testimony of others since the Team had not seen those themselves. As a result, a team of 3 officers, a Special Forces Colonel, a Marine Colonel, and an Air Force Colonel, were selected by General Gray from among the officers briefed and sent to Guatemala from 25 through 27 February to examine the air and ground forces personally. A subsequent report to the Secretary of Defense confirmed their finding that the forces were capable. (JCS Memo 146–61 of 10 March 1961, to Secretary of Defense; Subject: Evaluation of CIA Cuban Volunteer Task Force). This latter report recommended that an instructor "experienced in operational logistics" be assigned to the training unit "immediately for the final phase of training." A Marine Colonel with these qualifications was so assigned.

Thereafter, General Gray and his team were intimately connected with all plans and moves of Colonel Hawkins' PM Section. In fact, it would not be inaccurate to say that General Gray and his team were the equivalent of a full partner of the Agency in this phase from mid-February 1961 until 17 April. (This did not, of course, affect the primary CIA responsibility). During this period General Gray briefed General Lemnitzer at frequent intervals and also briefed the JCS at formal JCS meetings.

When DD/P headquarters elements went on 24-hour duty on 13 April 1961, General Gray's staff did likewise and assigned a full time liaison officer to sit with Colonel Hawkins' section in order to be able to brief General Gray fully each day. General Gray, in turn, briefed General Lemnitzer.

The Trinidad Plan was always the plan preferred by the military, i.e., the JCS, General Gray and Colonel Hawkins and his staff. It was, however, considered unacceptable in certain aspects for political reasons so that on or about 11 March 1961, President Kennedy decided that it should not be executed. A further study of the entire Cuban shore line was then conducted by CIA, mainly WH/4, from 13 through 15 March. As indicated in the Survey, this study resulted in a shift from Trinidad to Zapata. Two alternate concepts were sketched out but the Zapata area concept was the only one which met the political requirements and provided a reasonable chance of success. This concept was fully described to General Gray and his team and passed on by the JCS as the best alternate to the Trinidad plan (JCS Memo 166–61 of 15 March 1961 to Secretary of Defense; Subject: Evaluation of Military Aspects of Alternate Concepts of CIA Para-Military Plan, Cuba.) The covering memorandum from General Lemnitzer as Chairman of the JCS states in part:

"3. The conclusions of the evaluation of the military aspects of the three alternative concepts are as follows:

"c. Alternative III" (substantially the final Zapata Plan) "has all the prerequisites necessary to successfully establish the Cuban Voluntary Task Force, including air elements, in the objective area and sustain itself with outside logistic support for several weeks; however, inaccessibility of the area may limit the support from the Cuban populace.

"4. It is recommended that:

"a. the Secretary of Defense support the views of the Joint Chiefs of Staff as expressed in the above conclusions."

After 15 March, the JCS reviewed the Zapata plan as a body four times. The final plan was reviewed by individual Chiefs since it was only presented to the JCS on 15 April which was too late for its review by the JCS as a body.

The *only* reference in the Survey to JCS participation states that "members of the JCS" have stated "in the course of another inquiry (1) that the final plan was presented to them only orally, which prevented normal staffing; (2) that they regarded the operation as being solely CIA's with the military called in to furnish various types of support and the chief interest of the JCS being to see to it that every kind of support requested was furnished; (3) that they went on the assumption that full air support would be furnished and control of the air secured and on the Agency's assurances that a great number of insurgents would *immediately* join forces with the invasion forces; and (4) that, in the event the battle went against them, the Brigade would at once 'go guerrilla' and take to the hills."

Neither the "members of the JCS" nor the other "inquiry" are identified nor is there any citation supporting the alleged testimony. Being unable, therefore, to locate the full text from which the quotation was taken, it is not possible to analyze or clarify the points made. Presumably the "inquiry" referred to was that conducted by General Taylor although no verbatim minutes were kept. At least no transcript or full report of these hearings is available to the writer. In response, therefore, it can only be repeated that the JCS, as indicated, did review the Zapata plan and continued to be closely associated through their representatives and briefings with all actions taken thereon.

It is quite clear from the four memoranda supporting General Taylor's oral report mentioned above that the Cuban Study Group considered the operation to be one by the United States, not by the Agency, even though the Agency was the Executive Agent. Memorandum No. 2., entitled "Immediate Causes of Failure of Operation Zapata," says on this point:

"The Executive Branch of the Government was not organizationally prepared to cope with this kind of paramilitary operation. There was no single authority short of the President capable of coordinating the actions of CIA, State, Defense and USIA."

As far as the concurrence of the JCS is concerned, Memorandum No. 3, entitled "Conclusions of the Cuban Study Group," concluded:

"The Joint Chiefs of Staff had the important responsibility of examining into the history of the operation. By acquiescing in the Zapata plan, they gave the impression to others of approving it . . . ."

EYES ONLY

MEMORANDUM FOR:  Secretary of State
Secretary of Defense
Director of Central Intelligence Agency

SUBJECT:  Tasks, Para-Military Plan, Cuba

1. The Working Group assigned to work out the detailed tasks for the planning and conduct of the CIA Para-Military Plan, Cuba, and act as members of a Central Office for the operation, has agreed upon the tasks to be accomplished by the representatives of your respective departments and agency. The tasks are set forth for three phases: Pre-D-Day-Phase; D-Day and Post-D-Day Phase until Recognition; and Post-Recognition Phase.

2. The tasks for the Pre-D-Day Phase are set forth in Enclosure A hereto.

3. The tasks for the D-Day and Post-D-Day Phase until Recognition are set forth in Enclosure B hereto.

4. The tasks for the Post-Recognition Phase are set forth in Enclosure C hereto.

5. The proposed time schedule for the Pre-D-Day Phase is attached as Enclosure D hereto.

Department of State Representative
Department of Defense Representative
CIA Representative

Atts: Encls. A-D as stated

## PRE-D-DAY PHASE

1. Department of State representatives will:

a. Prepare White Paper for Presidential approval.

b. Provide assistance to Mr. Schlesinger in preparation of material for Presidential statements.

c. Provide Working Group with Policy Statement as to what "recognition" really means.

d. Determine action, if any, to be taken regarding disclosures to Latin American countries—e.g.,

(1) Guatemala
(2) Nicaragua

and other countries, e.g.,

(1) United Kingdom
(2) France

e. Provide policy guidance for all aspects of the development of the Free Cuba Government.

f. Prepare plans for overt moral and other possible nonmilitary support prior to recognition of the Free Cuba Government of the objectives of the Cuban Volunteer Force and of the Revolutionary Council, including possible action in the United Nations or in the Organization of American States.

g. Prepare plans for overt moral and other possible nonmilitary support of the objectives of the Free Cuba Government when established.

h. Provide policy guidance to USIA to support this plan.

i. Prepare plans for Post-D-Day actions.

2. Department of Defense representatives will:

a. Continue to provide training and logistic support to the Cuban Volunteer Force as requested by CIA.

b. Prepare logistics plans for arms, ammunition, and equipment support beyond the capabilities of the initial CIA logistics support.

c. Prepare plans for provision of support from operational forces as required.

d. Prepare letter of instruction to the Services, CINCLANT and CONAD for support of this operation.

e. Keep CINCLANT planners informed.

3. CIA representatives will:

a. Establish a Central Office from which Executive Department and Agency representatives will coordinate planning and conduct operations.

b. Continue to supply guerrilla forces in Cuba as feasible and required.

c. Assist in the organization of a Free Cuba Government.

d. Conduct an interrogation of two or three members of the Cuban Volunteer Force to determine full extent of their knowledge of actual facts and provide information to the President as soon as possible.

e. Finalize detailed plans for the employment of the Volunteer Force in Cuba and follow up plans. Execute these plans on order.

i. Continue to recruit, train and equip the Cuban Volunteer Force.

g. Prepare detailed plans for establishing contact with the internal opposition, establishing such control, coordination and support of this opposition as may be desirable and feasible.

h. Exert effort to arrange defection of key Cuban personnel. (N.B.: The defection of the military commander of the Isle of Pines, or at least officers who could control the Isle, would be particularly desirable.)

i. Continue detailed intelligence collection on Castro activities throughout Latin America particularly his efforts to export revolution.

j. Support the preparation of a White paper to be issued by the Free Cuba Government.

k. Review cover plans.

l. Coordinate with DOD representatives logistic follow-up support requirements.

m. Review and implement a pre-D-Day psychological warfare plan.

n. Review Psychological Warfare Plan for D-Day and Post-D-Day Phase.

o. Intensify UW activities in Cuba.

p. Prepare contingency plan for the disposition, if necessary, of the Cuban Volunteer Force.

q. Prepare final briefing on entire operation.

## D-DAY AND POST-D-DAY PHASE
### UNTIL RECOGNITION

1. Department of State representatives will:

a. Take such steps as may be feasible for the protection of U.S. citizens in Cuba.

b. Execute plans for support of the Revolutionary Council or Free Cuba Government in the United Nations or Organization of American States and to counter communist and/or Castro charges in the United Nations or Organization of American States, as appropriate.

c. Lend support to the objectives and actions of the Cuban Volunteer Force and the Free Cuba Government.

d. Revise plans as necessary for support of the Free Cuba Government.

e. Recognize Free Cuba Government as appropriate.

2. Department of Defense representatives will:

a. Provide follow-up logistic support as requested by CIA and/or in accordance with logistics plan.

b. Provide support from operational forces as directed.

c. Prepare detailed plans to support the U.S. aid plan for the Free Cuba Government for implementation when overt support is given.

d. Coordinate support by DOD agencies and commands.

3. CIA representatives will:

a. Execute and support over-all paramilitary plan.

b. Inform DOD representatives of logistics requirements.

c. Continue execution of psychological warfare plan.

d. Be responsible for the continuous operation of the Central Office and present briefings of the situation as required or directed.

e. Introduce representatives of the Revolutionary Council and of the Free Cuba Government into Cuba at an appropriate time.

## POST RECOGNITION PHASE

The Departments and the Agency will prepare, coordinate and execute, as appropriate, such contingency plans as may be required and will, moreover, plan for the resumption of their regularly assigned functions in relation to the new Cuban government.

## TIME SCHEDULE

1. *D-14*

   a. Department of State Representatives:

   (1) Complete White Paper for Presidential approval.
   (2) Provide policy guidance for all aspects of the Free Cuba Government (continuous).

   b. Department of Defense Representatives:

   (1) Continue to provide training and logistic support to the Cuban Volunteer Force as requested by CIA.

   c. CIA Representatives:

   (1) Establish a Central Office.
   (2) Continue to supply guerrilla forces in Cuba as feasible and required (continuous).
   (3) Assist in organization of Free Cuba Government.
   (4) Continue to train and equip the Cuban Volunteer Force.
   (5) Coordinate with DOD representatives logistic follow-up support requirements (continuous).
   (6) Intensify UW activities in Cuba.

2. *D-11*

   a. Department of State Representatives:

   (1) Provide assistance to Mr. Schlesinger in preparation of material for Presidential statements (continuous).
   (2) Complete plans for overt moral and other possible non military support of the objectives of the Free Cuba Government when established.

3. *D-10*

   a. DOD Representatives:

   (1) Complete letter of instruction to the Services, CINCLANT and CONAD for support of this operation.

4. *D-9*

a. Department of State Representatives:

(1) Provide Working Group with Policy Statement as to what "recognition" really means.

(2) Have approved policy position regarding action, if any, to be taken regarding disclosures to foreign countries.

(3) Complete plans for overt moral and other possible nonmilitary support prior to recognition of the Free Cuba Government of the objectives of the Cuban Volunteer Force and of the Revolutionary Council, etc.

(4) Complete plans for Post-D-Day actions.

b. DOD Representatives:

(1) Complete logistics plans for DOD follow-up support.

c. CIA Representatives:

(1) Finalize detailed plans for the employment of the Cuban Volunteer Force.

(2) Complete detailed plans for establishing contact with the internal opposition and for establishing such control, coordination and support of this opposition as may be desirable and feasible.

(3) Initiate effort to arrange defection of key Cuban personnel.

(4) Complete review and implement a pre-D-Day psychological Warfare Plan for D-Day and post-D-Day phase.

(5) Complete review of Psychological Warfare Plan for D-Day and post-D-Day phase.

5. *D-8*

a. CIA Representatives:

(1) Complete support of a white paper to be issued by the Free Cuba Government and arrange to have that Government issue same.

6. *D-7*

a. CIA Representatives:

(1) Complete review of cover plans.

7. *D-6*

a. CIA Representatives:

(1) Conduct an interrogation of two or three members of the Cuban Volunteer Force to determine full extent of their knowledge of actual facts and provide information to the President as soon as possible.

8. *D-5*

a. DOD Representatives:

(1) Brief CINCLANT and CONAD planners.

b. CIA Representatives:

(1) Complete contingency plan for the disposition, if necessary, of the Cuban Volunteer Force.

(2) Complete preparation of final briefing on entire operation.

9. *D-3*

a. Department of State Representatives:

(1) Provide policy guidance to USIA to support this plan.

b. CIA Representatives:

(1) Complete detailed intelligence collection on Castro activities throughout Latin America.

10. *D-2*

a. DOD Representatives:

(1) Complete plans for provision of support from operational forces as required.

b. CIA Representatives:

(1) Present final briefing on entire operation (if not given prior to this date).

## V. THE ASSESSMENT OF THE
## ADEQUACY OF THE PLAN

As stated above one of the considerations raised by the Agency's capability to perform the operation is the question of what it thought the chances of success to be and if, as was the case, these were thought to be good, how reasonable this conclusion was in the light of the known facts. An examination of the adequacy of the military plan is essential to a resolution of this latter point.

Whatever conclusions or inferences may be drawn from the defeat of the Brigade, no one can deny that, in the absence of the planned D-Day dawn air strikes, the operational plan was never tested. Perhaps those air strikes would have had no significant effect but in view of the essentiality of eliminating Castro's air force, it can be asserted that without these air strikes the plan never had a chance. No issue has received more thorough analysis since the failure of the operation than the decision to cancel. Although the Survey fails to tell the full story, it is felt that nothing can be gained from further review. There is no doubt, however, that the informed military view without exception and at all times was that complete control of the air was absolutely vital.

(N.B. The Survey's statement indicating that "two of the President's military advisors, both members of the Joint Chiefs" did not understand this principle is considered inaccurate.)

To the extent that there was a failure to communicate this to the appropriate political levels, blame should be attached. Quite candidly, it is unknown where this failure occurred, if, in fact, it did.

Before analyzing the reasonableness of the view that the D-Day air strikes could have changed the result it is important to examine the basic theory of the operation and what was accomplished, what failed and what was not tested. As to the last the only possible judgments are whether the theory based on existing evidence was sensible. The operational theory in outline was:

a. To destroy the enemy air force. *Not tested though partially accomplished.*

b. To land the Brigade on the Zapata beachhead achieving surprise. *Accomplished successfully.*

c. To maintain the Brigade on the beachhead perhaps for several weeks. *Not tested.*

d. To persuade the Cuban populace (both private individuals and governmental, including military) actively to oppose the regime. It was never expected that this would happen until the populace was convinced that an opposition force supporting democratic leadership receiving outside support was able to maintain itself on Cuban soil. How long this would take was unknown. *Not tested.*

The failure to knock out Castro's airpower (particularly his T-33 jets) was fatal. How reasonable was the assumption that the D-Day strikes would have eliminated this airpower or at least made it non-operational for a period of time?

The best estimates based on all sources, including photography, (later confirmed as substantially accurate) were that prior to D-2 Cuban combat aircraft strength was 36 aircraft, i.e.:

17 B-26's
13 Sea Furies
 5 T-33's
 1 F-51

All of those were at three airfields—San Antonio, Libertad, and Antonio Maceo. The in-commission rate was assumed to be 50% (believed to be slightly high) so that presumably 18 combat aircraft were operational at the time of the initial D-2 strikes.

Based on all sources reports, including COMINT and photography, the Cubans subsequent to the D-2 strikes were able to launch only 7 aircraft against the beachhead, namely:

2 B-26's
2 Sea Furies
3 T-33's

Photography, of course, cannot determine serviceability but photography of aircraft movements post D-2 were consistent with, and, it is fair to say, confirm the above figures.

In addition, these operational aircraft were concentrated by the Cubans at San Antonio with the possible exception of 1 B-26 at Libertad. With the potent fire power carried by the B-26's flown by the Brigade, and based on the results of the D-2 strikes, the elimination of these seven aircraft could reasonably have been anticipated assuming surprise. Since the landing achieved surprise and since the Cubans had no effective anti-air warning system, surprise would almost certainly have been achieved.

With regard to the ability of the Brigade to maintain itself once ashore (assuming the elimination of hostile aircraft), the theory was that the Zapata area was so difficult of access via only three exposed roads across swamps that a small force could easily defend it against vastly superior forces for "several weeks" as stated by the JCS. Hostile concentrations and artillery would have been almost impossible to conceal from the air due to the terrain and the B-26 fire power would have been devastating against these. This is confirmed by the one actual encounter of B-26's against Cuban tanks. The Brigade's fire power was also heavy and could have prevented passage of any Cuban troops or equipment down the narrow access roads. As long as the ammunition lasted the Brigade actually succeeded in doing this. Supplies, absent hostile air, could have been landed in large quantities since ships could have been brought in to the beachhead.

The accuracy of this conclusion depends, of course, on technical considerations and must be based on experienced military judgments assessing such matters as the terrain involved; the size and capacity of friendly and opposing weapons involved; and the capacity particularly of the attacking force to maintain logistic support. Such an analysis could again be made but it would seem sufficient to support the reasonableness of the judgment reached in April by reference to the judgments reached by the Agency military planners and supported by the JCS and its staff.

Although it was believed that the Brigade under the assumed conditions could maintain itself on the beachhead almost indefinitely, still for ultimate success internal support was obviously needed. The concept of the plan was as indicated that at some point (not immediately) the existence of the Brigade would be recognized and Castro's quiescent opposition would become active.

As far as internal opposition was concerned, there was essentially general agreement regarding the situation. Such disagreement as has existed has been with respect to the accuracy of the prognosis regarding internal support the Brigade might expect after landing.

The December 1960 U.S. estimate regarding the internal situation was that Castro was firmly in control; that his regime had consolidated its hold; that Cuban internal security was being rapidly built up; that Bloc assistance in the form of military technicians and instructors was about 200; that Cuban pilots and other specialists had been taken overseas by the Bloc for training; that the Cuban Communist Party controlled key positions; and that no one group or combination of the regime's enemies seemed well enough organized or sufficiently strong to offer a serious threat without outside help to Castro's authority (SNIE 85. 3 – 60: Prospects for the Castro Regime).

Essentially the same facts were presented in the pamphlet released in early

April by the State Department on Cuba, the facts in which were worked on jointly by all interested departments and agencies, (Department of State publication 7171, Inter-American Series 66, entitled "Cuba," pages 19–25).

Again the same conclusions were stated by the Agency in its presentations. An example is the memorandum, dated 17 February 1961, Annex B of the Survey which sets forth the view on these points consistently presented by the Agency throughout this period and up to 17 April 1961.

What then was the Agency prognosis? The Zapata plan took the view that there was evidence to justify the conclusion that once it could be shown to the Cubans that a Cuban force in opposition to Castro, having Cuban political leaders of political stature and democratic views, was capable of maintaining itself on Cuban soil, there would be substantial defections from the Castro regime in all walks of life, private and governmental.

In December the USIB had estimated that, despite the hold established by Castro and his regime, "Internal resistance to the Castro regime has risen sharply in the last six months."

"The Catholic Church, the only major institution not brought to its knees by the regime, has taken an increasingly firm stand against Castro."

"The middle and professional classes are now for the most part disaffected. Some *campesinos* are disgruntled, notably over the regime's failure to redistribute large landholdings as it had promised; thus far only token allotments have been made."

"A number of anti-Castro guerrilla groups are operating in the Sierra Escambray area and in Oriente Province, but the regime has demonstrated its ability to contain those bands."

"Within the Army, Navy, and Air Force, there probably remains a measure of dissidence and probably considerable resentment at the regime's decided preference for the civilian militia, but this may decline as more Bloc equipment is made available to them."

(The above quotations are all from SNIE 85-3-60, page 5).

The militia numbering at least 200,000 was estimated to have been drawn largely from the lower income peasants and urban workers.

"Thus far, the militia's overall combat efficiency is low; many units are still on a part time training basis. However, a basic cadre of well organized well equipped, and trained units is emerging and on a number of occasions the militia has been used effectively to control mobs and to perform other security duties."

"The regular forces are still disrupted as a result of successive purges, and rehabilitation has been delayed by the employment of substantial army and navy detachments in construction and other public works. At present, the combat effectiveness of the air force is virtually nil, that of the navy poor, and that of the army at best fair, although it probably now exceeds that of all but the best militia units."

(Above quotes from SNIE 85-3-60, pages 3-4. For similar conclusions approved by the USIB on 7 February 1961, see "A report prepared by an Ad Hoc Committee of the USIB." OCI No. 0592/61-C, Part I, para. 6, page 3, and Part I, para. 8, page 4.)

Further evidence of the instability of the Castro regime was apparent in the constantly growing list of individuals once close to Castro who were defecting from him. Many of these were referred to in the State Department pamphlet referred to above. Some significant examples (and only *examples*) are:

Dr. José Miro Cardona, once Prime Minister of the Revolutionary Government.

Dr. Manuel Urrutia y Lleo, hero of the Revolution, Provisional President of the Revolutionary Government. Under house arrest after being forced to resign.

Manuel Ray Rivero, organized anti-Batista underground in Havana. Castro's Minister of Public Works.

Humberto Sori Marin, Castro's first Minister of Agriculture.

Major Huber Matos Benitez, hero of Sierra Maestra, revolutionary *commandante* of Camaguey Province, then thrown in jail.

Manuel Artime      )
Nino Diaz          )   Sierra Maestra heroes.
Justo Carrillo     )

Raul Chibas, fund raiser for the Revolution and fought with Castro in the hills.

Felippe Pazos, represented the 26th of July on the Junta of Liberation, and was appointed by Castro as President of the National Bank of Cuba.

Pedro Diaz Lanz, chief of the Cuban air force and Castro's personal pilot.

David Salvador, labor leader, "anti-Yanqui" pro-Castro secretary general of the Cuban trade union federation. Castro intervened on the Communist side against Salvador's free labor movement and jailed Salvador.

Miguel Angel Quevedo, editor of *Bohemia*.

Luis Conte Aguero, radio and television commentator.

Jose Pardo Llada, radio official famous for attacks against U.S. on Castro's behalf.

Further available evidence supporting the conclusion that internal support would be forthcoming if an effective internal opposition force could be established was:

a. Many requests for aid during the period 22 March to 17 April were received through Agency communications channels, some of which are noted in the Survey at pages 108–109. The issue discussed by the Survey as to why aid was not given is not here involved. The messages, however, do emphasize the number of groups anxious to engage in active opposition. For example, between 22 March and 17 April there were 15 unfulfilled drop requests in support of a claimed total of 5,000 men. Even after the landing between 17 and 22 April seven groups totaling about 3,350 men begged for support in order to fight. These groups were in Oriente (2,500 men); Camaguey (two groups totaling 400 men); Las Villas (three groups totaling 400 men); and Pinar del Rio (50 men).

b. Manuel Ray Rivero, the organizer of the anti-Batista underground and a member of the Cuban Revolutionary Council took the view that the internal resistance was so strong that Castro could be overthrown without an "invasion" from the outside. His view was not officially accepted but represented the informed view of an individual experienced in this field regarding the opposition potential. The disagreement with his conclusion had to do with what action was necessary to persuade the opposition to rebel, not as to its existence.

c. Sabotage from October 1960 to April 1961 was evidence of internal opposition activists even though aside from psychological benefits to the opposition, the sabotage caused insignificant damage in and of itself to the regime. Examples were:

1) Approximately 300,000 tons of sugar cane destroyed in 800 different fires.

2) Approximately 150 other fires, including the burning of 42 tobacco warehouses, two paper plants, 1 sugar refinery, two dairies, four stores, twenty-one Communist homes.

3) Approximately 110 bombings, including Communist Party offices, Havana power station, two stores, railroad terminal, bus terminal, militia barracks, railroad train.

4) Approximately 200 nuisance bombs in Havana Province.

5) Derailment of six trains, destruction of microwave cable and station, and destruction of numerous power transformers.

d. The view of many of the Brigade who had been members of the militia which confirmed the official estimate mentioned above, i.e., that only a small percentage of the militia would fight against a resolute opposition with strong fire power. This hard core was considered to number 5,000 – 8,000 at the most. The Army was considered to have been too disrupted to fight.

e. Students and their professors were in revolt, e.g., two thirds of the faculty of the University of the Oriente in December 1960 openly condemned Castro in a public statement. Other students were actively engaged in acts of disruption and subversion working with groups supported by the Agency.

f. Labor was in opposition. Not only was David Salvador in jail as indicated above, but open acts of opposition occurred, e.g., the electrical workers in December 1960 marched from union headquarters in Havana to the Presidential Palace to protest reductions, while on 18 January 1961 workers' wives were attacked by Castro's strong arm squads for demonstrating against the execution of workers (as "traitors") alleged to have sabotaged the Havana power plant.

Since the issue of what the internal reaction would have been under the conditions assumed necessary for effective internal support never arose, it is impossible to evaluate the accuracy of the prognosis. It can be said that no one expected an immediate uprising; no advance warning was given to the internal resistance, as a security precaution, to avoid any disclosure of D-Day; ample supplies existed to support uprising had groups showed themselves; communications existed that could have identified areas of resistance (though no communicator was able to join the resistance in the Escambray); no one expected the resistance to join the Brigade on the beach in anything but very small numbers; and it was estimated that the psychological impact of unopposed heavily armed B-26 aircraft flying up and down the island would be significant—an assumption based, of course, on control of the air.

Whatever the correct conclusion, in fact, might have been, the situation was such as to render the judgment (mentioned above) regarding internal support a reasonable one. Surely it was one painfully reached by many informed observers.

Post-invasion planning did exist contrary to the Survey's contention.

Some of it has been discussed above. In addition plans for a breakout from the beachhead had been generally worked out recognizing that precise details had to await knowledge of the exact situation. As indicated, the Brigade, it was considered, could maintain itself on the beachhead for a substantial period assuming no hostile air. Consequently, large reserves of supplies and materiel could have been landed; air attacks against enemy concentrations could have been flown; and an attack following heavy air strikes could have been executed when the time was considered most propitious. Such attack could also have been supported by concurrent air strikes, plus, if desired, the dropping of a small airborne force back of the enemy lines to cause disruption. Similarly, air drops of individuals or teams plus supplies could have been made to any active resistance throughout the island.

A further possibility was overt U.S. support in the form of supplies on the basis that the opposition government (the Cuban Revolutionary Council) would have landed on the beachhead, declared itself as the rightful government of Cuba, and requested and received recognition from the U.S. Such recognition could have been accorded on the theory that Castro's regime was a Soviet-dominated dictatorship and, therefore, not representative of or the choice of the Cuban people while the opposition government was democratic, as representative as possible, and offered a program for choice by the Cuban people, if it attained power. Conversely, the Castro regime by its dictatorial actions had removed from the people all methods of effecting a change except forceful overthrow. Such U.S. recognition, it was believed, would justify U.S. materiel support, if not active support to an offensive. It should be emphasized that U.S. recognition was not considered an essential part of the plan (useful as it would have been) since materiel support could have been provided anyhow.

The planning for failure was, it is believed, all that was possible. If, as happened, the failure occurred before the consolidation of the beachhead, there was little that could be done except an effort to salvage what little was possible. Had the beachhead been established, a number of possibilities were planned, none too satisfactory because a failure of the beachhead was at any time a serious blow. If the Brigade or parts thereof could move together, they were to attempt to reach the Escambray. Assuming some help from the country people, this might well have been feasible. Another possibility was the removal of individuals, conceivably units, by air and sea while teams and materiel could have been airdropped in other parts of Cuba, if resistance had become apparent.

As to the Agency's capability and the adequacy of the plan, the best answer — since the military aspects are the sole consideration — is to refer to the supporting military judgments which were based on full knowledge of the facts. Some evidence of attitudes just prior to D-Day is the message sent by Colonel Hawkins from Puerto Cabezas regarding the desirability of despatching the Brigade. (Attached as Annex A). This message is significant as it received wide circulation at the time in Washington, including the White House, and was accepted as essentially accurate.

The allegation of failure to appraise the chances of success realistically may be accurate but it is submitted that the available facts at least made the judgments reasonable. Moreover, what actually occurred supports these judgments. The Brigade landed with the benefit of surprise; it held its own while ammunition lasted (even though it failed to land some of its firepower); the B-26's when they got a shot at the Cuban tanks demolished them; and the attitude of many of the militia during the early states of the fight was favorable to the Brigade, including defections by militia men to the Brigade even at this early indecisive moment of the engagement. All serious damage was inflicted by the Cuban's air, essentially the three T-33 jets.

The supporting memoranda to General Taylor's oral report are relevant on these points. Memorandum No. 1, in discussing the operation expresses the view in paragraph 75 on page 26 that "the beachhead could not have survived long without substantial help from the Cuban population or without overt U.S. assistance." Two of the Cuban Study Group (Admiral Burke and Mr. Dulles), however, differed with this statement on the grounds that there was "insufficient evidence to support the conjectures of this paragraph."

A footnote on their views at the foot of page 75 went on to say:

"The well motivated, aggressive CEF fought extremely well without air cover and with a shortage of ammunition. They inflicted very severe losses on the less well trained Cuban Militia. Consequently, it is reasonable to believe that if the CEF had had ammunition and air cover, they could have held the beachhead for a much longer time, destroyed much of the enemy artillery and tanks on the roads before they reached the beachhead, prevented observation of the fire of the artillery that might have been placed in position and destroyed many more of the local Militia en route to the area. A local success by the landing party, coupled with CEF aircraft overflying Cuba with visible control of the air, could well have caused a chain reaction of success throughout Cuba with resultant defection of some of the Militia, increasing support from the populace and eventual success of the operation."

Therefore, even in retrospect the Brigade's inability to hold the beachhead for some time was not clear to well-informed individuals who had soaked themselves in all the available evidence. A prospective judgment in favor of success prior to the event would, therefore, seem understandable.

Finally, regarding the question of intelligence failures, the supporting memoranda to General Taylor's oral report state that the effectiveness of the Castro military forces, as well as that of his police measures, was not entirely anticipated or foreseen. Memorandum No. 3, however, setting forth conclusions says:

"Although the intelligence was not perfect, particularly as to the evaluation of the effectiveness of the T-33's, we do not feel that any failure of intelligence contributed significantly to the defeat." (Memorandum No. 3., para. 1. i., page 3).

TIDE 519
(IN 3197)

13 April 1961

1. MY OBSERVATIONS LAST FEW DAYS HAVE INCREASED MY CONFIDENCE IN ABILITY THIS FORCE TO ACCOMPLISH NOT ONLY INITIAL COMBAT MISSIONS BUT ALSO ULTIMATE OBJECTIVE OF CASTRO OVERTHROW.

2. REF* ARRIVED DURING FINAL BRIEFING OF BRIGADE AND BATTALION COMMANDERS. THEY NOW KNOW ALL DETAILS OF PLAN AND ARE ENTHUSIASTIC. THESE OFFICERS ARE YOUNG VIGOROUS INTELLIGENT AND MOTIVATED WITH A FANATICAL URGE TO BEGIN BATTLE FOR WHICH MOST OF THEM HAVE BEEN PREPARING IN THE RUGGED CONDITIONS OF TRAINING CAMPS FOR ALMOST A YEAR. I HAVE TALKED TO MANY OF THEM IN THEIR LANGUAGE. WITHOUT EXCEPTION THEY HAVE UTMOST CONFIDENCE IN THEIR ABILITY TO WIN. THEY SAY THEY KNOW THEIR OWN PEOPLE AND BELIEVE AFTER THEY HAVE INFLICTED ONE SERIOUS DEFEAT UPON OPPOSING FORCES THE LATTER WILL MELT AWAY FROM CASTRO WHO THEY HAVE NO WISH TO SUPPORT. THEY SAY IT IS CUBAN TRADITION TO JOIN A WINNER AND THEY HAVE SUPREME CONFIDENCE THEY WILL WIN ANY AND ALL ENGAGEMENTS AGAINST THE BEST CASTRO HAS TO OFFER. I SHARE THEIR CONFIDENCE.

3. THE BRIGADE IS WELL ORGANIZED AND IS MORE HEAVILY ARMED AND BETTER EQUIPPED IN SOME RESPECTS THAN U.S. INFANTRY UNITS. THE MEN HAVE RECEIVED INTENSIVE TRAINING IN THE USE OF THEIR WEAPONS INCLUDING MORE FIRING EXPERIENCE THAN U.S. TROOPS WOULD NORMALLY RECEIVE. I WAS IMPRESSED WITH THE SERIOUS ATTITUDE OF THE MEN AS THEY ARRIVED HERE AND MOVED TO THEIR SHIPS. MOVEMENTS WERE QUIET DISCIPLINED AND EFFICIENT AND THE EMBARKATION WAS ACCOMPLISHED WITH REMARKABLE SMOOTHNESS.

4. THE BRIGADE NOW NUMBERS 1400 A TRULY FORMIDABLE FORCE.

5. I HAVE ALSO CAREFULLY OBSERVED THE CUBAN AIR FORCES. THE AIRCRAFT ARE KEPT WITH PRIDE AND SOME OF THE B-26 CREWS ARE SO EAGER TO COMMENCE CONTEMPLATED OPERATIONS THAT THEY HAVE ALREADY ARMED THEIR AIRCRAFT. GERMOSEN INFORMED ME TODAY THAT HE CONSIDERS THE B-26 SQUADRON EQUAL TO THE BEST U.S. AIR FORCE SQUADRON.

6. THE BRIGADE OFFICERS DO NOT EXPECT HELP FROM THE U.S. ARMED FORCES. THEY ASK ONLY FOR CONTINUED DELIVERY OF SUPPLIES. THIS CAN BE DONE COVERTLY.

7. THIS CUBAN FORCE IS MOTIVATED STRONG WELL TRAINED ARMED TO THE TEETH AND READY. I BELIEVE PROFOUNDLY THAT IT WOULD BE A SERIOUS MISTAKE FOR THE UNITED STATES TO DETER IT FROM ITS INTENDED PURPOSE.

*Requested if experiences the last few days had in any way changed Colonel Hawkins' evaluation of the brigade.

## VI. ORGANIZATION AND COMMAND RELATIONSHIPS

The Survey reaches the flat conclusion that the project was "badly organized." The reasons given are:

"Command lines and management controls were ineffective and unclear. Senior Staffs of the Agency were not utilized; air support stayed independent of the project; the role of the large forward basis was not clear."

The Survey directs these criticisms exclusively at the Agency structure making essentially no effort to relate Agency organization and managerial problems to the participation in the project by other elements of the Government. Before responding, therefore, it should be stated that we share the views set forth in one of General Taylor's supporting memoranda and quoted in another section of this paper that "the Executive Branch of the Government was not organizationally prepared to cope with this kind of a paramilitary operation" and that "there was no single authority short of the President capable of coordinating the actions of CIA, State, Defense, and USIA." In other words, it was a U.S. rather than a CIA project.

The real organizational problem is one of the basic dilemmas of the U.S. Government, namely, how to manage military or quasi-military operations in peacetime—a dilemma accentuated in those instances involving an effort to maintain clandestinity. Since most of the operational acts involved in paramilitary projects of this nature raise or could, under certain circumstances, raise significant political issues, they normally require high level political clearance prior to being undertaken. Such clearance involves at least the State Department, often the White House, and, due to military implications, the Defense Department plus one or more of the military services. The description in another section of this paper of the extensive participation by and with other elements of the Government indicates that the Cuban project was clearly of this troublesome type.

The Survey's failure to examine or consider these relationships means that most of its criticisms limited as they are to Agency consideration alone, are too localized or provincial to be realistic or fully understandable. An analysis will, however, be attempted.

The criticism of command lines is, if properly understood, directed essentially at two major defects, one that the project lacked a single, high-level full time commander possessing stated broad powers and abilities sufficient for carrying out the mission; the other that there was a fragmentation of authority between the project chief, the military chief of the project's Paramilitary Staff and several high level officials, whose wide responsibilities elsewhere in the Agency prevented them from giving the project the attention it required.

The DCI allegedly "delegated his responsibility for major project decisions to a considerable extent." The Survey appears to support this statement on two grounds, first that the DCI relied on the DDCI "for policy matters involving air operations" and for "military advice he relied on the military officers detailed to the project." The consequence of this "reliance" according to the Survey was that the DCI was deprived "of completely objective counsel."

"Reliance on," according to normal usage, does not mean the same thing as "delegation of responsibility." Whatever the Survey intends to say in this connection, it is a fact that the DCI *never* delegated any portion of this responsibility at any moment during the project. Naturally he relied on others for many things (he could hardly run the entire project himself) and he even delegated *authority* (not *responsibility*) in some limited respects.

He did, for example, authorize within clearly understood limits the DDCI to approve certain aspects of Cuban overflights for him. It should be noted in this connection that the clearance of overflights resided in the first instance with the Special Group or the White House and was requested through briefings by the DCI or the DCI plus one of his people, normally the DDCI, the DD/P or both. Thereafter, whether or not an overflight was within the terms of the top level approval and was operationally sound was cleared by the DDCI on behalf of and at the direction of the DCI.

The DCI never released the authority regarding over-all air planning recommendations. The word "recommendations" is used because final air plans decisions lay at a higher level outside of the Agency. Before presentation to such outside authority (the Special Group or the White House) these recommendations were first passed on within the Agency by the DCI.

As far as reliance on military officers is concerned, the DCI obviously received briefings which were mainly given by the DD/P but often the DD/P presentation was expanded by statements from C/WH/4 (the Task Force Commander) his Paramilitary Chief or other individuals connected with the project as appropriate.

Both with regard to air and ground, the DCI also insisted upon and received the advice and judgment of air and ground military officers assigned by the Pentagon to study project plans and activities; of the JCS as a body, and of individual members of the JCS. This entire process has been explained elsewhere in this paper and is developed in considerable detail in the supporting memoranda to General Taylor's oral report.

Moreover, the DCI, almost without exception, held three staff meetings a week attended by his senior officials including the DD/P, COPS, and A/DDP/A. When any significant matter relating to Cuba needed approval or clarification, the DCI was briefed after one of these meetings. These briefings and meetings plus continuous telephone communications, plus cable traffic, kept the DCI current on all but the smallest details.

The DD/P is criticized by the Survey for "in fact directing the project, although this was only one of his many responsibilities." Presumably the Survey did not mean to suggest that the DD/P should have given up his other duties to be full time Task Force Commander. Consequently, his alleged fault must have been a failure to make a broad enough delegation of authority.

The Survey defines the limitations on the DD/P delegated authority by stating that C/WH/4 had "to apply constantly for the decision of policy questions and important operational problems" to the DD/P. It is suggested that, except in very unusual or certain "hot war" situations, such reservation of authority is the normal one between any unit commander and his next higher echelon. Moreover, until 17 April 1961 (the landing date) urgencies, although great, were never such as to make this sort of review impossible. Undoubtedly it was irksome to C/WH/4 in the same way that any higher authority is considered a problem to a commander who is anxious to push ahead without hurdles or outside restraint.

Quite apart from these considerations, however, the DD/P, because of the requirement to clear outside of the Agency many issues (including details) as policy questions, had to maintain a close control over the project in order to guard against omissions of such outside clearances and to be in a position to request them through the DCI.

To avoid delays in communications between WH and the DD/P, the A/DDP/A spent substantially full time on the project. His position was thoroughly understood by all involved though a purist chart-maker might have felt some concern as to the proper designation of the job on a chart. A/DDP/A was, in fact, an extension of the DD/P arm. He was physically located next to the DD/P; saw him constantly; had immediate access to him whenever he was available, and, therefore, knew instinctively what the DD/P reaction to most problems was and would be. Consequently, he could act for him in many instances while at the same time being fully aware of those situations which should be brought to the DD/P for decision. If chart terms are necessary, he was a senior special assistant with a perfectly clear and understood delegation of authority on matters which he could decide for the DD/P. This individual's availability plus the amount of time accorded the project by the DD/P personally meant that the Task Force was able to obtain decisions from the DD/P level rapidly provided that they were in the DD/P's jurisdictional competence. The many decisions already mentioned which required outside clearance had to be obtained either in accordance with regular procedures as in the case of the Special Group or by special arrangement if some other tribunal such as the White House was involved. The DD/P and the A/DDP/A were both positioned effectively with respect to the senior Agency or non-Agency officers involved to be able to arrange on the most expeditious basis possible whatever high level consideration might be required in given situations.

All existing decision-making procedures were, it is believed, well understood or if a new clearance procedure was needed for recurring activities, a special procedure was created. An example is the procedure for clearance of Cuban overflights, dated 24 October 1960, which is attached as Annex A.

The Survey criticized C/WH because he was "in the chain of command but "only in a partial sense." He signed many outgoing cables, supervised staffing activities and attended some of the meetings of the Special Group. "But the DD/P and his deputy dealt directly with the project chief, and gradually the Chief of WH Division began to play only a diminished role." All of this is essentially true (C/WH, however, was not in the chain of command except on certain specified well-understood matters) although the Survey fails to state that C/WH also sat in on substantially all of the DD/P and DCI meetings on the project attended by any WH personnel, and handled many of the policy negotiations with the State Department as well as some of the more difficult special problems with the Cuban political leaders and some other special negotiations, i.e. those involving possible economic sanctions (with the Treasury and some leading U.S. businessmen and lawyers) and those with particular individuals such as William D. Pawley. Also, of course, interrelationships with the many Agency stations throughout the Hemisphere and their activities were supervised by C/WH.

Even in retrospect, this arrangement with C/WH is believed to have been organizationally sound and would again be adopted under similar circumstances. Black and white organizational answers often do not meet the complex interplay of problems in a project involving as many facets as the Cuban one. Granted, each echelon, starting with the DCI, should have one individual in the next lower echelon to hold responsible for all decisions of that echelon but such individual responsibility was quite clearly identifiable in the project.

C/WH could have been the Task Force Commander but the DCI, having discussed the matter with C/WH, decided that, since C/WH could not be the Commander and also run the rest of WH Division, it was preferable for him to do the latter. Nevertheless, C/WH had long and wide experience in the WH area; connections with many Latin Americans as well as Americans with WH associations; intimacy with the WH Division, its personnel and activities, and had been for many years at a policy level in the Agency. Consequently, his advice and reactions were wanted in the Cuban project and he was asked to stay as close to project activities as he could while performing his other duties. The matters listed above were, therefore, covered by C/WH pursuant to this concept. Actually, C/WH had substantially the same relationship to this project as he had to the Guatemalan anti-Arbenz project which worked well. Nothing new, therefore, was involved.

The Chief of the Task Force (i.e. C/WH/4) is not criticized but his superiors are criticized for selecting for this post only a GS-15 at the fourth echelon in the organization of the Agency. With regard to grade, the C/WH/4 was a senior GS-15 or, in other words, the equivalent of a senior full colonel in the Army. More grade could hardly be required for the top operational command job. As to competence and experience for the post, it is felt that he will compare favorably with any officer in the CS.

Perhaps the echelon was too low but this is a matter of judgment. Actually the C/WH/4 was at the third not the fourth echelon, the first being the DCI and the DDCI and the second the DD/P. If the Agency alone is considered, it is believed that the echelon was not too low. If all of the Executive Department elements involved are considered, numerous other factors are introduced which involve so different an organizational concept as to make any relative analysis impossible. This overall organizational problem has been mentioned and is now under Governmental study so that it would seem preferable here to discuss only the internal Agency relationships.

At any rate, C/WH/4 for reasons already discussed was obviously not free to make all decisions on his own whatever the Survey may advocate in this respect. He was, however, very much the Task Force Commander. All elements of WH/4 in and out of Washington responded to his command. The extent to which he had to clear decisions with higher authority has been indicated. It is a matter of judgment whether or not the delegation of authority was adequate but it must be re-emphasized that the judgment of most non-delegated items lay outside of the Agency (i.e., as General Taylor's memorandum said, "there was no single authority short of the President capable of coordinating . . ."), and within the Agency (once the problem of non-Agency clearances is recognized and accepted) the powers reserved by the DD/P and the DCI were in keeping with normal relationships between command echelons. Moreover, the DD/P, supplemented by the A/DDP/A, was able to expedite decisions so delay was held down as much as possible. Admittedly, the U.S. organizational structure as a whole was not satisfactory for this type of operation. The Government, as indicated, fully appreciates this and is attempting to find a solution.

The Survey makes another point regarding too many echelons, namely, that "the top level had to be briefed by briefers who themselves were not doing the day-to-day work." This conclusion is another statement of a troublesome problem of senior governmental management in the complex modern world. How can the individuals informed on details communicate to the top policy decision makers the relevant parts of their knowledge in a timely and fully informative way? In the Cuban project, it can only be said that the top level saw more of the detail people than is usual. The DCI and the DD/P brought C/WH/4 or the project's Paramilitary Chief with them to substantially all the Presidential meetings on Cuba. Moreover, the Chairman of the JCS brought General Gray (and often another member of his team) with him. Detail knowledge was, therefore, represented.

Moreover, of course, briefings at high levels within each interested element were numerous. General Lemnitzer and the Secretary of Defense received daily briefings in the period immediately prior to 17 April. The Assistant Secretary of State (ARA) and the Secretary of State were constantly briefed throughout the project. McGeorge Bundy, Rostow and Schlesinger had almost daily contact with the DD/P or the A/DDP/A. The DCI and the DDCI, of course, also were kept current on details. In view of this and the extensive interdepartmental coordination involved in this project and described in another section, the amount of top level detailed information was unusually complete. Admittedly, however, this does not mean that it was satisfactorily complete on all issues and this is one of the problems involved in the above mentioned Governmental study on organization for projects of this nature.

Three other Washington Headquarters factors are described as "extraordinary" by the Survey, namely, that:

1) COPS played "only a very minor part in the project." COPS also allegedly "declined to involve himself with the project" although on at

least two occasions he was given "express warning that the project was being perilously mismanaged";

2) The DD/P Senior Staffs, the Agency's top level technical advisors, "were not consulted fully" but "they allowed themselves to be more or less ignored"; and

3) The Project Review Committee did not review the project.

These allegations are so "extraordinary" (to borrow the Survey's word) that it is difficult to accept a serious intent on the part of the Survey's authors. Quite naturally COPS spent little time on the project. The DD/P office was a three-man office, one of whom (A/DDP/A) was spending essentially full-time on the project and another of whom (DD/P) was spending a very substantial part of his time. Consequently, it was only logical, if not essential, that COPS devote his time to the rest of the world as well as to the numerous remaining issues of internal management.

As to the statement about express warnings of perilous mismanagement, it is indeed strange that such a charge should not be identified at least sufficiently to permit some assessment of how responsible the warnings were and of what they consisted. COPS remembers receiving no such warning. Of course, COPS, as well as many other people were told on numerous occasions that some mismanagement as well as other mistakes were occurring in the project. In what project does this not occur, particularly if it is urgent, complex, and disruptive of normal procedures? These "warnings" were given such attention and recognition as the facts in each instance warranted. Actually, the Survey is unclear as to what it believes COPS should have done though the inference is that he should have used the alleged "warnings" as a basis for taking the project away from the DD/P.

The criticism regarding consultation with the Senior Staffs obviously is directed at a failure to obtain available competent advice. Undoubtedly, the Senior Staffs had good officers who could have been helpful. The judgement involved, however, was at what point do you draw the line when you have operational activities to be accomplished. Each of the Senior Staffs assigned officers to work with the project staffs. No Senior Staff officer not so assigned could have been kept sufficiently well-informed without full and constant briefings. In view of the briefing obligations already in existence, it was decided that additional briefing burdens were unacceptable. Moreover as indicated above, a line had to be drawn and it was felt that sufficient senior personnel were fully involved. The Survey's criticism in this connection is based on a concept of a normal DD/P project rather than an extraordinary one like Cuba. In this connection, it should again be emphasized that participation by other elements of the Government is wholly omitted by the Survey.

The Project Review Committee's (PRC) clearance at the most under PRC procedures would have involved a review of the proposed project in its early stages with a view to determining whether or not it should proceed. The peculiar nature of the Cuban project resulted, as already indicated, in clearances throughout the Government at levels which make it hard to comprehend how the PRC would have affected the process. Moreover, even internally in the Agency, the PRC is only advisory to the DCI and it is doubtful if its normal procedures were intended to apply to this type of project.

The Agency, particularly the DD/P, is criticized for failing to deprive the Development Projects Division (DPD), the Agency's air arm, of its independence by placing it within the organizational structure of the project. The proper organizational positioning of an air commander in relation to the ground commander has long been a matter of argument in the Armed Services. The same difference evidenced itself in the Cuban project with WH-4 favoring the Marine view of complete subordination of air conflicting with the DPD air view advocating a separate command with responsibility to support. This conflict was never fully settled and did cause friction (and probably in a broader sense never will be to the full satisfaction of all the services). It is not felt that it created any more serious difficulties. At any rate, the DD/P dealt with this difference in the only possible practical way in early October 1960. On 5 October the Paramilitary Chief sent a study through C/WH to DD/P expressing at length his views on the command relationships for air operations. On 12 October 1960, the DD/P wrote an answer which set forth the controlling decisions. A copy of this memorandum is attached as Annex B. Operational control of air forces and facilities required for the project was assigned to Chief of the Task Force. An air staff section for air operations was created in the Task Force. The Acting Chief of DPD was designated chief of the new air section which was to include all DPD personnel when actually employed on project business.

Since DPD had many air commitments to service outside of the Cuban project, AC/DPD was directed to report to the DD/P in the usual manner as to this non-Cuban business.

In view of the foregoing, the Survey is simply wrong when it says "The project chief had no command authority over air planning and air operations. The DPD unit established for this purpose was completely independent."

The Survey is also wrong in stating that there was no day-to-day continuing staff relationship. Two DPD officers (one, an air operations officer) were assigned full-time from DPD to the project and were physically located with it. In addition, a senior air operations officer attended daily staff meetings. He also spent all of his time with and on the project. Consequently, the air unit was organized to be completely responsive to the requirements of the Task Force with the exception of air safety considerations. In addition, DPD facilities (e.g., weather, communications mapping and planning air operations, photographic intelligence and related interpretation services) were made available as needed. These were not physically moved as they were more effective in place and were able by remaining to service other Agency requirements as well. In fact the DPD relationship with WH was much closer than quite effective relationships which it had with other Area Divisions having similar requirements.

The Survey devotes several pages to criticism of the WH-4 intelligence collection covering a number of points. The most serious allegation is that the interpretation of intelligence was "entrusted to officers who were so deeply engaged in preparations for the invasion that their judgments could not have been expected to be altogether objective." One of the essential items referred to is the estimate regarding the effect of the strike force landing in triggering "an uprising among the Cuban population." The Survey's lack of understanding of the project's theory on this point and the evidence for the judgments reached has been discussed in detail elsewhere.

It might be noted again that one of the supporting memoranda to General Taylor's oral report concluded "we do not feel that any failure of intelligence contributed significantly to the defeat." Moreover, two members of General Taylor's four-man Cuban Study Group, even in retrospect, still felt after hearing all the evidence that the operation might have been successful had the Cuban air power been eliminated.

Probably if any similar effort were to be attempted in the future an even greater association between DD/P and DD/I should be worked out for evaluation purposes. In view of the above conclusions, however, it would seem fair to say that admitting failures (which indeed is done) they were not as obvious as the Survey suggests. In fact a case can still be made that the estimates were right.

The Survey's other criticism regarding WH/4 intelligence activities will be dealt with briefly. The creation of a G-2 in the paramilitary unit rather than with the Project FI Section is strongly criticized. The alleged bad consequence of this error, i.e., improper estimates, has just been discussed. In other respects on this point the Survey is inaccurate. The Chief of the FI Section did attend WH/4 staff meetings. There was liaison between the G-2 and FI Sections. They both saw cables. They exchanged intelligence and generally supplemented each other.

The remaining criticism regarding intelligence is directed at a failure to support the Miami Base. Since the Base raises a number of other considerations, they will be discussed together.

The Survey, in effect, commends many of the operational results achieved by the Miami Base. The FI and CI activities are mentioned in paragraphs 10 and 11 on page 70 and, it is believed, that these accomplishments are commendable.

The PM side involves a more complicated picture. The Survey is critical of the fact that Headquarters in Washington kept too tight a control on Miami. Consequently, too little authority was delegated to enable Miami to function effectively. There is no doubt that a number of Miami officers felt that they were being over-controlled. No good operations officer ever feels differently or if he does, he is not doing his job. Consequently, the normal, healthy operating effort to shake the bit and run free was part of the attitude held by Miami operators in relation to Washington.

Washington, on the other hand, was anxious to avoid moving Headquarters functions to Miami or treating Miami as a field station which it clearly was not. Miami was not Cuba. Communications from target areas could be received and handled just as fast in Washington as in Miami. Many aspects of operational planning could be handled just as well, if not better, in Washington than Miami. Coordination with other operating areas was better handled in Washington. There were, of course, exceptions. Some of the more obvious exceptions were that Miami was a center for Cubans and an active interchange by sea between Miami and Cuba was a fact of life. The project organizational concept, therefore, was to provide Miami with people and the authority needed to take advantage of these potentials. Mainly, of course, this meant FI and CI activities, some propaganda activities, some special training, and the handling of the Cuban exile leaders. The Survey apparently does not find major fault (except as noted in the following paragraphs) with respect to Headquarters-Miami organizational relations in these fields, whatever the Survey may say about these activities in other respects.

The Survey does to some extent criticize the training run by Miami by saying that there was no full-time chief of training, no training objectives or plan and that much of it was merely a case officer doing the best he could. The results allegedly were haphazard. For example, "one man was trained in a hotel room to make a parachute jump." Obviously a full jump course would have been preferable but the Survey's comment indicates a lack of under-standing of the problem. In WW II, many officers did successful operational jumps with only minimal ground training. Combat pilots and air crews, when forced to jump, did so without having even been trained in a hotel room. Anyhow, as the Survey says the hotel-trained jumper "made one (jump) suc-cessfully!" It might also have been stated by the Survey that the man in ques-tion was in his early thirties, in excellent physical condition and an *expert tumbler*. Moreover, his one successful jump was the only one he was asked to do. This case, unimportant in itself, is referred to because it brings out several relevant points, i.e., in projects of this kind operating necessities are handled in the best possible way. Agents are often used without adequate training in the hope of getting some benefits; training sites are often inadequate but are accepted as the only available ones in view of all applicable conditions; op-erational equipment is not selected as being the best for the job but the best for the job in the light of applicable limitations; drop zones, reception com-mittees and internal organization are rarely what would be described as ideal in the training text book. Communications are difficult, zones hard to iden-tify and agents are on the run and harassed. Since the Survey at no point suggests the existence of those problems, some reference to their presence seems essential.

The hotel room as a training site for parachute jumping is only one of many examples of the Survey applying unrealistic criteria. We repeat what has been previously stated that the project surely had many faults but they should be tested against what was possible not against a theoretical and im-possible ideal.

Moreover, the Survey provides some evidence inconsistent with the fore-going. In paragraph 5 on page 126 the care taken in selection and screening of Useppa Island trainees is described. Paragraph 12 on page 129 sets forth the training given to 178 trainees originally prepared for infiltration. "In all," the Survey states, "178 men (including 23 radio operators) had been trained in security, intelligence collection, and reporting, propaganda and agitation, subversive activities, resistance organization, reception operations, explo-sives and demolitions, guerrilla action, and similar matters." This would seem reasonably complete and organized. Granting a normal complement of faults and failures, it is still believed that the Miami PM operational and train-ing record is a good one and that this will be supported by the results.

After November 1960 the PM focus was away from Miami. Under the "in-vasion" concept training, air operations, and planning were the major problems and these were primarily located outside of Miami. Nevertheless, Miami had much to do in connection with portions of these activities. Recruitment was largely done in Miami. Despatching of materiel and recruits took place from Opalocka; PM agents were infiltrated from and exfiltrated to Miami; communications and certain other limited training was handled in Miami, and the efforts to find and maintain maritime assets centered in Miami.

As between the two offices, Headquarters retained the final decisions on any operation activity directly involving Cuban soil or territorial waters. The concern of non-Agency elements of the Executive Department, already described, meant that it was inadvisable to permit operational decisions involving Cuba to be made outside of Washington. Moreover, with the speed of communication the extra time required was normally acceptable, since not operationally fatal, even though aggravating to those involved (i.e., mainly Miami officers). Of course, overflight decisions *had* to come to Washington as did landings of any substantial amounts of materiel. Small exfiltration and infiltration operations could have been decided in Miami but policy limitations, such as no entry into Cuban territorial waters of boats having Americans aboard, made close Washington supervision advisable. Moreover, delay in obtaining decisions on these latter type operations was especially minimal since in substantially all of these cases WH/4 was authorized to make the decision. Actually, as pointed out by the Survey, Headquarters seldom had any difference of view with Miami.

As far as PM results were concerned, the statistics were that in mid-April 1961, 43 trained PM agents (these are in addition to the 31 FI agents mentioned in Para. 10, page 70 of the Survey) were on the ground in Cuba of which 13 were regularly functioning, non-doubled radio operators and four more were radio operators but in reserve since they had no sets of their own. The geographic distribution of both these agents and radio operators was pretty good, covering most of the island.

The maritime operations handled by Miami had by mid-April landed 88,000 pounds of materiel (which with the 27,800 lbs. actually delivered by air provided the resistance up to 17 April with a total of 115,800 lbs.), had infiltrated 79 bodies and exfiltrated 51 bodies. Admittedly, much of the material, though by no means all of it, was landed on the north shore in Havana Province since this was a resistance center. Consequently, those who wanted it and those who could handle it were concentrated there—particularly in the early days. Of the 88,000 lbs. total, however, about 45,000 lbs. was in provinces other than Havana, i.e., about 19,000 lbs. in Matanzas and 26,000 lbs.

in Pinar del Rio, Las Villas and Camaguey. In addition, some materiel was landed on the south coast at both the west and east ends, i.e., a small amount, perhaps 800 lbs. in Oriente and 20,000 lbs. in Pinar del Rio. In the early days after a ship with the range was available, a few efforts were made to land some materiel in the central part of the south coast but connections were never made with the reception parties. For a substantial period (at least two months) prior to the landing the central south coast was intentionally avoided since it was felt to be vital not to provide even the slightest suggestion of operational interest near possible landing areas.

Some of the specific criticisms of the Miami Base should be mentioned.

1.) Conflict and confusion between Headquarters and Miami was said to exist, resulting in duplication of effort and division of control as to both agents and in the maritime field as well as high phone bills and unnecessary cables. The duplication of effort undoubtedly existed to some extent, particularly in the summer and fall of 1960 as the organization was being set up, but the Survey does not give enough specifics to enable direct answer, and undue or serious duplication is not remembered. As to confusion of channels, there was surely some confusion in the early days on Washington-Miami calls, but in the fall of 1960, rules were established which, it is believed, adequately clarified this problem. The division of control on maritime assets was intended, namely, the small boats were considered tactical and were under Miami control, the big boats strategic and were, therefore, kept under Headquarters control in order to keep them available for and ready to support the main landing. As far as is known, this division of control, which is considered to have been sound, caused no real difficulty.

2.) Miami allegedly received almost no intelligence support. The general nature of these allegations plus a failure to indicate what the alleged consequences of the errors were once more make it difficult to answer directly. Obviously, there was no intention to deprive Miami of needed support and no Miami operation is known to have failed because of lack of operational intelligence. Beach areas and the internal Cuban situation were as well known to Miami as to Washington. U-2 photography did not go to Miami, but it was not needed for any of the Miami decisions. Also, it was available in Washington to Miami officers. As to Special Intelligence, the Miami Base was supported by a whole Staff D unit at another location. Miami did not, it is true, have a Staff D officer in Base Headquarters. An FI officer, however, was given the responsibility of digesting all Special Intelligence material in order to pass it to operations officers if important. In addition, he briefed the operations officers on this material twice a week.

3.) Security is attacked. Obviously many aspects of the Cuban project were public knowledge. With the required relations with many Cubans, politicians, military, and otherwise; recruitment efforts; press, magazine, radio and other propaganda programs, a substantial amount of undesired publicity along with the desired was unavoidable. Otherwise, it is believed that the security record of the project was not too bad. For example, it is now known that any case officer was ever "blown" by true name. The Useppa Island operation was never disclosed. U.S. training sites were mentioned in the press but not located specifically and were not, it is believed, identified. The movement of the brigade from Guatemala to Nicaragua and from Nicaragua to Zapata was not discovered. In view of the efforts to find out everything by the Cubans and the U.S. press, these were significant accomplishments. Sending agents to Cuba who had known each other in training is criticized and blame is registered for one radio operator who knew "almost every paramilitary operation in Cuba from the beginning of the project." In reply, it can be said that every effort was made to send agents trained together to different parts of Cuba. Admittedly, there were cases where they may have moved together after arrival (e.g., working their way into the city of Havana). No case is known, however, where two agents trained together were despatched together to the same place. As to the knowledgeable radio operator, it is quite true that there was a man with exclusive knowledge of operations. He served under three resistance chiefs, the first two having been killed. Each of these chiefs chose him as their command communications channel, thereby evidencing the utmost confidence in him. He managed to escape and is now an instructor for the Agency. No reason is known as to why the belief in him was not justified. The disregard of security rules by trained agents was regrettable but Cuban, or indeed human, discipline is fallible. No instance is reported or known where such indiscipline was too serious or could have been avoided. As to American lack of discipline the Survey cites only one case, i.e., that of a case officer in a Miami motel. The Survey might also have said that this case was *thoroughly* investigated immediately and reported on long before the project was completed. Had the Survey mentioned this, it might also have indicated that unfortunate as the incident was, the DCI on the recommendation of the DD/P, decided that in view of all the circumstances the officer had made a mistake but an understandable one and not one requiring action other than a warning to increase future safeguards. As to screening recruits, it was impossible to use the same precautions regarding recruits to the camps, particularly toward the end when the recruiting rate was high, as was used with individual agents. In camp, however, they were members of a group making individual activity difficult and even if they had known something, they had no means of communication. The pre-landing movements and the landing, it must be remembered, remained unknown. Also, the brigade members discharged their duties well. Bad consequences, therefore, of the looser procedures were not too evident.

SECRET

24 October 1960

EYES ONLY

MEMORANDUM FOR:   A/DDP/A
C/WH Division
C/WH/4
AC/DP Division

    The following procedures shall apply to all Cuban overflights undertaken under the Cuban Project, with the exception of any U-2 reconnaissance missions. Approval for the latter shall be obtained and instructions issued in accordance with standard U-2 procedures.

    1. Prior to sending any notification to the field, the DD/P and A/DDP/A (or one of them if either is unavailable) shall be briefed on the operational plan. If possible DDP/EBM shall be included in the briefing in order to be informed when the matter is presented to the Special Group.

    2. WH/4 should be responsible for arranging this briefing. As a rule it should cover at least the following aspects of the proposed operation:

    a. Status and means of communication with reception party.
    b. Detailed flight plan.
    c. Communications plan.

A representative of DPD should always be included to cover the second aspect.

    3. The DD/P, or A/DDP/A on his behalf, shall make arrangements for an appropriate briefing of the D/DCI on each such flight. Normally such briefing will occur after a DD/P plan has been decided upon following the briefing referred to in paragraph 1 above. In case of urgency, however, the DD/P, or A/DDP/A on his behalf, may decide to combine these briefings into a single briefing in order to save time. /N.B.: All briefings of either the DCI or the D/DCI on Cuban Project matters including the above shall be arranged through the office of the DD/P./

    4. Following the above briefings an appropriate message, or messages,

will be sent to the field. Since an approval of the operation and of specific operational plans will have been obtained in the briefings, messages may be released by C/WH/4 (and AC/DPD as appropriate), provided they communicate plans reviewed at the briefings. If, however, any message includes important instructions the substance of which has not already been reviewed then it should be released by the DD/P or D/DCI as appropriate.

5. No flight shall be dispatched until the Special Group has been advised of the plan or the DCI has specifically waived this requirement.

RICHARD M. BISSELL, JR.
Deputy Director
(Plans)

TOP SECRET

12 October 1960

MEMORANDUM FOR:    Chief, WH-4

SUBJECT:    Organization and Command Relationships WH-4 and Development Projects Division

REFERENCE:    Memo for C/WH-4, dated 5 October 1960, from C/WH/4/PM, subject: Study on "Organization and Command Relationships of Cuban Task Force (CTF) for Air Operations"

1. *Comment on Reference*: The referenced study I find penetrating and well expressed. The facts set forth in paragraph 2 are accurately presented and the considerations elaborated in paragraph 3 have great force. On the other hand, certain additional considerations bearing on the problem appear to have been ignored. When these are taken into account, the conclusions as stated in paragraph 4 require slight modification and the recommendations set forth in paragraph 5 must be substantially modified in order to be acceptable.

2. *Additional Considerations Bearing on the Problem*:

a. As stated in the reference present command relationships do not give the Cuban Task Force Commander (C/WH/4) control over all the major assets committed or proposed to be committed to this operation. In particular, air capabilities are under the control of AC/DPD, a separate component subject to no common command below the level of the DD/P. Although the referenced paper does not specifically refer to other resources required for the CTF which are not under the command of C/WH-4, it is important to emphasize that this project will require extensive support from other organizational components and that no contemplated arrangements will give C/WH-4, command authority over all the resources and supporting activities upon which the success of the project depends. Accordingly, the issue raised by the paper is whether with respect to air assets the dividing line between assets under the command of the C/WH-4 and other assets remaining under separate command but used in support of the Cuban Project should be drawn as at present or should be redrawn in such a way as to place part of DPD under command of C/WH-4.

b. The reference argues that the proper place to draw the line is between the Air Support Section of DPD, which should be transferred to the control of C/WH-4, and the other elements of that component. It is believed that this judgment is erroneous. In actual fact, the Cuban Project will require at one time or another the performance of operational and supporting activities by most of the branches of DPD. The reason is that DPD has been developed as a largely self-sufficient, integrated organization which includes staff sections for not only operations, but logistics, personnel, finance, security, and administration—all of which may have some part to play in the Cuban Project. Specifically, it will probably be desirable for logistic support of air operations to be managed by DPD. As for operational planning and Headquarters monitoring of operations, it may well be desirable to use the DPD control room and communications facility. The DPD Cover Officer certainly has important contributions to make as does the Security Section. Even the Air Proprietaries Branch will be concerned with the Cuban Project because of the need for some of its resources. In order, therefore, to place under the command of C/WH-4 all of the air assets he may require it would be necessary to transfer a substantial part of DPD.

c. The foregoing suggests that the proper dividing line between the authority of C/WH-4 and that of AC/DPD should be redrawn in such a way that perhaps half of the latter component would be under the command of the Cuban Task Force Commander. In fact, however, it would be inefficient and probably wholly infeasible to draw a dividing line in this fashion. All of the Branches of DPD which have responsibilities for the Cuban Project, and most of the personnel who will discharge those responsibilities, also have concurrent duties which fall outside of the responsibility of C/WH-4. If DPD were a large Headquarters it would at least be feasible to split each Branch into two pieces but such is not the case. Moreover, the burden of the Cuban Project activities and of other business will vary from day to day and week to week. Efficient utilization of personnel requires that in many cases the same individuals perform both sets of duties.

3. *Supplementary Conclusions*: It is concluded that DPD as an organizational unit cannot be split into two parts, one of which would have full and

exclusive responsibility for Cuban Project activities and be placed under the command of C/WH-4. Taking this conclusion in conjunction with those stated in paragraph 4 of the reference it would appear that a solution must be sought not by splitting DPD, but by placing the whole of that Division under the control of the CTF Commander with respect to air activities which are in fact Cuban project operations. This solution will have the added and vital advantage of making available to C/WH-4 as a senior staff officer, AC/DPD who is the senior air commander in the Agency.

4. *Physical Separation*: The considerations set forth in paragraph 2 above suggest that no modification of command relationships will overcome the major difficulties that grow out of the physical separation of WH-4 and DPD. It is manifestly infeasible to house the whole of DPD in the Cuban Project headquarters. The physical location of the DPD Air Support Section with WH-4 may be desirable but obviously will leave the DPD Operations Control Room and its Logistics and Administrative Branches in a remote location. Accordingly, such matters as the devising of cover stories, the working out of budgets and funding arrangements, certain security business, and the clearance of many cables will still have to be done between officers who are housed some distance apart. It should be emphasized that this is inherent in any arrangement whereby the full resources of DPD are employed in support of the Cuban Project. Perhaps the most serious problem is that presented by the remoteness of AC/DPD's office from that of C/WH-4. This can only be overcome by reasonably frequent meetings between those two individuals. The inconvenience which is the cost of this solution is the price that must be paid for the employment in the Cuban Project of the best technical talent available to the Agency under circumstances that will permit that talent to be used parttime for the performance of other essential tasks.

5. *Task Force Concept*: A solution along the lines outlined in paragraph 3 above is in the main consistent with comments on the military tank force concept contained in paragraph 3.b. of the reference. In particular, the proposed solution will permit unity of command. It must be recognized, however, that this solution will in effect provide C/WH-4 with a large air section and with the services of a senior staff officer for air activities. It is the size and competence of the air section thus provided that precludes physical integration as explained in paragraph 4 preceding. Moreover, if such an air section is to be used efficiently and to make its full contribution, C/WH-4 must practice substantial delegation to his air section and should recognize that it is com-

petent to handle details in the implementation of broad instructions issued by him. It is especially desirable that full use be made of DPD in its capacity as the air section of the Cuban Project, along with other staff sections of WH-4 as appropriate, in the development of military plans. It will be necessary, if high professional standards are to be maintained, for several military specialists, of which air represents one, to be made use of in planning as well as in operations .

6. *Approved Action*:

a. Operational control of all air forces and facilities required and employed in the Cuban Project will be assigned to Chief, CTF.

b. Chief, CTF will exercise this control through a newly created staff section for air operations in the CTF.

c. AC/DPD will serve as the Chief of the CTF Air Section. The staff of the Air Section will include any and all DPD personnel when actually employed on Cuban Project business.

d. For DPD business unrelated to the Cuban Project, AC/DPD will continue to report in the usual manner to the DD/P. When and if questions arise concerning the allocation of DPD resources as between the Cuban Project and other requirements and activities, such questions will be resolved by the DD/P.

e. The Cuban Task Force as presently constituted has a unified force with a single Headquarters. If and when it should seem desirable to establish a forward Headquarters or a Field Command having responsibility for military operations in which air and other forces will be employed, the constitution of any such Field Command and its command channels to CTF Headquarters will require careful consideration. The desirability of such a combined Field Command and relationship between the CTF Air Section (DPD) and air assets committed in Field operations will be considered when military plans are more nearly complete.

(signed)
RICHARD M. BISSELL, JR.
Deputy Director
(Plans)

## VII. PERSONNEL

The Survey is critical of the Project's personnel management in two major respects:

1) The Project was not staffed throughout with top-quality people; and

2) A number of people were not used to the best advantage.

There are three basic difficulties common to the entire Survey which are equally and perhaps especially applicable to the sections on personnel and which make specific responsive answers almost impossible. They are the existence of:

1) Unsupported allegations of fact as in paragraph 5 on page 42, which will be discussed further below.

2) Conclusions unsupported by facts as in paragraph 13 on page 45 where a number of "obstacles" are stated in such general terms as to make their understanding difficult or in paragraph 3 on page 42 where it is stated that as a result of a number of factors "*none* of the most experienced, senior operating officers of the Agency participated full time in the project." (Underlining supplied).

3) An admixture of allegations some of which apply to the DD/P generally (e.g., lack of Spanish linguists; defective nature of entire CS staffing system; some of which apply to the government or the Department of Defense (e.g., problems with Armed Forces; and some relate to the Project.

An effort, however, will be made to be specific in reply and where this is impossible to indicate the difficulty. Regarding inadequate competence in staffing, it should be stated that the Survey mentions no names. A somewhat general response is, therefore, unavoidable, but to be reasonably specific, it has been felt that the names and the backgrounds of a number of the senior officers in the project, excluding the DD/P, A/DDP/A, and C/WH, would be helpful in determining the managerial judgments in this selection. (See Annex A). Support personnel, including communications, have not been included since the Survey is rightly complimentary of their performance.

A major criticism by the Survey in connection with personnel assignments was an alleged failure to carry out a statement made by the DCI in April 1960 that he would do anything necessary to provide the personnel needed for success. In fact, this was given substantial recognition. On 15 April 1960, the practice was established that if the Project wished to secure the services of a particular individual about whose release there was some question, C/WH would advise the A/DDP/A who would examine the case with the DD/P.

Obviously *carte blanche* could not be given but a rapid procedure was established for resolution of difficult cases. In this connection, it is not clear if the Survey in paragraph 1 on page 41 is criticizing a failure to give *carte blanche*, but, if so, the conclusions suggest an organizational concept with which we disagree.

The Chief of the Clandestine Service Personnel Office (CSPO) also had meetings with the A/DDP/A in which the DCI's views were discussed (at least one of which is recorded in a Memorandum for the Record, dated 22 April 1960) and the CSPO arranged a procedure with WH-4 whereby personnel requests were brought to him either by name or by skill requirement, then by him to the appropriate Panel and finally to the element in question. The understanding was, as indicated above, that difficult cases would be brought to the DD/P via the A/DDP/A. The purpose of this procedure was to avoid the need for WH-4 negotiating directly with other elements regarding personnel thereby eliminating any potential divisional conflicts.

On 16 May 1960, COPS sent an EYES ONLY memorandum to Staff and Division Chiefs and Chief, Operational Services indicating the need of WH for clerical assistance as well as imposing certain requirements on the addressees for help in this request. A copy is attached as Annex B.

Again on 25 August 1960 at the DD/P weekly staff meeting attended by Division and Staff Chiefs of the CS, COPS, in order to reemphasize the above, announced that the DD/P wanted to be sure that WH-4 was receiving "enough first class people to assure success in their efforts." The solution announced was:

"We have staffed WH-4 thus far without seriously interfering with other operations and activities. The seriousness of the situation demands your most sympathetic consideration of requests for temporary assistance to them. They now have about a dozen critical officer vacancies. We have agreed to having WH-4 suggest the names of those officers whom they would prefer to have particular jobs. The CS Personnel Office will be in touch with you on the names produced by WH-4 and on others identified as being qualified. If you can possibly spare them for the next few months, I urge you to do so. If you feel you cannot spare them, please tell the CSPO your reasons. Mr. Barnes, Mr. Bissell or I will then attempt to judge the relative priorities and make a decision respecting such assignments."

In view of the foregoing, there can be little doubt that senior CS officers knew of the CIA policy to support WH-4 in its personnel requirements. The success or failure of the application of the policy is, of course, a matter of judgment. Obviously no personnel roster is ever wholly satisfactory. Conversely, no project can take *any* officer regardless of other commitments. The attached roster, it is believed, establishes that on an impartial judgment the project was served with officers of experience and competence.

Obviously the requirements of the Project were unusual and urgent, but a review of the pace at which officers (i.e., staff not contract) were assigned and detailed has revealed no more than the usual problems, e.g., a requesting officer wanting help more rapidly than provided and some junior officers being less qualified than desired. On the whole, however, assignments and details were kept pretty well up-to-date and the caliber adequate. In a number of cases the performance of many officers responded to the challenge of the project, and, consequently, was better than might have been anticipated. In this connection, it might be noted that despite the enormous time demands, inconveniences, family separations, and other difficulties imposed on personnel the project's record for sick leave or absenteeism was so good as to be spectacular.

It might be noted that the CSPO, one of the few senior officers with whom the I.G. or his representatives had any discussions on this matter, asked the chief investigating officer what officers were considered poor. One PM officer was named. The CSPO then demonstrated that, although this officer was disliked by some people, he had been specifically requested by WH-4, had performed extremely well and in fact was continued in WH-4 after the misfortunes of April 1961 because of his performance in the project. No more was then said about this individual but no other examples were offered despite a specific request for names.

In view of the foregoing, it is suggested that the Survey allegations be at the very least set aside until specific evidence be introduced to which an answer can be addressed. The few minor points listed by the Survey regarding personnel are discussed below:

1. A basic mistake was made by filling key spots early without realizing how much the project would grow with the result that officers often ended up supervising three to four times as many people as originally anticipated.

The inference of supervisors beyond their depth is clear. It can only be said that supervision during the project in no place seemed to require change due to inability. Moreover, it must be recognized that in a fast moving situation an informed junior officer, who has lived with the project often is more effective than an uninformed senior officer. At any rate, further factual support of the criticism must be produced before any more thorough answer can be provided.

2. None of the three GS-16 officers assigned to the project was given top-level managerial responsibilities

Actually, there were four GS-16 officers with the project. One, however, was detailed for a special assignment. One of the other three was Chief of Station, Havana until the Embassy was closed in January 1961 when he returned and became the senior man dealing with the Cuban political elements. Another GS-16 was Deputy Chief of Station in Miami. The Chief in Miami was junior to him in grade but he had been with the project from the start (having initially been the project deputy); he was an old hand in the WH area and was performing well. All, including the GS-16, agreed that the Deputy Chief of Station, Miami was appropriate for the GS-16 since it was a high enough post to permit him to be effective and still did not upset a situation by changing purely for reasons of grade an officer, performing well, in favor of a latecomer who was not an area expert. The third GS-16 was a DD/I officer, not a DD/P officer, who performed well in a responsible overt post. To have made him a manager would have created problems since he did not have operational experience.

3. Of the 42 officers "holding the principal operational jobs in WH-4 in Grade GS-12 through GS-15" a large percentage were rated in a low position in the *initial* "Relative Retention Lists."

Without analyzing specific cases, it is submitted that these statements are completely deceptive as possible evidence of poor quality of personnel. The reasons are:

a. The ranking of individuals under the above procedure in many cases had nothing to do with competence or ability in given assignments. Rather the criteria were the needs of the service over the years to come. A high grade specialist in a little needed field, therefore, might be rated very low. A specific example is a paramilitary officer assigned to WH-4 from another division who served in the project with distinction. Nevertheless, since his parent division had no foreseeable need for such officers, he was ranked low in the *initial* list. More generally a similar result might well be true of paramilitary officers since the feeling is that the Agency, particularly post-Cuba, will in all likelihood have few similar projects in the future. Surely this view would be reflected in initial lists prepared by Divisions and would tend to be corrected as necessary during the elaborate policy level review of the lists.

b. Ranking is competitive, and since many of the project officers were not WH officers, they were ranked in the retention lists *initially* by WH officers in competition with WH officers for long term WH assignments. On this scale, they might well come out badly regardless of their competence for the Cuban Project. In the first place, if paramilitary officers, their speciality is not in future demand; and if not WH area specialists, they would be poor competitors with area specialists looking to a long term future. They might, however, have been excellent officers in many Cuban Project assignments without area knowledge.

c. The *initial* lists were substantially revised for the above and other reasons in subsequent reviews. Consequently, by themselves they are of little validity.

Again, therefore, it is recommended that at the very least the Survey's allegations in this respect be set aside until a more detailed examination is possible covering the specific individuals in question; why they were rated low on *initial* lists; did their ratings change on later lists and, more specifically, what relation the rating for retention purposes had to the performance on the Cuban Project. Obviously, the reverse might also be true, i.e., an officer could receive a top rating for retention purposes but still have poor qualities for the type of urgent rather peculiar requirements existing in the Cuban Project.

4. "A very few project personnel spoke Spanish or had Latin American background knowledge."

Obviously, it would be desirable for most officers in a project of this sort to have both the language and area knowledge. Admittedly, the Agency has not achieved this capability to the extent desired, and probably never will. It must also be recognized that in special projects like Cuba the personnel demands must be met in substantial part by assignments based on functional experience even though the individual assigned lacks area or language qualifications.

As to the Project itself, the need for Spanish should also be analyzed. Obviously it was necessary primarily for those dealing with Cubans. Not all such officers, however, needed Spanish, since, for example, PM instructors were quite able to perform effectively without the language since they taught by showing and example. Actually, there were Spanish-speaking trainers in Guatemala so this point is made only for purposes of analysis. Moreover, the training job both on the ground and in the air was never an issue as it was generally conceded to have been excellent.

As to others dealing with the Cubans, the officers working with the Cuban politicians were all fluent in Spanish with one exception, a senior officer who had no difficulty dealing with the Cubans in English and who was relied on very heavily by many of the senior Cubans. His lack of Spanish, therefore, did not prevent his achieving a position of personal confidence.

The officers in propaganda had native Spanish and in addition the publications, the newspapers and the radio scripts were written and produced by Cubans who, in the case of most of the newspapers and publications, had run and produced the same items in Cuba immediately prior to defecting.

The senior FI and CI officers had fluent Spanish. In Miami, an officer with native Spanish organized a corps of 35 to 40 Cubans into a CI organization of considerable competence. Even the Survey called this a "responsive and useful instrument."

C/WH-4 and his Paramilitary Chief had fluent Spanish, as did the Chief in Miami. To generalize, of the sixteen senior managerial officers listed in Annex A, eleven had fluent Spanish. During the last four months, the Project operated its own Signal Center and its own Cable Secretariat providing 24-hour coverage. Two of the three post-duty Duty Officers had fluent Spanish. Also, a Translation Unit of seven people was developed to provide 24-hour coverage of direct communications.

It can be asserted that Spanish speakers were available for all needed uses. Some inconvenience may have been caused on occasion due to not having even more Spanish speakers, but a lack of adequate Spanish speakers cannot honestly be alleged as a ground for any major failure in the project.

5. "Some of the people who served the project on contract were incompetent."

Undoubtedly, this statement has some basis in fact, but since no more is said and the consequences to the Project not explained, a reply is not possible in any manageable context.

6. Regarding the improper use of skilled personnel, the Survey has little to say. Inadequate use of GS-16's is discussed above. The only other comments in the Survey are:

a. "In a number of instances, those senior operating personnel in the field stations that did speak Spanish had to be interrupted in their regular duties merely in order to act as interpreters." This is answered above.

b. "In many instances, case officers were used as 'hand-holders' for agents and technical specialists as stevedores." Surely any case officer does some handholding. Wherein this was particularly serious in the project is not known nor indicated by the Survey. The "stevedore" reference is elsewhere expanded by the Survey to the effect that the "technical

and training abilities" of several Navy Chief Petty Officers who were borrowed in connection with work in certain of the Project's ships were
"grossly misused" as "much of their time was spent at stevedore or deckhand labor." It is quite true that some Navy personnel on duty with the
Agency were made available by their components to represent the Agency
interests and keep an eye on maritime repairs and modifications. Unquestionably, they were not fully employed though their presence at moments
was very important. In all likelihood, therefore, this was a situation where
some inefficiency of employment resulted. One Chief Petty Officer was
upset by the assignment and asked to be returned to his regular duties.
Others, however, accepted the situation as special and largely unavoidable, and served without complaint as long as their experience was
needed.

c. The Navy Captain assigned at Agency request to the Project to
handle maritime activity was "reported to have been not entirely happy
with his brief Agency tour. In any event, he was another example of poor
handling of people in this project, and he was not given a chance to solve
the problems of maritime operations." It is not known who "reported" the
Navy Captain (Captain Scapa) as "not entirely happy," but we are sur-
prised at the statement since Agency officers close to him thought that he
left in a pretty good frame of mind. Of course, it must be remembered that
his experiences might well have caused some discouragement. He was
flown on short notice from his shipboard Navy assignment to detail with
another Agency with which he had no previous experience. He arrived in
February 1961 so that the project was well along and he had to fit himself to
it in a great hurry and under pressure. He was, however, able to provide
substantial help and his assignment was distinctly worthwhile. He examined such ships as the project had; went to Vieques and inspected the
Cuban crew training; spent a substantial amount of time at Project Headquarters working on the maritime aspects of the Trinidad and Zapata
plans and finally accompanied the Paramilitary Chief to Puerto Cabezas to
participate in the final briefing of the Brigade and the ships' crews. Thereafter, he returned to Project Headquarters and spent night and day in the
war and operations rooms working on all maritime aspects of the final days
of the effort. Such employment of Captain Scapa, it is submitted, was sensible and constructive.

*Biographic Summary of Certain Senior Officials*

*Jacob D. Esterline* E.O.D. February 1951 *Chief, Cuban Task Force*

Mr. Esterline's prior Agency experience included an assignment as a senior official on the anti-Arbenz project in Guatemala and [excised] Mr. Esterline had fluent Spanish. He has since been assigned as Chief of Operations, WH Division.

During World War II he had 20 months with OSS including two tours behind the lines in Burma. He was a Captain and commanded guerrilla units up to battalion strength.

1951–52, Chief Instructor at Guerrilla Warfare School at Fort Benning

1953, Chief Instructor in Guerrilla Warfare

*Edward A. Stanulis* E.O.D. September 1952 *Deputy Chief, Cuban Task Force*

Mr. Stanulis served in succession as Chief, Plans and Programs, Chief of Operations, and ultimately as Deputy Chief of the Cuban Task Force.

His military service was with the U.S. Army from 1942 to 1950 wherein he progressed in rank from 2nd Lt. to Major. He is now permanently retired for combat incurred disability (loss of leg). His assignments prior to combat duty included:

Asst. Reg. Intelligence Officer, Eastern Defense Command

Regimental Adjutant, Instructor, Intel. School

Asst. Plans and Ops Officer

Training Officer, Infantry Tactics

In combat (ETO), with the rank of Captain and Major, he served as Commanding Officer of an Infantry Co. (Rifle) with tactical control of battalion attacking elements. Having been wounded, he was a POW for six months.

On return to active duty in Washington he served as a Major in Public Information Divisions of the Army and the Department of Defense until his discharge in 1950.

He has also had broad experience in public affairs, writing, editing, and publishing. His prior Agency experience included assignments to OPC/PW, P&P Staff, and PP Staff. Assigned as an instructor and ultimately Chief of

Headquarters Training, Ops School/OTR. Mr. Stanulis instructed in and assisted in the revision of PP, FI, and PM courses.

*Richard D. Drain* E.O.D. March 1951 *Chief of Operations, Cuban Task Force*

Mr. Drain reported to the Project from an overseas assignment in [excised] where he was Chief of Internal Operations and on occasion [excised].

His military record includes service as an officer with the U.S. Army, Field Artillery (Armored). His active duty extended from April, 1943 to May, 1946. His training included the *Ground Forces Intelligence Course #1*, with special emphasis on O.B. and the *Armored Command Hqtrs. Combat Intelligence Course.*

Among other assignments he conducted Basic Training; served as Assistant and Acting Battalion S-3; was an Instructor at the Armored School; and was Battery Officer in Advanced Training.

In combat (ETO) he was Forward Observer with a Combat Team and a Platoon Commander.

His decorations include the Silver Star and Bronze Star.

He is a lawyer and practiced in D.C. prior to Agency EOD. His Government experience also included Agency assignments as Executive Asst. to the DD/I, Staff Officer for O/IC (Office of Intelligence Coordination), Secretary, Intelligence Advisory Committee; and he was detached from the Agency for two extra-Agency assignments. In the first he served on the White House Staff of the Planning Coordination Group under Mr. Nelson Rockefeller. In the second he served with the Department of State as a Special Asst., Multilateral Affairs.

*John F. Mallard, Col., USMC* E.O.D. August 1957 *SA Military, Cuban Task Force*

Prior to his assignment win this Agency, Col. Mallard had served with the Office of the CNO, Assistant Head Naval War Plans Section. His performance was outstanding with comments indicating an excellent background of staff experience and professional capabilities. Noted as diligent, thorough and possessing mature judgment. He had earlier served as Assistant Plans Officer on the staff of the Commander, 7th Fleet, where he also received an outstanding rating and was looked upon as a source of strength on the staff. Had earlier been a Battalion Commander and was rated an outstanding Artillery Battalion Commander. Col. Mallard carried the brunt of liaison with the military service and heavy responsibility with the State Department on military matters.

[Excised] E.O.D. June 1951 *Chief/Intel/PM Section/Cuban Task Force*

[Excised] reported to the Project from the FI Staff. His earlier assignments had included that of senior FI Case Officer in [excised], Chief/[excised] and Chief Instructor, Resistance Ops course/OTR. He has received numerous commendations for his performances in Headquarters, in the field, and in Agency liaison activities.

His military service was with the USMC where he served overseas as Bomb Disposal Officer from 1943 to 1945 at New Caledonia, Guadalcanal, and Northern Solomons. He is a Major in the USMCR.

*Albert C. Davies, Lt. Col., USA* E.O.D. March 1960 *DC/Intel/PM Section/ Cuban Task Force*

At the time of his assignment to the Project Col. Davies (a regular infantry officer) had been serving as Army G-2, USACARIB from 1956. He is rated by his service as an Infantry Staff Officer. Served in the European theatre during World War II and in Korea. He holds the Silver Star and the Bronze Medal with two oak leaf clusters. Prior to his assignment to USACARIB he had been an infantry instructor at Fort Leavenworth, Battalion Executive Officer, and Battalion Commander in the Far East, and had been a student at the Army Command and General Staff Officers Course in Oklahoma. Col. Davies' assignment with the Cuban Task Force included that of Post Command at Ft. Randolph and later deputy chief, Intel Unit-PM Section. He has broad area familiarity with Latin America and has some fluency in the Spanish language. He is currently serving as Chief/Intel, Research, and Reports/WH/4.

[Excised] E.O.D. February 1952 *C/FI Section/Cuban Task Force (Later DC/WH/4)*

[Excised] experience included ten years with the Department of State with whom he served in Tegucigalpa, Madrid, and Santiago, Chile, the latter two as Second Secretary. He has fluent Spanish, Portuguese, and French, and has wide experience in Latin American affairs with a thorough knowledge of economic matters.

His WH Division assignments include the following

    [excised]

    [excised]

    [excised]

He is now preparing to assume duties of [excised].

*Ralph G. Seehafer* E.O.D. August 1952 *DC/FI Section/Cuban Task Force*

Mr. Seehafer entered on duty with the Agency in August of 1952 and has served exclusively with WH Division. His overseas tours of duty included an assignment as [excised]. He possesses fluent Spanish and also speaks Portuguese and German. Mr. Seehafer took his undergraduate degree in Hispanic studies. He is noted for his deliberate and untiring efforts and was a source of strength to the several senior officers who served as Chief of the FI Section.

*David A. Phillips* E.O.D. April 1955 *C/PP Section/Cuban Task Force*

Originally a contract agent and covert associate in [excised], Mr. Phillips became a staff employee with the Agency on assignment to P&P Staff and PP/Operations. He then had assignments to the Havana Station and [excised]. Noted as an outstanding propagandist with excellent supervisory qualities. Mr. Phillips has fluent Spanish with excellent area knowledge as evidenced by the fact that he often speaks publicly on the area, including having been on the "Town Hall of the Air."

*Philip A. Toomey* E.O.D. December 1951 *DC/Propaganda Section/Cuban Task Force*

Entered on duty with the Agency in December 1951 and has had prior assignment with OPC/WE/Plans and Ops, served abroad [excised] as a PP Ops Officer, returned to the PP Staff in Headquarters and was serving with WH/3 at the time of his assignment to the Project. He has native Spanish and possesses ability to handle a tremendous amount of work. Mature judgment and skill in the propaganda field are only a couple of his attributes.

*Jack Hawkins, Col., USMC* E.O.D. October 1960 *C/WH/4/PM*

Col. Hawkins was serving on the staff of Marine Corps School, Quantico, Virginia at the time of his appointment by Commandant, USMC to the Cuban Task Force. He is a Naval Academy graduate and saw service in the Philippines at Bataan and Corregidor until taken prisoner. Having escaped from his prison camp, he joined guerrilla forces and led raiding parties in attacks against the enemy for which action he was awarded the DSC. He was later awarded a Bronze Medal for the Okinawa campaign. Following World War II he served as a member of the Naval Mission to Venezuela and later as Commanding Officer, 1st Battalion, 1st Marines in combat in Korea. He was there awarded the Silver Star. Served as an instructor in Quantico for three years and then as G-3 at Camp Lejune where he was promoted to his present rank of Colonel. Col. Hawkins possesses native fluency in Spanish. He was personally selected for the assignment by General Shoup, C.G., USMC.

*Frank J. Egan, Lt. Col., USA* E.O.D. June 1960 *C/SPU/PM/WH/4*

Col. Egan reported to the Cuban Task Force with a background of experience in Special Forces, U.S. Army. He had on earlier occasion worked in a liaison capacity with this Agency and always showed a true appreciation of the peculiar requirements of covert action. Serving originally as Chief of the Strikes and Plans Unit/PM Section, Col. Egan later proceeded to Guatemala where he assumed command of all indigenous Brigade training. He held this position with the help of a few staff and contract employees until the arrival of the group of Special Forces Trainers. His capacity for work was outstanding and the rating he received by his senior officer, Col. Hawkins, reflects Col. Hawkins' respect for his abilities. Comments particularly pertinent refer to his ability to influence and inspire the confidence and respect of troops.

*Ernest Sparks* E.O.D. August 1954 *Sr. Cuban Task Force Rep/Guatemala*

Entering on duty as Ops Instructor in 1952, Mr. Sparks departed for Korea with the USMC and remained there as an IO/PM and Maritime Officer until 1954. He then served at [excised] until 1958 first as an Instructor, then Chief of the Maritime Branch, later as Instructor, and ultimately, Chief of the Ops Course. He was commended as an outstanding instructor and capable administrator. Prior to his assignment to the Cuban Task Force he served as Chief/Cover Training ([excised]) where he set up and administered a highly competent tutorial facility. His performance was noted as being outstanding.

*Jacob Scapa, Capt., USN* E.O.D. February 1961 *C/Maritime Ops/Cuban Task Force*

Assigned to the Cuban Task Force as a Special Assistant for Military Matters by the CNO, Capt. Scapa appeared on the scene in the late stages of Project development. He was at the time of his assignment on the Staff of the Commander, Amphibious Training Command, Atlantic Fleet. He had earlier served as Commanding Officer of the USS Walke and served aboard the USS Wisconsin, and had been on the Staff of the Supreme Allied Command, Atlantic. Capt. Scapa quickly reviewed and made himself familiar with all maritime operations and plans. He participated in pre-invasion briefings and added a significant touch of professionalism to maritime matters.

TDY visit to Miami Base/[excised] to review problem of Maintenance Facility for LCI's and Small Boats. On return recommended and assisted in acquisition of Navy CPO's (Machinists).

Then assigned to Plans and Strike Operations Unit where he assisted greatly in liaison with Navy components and in preparation of sailing instructions, etc. He participated in final briefings of Brigade and maritime personnel. Active during actual strike in War Room, Headquarters, Cuban Task Force. Currently, Chief of Naval Mission, Ecuador.

[Excised] E.O.D. September 1951 *C/CI Section/Cuban Task Force*

Entered on duty with the Agency as an instructor in the Ops Course in 1951. He remained with OTR until his assignment to [excised]. He served there as a Training and Intel Officer and Director of FI Operations. Returning to OTR in 1956 as an instructor in the CE/CI Training Course, he was responsible for the training of two [excised] services. He became Chief Instructor in the Agency Orientation, CI Familiarization and Security Officer Courses. All reports indicate he was a superb instructor, a good executive and supervisor. He has been noted as being the Outstanding instructor on the Headquarters Operations School faculty.

*Gerard Droller* E.O.D. September 1949 *C/PA/Cuban Task Force*

Extremely capable PP Officer, original, enthusiastic, aggressive. Requires challenge. Outstanding PA man. Long time EE Officer. Entered on duty with the Agency in 1949 in OPC tour in [excised]—52–54 excellent reports. Respectively C/Ops/[excised], C/[excised], DC/[excised], C/[excised].

*Bernard E. Reichhardt* E.O.D. November 1947 *P&P Officer/Cuban Task Force (Later C/FI Section)*

Mr. Reichhardt's earlier Agency assignments included that of Finance Officer, later Chief/Cover Division. He served FE Division in [excised] and as Chief/Branch 1/Headquarters. Later assignments were to the PP Staff and with Branch 3 WH Division. His assignments with the Project included a stint of duty at Miami Base before returning to Headquarters as DC/PA Section/Cuban Task Force. He was then moved up as Plans and Policy Officer and ultimately served as Chief/FI Section. Mr. Reichhardt has native fluency in Spanish. He is currently [excised].

[Excised] E.O.D. September 1947 *Special Asst/WH/4/Cuban Task Force*

Prior assignments included [excised] and Department of State (Mexico) 1931–41. [Excised] has fluent Spanish. Was commended for extraordinary performance [excised] by C/WHD. Characterized as dependable and resourceful, and having the ability to get the most out of employees.

*E. Howard Hunt* E.O.D. November 1949 *PP/PM/Cuban Task Force*

Mr. Hunt's background prior to his service with the Agency was working as a writer and as a correspondent for *Time, Inc.* He was assigned to OPC and served in [excised] for three (3) years, was then reassigned to SE/P & PW Staff. He was then assigned as a PP Officer to [excised] before being selected as [excised]. He was rated, before his assignment to the Cuban Task Force, as having outstanding ability in the covert action field. He is exceptionally talented and imaginative in the PP field. His assignment in [excised] drew outstanding reports. He has fluent Spanish.

*B.H. Vandervoort* E.O.D. September 1947 *C/SI Unit (FI/D), Cuban Task Force*

Mr. Vandervoort's outstanding military background is well known to all in the Clandestine Services. He possesses area knowledge in WE, FE and WH Divisions and he has good Spanish. He is a competent reporter. Earlier personnel reports note his exceptional qualifications for participation in contingency task force operations. He had also earlier been recommended as a Senior War Planner.

U.S. Army service from 1939 to 1946 and was discharged with the rank of Lt.Col. He gave outstanding service in the ETO and was decorated by Generals Gavin and Ridgeway as "outstanding WW II Battalion Co., 82nd Airborne." Decorations: two DSC's, two Bronze Stars, three Purple Hearts, plus French, Dutch, Belgian Decorations.

*Robert Reynolds* E.O.D. October 1949 *COB/Miami Base*

Mr. Reynolds' career has been spent largely with WH Division beginning with his assignments in OSO. He served in [excised], [excised], and later as [excised]. Mr. Reynolds had returned to WH/3 at the time of his assignment to the Project and was one of the first senior officers so assigned. Serving first as DC/Cuban Task Force he was later transferred to Miami Base as Chief of Base. Mr. Reynolds possesses fluent Spanish ability.

16 May 1960

E Y E S   O N L Y

MEMORANDUM FOR:    Chiefs of All Special Staffs and Operating Divisions

SUBJECT:    Clerical Assistance for WH Division

1. Certain activities of the WH Division require experienced clerical personnel. It is desired that all CS components contribute to this effort to the maximum extent possible.

2. Requirements now exist for first-class stenographers and typists, grade immaterial, who have had general experience in the Clandestine Services for temporary detail to WH Division for an indefinite period. It is requested that you provide at least one such person from your component. Please notify the Clandestine Services Personnel Office (Ext. 4541) of your selection so that the necessary arrangements may be made. The CSPO will notify you several days in advance of the date when your nominee should report to WH for duty.

Richard Helms
Chief of Operations, DD/P

## VIII. THE POLITICAL FRONT AND
## RELATIONS WITH THE CUBANS

One of the conclusions of the Survey (as stated in para. 3 on page 143) was "as the project grew, the Agency reduced the exile leaders to the status of puppets, thereby losing the advantages of their active participation." This summarizes the Survey's general criticism of the handling of the Cuban leaders. Two more specific criticisms are made at least by inference in the discussion of this matter in the body of the Survey. The first was that the decision in November 1960 to consider requests for paramilitary aid from groups other than the FRD "complicated relations between Project case officers and the FRD leaders," and "appears to have resulted in some diffusion of effort." It also "seriously hampered progress toward FRD unity, sharpened internal FRD antagonisms, and contributed to the decline in strike force recruiting efforts." The second criticism is that the Agency prevented close contact between the political leaders, first of the FRD and later of the CRC, and the military forces in training in Guatemala. The Survey states that "this was probably a mistake and an unreasonable interference in the Cubans' management of their own affairs. Controlled contact between the FRD and the troops would have done much to improve morale and motivation of the troops and make the training job easier."

As will be shown in the following paragraphs, the generalized criticism that the exile leaders were treated as puppets has little if any basis in fact. As to the two more specific criticisms, the facts are correctly stated, but as explained below there were plausible reasons for both decisions and even with the benefit of hindsight these decisions appear to have been wise. This does not mean that no disadvantages attached to them. The Survey is correct in pointing out that relations with the FRD were strained by the decision to support certain non-FRD groups and that the lack of contact between the political leaders and the Brigade gave rise to difficulties on both sides. What is omitted from the Survey's discussion, however, is any explanation of the considerations that made those two decisions seem necessary, let alone any attempt to balance the risks and costs of different courses of action against the disadvantages of those actually pursued.

The press has carried many stories especially after the events of April 1961 citing the sentiments of Cuban exiles to the effect that they were disenchanted with their role in the affair. It is understandable that after the defeat those Cubans would look for scapegoats and allege that they had been used as puppets. It is, on the other hand, disturbing that these Cuban utterances in the press are accepted as fact in the Survey, particularly when considerable documentary evidence to the contrary was available to the Survey team.

Before analyzing the Survey's above conclusions, it is important to examine various aspects and complexities of what the Survey calls "exile leaders." First, one must differentiate between the political and military leaders. Second, one must recognize the pressures which existed within each of these two groups. Third, one should understand what the term "leadership" meant within the Miami Cuban exile community.

From the very beginning of the Project it was evident that there were considerable differences of opinion—on almost all important questions—among Cuban exiles of varying political shades and leadership capabilities. Clearly, there was unanimity on the desirability and need to overthrow Castro; but during the great debate on how to accomplish this, two main trends became discernible: the activists, principally the military element in this category, wanted to fight. Political considerations meant little to this segment of exiles who believed political solutions would evolve automatically after Castro's demise. As a matter of fact, they had the greatest contempt for "the politicians." On the other hand, the politically-minded exiles realized that the overthrow of Castro without specific plans and preparations to fill the vacuum created by his departure would be an immense error. They agreed with the activists that the overthrow could only be accomplished by violent action but they feared that during the fighting one or more of the military leaders would emerge whose politico/economic postures were unknown quantities and who—in the exuberance of victory—might be accepted by the population as the new political chief of Cuba. Consequently, the political and military exile elements grew apart despite the existence of bonds of friendship and loyalty between individuals in one element and people in the other. Thus, when speaking of "exile leaders" a distinction must be made between political and military leadership.

Also within the political and military groups a high degree of competition existed. Personal ambitions were rampant. Each individual claimed larger followings inside and outside Cuba than the next man, each tried to belittle the potential and capabilities of the other; each proselyted the other's assets. In the early autumn of 1960, over sixty different anti-Castro political groups were active and vocal, almost all of them in the Miami area. They ranged in size from an individual exile with three or four personal henchmen to sizeable bodies with substantial organizations still active within Cuba itself. The Agency representatives were in contact with many of these and its constant effort was to induce as many groups and individuals as possible to support a broadly based unified movement which would exclude only the supporters of Castro on the left and the Batistianos on the right. The Agency exerted pressure on the Cubans throughout the whole period from mid-1960 up to the invasion in only two ways: to promote the greatest and most inclusive unity of effort and to promote the greatest feasible effectiveness. Decisions, however, as to who should be the dominant leader and what the political platform of the opposition should be were studiously left to the Cubans themselves.

Despite the pressure for unity, it remained true up to the election (by the Cubans) of Jose Miro Cardona as president of the CRC in March 1961 that exile Cuban leadership—if taken in the broadest meaning of the term— consisted of the spokesmen of a great number of anti-Castro groups whose prominence, importance and capabilities for active participation in the operation varied greatly and whose claim for leadership remained highly controversial. If the term is to connote the FRD Executive Committee then it is highly pertinent to keep in mind the barrier between the "Politicians" and the "Militarists" mentioned above and the very remarkable checks the FRD Executive Committee members imposed on each other. For rather obvious reasons they attempted to make the FRD an "Exclusive Club" by restricting, if not closing, membership in it and they insisted on a system of parity throughout all FRD working elements, that is to say that each Executive Committee member placed the same number of his followers, as did any one of his follow members, on any working group. This concept of leadership—not surprising in exile politics and somewhat reminiscent of past Cuban history and practices—had, of course, its effect on dynamic action and puts the term leadership in a somewhat different context. Moreover, the U.S. and the Agency did not feel that a different concept could be forced on the Cubans.

As the pace of the build-up and of current operations accelerated in the autumn of 1960, it became increasingly apparent that any approach to the effectiveness which was the second of the two objectives of Agency pressure would require a higher degree of control over and direction of the anti-Castro movement by the Agency than had originally been hoped. The Cubans never did succeed in creating a Cuban organization sufficiently free of internal divisions and competently enough staffed to perform the rapidly expanding operational tasks. Radio broadcasts had to be organized, publications arranged, and propaganda material prepared. Paramilitary personnel had to be recruited, screened, and trained. Boats had to be procured, crewed, and maintained. Air crews had likewise to be selected and trained and air operations mounted. Two bases had to be built in Guatemala. There was the large and continuing task of logistic support. All of these tasks would have had to be performed in one form or another even if the major emphasis had continued to be on the internal resistance rather than on the preparation of a strike force. The FRD never came close to achieving the capability to take the major initiative in planning, directing, or conducting these activities. The hope entertained in the summer of 1960 that the FRD would soon evolve into an organization which could take increasing responsibility for the direction of the effort, relying on the Agency mainly for financial and logistic support and for some help in training, proved completely illusional. It is fair to say that by mid-autumn of 1960, the choice was between a degree of initiative and control by the Agency recognized at the time to be undesirable and, as the only feasible alternative, the abandonment of any serious effort to accomplish the end in view.

Against this background one can examine whether the FRD's political and military elements were reduced to the status of puppets and whether the advantages of their active participation was lost by this.

## 1. The FRD Political Element.

a) From the outset, the basic principle was established to respect the independence of the Project's Cuban collaborators and, for all intents and purposes, to treat and deal with them as equals; no orders were to be issued, results were to be accomplished by persuasion and by the application of normal, generally accepted practices of political intercourse. The 11–12 May 1960 New York meeting which resulted in the formation of the FRD is but one example of the application of this Agency's posture: Agency representatives served as hosts for the assembled Cubans, stated unequivocally the view that formation of a unified opposition to Castro was strictly a Cuban affair and then withdrew leaving it to the delegates to establish their organization in terms upon which they could agree.

b) The staffing of the FRD working elements and the initiation of activities via those elements was in the hands of the Cubans who were not obliged to check their moves with their U.S. contacts. In fact, the inclusion of Aureleano Sanchez Arango in the Executive Committee on 10 June 1960, which took place without Agency consultation and was at that time at least considered an undesirable development, is another example of the freedom of action the Cubans enjoyed. It might also be said that Sanchez Arango never had any assets of any kind to offer. He had a long-standing friendship with "Pepe" Figueres of Costa Rica and President

Betancourt of Venezuela which enabled him to muster some pressure in the early days for a high position. In view, however, of his lack of following, his resignation was of no significance whatsoever contrary to the statement of the Survey.

c) From the moment the FRD was formed in May 1960 in New York, the Cubans were aware of the importance attributed in the early stages of the Project by their U.S. contacts to having FRD Headquarters moved to Mexico. The Cubans opposed this move for a variety of reasons — mostly personal and some, from their view point, political. Had the Agency treated its counterparts as puppets, this move could have been accomplished within a matter of weeks. However, in spite of considerable pressures on the Agency, the principle of tactful persuasion was relied upon and it was not until August 1960 that the FRD got to Mexico and then it was only for a short time.

d) The establishment of FRD branch offices in numerous Latin American countries was accomplished by the FRD Executive Committee, with U.S. contacts merely playing an advisory role.

e) The aforementioned self-imposed system of parity and of running the FRD by Committee resulted in less dynamic action than was desirable. A partnership with divergent views among the partners is not the best mechanism for decisive action. Thus, U.S. contacts suggested in September 1960, the creation of the position of an FRD General Coordinator, a suggestion accepted in principle by all Cubans concerned. The Cubans, however, wanted their U.S. colleagues to declare their preferences for a particular person. Again this was not done because of the principle of non-U.S. interference in strictly unilateral exile Cuban affairs. The exile internal warfare on this leadership issue assumed rather remarkable proportions but finally the FRD Executive Committee selected Antonio de Varona as General Coordinator on 27 September 1960.

f) The concept of permitting the FRD Cubans to run their own show as much as possible coupled with their own preoccupation on mending their political fences and creating their own political machines, caused many tactical difficulties to those Agency elements charged with day-to-day propaganda activities whose successful implementation hinged on immediate action without protracted negotiations on each detail. Thus, of necessity unilateral Agency operations had to be created in substantially all the action fields (e.g., propaganda, intelligence collection, paramilitary) which were impossible to conceal from the FRD. The FRD leadership resented what they considered competition and demanded exclusive control of these activities; they also demanded that the FRD be the only channel for U.S. dealings with any segment of the internal Cuban opposition or the Cuban exile community. On the latter point the Department of State did not agree; on the former, the Agency could not acquiesce because of operational considerations. Moreover, on the former point there was a strong feeling throughout the U.S. Government that it would be wrong to permit the FRD to be in a position to rule out any Cuban elements which might have usable internal Cuban assets. It was clear at least by December 1960 that the effort to broaden the membership of the FRD to the point where it included all political acceptable elements of the opposition had failed and that the effort of its members to use it to advance their own political fortunes within the exile community was resented. All elements of the U.S. Government were agreed that it could not be an exclusive chosen instrument with a monopoly of governmental support. These problems were certainly not the product of coercion.

g) The inability of the FRD Cubans again—because of their incessant preoccupation with political advantage—to establish an effective paramilitary recruiting mechanism within the Project deadlines called for the utilization of Cuban officers and men outside the FRD channel. This action was in line with the realities of the situation, i.e., the inability of the political elements to tackle the military tasks as speedily and effectively as necessary and the aforementioned unwillingness of the military (or activists) to accept the political leadership. (Only after the election of Miro Cardona as CRC President did the Liberation Army support and accept the political structure.) Thus, political personalities retained their independence in their specialty and the military (and activists) worked—with the guidance of U.S. military specialists—in theirs. If closer coordination had been possible between the political and the military it would clearly have been desirable. Only the political urgencies of an actual attack were sufficient to achieve any real unity and this was in many ways a mirage and a "sometime thing."

It is true as stated in the Survey that the Agency intervened actively to prevent visits by the political leaders to the training camps in December and January, and that this was deeply resented by the political leaders. It is also true that this lack of contact with the political leadership left the Cuban military personnel unsure of what and for whom they were going to fight, even though being activists not political scientists they were generally satisfied with a mere "Down with Castro" slogan. There were, however, the most specific and urgent reasons for following this policy. During these months, as the crucial role of the strike force was recognized by all concerned, the competition between the political leaders to secure control of it was at its maximum. Varona used the FRD recruiting machinery to try to insure a preponderance of loyal personnel that would be acceptable to and have some loyalty to him. Other members of the CRC were equally anxious to insure the inclusion of recruits loyal to them. Most (but not all) of the FRD leaders resented the inclusion of men who had not been supplied through their own recruitment machinery. The FRD leadership, and later some members of the CRC, were determined to try to displace the senior military officers of the Brigade with political appointees acceptable to them. During the four months before the invasion, no one of the political leaders could have been allowed to visit the camps alone without accusations of favoritism. Meanwhile, the Cuban military leaders in training and the American training officers who were endeavoring to fashion the Brigade into a cohesive and powerful force, feared above all any encouragement of factionalism in the ranks. Moreover, although the troops needed indoctrination in the ideology for which they were going to risk their lives, it was known that some members of the FRD and later of the CRC were unpopular in the camps. There was a real possibility that if there were many visits of the political leadership, and if those visits were not carefully controlled when they were permitted, a real cleavage would have opened up between the military force and the political committee with the possible disruption of the Brigade, the one essential asset at the time. The decision to isolate the Brigade from the political leadership for a considerable period was obviously a difficult one and no one can state with certainty that the course of action actually followed was the wisest. It did, however, produce a situation on D-Day in which the Brigade was unified and the political leadership had, at least superficially, accepted their relationship to it.

h) As the deadline for the Project approached the need to broaden by democratic means and strictly by Cuban action the FRD base and to evolve a provisional government became pressing. Continuous negotiations were conducted during February 1961 and March 1961, and on 22 March 1961 the CRC was created. Every Agency position paper prepared on this matter stressed the need for letting the Cubans have their own say. Indeed it was felt that *only* Cuban selection could have any real value. This policy had the approval of the Department of State and was carried out to the letter. The following excerpts from an address by an Agency representative to the Cuban Revolutionary Assembly on 18 March 1961 just prior to the start of the selection of the CRC exemplified this: "Naturally, the procedures employed in the election of your leader or Provisional President must remain entirely in your hands . . . Obviously we are not trying to tell you whom you should elect—that is your responsibility and yours alone . . . The decision is up to you. I am confident you will make the right one." Thus, acting independently the Cuban exiles elected Miro Cardona as their provisional President.

i) It is quite true that CRC members went into isolation during the 17 April invasion; it is also true that statements on the invasion were issued in their names. On the former, CRC members were briefed and counseled by two high ranking Agency officials and the Cuban agreement was given voluntarily and without coercion and in recognition of the demands of the hour. In fact Miro Cardona was told that he might stay in New York City over the fateful weekend of 14–17 April. He, however, asked to be isolated with the other members of the CRC.

j) In summary, the facts prove that FRD (and later CRC) members were not reduced to the status of puppets—regardless of their feeling in the ice cold reality of defeat—and that their action capabilities were exploited to the fullest (an outstanding example is the great number of laws and plans which were ready for promulgation and implementation upon the assumption of power in Cuba by the Provisional Government). Such limitations as existed on active participation by Cubans in post-Castro plans for Cuba were created by their own preoccupation with matters relating to personal ambitions, long-standing personal biases and exile politics Caribbean style. Indeed as pointed out above, politicians had little to do with the military aspects of the operation since they lacked by their own admission technical competence. Just before the landing, however, the politico-military understanding was at its best. The Brigade and its leadership recognized the political leadership of the CRC and Manuel Artime, a leading member of the CRC, stayed and landed with the Brigade as a representative of the CRC.

## 2. The FRD Military Element.

a) The military element similarly enjoyed freedom of action consonant with traditionally accepted rules of military discipline and order. Although American advisors, of necessity, directed the planning of the troop training from the basic stage through advanced large unit exercises and maneuvers, the Cuban military leadership participated in this planning and was solely responsible for the conduct of the training and for the control of the troops. In this latter connection, the Cuban military leaders were responsible for the maintenance of law, order and discipline and in the discharge of these responsibilities meted out disciplinary punishment ranging from "company punishment" to incarceration.

b) Without coercion on our part, the Liberation Troops pledged their loyalty to the Cuban political leadership as represented by the Cuban Revolutionary Council.

c) The traditional cleavages of military versus political leadership naturally were evident in this operation as they are in almost any organized state in the world. There is no evidence, however, to support any contention that the gap between their respective objectives and methods to be employed to achieve these objectives was any wider than would be expected given the circumstances that existed. Merely because those like Manuel Ray who never favored an invasion said after the defeat "I told you so" to all available newspapers did not mean that the D-Day unity was not sufficiently strong to have provided a platform on which to build. Failure, quite naturally, provided the most potent fuel to the flames of dissension which lay only just below the surface.

3. *Miscellaneous.* Other than the main conclusion mentioned above, there are some minor criticisms in the Survey. Project officers are criticized for not speaking Spanish. This point is discussed elsewhere but it might again be noted that of the six senior officers dealing with the Cuban leaders, five had fluent Spanish and the one officer who did not succeeded nevertheless in achieving a close relationship with a number of the top Cubans including Miro Cardona.

Paragraphs 42–50 on pages 94 to 97 of the Survey contain a series of criticisms and preachments which are so general, unsupported or unconnected to some specific consequence that we can only comment that they have been noted with dismay and that we regret that until more detail is furnished, an answer is not possible.

The remainder of the Survey's section on the political front and the relations to the Cubans starting on page 81 is mainly factual. It is only unfortunate that it treats so complex a problem so superficially and fails to include any of the extensive Agency relationships with the State Department and the White House with respect to the proper line to take with the Cuban leaders and the correct interpretation of the political views of these leaders. Also, what political attitudes were the most desirable from the point of view of the

U.S.? In addition, the Agency did considerable work on the preparation of political documents. Moreover, some non Agency experts were obtained to work with the Cuban leaders at their request in the development of the planks for their political platform. The absence of this whole story and the problems faced as it unfolded makes it difficult to have any real understanding of what was involved on the political side.

## IX. AIR MARITIME OPERATIONS

The Survey only has a one sentence conclusion regarding the carrying out of paramilitary operations (as distinguished from the basic military concept), namely, "Air and boat operations showed up poorly." The body of the Survey, however, has three chapters on this point dealing with "Air," "Maritime," and "Training Underground Leaders." The major points in those chapters will be considered below.

[NB: Three maps have been kept and are available, if desired, which show all air and maritime deliveries into Cuba plus all PM assets on Cuban soil as of 17 April 1961. These can be examined at any time. They are believed relevant to these paramilitary points.]

### A. AIR

1. Before discussing the many specific criticisms of the Survey, a few background points shall be presented.

    a. For reasons already discussed, U.S. bases could not be used. Consequently, drop missions had to be flown the longer distance from Guatemala, the only foreign soil within range for which permission from the local government was possible. Conceivably, President Somoza might have approved Nicaragua, but for many reasons Guatemala was preferable for these missions, e.g., a usable base in Nicaragua was not ready until late in the project; Nicaragua was farther from the U.S. and during this period supplies had to come from the U.S.; the trainees were in Guatemala, so that by using the same country the logistic support was simplified; and a separate country for the strike base was desired. Moreover, it was advisable to keep pre-strike activities out of the country providing the strike base.

    b. U.S. airmen could not be used. The Cubans recruited had extensive experience and were given a lot of training. Their air background, however, was commercial flying which, as it turned out, did not provide them with the kind of night flying navigational precision desired. Moreover, being Cuban and emotionally involved, their discipline was not good. For example, they often violated orders by remaining over targets too long in an effort to find the DZ and help their countrymen.

    c. Reception committees were either untrained or performed under difficult conditions. Even a trained individual, other than perhaps a surveyor, can make a slight error in figuring the coordinates of a DZ, particularly in rough terrain. A small mistake is enough to destroy the effectiveness of an air drop.

d. The recent and productive experience of making drops in difficult areas, such as [excised], has convinced us that communications with the receiving group, including ground to air communications from the DZ to the dropping aircraft (whether by radio, W/T or beacon), is essential to any assurance of success. In the Cuban situation, communications at best were difficult. For example, although contact was established with groups in the Escambray by courier, efforts to infiltrate a trained radio operator with equipment were never successful. In other cases it was advisable, if not necessary, to keep the radio operator away from the DZ in order to avoid risking so scarce a commodity. This meant an unavoidable delay with respect to last minute messages between the senders and the actual receivers. In no case were the desired communications mentioned above ever possible.

e. The Cuban land mass is not easy for drops. Either the terrain is rough and DZs are few as in the Escambray or the area is relatively crowded making an isolated spot difficult to find. In addition, Castro, as a former guerrilla leader, had surveyed possible DZs and was thoroughly familiar with their location.

f. Drop operations without all aids are inherently difficult. As already stated even toward the end of WW II skilled crews dropping to skilled and experienced reception committees were accorded, as a rule of thumb on the basis of lessons learned, only a 50% chance of success. The technical facilities in Cuba were less good than those in France in 1944–45 and the human capabilities much less good.

Having made the foregoing comments, it should then be admitted that the drop record in Cuba was poor. Efforts to improve it, however, were not successful, nor is it clear that any permissible action would have done any good. Some 27,800 lbs. of materiel were actually delivered (somewhat more than stated by the Survey). The major deliveries, however, as already explained, were by boat. Only one body drop was made. The reason for this was that drops were obviously going badly and individuals could be infiltrated more successfully by boat.

2. Specific allegations of the Survey follow:

a. The first drop was close but missed by 7 miles as stated by the Survey. A contributing factor was an unknown dam construction marked by lights. No U-2 flights had been approved at this stage of the project and knowledge of the construction was not available. On return the plane hit the proper coast-in point in Guatemala, and the crew captain then turned the plane over to the co-pilot. The latter took a short cut, climbed above some cloud cover, was lost when he came down and landed on the first field he found, i.e., in Mexico, even though he still had sufficient fuel to return to Guatemala. Obviously, this was bad procedure and poor crew discipline.

b. The rice and beans drop is an exaggerated case. In order to fill out the load, the DDCI decided to drop some food, as food shortages were clearly a problem with the resistance. Probably too much food was dropped and the agent was disturbed and angry. He continued, however, to work for the resistance and with the Agency, coming to Miami at a later date and returning again to Cuba thereafter.

c. Reception procedures were the best that could be devised in each instance, given the circumstances, i.e., the DZ, the local situation, the communications and the materiel available or that which could be used, (e.g., bonfires often were impossible, thereby making flashlights necessary). As to differences of view, there is no doubt that before a final flight plan was decided upon in particular cases there were often varying suggestions as to what should or should not be done. The clearance procedures already described were fully understood, however, and, it is believed, worked. In view of all the circumstances, they were not "cumbersome," as alleged by the Survey. The Special Group gave the overall clearance; the Task Force made the request for a drop and recommended the time, the place and the load; DPD handled the preparation of the flight plan and suggested any changes prompted by air safety considerations; and the DDCI gave the specific flight plan and final operational clearance. The crews were briefed in Guatemala. Their air discipline, as already indicated, was poor but how to correct it was difficult. Pilots and crews were hard to find so that they could not be fired. Navigation also was faulty though usually mistakes occurred in the difficult area after hitting the Cuban coast-in point.

d. Pilots were often told, as indicated by the Survey, to drop if they had any reason to believe that they were close to their targets. Often the need was so urgent that any effort to deliver supplies was justifiable. Moreover, capture of materiel by Castro's forces was a matter of no consequence as the Cubans had more equipment than they could use. Also, there were cases where recovery was by non-resistance Cubans who then passed the materiel to the resistance. Consequently, this chance was always present. If the blind drop theory was wrong, at least it was consciously adopted by all concerned at the time.

e. The so-called "tardy corrective action" was misunderstood by the Survey. In late February or early March a review of drops was made to try to see what, if anything, could be done to improve results. The findings merely confirmed the problems but really provided no solutions. Some suggestions were made which, in effect, were merely a restatement of existing procedures. Blind drops, as already indicated, were continued as a matter of policy when conditions were urgent, even though the review recommended their elimination. The other study made in January 1961 was stopped by the Paramilitary Chief as he knew that a solution by use of American pilots was politically unacceptable no matter how desirable operationally.

In conclusion it might be said that the DPD overall air drop record is a good one and will stand close examination. The failures in Cuba were not the result of lack of competence nor of poor organization. They were rather the result of many complex factors, some beyond Agency control, some undoubtedly within Agency control. During the project, the only real solutions were believed to be in the area of political infeasibility, although an improved record might have otherwise been achieved. Surely if better communications could have been provided with the resistance elements at the time of drops, there would have been greater success. It must be remembered in this connection that during the early months in 1961 the communications picture improved materially. Moreover, during the last two or three weeks before the invasion some 15 drop requests were received which could not for other reasons be fulfilled. The groups making these requests were, however, well equipped and capable.

## B. MARITIME

In the maritime field, it should be noted that the Survey makes no mention of the operational atmosphere or difficulties. This, of course, is true throughout the Survey, but, because of the particular difficulties encountered in connection with ships and crews and the amounts of money involved, the omission of realities seems perhaps more conspicuous in the maritime field. One major omission, for example, is the effort made by the Agency to find boats in the Navy and the Coast Guard. Although such effort was made and both Services were thoroughly cooperative, no usable boats could be found. Consequently, although the Agency fleet was not what might have been desired, it was, of necessity, obtained out of what could be found.

Another omission is any review of performance in relation to difficulties. For example, under the circumstances, it is suggested that the infiltration of 88,000 lbs. of materiel plus 79 bodies and the exfiltration of 51 bodies is a perfectly reasonable performance. Moreover, the transportation of the Brigade to the beachhead without hitch was surely a commendable operation.

As to supplies, the Survey criticizes the limited distribution achieved geographically in Cuba, but the fact is that the distribution was fairly good. This has been explained in an earlier section along with the reasons why the central south coast was not covered.

As to the condition of ships and the money required for their purchase and repair, no detailed discussion seems justified, although the Survey devotes considerable space to these items. The only significance of these allegations, it is felt, would be if, in the light of the existing requirements, urgencies and availabilities (i.e., of both equipment and people), the judgments exercised were reprehensible. Admittedly, the Agency fleet cost a substantial amount of money. Moreover, as stated, the craft were not ideal. The issue, however, is what else was possible. It is doubted that anything could have been done at the time which would have materially altered the situation.

Admittedly, as indicated in the Survey, the Agency capability in the maritime field at the start of the Cuban project was not very substantial. This, however, is no great surprise in view of the unlikelihood pre-Cuba that the Agency would become involved in a project requiring this type of maritime capability. It should be noted that for two years prior to Cuba DD/P officers examined all aspects of PM requirements, including maritime to determine what preparatory stops, if any, could be constructively taken in advance of an actual project requirement. Although a number of actions were taken, the Cuban maritime needs were not anticipated. In this connection, in retrospect it would probably have been wise to have requested Captain Scapa or some other senior Navy officer earlier in the project. A Marine Colonel was, of course, the Paramilitary Chief and had charge of maritime operations. Also, continuous liaison with the Navy and Navy officers in Defense was taking place. Nevertheless, a full time Navy Captain in the project could have resulted in the adoption of more imaginative methods which might possibly have produced greater performance. Even in retrospect, however, it is not known what those would have been.

## 1. The main specific criticisms of the Survey are:

a. Difficulties with crews particularly the "Barbara J." There is no question that trouble was experienced with the Cuban crews. One problem was that the Cubans, when recruited, thought that they were going to control the ships. This impression could have been given by Agency officers in good faith. At any rate, it soon became apparent that such control was impossible, particularly for the landing operation. Clearance was, therefore, requested by the Agency and obtained to hire American masters plus a few American officers for special posts (e.g., chief engineer, communications) on the main landing ships. The heads of MSTS went to extensive pain and trouble to help the Agency find such officers. When hired, however, they were resented by the Cuban seamen, who felt that they had been deprived of their own command and control, and time and circumstances did not permit shakedown cruises. The consequence, particularly when the crews were first put on board ship, was trouble, partly for the reason given and partly because of differences between the Cubans themselves. These latter conflicts were unfortunate, but it is unknown how they could have been discovered or anticipated during the recruitment unless more time had been available. These problems, moreover, were ironed out before the landing movement in which these particular ships were involved. In addition, the crews were effectively given good training at Vieques as evidenced both by Captain Scapa's examination and the later performance of the crews.

b. The Survey makes a great deal of the case of one of the Masters of the "Barbara J" who was discharged and subsequently had his name included in a letter of commendation. This case had a long history known to the inspectors which unfortunately the Survey does not choose to mention. Briefly, the Master was considered by MSTS as one of their best men. In fact he was one of the youngest of their men (about 35) to be made a Master. A strong personality difference arose between him and one of the senior Agency contract employees who was to be a central figure in the landing. This employee made charges against the Master including a charge that the Master had been drinking on an operational trip. He, therefore, demanded that the Master be discharged. The case was such that under the circumstances the Agency employee had to be backed or lost. Due to the employee's importance to the mission, the fact that he was a very good officer, and the shortness of times he was backed and the Master discharged. On further investigation, it was found that the Master not only denied all the allegations against him but claimed that he could find men to substantiate his story and asked in writing to vindicate himself. In view of his superior MSTS record and faced with serious issues of fact plus obvious security problems and with no time or opportunity to hold hearings to resolve those issues, it was decided to give the Master his contract pay and to explain the facts to the Industrial Relations Officer of MSTS. This was done. Thereafter, at the last moment it became essential to obtain a Master for one of the reserve supply ships. Due to the urgency of the situation, the Master's background and the very good impression that the Master had made following the other incident he was asked to take the job. Knowing of the problems at the beachhead including the dangers from enemy air attack and despite his strong disagreement with the decision resulting in his discharge, the Master still immediately accepted, took command of the ship and put to sea. Due to subsequent events beyond his control, he was recalled. In view of all these facts, his name was later included in the general letter to MSTS commending the performance of the more than 20 officers provided by MSTS. On this record, the action taken still seems correct.

c. As to infiltration of teams, there were some difficulties but again the situation must be examined in regard to all the existing facts. In the first place through the summer, fall and early winter of 1960, the Havana Station was in existence (the Embassy and thus the Station was closed in early January). Consequently, internal Cuban contacts and communications were excellent. Moreover, legal travel was relatively easy and as pointed out by the Survey, some 8 radio operators were put into Cuba legally. In addition, defectors, as indicated in an earlier section, were exfiltrating in large numbers. Many of these held responsible positions in the Castro Government or in the community and were in close touch with resistance groups. Moreover, the Miami exile community, many of whom were U.S. representatives of internal resistance groups, had their own communications through couriers or otherwise. Consequently, the six maritime operations mentioned by the Survey in September, October, and November must be assessed in relation to this background. Also, in addition, in the summer and fall of 1960 (ending in December) the RIO ESCONDIDO was used to infiltrate and exfiltrate as many as 16 people. The ship had a smuggling compartment in the boiler room which could take two individuals, preferably one. The Survey does not mention these move ments, probably because they were not considered maritime operations, rather arrangements with the ship's captain. Five of the 16 people infiltrated during this period were key resistance leaders and their W/T operators. An-other factor during this period was that legal movement was relatively easy for individuals legally in Cuba so that the desirability of putting in indi-viduals who had to live and leave black was reduced. In view of all these factors, it was decided to keep out many of the teams originally planned for infiltration. The reaction of trained teams to such inactivity was, what might have been expected, anger, discouragement and lowered morale. On top of this the ill-fated trip of the "Barbara J" was unfortunate since 3 teams were aboard who were not put ashore in Cuba. Consequently, the attitude of this group of Cuban trainees was at times bad. After the Havana Station was closed, however, the infiltration efforts picked up despite be-ing thwarted by bad weather through January. By the end of March or early April, the paramilitary agent infiltration had achieved an adequate total. Moreover, thirteen communicators was a satisfactory number al-though it is probably fair to say that there is no such thing as too many communicators.

d. The Survey alleges that small boat operations were not planned. Probably under the press of events the paper work was not as tidy as might be found in normal charter parties. Planning, however, was, it is believed, what was possible. Maritime operations can only be planned in relation to known facts such as an available reception, an available boat and a moment timely for a mission. Overall plans are obviously possible and it is believed that it can be shown that such plans existed. In the same way what was desired in the way of boats was known but actual purchases were only feasible as particular craft materialized on the market.

## C. TRAINING UNDERGROUND LEADERS

The major criticisms of the training were that the sites were inadequate and in some cases too remote; training on foreign soil would have been better accomplished in the U.S.; some of the U.S. training was with haphazard fa-cilities and trainers; and the training was piecemeal without plan.

Before responding to the particular allegations, it must be noted that, with all due respect, the Survey's criticism suggests the attitudes of a dweller in a secure and well-ordered academic "Never- never Land" who assumes that all training must be similarly conducted or it is poorly managed. It is the Har-vard Law School trying to comment on the advantages of sandlot training for baseball players. The only difference being that the HLS would be judi-ciously analytic which is a point of view never achieved by the Survey.

The facts are that none of the project's training sites were ideal or picked solely for the accomplishment of the training involved. Security considerations, or, in other words, political concerns, played a vital role.

Moreover, if results are any criteria, the training sites were adequate. As far as the Brigade and its air arm are concerned, the conclusions of impartial experts (i.e., the JCS team) regarding the competence achieved are recorded in writing. The performance of the trainees on the beachhead is further proof. The training of the landing ships' crews at Vieques was good and effective in operation. The training in Panama was excellent on all reports as was the screening and handling of personnel to be trained at Useppa Island. The Nino Diaz group at New Orleans was, according to all observers, well trained and ready to fight. Its failure to land was due to poor leadership and not the fault of the troops.

The communications training has always been reported as excellent and the Survey itself commends the communications effort. Practice also established that the trained agent communicators in Cuba had far fewer garbles in their messages than normally found in such transmissions.

The agents, who were trained (and all those who were infiltrated as agents were given training), received courses in how to live black; some weapons and demolitions training; some CE; air reception and how to handle drops; resistance organization and how to contact underground groups. The teams who were to be infiltrated received, as stated by the Survey and mentioned earlier, training in "security, basic clandestine tradecraft, intelligence collection and reporting, propaganda and agitation, subversive activities, resistance organization, reception operations, explosives and demolitions, guerrilla action and similar action."

There was, therefore, no lack of training doctrine or planning. Incidentally, since it has been raised by the Survey, the air reception procedures taught to all agents were those taught in the Agency School on this subject.

Regarding sites, it should be pointed out that, whether good or bad, the Guatemala sites were the *only* ones available. The U.S. was politically unacceptable and the Guatemala government was the deciding element as to the sites in Guatemala that could be used. The Survey says that the ground training base in Guatemala "obviously . . . could not" accommodate 500 individuals. The fact was that it did plus many more and worked.

Similarly the initial situation at New Orleans was difficult. Again, however, the problems were adequately corrected to provide adequate training. It took work and some help from the Armed Services to get the base functioning but both occurred and prevailed.

The Survey, as indicated, also alleges that training could have been more effective and secure if done in the United States. The Survey points to tank and communications training which did take place in the U.S. to support its conclusion. What is not said is that the tank training only involved 25 men and was done at a U.S. base accustomed to training foreign groups and quite able to assimilate a small group of this size. Similarly, communications could be and were taught in small classes. Political clearances, therefore, were granted specifically for these classes, i.e., a U.S. base for tankers and U.S. safehouses for communicators, but as a recognized exception to the basic rule of generally denying the use of the U.S. for any kind of training. The Nino Diaz group at New Orleans was obviously another exception and one which was somewhat inconsistent with the general rule, but the clearance was given nevertheless because time was short (the invasion was imminent) and an attempted diversionary operation was considered important. Moreover, no other site was available that was either better or usable, taking all factors into account.

The question of haphazard facilities and trainers has been discussed earlier. Obviously, there is a good deal of adjusting to the needs of the moment in a project of this sort. It is believed, however, that the record will show that the training plans were reasonably detailed and complete. Moreover, that wherever a training course of any length was involved, there was a specific training plan.

# Associated
# Documents

20 November 1961

MEMORANDUM FOR:    Mr. McCone

SUBJECT:    Survey of the Cuban Operation

1. Presented herewith is a 150 page survey of the Cuban Operation, together with the most important basic documents on the Operation which are included in the five annexes. In this report we have not attempted to go into an exhaustive step by step inspection of every action in the operation. Nor have we tried to assess individual performance, although our inspection left us with very definite views. Rather, we have tried to find out what went wrong, and why, and to present the facts and conclusions as briefly as possible. This report has been double-spaced for ease in reading. The ten recommendations for corrective action start on page 148.

2. In conducting this survey we reviewed all of the basic files and documents, including all of the material prepared by the Agency for General Maxwell Taylor's Committee, as well as the minutes of that Committee which were made available to us. In addition, we conducted extensive interviews with all of the principal officers on the project from the DD/P on down, and made detailed memoranda for our files on all of these discussions; e.g., my meeting with the top three officers of the Branch reviewing the operation the week after the landing failed is reported in some 70 pages. Thus, while the analysis and conclusions presented herewith regarding the operation are those of the Inspector General, the bases for these conclusions are extensively documented in the files.

3. This, in my opinion, is a fair report even though highly critical. Unfortunately, there has been a tendency in the Agency to gloss over CIA's inadequacies and to attempt to fix all of the blame for the failure of the invasion upon other elements of the Government, rather than to recognize the Agency's weaknesses reflected in this report. Consequently, I will make no additional distribution of this report until you indicate whom you wish to have copies. In this connection, the President's Foreign Intelligence Advisory Board has requested a copy in time for Mr. Coyne to give a brief report on it at their December 9 meeting. I will await your wishes in this regard.

/s/ Lyman Kirkpatrick
Lyman B. Kirkpatrick
Inspector General

Attachment

24 November 1961

MEMORANDUM FOR:    Director of Central Intelligence

SUBJECT: Report on the Cuban Operation

    1. The report on the Cuban Operation, as is true of all Inspector General reports, was prepared under my personal direction and worked on by myself and my deputy, Mr. David McClean, as well as the three officers who did the principal collecting of information and preparation of the text: Messrs. [excised], [excised] and [excised]. The final editing was done by myself personally and the report represents the views of the Inspector General.

    2. In preparing the report we had access to all of the material prepared by this Agency and submitted to the Taylor Committee, as well as the minutes of the Taylor Committee meetings, and a chance to see their final conclusions and recommendations. In addition to this we had all of the documentary material available in the WH Division, WH-4 and other staffs and divisions of the Agency who had cognizance of or prepared material for WH-4. These particularly included ONE, OCI, and Staff D of the DD/P.

    3. As is noted particularly in our report, we did not go outside of the agency in any respect and tried to confine our inspection to only internal Agency matters, except where reference had to be made to outside actions that affected the operation. In interviewing persons connected with this operation, we talked initially to three of the top officers in the operation, commencing with Mr. Esterline and Colonel Hawkins, and having our initial lengthy discussion with them within a week of the operation. We interviewed all of the appropriate supervisors in the DD/P, starting with the DD/P himself and including the A/DDP/A, Chief, WH, Chief WH-4, and some 130 other officers and employees directly involved in the operation. We kept extensive notes and material of all of these discussions which are documented in our files.

Lyman B. Kirkpatrick<br>Inspector General

cc: DDCI
DD/P

28 November 1961

MEMORANDUM FOR THE RECORD

General Cabell called Mr. Kirkpatrick to state that the fact of the IG's report on Cuba should be restricted on a must-need-to-know basis. No copies other than those that have been distributed to Mr. McCone, Mr. Dulles, General Cabell, Mr. Bissell, Colonel King, and Mr. Esterline will be distributed without authority of the DCI or DDCI.

This restriction also specifically applies to distribution to the President's Board of Intelligence Advisors, and Mr. Kirkpatrick so informed 27 November.

General Cabell has discussed holding this report tightly with Mr. Dulles and Mr. Bissell, and the latter is to pass on the guidance to Colonel King and Mr. Esterline. (Accomplished per report to DDCI 27 November.)

/s/ CPC
C.P. CABELL
General, USAF
Deputy Director

1 December 1961

MEMORANDUM FOR:    Director of Central
Intelligence

SUBJECT: Report on the Cuban Operation

1. In our conversation on Friday morning, the first of December, you mentioned your concern that the Inspector General's Report on the Cuban Operation, taken alone, might give an erroneous impression as to the extent CIA is responsible for the failure of the operation. In my opinion the failure of the operation should be charged in order to the following factors.

a. An over-all lack of recognition on the part of the U.S. Government as to the magnitude of the operation required to overthrow the Fidel Castro regime.

b. The failure on the part of the U.S. Government to plan for all contingencies at the time of the Cuban operation including the necessity for using regular U.S. military forces in the event that the exiled Cubans could not do the job themselves.

c. The failure on the part of the U.S. Government to be willing to commit to the Cuban Operation, as planned and executed, those necessary resources required for its success.

/s/ Lyman Kirkpatrick
Lyman B. Kirkpatrick
Inspector General

15 December 1961

SUBJECT:   The Inspector General's Survey of the Cuban Operation

To comment on the subject report in detail would result in a paper approaching in length, that of the survey itself. Such a commentary would have to deal in depth with the aim of the survey, its scope, and the method used in compiling it. Such a commentary would, at a large number of pages, be required to note inaccuracies, omissions, distortions, unsupported allegations, and many erroneous conclusions.

A detailed inquiry on the Cuban operation on elements other than clandestine tradecraft, has already been completed by the group headed by General Taylor. General Taylor's report was based on testimony by all the principal officers involved in the Cuban operation. The Inspector General's report is not based on complete testimony; some of its conclusions are in conflict with General Taylor's conclusions.

It is not clear what purpose the Inspector General's report is intended to serve. If it is intended primarily as an evaluation of the Agency's role, it is deficient. Neither Mr. Dulles nor I was consulted in the preparation of the Inspector General's report. As a result, there are many unnecessary inaccuracies.

The report tries to do both too much and too little.

On the one hand, it attempts to describe the processes of national security policy-making as though this were a process in logical deduction like working a problem in geometry. According to the Inspector General's account, firm propositions should be laid down in writing and in advance from which correct conclusions as to proper actions must inevitably be drawn. In this respect the report goes far beyond an analysis of the Agency's role, and it is not accurate. It tries to do too much.

On the other hand, the report treats the preparations for the April landings as if these were the only activities directed against Castro and his influence throughout the hemisphere and the world. It chooses to ignore all other facets of the Agency's intelligence collection and covert actions program which preceded, accompanied, and have followed the landings in April of 1961. Thus, it does too little.

The report misses objectivity by a wide margin. In unfriendly hands, it can become a weapon unjustifiably to attack the entire mission, organization, and functioning of the Agency. It fails to cite the specific achievements of persons associated with the operation and presents a picture of unmitigated and almost willful bumbling and disaster.

In its present form, this is not a useful report for anyone inside or outside the Agency. If complete analysis beyond that already accomplished by General Taylor and his group is still required, then a new kind of report is called for, —a report with clear terms of reference based an complete testimony. Such a report could concentrate on clandestine tradecraft, an asset for which the Agency remains uniquely responsible.

/s/ C.P. Cabell
C.P. Cabell
General, USAF
Deputy Director

19 January 1962

Dr. James R. Killian, Jr.
Chairman, President's Foreign Intelligence Advisory Board
297 Executive Office Building
Washington 25, D.C.

Dear Dr. Killian:

Attached is copy of the CIA Inspector General's "Survey Of Cuban Operations" together with comments thereon by General C.P. Cabell, Deputy Director of CIA and "Analysis Of the Cuban Operation" by Deputy Director (Plans). This latter report is intended as a comment on the Inspector General's report.

As you readily understand, I am not in a position to render a personal opinion concerning the validity of the IG's report or the statements by the DDCI and the DDP because I was not in CIA at the time. Moreover, it is my personal opinion as a result of examinations I have made of this operation after the fact that both the report and the rebuttals are extreme. I believe an accurate appraisal of the Cuban effort and the reasons for failure rest some place in between the two points of view expressed in the reports.

I believe it is safe to say the failure of the Cuban operation was Government-wide and in this respect the Agency must bear its full share (though not the entire) responsibility.

For this reason I would recommend that your board, in reviewing the Inspector General's Survey also review the comments and analysis of the DDCI and the DD/P.

Yours very truly,

/s/John A. McCone

John A. McCone
Director

Attachments
    As stated

19 January 1962

MEMORANDUM FOR:    Deputy Director (Plans)

SUBJECT:    Survey of Cuban Operation

1. My work in support of your "Analysis of the Cuban Operation" gave me an unusual opportunity to study with care the document which caused the Analysis to be written, namely, the "Inspector General's Survey of the Cuban Operation, October 1961."

2. My consideration of the Survey has forced me to reach certain conclusions which I feel that I must record. I do so in writing because these conclusions are, in my opinion, of sufficient significance to demand the discipline of a written expression. Moreover, I feel that those who disagree with me should have the opportunity to direct any replies that they may choose to make to specific identifiable comments.

3. I may say that my decision to write this memorandum was reached with considerable reluctance and only after long deliberation. The deciding factor was my belief that the suggestions for action in paragraph 6 below are worthwhile and should be submitted. They would have been meaningless without the reasons set forth in the earlier paragraphs. The views expressed are, needless to say, exclusively mine.

4. In my opinion the I.G. Survey is most unfortunate for three reasons:

a. It is an incompetent job. The authors never understood the problems with which they were dealing and failed to express their views with any precision or proper use of relevant facts.

b. It is biased. Basically relevant evidence on vital issues was not only left out but never even mentioned. The Survey undertook only to present those items which suggested failures or inadequacies. These items, however, were not fully depicted so that a false picture was given. Admittedly, an I.G. must expose fault but it is also his job to do so accurately.

c. It is malicious, or, to put it alternatively, it is intentionally biased. Admittedly, this is a serious charge and is, at best, merely a statement of opinion. I can only say that I hold such opinion firmly. In my view it could be supported solely on the basis of the Survey's total omission in many places of significantly relevant evidence. Such omissions are so excessive and one-sided as to substantiate the conclusion that they must hare been intentional. In addition, however, I would like to mention four other points:

1) The fact that the inspectors, in making their investigation, omitted any discussions of their findings with the senior officers responsible for the project. Although, technically, the I.G. can accurately state that he talked to the DD/P and the then A/DDP/A about the Survey, the fact is that these discussion were exceedingly brief and covered none of the real issues in the Survey. The AC/DPD was not spoken to at all. The Security Officer of WH/4 was not spoken to at all. Other senior officers, such as C/WH and C/WH/4, were never given an opportunity to express their views in relation to statements in the Survey.

2) Some officers with whom the inspectors had discussions felt after they had a chance to see the Survey, that it did not impartially express the information which they had provided and left out much of the relevant information given. Moreover, some officers have reported that the attitude of the inspectors and their line of questioning indicated a desire to obtain facts or views to support judgments already formed. Opinions contrary to these judgments were not only disregarded but resisted.

3) The distribution of the final Survey was so peculiar and contrary to norms, practice that it raises an inference of intended partiality. The method of distribution is known and will not be repeated here. It might be added that there were other facts with respect to the distribution of the Survey worthy of mention. C/WH/4 was called one day and asked if he wanted to read the Survey. He said that he would like to do so but since both C/WH and DC/WH were away he could not leave since he was Acting Chief of the Division. Particularly, he could not meet the requirements of the offer which were that he would only have an hour from the time of the telephone call to see the Survey (including travel time) since it then had to be sent to the printer. Why the urgency was so great is not clear. As far as is known, only one individual outside of the I.G. Staff saw the Survey in final or substantially final form before it was distributed, namely, an Officer who was the Chief of Operations for WH/4 during the project. Why he was selected instead of one of his superiors who was connected with the project is not known.

4) Since this particular operation, without question, involved more political interest and dynamite than any in which the Agency has ever

participated, there was every reason for following regular procedure meticulously. In addition to the distribution point mentioned above, it seems relevant to wonder how Dr. Killian and the Attorney General knew of the Survey's existence so as to request a copy.

5. I should say that, whatever the appearance of the foregoing, I have not been trying to I.G. the I.G. The information reported came to me unsolicited and in the normal course of my work with you and your Analysis. Maybe there is additional evidence of importance, but I have not looked for it and do not plan to do so.

6. The significance of the foregoing is to provide the reasons for the main purpose of this memorandum, i.e., the submission of the following recommendations for action.

a. The DCI should resolve to his own satisfaction the conflicts on major issues between the I.G.'s Survey and your Analysis. Since both these documents are internal to the Agency, there is no Agency position on the Cuban operation unless the conflicts are resolved. In view of the importance of and the continuing interest in the operation at high levels of the Government, an Agency position seems essential. Such a position is also important for the future. The operation is bound to be studied for various reasons and there should be an Agency position at least as to what happened, what were the mistakes and what were the lessons. Moreover, the DCI, having assigned office after the operation was thoroughly finished, has every reason for wanting to have some definitive findings and conclusions.

b. If the DCI agrees with a. above each recipient of the Survey and Analysis (and it is understood that they will only be distributed together) should be advised of the fact that such an Agency position is being sought. This might help to avoid independent conclusions outside of the Agency being reached first.

c. The following requirements should be imposed on all future I.G. surveys at least on any aspects of the DD/P area of responsibility.

1) No survey shell be undertaken without specific written terms of reference approved by the DCI.

2) The DD/P shall be satisfied that in each future survey covering any portion of his area of responsibility the I.G. or his staff will interview at least all officers having had responsibility for any part of the activity inspected by the I.G. and prior to the distribution of the survey

the DD/P and each such officer will be given an opportunity to express his views on points included in the Survey. Obviously the I.G. need not accept those views. Such procedure, however, will save an enormous amount of time required to answer surveys such as the Cuban one which fail to present a full factual picture regardless of the conclusions reached.

7. I am addressing this memorandum to you as my immediate superior. I hope, however, that you will agree with my request that the memorandum be passed to the DCI for his consideration. I do not, of course, ask that you associate yourself with it or any part of it merely because you transmit it.

/S/C.T.B.
C. TRACY BARNES

*PERSONAL & CONFIDENTIAL*

MEMORANDUM FOR:   Mr. C. Tracy Barnes

Dear Tracy:

Thank you for your courtesy in sending me a copy of your memorandum of 19 January concerning the Inspector General's Survey of the Cuban Operation. I do hope that Dick forwards it to the DCI, and I am enclosing a copy of this note to you in case you wish to send a copy to Dick.

I have not had time to study your memorandum, or even in fact do more than glance at the DD/P analysis in view of the meeting with the President's Board all day Friday and the fact that I am going to be away all this week. However, I will make the following comments. Needless to say, I completely disagree with your statement that it is an incompetent job. I feel that it is competent and I believe that the more than one file cabinet drawer full of background documents will prove its competence. I do not believe that it is biased. We made it very clear at the start of the report that it would only deal with inadequacies and failures and would not purport to be a thorough analysis of the operation.

Most of all I object most strongly to your third observation, namely that it is malicious and intentionally biased. I have asked the men who did this survey to review your memorandum and comment on the reasons you believe that it is biased. I should perhaps acknowledge that more time should have been spent with you or Bissell, but inasmuch as this devolved on me, if there is a fault, it is mine personally. But to imply that for some reason, unknown to me, that we would slant this report is an unfair comment. You apparently feel there was something unusual in the distribution of the final report. The only thing unusual in it was that we had two Directors at the time, and Mr. Mc-Cone having asked for it received it as he was leaving for the West Coast on the day before Thanksgiving and everybody else got their copies on the day after Thanksgiving. Your concern as to how the President's Board and the Attorney General knew of the survey's existence can be answered very simply. In 1956 the Presidents Board in writing advised all agencies that all inspector general reports should be forwarded to them automatically. I don't believe it was a week after the Cuban operation that the direct question came from that Board as to whether an inspection was going to be done to which an affirmative reply was given. The Attorney General's source I do not know.

Finally as far as to what should be done next, you and Dick should know that at the conclusion of my discussion with the President's Board I urged that a group, or individual, who had not in any way been associated with the operation be charged with taking the Taylor Report, our report and your comments and all background material and writing a truly national and detailed report. I believe that would be a far better solution than trying to develop a CIA position, which really is not very practical inasmuch as there were so many outside factors affecting this operation.

/s/ Kirk
Lyman B. Kirkpatrick

MEMORANDUM FOR:   Mr. Kirkpatrick

SUBJECT:   The IG's Cuban Survey and the DD/P's Analysis of the Cuban Operation

1. The scope of the IG Survey is briefly and clearly stated in the Introduction. The Survey's intent was to identify and describe weaknesses *within the Agency* which contributed to the final result and to make recommendations for their future avoidance. The IG had no authority to conduct survey of the machinery for making decisions and policy at other levels of Government. This field was covered by the group headed by Gen. Taylor. The Survey expressly avoided detailed analysis of the purely military phase of the operation.

2. Much of the DD/P's Analysis is devoted, however, to a discussion of governmental decision-making and to a rehash of the military operation. It criticizes the Survey for insufficient attention to those matters, putting the major blame for the operation's failure on factors beyond the control of the Agency.

3. The Analysis attempts to refute most of the weaknesses described by the Survey. The few which it admits were, it contends, not significant to the final result. It rejects the Survey's statements that intelligence was inadequate and misused and that staffing was inadequate. It blames the failure of the air drops on the Cuban reception crews and air crews. It states that small boat operations could not well have been handled in any other way. And it states that other weaknesses were not important because they were not the decisive reason for failure.

4. There is a fundamental difference of approach between the two documents. While the Analysis is preoccupied with interdepartmental policy making and military strategy, the Survey is mainly concerned with the failure to build up internal resistance in Cuba through clandestine operations. The Analysis fails to shed any further significant light on this fundamental issue.

5. The Analysis shows a poorer grasp of what was going on at the case-officer level than of events in policy-making circles. This is apparent in a number of inaccuracies in the Analysis. For example, the discussion of activities in Miami is inaccurate and misleading. Conduct of training in Miami

is defended although it was not criticized by the Survey. The 178 trainees alluded to in the Analysis as trained in Miami were in fact trained in Guatemala. The PM section in Miami was being *built up* beginning in November 1960, rather than being de-emphasized. These and other inaccuracies suggest that the Analysis should be read with caution where it deals with events on the working level of the project.

6. The IG investigators centered their inquiry on certain phases which are significant to the success or failure of any operation and of the Agency's overall mission itself. They cannot be ignored or argued away just because of policy decisions made outside of the Agency.

[Excised]

/s/

[Excised]

[Excised]

/s/

[Excised]

[Excised]

/s/

[Excised]

27 January 1962

MEMORANDUM FOR:    Director of Central
  Intelligence

SUBJECT:    Mr. Barnes' Memorandum on the IG
  Survey of the Cuban Operation

1. As you are aware, Mr. Tracy Barnes did a major part of the work in preparing our comments on Mr. Kirkpatrick's Survey of the Cuban Operation. At the conclusion of the task, Mr. Barnes wrote me the attached memorandum which I hereby pass on to you.

2. I may say that I am in agreement with Mr. Barnes that the Survey, largely by reason of the omission of material relevant to its conclusions, constitutes a highly biased document and that the bias is of such a character that it must have been intentional.

3. I will be glad to discuss this with you if you so desire.

/s/ Richard M. Bissell, Jr.

RICHARD M. BISSELL, JR.
Deputy Director
(Plans)

Attachments
1. Barnes' Memo
2. IG Memo to Mr. Barnes

TOP SECRET

15 February 1962

MEMORANDUM FOR: Mr. John McCone
Director of Central Intelligence

SUBJECT: The Inspector General's Survey of the Cuban Operation

1. Upon receipt of the Inspector General's report of October 1961, on the Cuban Operation which reached my desk prior to my resignation as Director of Central Intelligence, I immediately transmitted a copy to the Deputy Director (Plans) for his comment. This was in line with the practice I had consistently followed in dealing with the reports of the Inspector General: namely, the Office which is the subject of the inspection is given an opportunity to comment on the I.G. report before the Director determines the action to be taken thereon. The reply of the Deputy Director (Plans), dated 18 January 1962, of which I have received a copy, was submitted to you following my resignation.

2. Meanwhile, I have also received and considered the comments of the Deputy Director of Central Intelligence, General Cabell.

3. I remain at your disposal for any comments you may wish me to submit on any phases of this matter relating to C.I.A. responsibilities. Hence I will not submit detailed written comment on the Inspector General's report.

4. At this time, however, I wish to make certain general comments:

a. As a member of the Taylor Committee appointed by the President, I participated fully in the work of his Committee and joined in his Memorandum and oral reports to the President on this subject. While I do not nor have a copy of these documents, I made only one or two reservations to the general conclusions and recommendations of those reports. I consider them to be sound and believe they should be accepted as the best available Survey of this particular operation.

b. The Inspector General's report suffers from the fact that his investigation was limited to the activities of one segment of one agency, namely, the C.I.A. Opinions based on such a partial review fail to give the true story or to provide a sound basis for the sweeping conclusions reached by him.

c. Judgments could not properly be rendered in this matter without a full analysis, as was made by the Taylor Committee, of actions of all of the participating elements in the operation and the influences brought to bear outside of the Agency which affected the operation. This applies particularly to the participation of the Department of State, the Department of Defense, the Joint Chiefs of Staff and to certain elements of the Executive Department of the Government.

    d. At no time during the preparation of his report did the Inspector General request any information from me and he makes certain serious errors in areas where my direct responsibility was clearly involved.

5. Two major areas of criticism in the I.G. report cover (1) the operational arrangements for the organization, training, transportation and deployment of the Brigade and, (2) the relations of Agency personnel to the Cuban emigration and their political organization. As to these points, I submit the following:

    a. First, while certain organizational matters, in the light of developments, may be open to some criticism, the Brigade with its entire complement of men and equipment reached the landing area on schedule and under circumstances which achieved complete surprise. The situation in the landing area was substantially as predicted. The enemy battle order intelligence was essentially correct. The failure to get the ammunition and supplies ashore was due to circumstances beyond the control of the Brigade commander or its personnel.

    b. Second, with respect to the organization of a Cuban emigre political committee in support of the operations, I would point out that prior to engaging in the operation a broad coalition of Cuban leaders, and one acceptable to our State Department, was realized.

These two important achievements covered major areas of C.I.A. responsibility.

6. As Director, I deemed it desirable and necessary in view of my other duties to delegate certain responsibilities within the Agency for the day-by-day management of the operation, and on military matters and judgments I relied heavily on military personnel assigned to C.I.A. and on Department of Defense personnel and the Joint Chiefs of Staff. However, I assumed throughout full responsibility for the Agency's participation and actions and kept currently advised of all important developments. During the concluding days of the operation, I was particularly influenced by the judgments in Col.

Hawkins dispatch, dated April 13, 1961, relating to the high state of readiness of the Brigade (Annex A to Chapter IV of DDP report).

7. Whether or not the operation would have succeeded if the Brigade had landed with its entire personnel and equipment is a matter which can be debated and on which even today military experts differ. Certainly, the responsibility for failure does not lie primarily in the main areas of criticism stressed in the Inspector General's report.

8. Of course, there are lessons to be learned as pointed out in the Taylor Reports. These Reports, I believe, should be taken as the main basis for any review of the Agency's actions in support of the operation.

/s/ Allen W. Dulles
Allen W. Dulles

19 February 1962

The Honorable Allen W. Dulles
Washington, D.C.

Dear Allen:

I have received your memorandum of 15 February 1962 containing your comments on the Inspector General's Survey of the Cuban Operation. Copies of this memorandum, together with the DD/P analysis of the survey, the comments made by General Cabell, Mr. Kirkpatrick, and the personal views expressed by Mr. Tracy Barnes, will be bound in the report—and therefore will be known to anyone who might have occasion to read it.

Sincerely,

signed

John A. McCone
Director

DD/P-2-0779
23 February 1962

MEMORANDUM FOR:   Assistant to the DCI, Mr. Chapin

SUBJECT:   Return of Available Copies of "An Analysis
of the Cuban Operation by the Deputy Director
(Plans)," TS #181884.


1. Transmitted herewith are all the completed copies available to us of subject document. Included are copy 5 and copies 7 through 20.

2. To confirm our original understanding: Copies 1, 2, and 3 went to the DCI on 18 January; copy 4 went to Mr. Dulles on 18 January; copy 6 went to the Inspector General on 19 January; and copies 21 through 25 are unassembled, with the pieces residing in the DD/P Registry. We will destroy those latter materials if you have sufficient copies without assembling the last five.


ROBERT W. KING
Assistant to the DD/P

Attachments:
    As stated

*DD/P Registry (Margaret Porter) advised that those copies were being destroyed.

# The Bay of Pigs Revisited

*An Interview with Jacob Esterline and Col. Jack Hawkins*

In October 1996, the two chief managers of the Bay of Pigs operation met in a Washington D.C. hotel to conduct a lengthy interview on the invasion. The meeting marked the first time they had seen each other since the weekend of April 17–19, 1961, and the first time they had recalled, together, the events surrounding the failed invasion. The interviewer is Peter Kornbluh.

About JACOB ESTERLINE: Jacob D. Esterline, aka Jake Engler, served as chief of the special Cuba Task Force established to run the Bay of Pigs operation (C/WH/4). In 1954 he had held a similar position during Operation PBSUCCESS, the CIA effort to overthrow the government of Jacobo Arbenz; he served as the first post-coup chief of station in Guatemala City from 1954–1957, and then chief of station in Caracas, Venezuela until 1960 when he was selected for the Cuba Task Force. After the Bay of Pigs he had several assignments, including chief of station in Miami from 1967–1972. He retired from the CIA in 1973.

About Col. JACK HAWKINS: Col. Hawkins, aka John Haskins, served as the chief paramilitary specialist on the Cuba Task Force in charge of the invasion (C/WH/4/PM). In October, 1960, when the concept of the operation expanded from an infiltration plan to an amphibious assault, he was detailed from the Marine Corps to the CIA. Awarded a Bronze Medal and Silver Star in World War II and Korea, he retired from the Marines in 1965.

\*\* \*\* \*\*

**Q.** Do you recall how you became involved in the Cuba operation?

**Esterline:** I was finishing a tour in Venezuela. [CIA Deputy Director Frank] Wisner came through in and around that time and mentioned that they were probably going to be doing something about, about Castro, beginning to think about it at least. And I said, well, if there's anything I can do when I finish my tour here let me know. Those were fatal words because a month or so later I was told that upon my return to the United States I was going to be put in charge of the initial thinking about what we were going to do about Castro.

**Hawkins:** I reported to the [Marine] Commandant in his office, General David Shoup, and he said the CIA wants to land a few Cuban exile troops in Cuba and they have asked for a Marine colonel to give them some help on this. And he says, "I'm going to send you over there on a temporary basis."

**Q.** What covert warfare experience did you draw on for the initial planning on Cuba?

**Esterline:** We thought back to the original things we had tried in terms of Guatemala in the broad sense of the word, not in the specific. We would have to begin to develop a fairly substantial cadre of military specialists and to that end we began the selection process of people who were available or would be available either outside of Cuba or inside of Cuba — people that we could exfiltrate. Also in that timeframe we had to begin to look for places that we could securely train these people and, as I recall, the United States, in the early stages, the United States was absolutely verboten in terms of where we would train. Having had a long experience in Guatemala and [previously] being chief of station, I was in the strongest position in terms of getting the real estate and the kind of support that would be necessary in Guatemala. To that end I went to Guatemala with the then chief of station who had actually replaced me there. We began to develop the ties to the folks in the Guatemalan government, namely Ydigoras Fuentes — that was the president — that would enable us to obtain relatively secure training camps.

**Q.** The initial landing site was the city of Trinidad. Why did you pick that location?

**Esterline:** I wanted to be absolutely sure that we didn't take any step that we couldn't back away from and to that end that is the reason that I had very early on developed a fondness for the eastern end of the island of Cuba, the Escambray mountains, what they now call the Trinidad area, because I thought if we could put people in there, they could survive and we could think very seriously about a greater effort.

If these teams that we put in survive, they would proliferate if the situation was correct and we could then begin to put in whatever additional material support we needed to be dictated by the situation. And I still think that that approach was right except that there was no question that time was not on our side.

**Hawkins:** My understanding after arriving there was that the original concept was, as Mr. Esterline says', primarily to develop guerrilla warfare within Cuba through the medium of the agent teams, who would have radio contact with the CIA in the United States and to whom we would deliver arms through overflight airdrops. This was the major effort of the plan to start with and Mr. Esterline proposed that a small infantry force of perhaps 300 men would be organized for possible employment but in conjunction with guerrilla warfare that was already going on in Cuba or had been developed by the teams.

**Q.** You both drafted a key planning paper in January 1961, laying out some of the assumptions and necessities of a successful invasion. Could you read the most important passages and comment on their significance?

**Esterline:** [reading from document] "It is expected that these operations will precipitate a large uprising throughout Cuba and cause a revolt of a large segment of the Cuban Army and Militia. An internal revolt in Cuba, if one is triggered by our actions may serve to topple the Castro government within a couple of weeks."

We had reason to believe that there was a fairly active and fairly sizable resistance at least in spirit opposed to Castro at that time but we did not know it definitively. The problem was how to begin operations that would allow us to get a better feeling for how serious and how successful—what the chances of success would be.

**Hawkins:** We did have intelligence from our agents that the whole province of Las Villas was anti-Castro for the most part and were sympathetic to the guerrillas then operating in the Escambray Mountains. We thought that we would have the opportunity to arm considerable numbers of them but, if not, the brigade would enter the mountains and begin guerrilla activity.

My belief and hope at the time was that we would have established absolute control of the air before we ever landed this force which I described as being absolutely essential and that the air operations in support of our force in the Trinidad area would be very spectacular in Cuba and inflict serious casualties on Castro's forces, the Militia. We thought that this would gradually produce unrest and further uprising. I still believe that that probably would have occurred had we done it as we recommended.

**Hawkins:** [reading from document] "If matters do not eventuate as predicted above, the lodgment established by our force can be used as the site to establish a provisional government which can be recognized by the United States and other American states and be given overt military assistance. The way will then be paved for United States military intervention and the pacification of Cuba. This will result in the prompt overthrow of the Castro government." So even in that time in January, I visualized the possibility of a provisional government in the Escambray Mountain area which would at that time be assisted by the United States, at least logistically.

It really was essential to overthrow Castro. I thoroughly believed in that objective and of course it later proved, later on, that that should have taken place. We should have gotten rid of that communist regime. I really assumed that the national government meant what it said when it said "We want to overthrow Castro." Now, of course, we had a change of administration in there [when Kennedy was elected] and that changed things considerably.

**Q.** Kennedy defeated Vice-President Nixon in November 1960. Where did that leave preparations for the Cuba operation?

**Esterline:** I really thought that what we were doing should stop and that this new administration coming in should have time, in an orderly manner, have time to develop their own options and think about how they might want to deal with this problem. I put that forward to [Deputy Director] Bissell in writing and I got nowhere. I was told that it was not good to be that way and that we would go ahead and develop and continue with our plans that would be put to this new administration. I was very uneasy about it because I just . . . it was such a hairy thing to begin with.

**Q.** Were you involved in any direct briefings for President Kennedy?

**Hawkins:** I did go with [CIA Director] Dulles two or three times over to the White House meetings in the Oval office with President Kennedy and members of this cabinet. Mr. Rusk spoke out more than any of the other cabinet members and he was adamantly opposed to this operation and to the use of any aircraft whatever.

I don't believe that anyone was explaining to him that you can't take a thin-skinned troop transport onto a hostile beach and drop anchor and start unloading troops with hostile fighters and bombers overhead. It can't be done. Nobody in the administration at high levels seemed to know that and nobody made it clear to President Kennedy that I know of.

**Q.** Did you brief the President on the Trinidad Plan?

**Hawkins:** The area lent itself to what we call in military terms isolation of the area. In other words, we could take certain measures that would make it difficult for the enemy to come into that area. The mountains on the west, that was one barrier and there was an unforgeable river on the north and east that had only two bridges over it. One of them was a railroad bridge and we thought we could knock those out. Tanks and vehicles would then not be able to come into Trinidad.

The plan was to land there at Trinidad; that location had good landing beaches, good defensible terrain; and we were going to block these ways for vehicles to come in there and we were going to hold there as long as we could and we were going to try and arm some of the residents and if we weren't having any luck or we were being pressed, we go right up into the western mountains and join the guerrillas already there.

**Q.** But Kennedy objected to Trinidad.

**Hawkins:** Well [Richard Bissell] came and told me that the president had completely rejected the Trinidad plan because it was too noisy and looked too much like an invasion. And he told me that the State Department and the president had imposed conditions on the landing—that we had to capture on the first day an airfield capable of supporting B-26 operations.

He wanted me immediately, that night, to find out such a place where that could be done. There was only one such a place that we could seize and hold for a limited time and had such an airstrip and that was the Bay of Pigs.

The president only gave [Bissell] three days to come up with a plan and so we told him what I had just said that this was the only place that satisfied this requirement. Now I made it clear to him that, yes, we could land there and hold this area for a little while anyway because of the narrow approach through the swamps and a third along the coast from Cienfuegos. Now we can hold this for a while but not very long. Moreover, the brigade has no chance whatever of breaking out of there. In spite of these warnings that I gave him, about the military dangers involved in this area, [Bissell] said if this is the only place that satisfies the president's requirements then that's what we're going to do. And he said go ahead and develop a plan on the Bay of Pigs.

**Q.** What was your reaction when you found out about the change of landing site?

**Esterline:** Jack said [pointing to a map] the Bay of Pigs, and I looked down and I said "Bay of Pigs, that's not a very good name for success." But I looked at it and I thought to myself, it does look very secure, no one is going to get in there very easily but how are we going to get any more recruits, how are we going to expand this front because there is nobody there except alligators and ducks.

**Q.** Your superior, Richard Bissell made some critical decisions that affected the invasion. What were your opinions about him?

**Esterline:** I guess I have to say that he used us just as he used a lot of other things to his own advantage entirely.

**Hawkins:** Mr. Bissell acted unwisely in not defending the Trinidad operation. If they wanted to really get rid of Castro, he should of defended that, 'cause that was the only chance.

Later on, he didn't defend the need for air operations. I didn't know that the president had never really been informed about the necessity for eliminating Castro's air force and apparently he wasn't. And I didn't know that. I resented the fact that at the last moment Bissell did not fight harder to preserve our own air capability and particularly not to allow the final strike to be completely canceled. I thought that it behooved us to have enough honor not to do that to those Cuban troops. I would never have done it, and neither would Mr. Esterline.

**Esterline:** I am forced to a very unhappy conclusion and that is that he was lying down and lying up for reasons that I don't yet totally understand. I am convinced of this right now. I think the fact that someone would deliberately misrepresent a situation like that to the ultimate head of state, that's pretty unforgivable, I think.

**Q.** In early April, you both actually went to Bissell's house and said you were resigning because the invasion was going to be a disaster.

**Esterline:** We looked at every aspect and the odds and the percentages of success and we finally decided that we couldn't deliver on them.

**Hawkins:** I finally came to the conclusion that this could not work and was going to be a disaster.

**Esterline:** I called Bissell directly and said that we simply had to sit down with him. And I said that we can't tell you in good faith that we can give you any reasonable expectation that this thing is going to come to a successful conclusion as it stands. And he kind of impugned our loyalty. I certainly get the feeling that he impugned my loyalty, that because I didn't like something I was deserting a ship.

**Hawkins:** I remember this: Bissell said that as far as the air is concerned, he said I think I can persuade the president to allow us to conduct enough air operations to get rid of the Castro air force. He said he thought he could.

**Esterline:** I know he promised us that there would be no further reduction. And I said well if you promise there'll be no more reductions on air strikes as we lay them out, then I'll go along.

**Q.** Bissell may have expected Castro to be assassinated prior to the invasion. Were either of you aware of the assassination plot that was part of his Bay of Pigs planning?

**Esterline:** All of a sudden I started getting requests to authorize big payments, $60,000, $100,000, and I refused them. I just put them aside. And J.C. King [head of the CIA's Western Hemisphere division] called me and he said, "say, you're going to have to sign these things." Well I said that you'll have to tell me what I'm signing or I won't. He said: "well I can't because your not cleared." Get someone else to sign them, then, and he said, "Oh no, we can't do that."

A few days later I got a call and he said "you're going to be briefed," and so Shef Edwards, who was then the chief of security and one of his aides came over. I met with them and they unfolded to me. I couldn't believe they were telling me! This plan that they had laid out with Sam Giancana, their gambling interests—Traficante was another name that comes back to my mind. They [the Mafia] were being threatened, their interests were being threatened in Cuba, and therefore they had decided they were going to do something about Castro. So all of a sudden the agency gets sucked into being a part of it, which I never could understand how this made any sense, how this added up, but in point of fact, [the CIA] had the relationship with Giancana and he needed half a million dollars to perform his part of this.

When I went back to J.C. and I said, "J.C." I said, "do you realize that this is going to make people take this whole thing less seriously if somebody thinks there's an easy way out with Castro being killed?" And he said, "Nobody's going to find out" and I said "What are we going to tell Bissell?" And he said "Don't tell Bissell, Bissell's not cleared." It wasn't till years later that I found out Bissell was the guy behind it.

I thought it was absolutely amoral that we involve ourselves for the record in anything of this sort. Number one, I was just having trouble coming to grips with that, but number two I thought it would also be the most self-defeating thing for the operation which was going to be [difficult] at best. . . . I was saddled with this, I never told Jack [Hawkins].

Q. What factors, in your opinion, led to the failure of the invasion?

Hawkins: We should have done it so we could succeed. That was the whole thing. No one seemed to have success in mind. What they had in mind was is someone going to know about this. Success was what they should have been thinking about. It was a fundamental error that was really the underpinning of all the other errors made because everybody at the political level was trying for plausible deniability and that caused so many restrictions that the operation really could not be successful.

**Esterline:** It failed, I guess, primarily because starting at the top of government nobody wanted to do it so badly that they were prepared to take the steps to ensure success.

**Hawkins:** We wanted to use enough aircraft to do what had to be done. State opposed that from the very first they every heard about it and never stopped opposing it. They opposed the use of American pilots, they opposed the use of American bases. It was really State that convinced the president to cut down the airstrikes. That was Mr. Rusk, the Secretary of State. So the Department of State crippled and destroyed this operation. That is my considered judgment that I thought at the time and for years after, and they were never blamed for anything.

**Q.** And today? What do you think about current U.S. policy toward Cuba?

**Hawkins:** I think we should be willing to act like the great power that we are and make it felt wherever our interests are at play. I don't think we need to sneak around about anything.

**Esterline:** All I know is that this is a ridiculous situation we're living in now. It doesn't serve anyone. It doesn't serve us. It doesn't serve the Cuban people. We need some kind of a knight in shining armor who says "all right, lets get this thing under control," but I'm not volunteering for the job, believe me.

** ** **

# —The Bay of Pigs Invasion

*A Comprehensive Chronology of Events*

**JAN 1, 1959:** The 26 of July Movement, led by Fidel Castro, succeeds in forcing General Fulgencio Batista into exile. Fidel Castro gives a victory speech from Santiago: this new revolution, he states, will not be like 1898 "when the North Americans came and made themselves masters of our country."

**JAN 7, 1959:** Washington officially recognizes the new government; early the next day, Castro's victory caravan finally reaches Havana, and the new regime takes power.

**APR 19, 1959:** During Fidel Castro's first post-revolution trip to Washington, he meets with Vice President Richard Nixon for three-and-a-half hours. "I spent as much time as I could trying to emphasize that he had the great gift of leadership, but that it was the responsibility of a leader not always to follow public opinion but to help to direct it in proper channels, not to give the people what they think they want at a time of emotional stress but to make them want what they ought to have," the Vice President reports in a four-page, secret memo to Eisenhower, Secretary of State Christian A. Herter, and Allen Dulles. "It was apparent that while he paid lip service to such institutions as freedom of speech, press and religion that his primary concern was with developing programs for economic progress." Nixon concludes that Castro is "either incredibly naive about Communism or is under Communist discipline." In the wake of the meeting, Nixon later writes, "I became a leading advocate for efforts to overthrow Castro." (Richard M. Nixon, *Rough Draft of Summary of Conversation Between the Vice President and Fidel Castro*, April 25, 1959)

**LATE OCT 1959:** President Eisenhower approves a program proposed by the Department of State, in agreement with the CIA, to support elements in Cuba opposed to the Castro government. The operations are intended to make Castro's downfall seem to be the result of his own mistakes. As a part of this program, Cuban exiles mount seaborne raids against Cuba from U.S. territory. (Wyden, pp.28-29; Gleijeses, p.3; Taylor Report, pp.3-4)

**DEC 11, 1959:** J.C. King, head of the CIA's Western Division, writes a memorandum for Richard Bissell and CIA Director Allen Dulles stating that

Castro has now established a dictatorship of the far left. The intelligence community predicts an increase in Cuban support for other revolutionary movements in Latin America and "rapid nationalization of the banks, industry and commerce." The memorandum states that "violent action" is the only means of breaking Castro's grip on power, listing as the U.S. objective "the overthrow of Castro within one year." King also recommends that "thorough consideration be given to the elimination of Fidel Castro," marking the first time that the idea of assassination is committed to paper. (*Cuban Problems*, 12/11/59)

## 1960

**JAN 1960**: The CIA sets up Task Force WH/4, Branch 4 of the Western Hemisphere Division to implement President Eisenhower's request for an ambitious covert program to overthrow the Castro government. Jacob Esterline, Guatemala station chief between 1954–1957, is put in charge of WH/4. (Wyden, pp.28–29; Gleijeses, p.3; Taylor Report, pp.3–4)

**FEB 1960**: The Movement for Revolutionary Recovery (MRR) releases its "Ideario" of basic points. In the preamble, Manuel Artíme writes that MRR has been formed "not only to overthrow Fidel Castro, but to permanently fight for an ideology of Christ; and for a reality of liberating our nation treacherously sold to the Communist International." ("Ideario: Puntos Basicos.")

**MAR 1960:** The CIA begins training 300 guerrillas, initially in the United States and the Canal Zone. Following an agreement with President Ydígoras in June, training shifts to Guatemala. (Gleijeses, p.6)

—Rafael Rivas-Vasquez sends a confidential memorandum to Artíme on "Propaganda and Psychological Warfare of the F.R.D. (Revolutionary Democratic Front) in Cuba." The goals, he writes is to make the F.R.D. known inside of Cuba, win over sectors of the country, and "break the red power through creating a mystique [to oppose Communism] based on Christian principles and the democratic traditions of our people." Propaganda will be written and by radio. Psy-ops should include a "campaign directed a demoralizing the military . . . based in terror," a radio and flyer campaign to identify Castro's intelligence officials and Communist spies, promoting civic resistance, and spread the word about the resistance and its operations. Among the recommendations are to "blow up" Castro's radio station, the Voz del INRA, which is interfering with Radio Swan's transmissions. "Actions and sabotage, coordinated with written and radio propaganda . . . give life to the slogans and civic resistance," Rivas Vazquez writes. (*Propaganda y Guerra Psicológica*, 3/60)

**MAR 4-5, 1960:** An explosion aboard a French ship, La Coubre, in Havana harbor kills about 100 people and wounds some 300. The following day, at funerals for the victims, Fidel Castro accuses the United States of responsibility for the action. (*Informe Especial: 1960*)

**MAR 9, 1960:** At the first meeting of Branch 4 Task Force, the head of the CIA's Western Hemisphere division, Colonel J.C. King predicts that "unless Fidel and Raul Castro and Che Guevara could be eliminated in one package . . . this operation can be a long, drawn-out affair and the present government will only be overthrown by the use of force." King also discusses the training of instructor cadre to train other Cuban covert action groups and warns other members of the group not to underestimate the capabilities of the Cuban government, which is well armed and enjoys 60 to 70 percent support in Cuba. (Memorandum, *First Meeting of Branch 4 Task Force*)

**MAR 17, 1960:** At an Oval Office meeting with high-ranking national security officials, President Eisenhower approves a Central Intelligence Agency policy paper titled "A Program of Covert Action Against the Castro Regime." The plan suggests that the CIA: (i) form a moderate opposition group in exile whose slogan will be to restore the revolution which Castro has betrayed; (ii) create a medium wave radio station to broadcast into Cuba, probably on Swan Island, south of Cuba; (iii) create a covert intelligence and action organization within Cuba responsive to the orders and directions of the exile opposition; and (iv) begin training a paramilitary force outside Cuba and, in a second phase, train paramilitary cadres for immediate deployment into Cuba to organize, train and lead resistance forces recruited there.

During the meeting, Eisenhower states that he knows of "no better plan" for dealing with this situation but is concerned about leakage and breach of security. He argues that everyone must be prepared to deny its existence and only two or three people should have contact with the groups involved, agitating Cubans to do most of what must be done. The President tells CIA Director Allan Dulles that he thinks he should go ahead with the plan and the operations but that "our hand should not show in anything that is done." (*Memorandum of Conference with the President*, 3/18/60; CIA, *A Program of Covert Action Against the Castro Regime*, 3/16/60)

**MAR 27-28, 1960:** Fidel Castro speaks to a gathering of militia in Ciudad Libertad: "We also are organizing ourselves . . . In the first place so that they do not carry out aggression against us, and in second place, if they do, they will have to pay very dearly for their impudence and audacity in finding themselves on the soil of our country."

The following day, Castro warns that "if there is an invasion, the war, they can be sure, will be to the death." (*Informe Especial: 1960*)

**LATE MARCH 1960:** David Atlee Phillips, a CIA contract employee who until recently had maintained a public-relations company in Havana, is selected by the CIA as chief of propaganda for the Cuba project. At operation headquarters in Washington, Phillips is told that the Cuba project will go by the Guatemala scenario. (Phillips had performed the same function in PBSUCCESS, the 1954 operation against Guatemalan President Jacobo Arbenz. During the coup by a CIA-directed exile force, Phillips had operated a clandestine station supporting them.)

CIA operative E. Howard Hunt, also a veteran of the Guatemala operation, is assigned the position of chief of political action for the project. His primary responsibility is to form a government-in-exile to replace Castro's government following the invasion. (Wyden, pp. 20-22; Hunt, p. 23)

**APR 14, 1960:** At a National Security Council meeting, Eisenhower administration officials weigh options for broadcasting propaganda into Cuba. U.S. Information Agency Director George Allen reports that USIA is considering establishing a Cuba-directed station in Florida and buying time on commercial stations there. Also under study is a proposal to fly an aircraft over Key West for the purpose of beaming television programs into Cuba. Meanwhile, Allen says, USIA's short-wave broadcasts to Cuba have been augmented. CIA Director Allen Dulles reports that "some Cuban intellectuals [will] soon be broadcasting to Cuba from Boston at night, and that it is likely that a second radio station over which Cuban refugees might broadcast will be installed in five or six weeks." (NSC, *Discussion at the 441st Meeting of the National Security Council*, April 14, 1960.)

**MID APRIL 1960:** David Phillips meets with the CIA official in charge of the Cuba operation, Deputy Director for Plans Richard Bissell. When Bissell asks how long it will take to create the proper psychological climate, Phillips says it will take about six months. Bissell directs the propaganda chief to have Radio Swan up and running in one month.

On Swan Island, a tiny, contested territory located about 100 miles off Honduras, the CIA begins construction of a 50-kilowatt, medium-wave radio station. The island had served as a base for CIA broadcasting during the agency's successful campaign to oust Guatemala's President Arbenz, and some radio equipment used in that operation is still on the island. Phillips obtains a transmitter from the U.S. Army in Germany, which was preparing to make it available to the Voice of America. A detachment of Navy Seabees constructs a pier at Swan Island to facilitate the unloading of the equipment. (Phillips, pp. 112, 114; Wyden, pp. 22–23; Gleijeses, p. 6)

**APR 23, 1960:** Cuba's Foreign Minister Raúl Roa declares that "I can guarantee categorically that Guatemalan territory is being used at this very time with the complicity of President Ydígoras and the assistance of United Fruit, as a bridgehead for an invasion of our country." (*Informe Especial: 1960*)

**APR 25, 1960:** The MRR sends a memorandum to the CIA, summarizing the history, motivations, positions and goals of the organization. The document describes six major points of the MRR platform: respect for the dignity of the individual; firm devotion to representative democracy; unbreakable faith in the concepts, of private property, free markets, the development of capitalism, political pluralism, and the democratic credo against totalitarian communism. (*MRR, Memorandum Personal y Confidencial*, 4/25/60)

**MAY 1960:** CIA operative Howard Hunt spends several days in Cuba on an undercover visit, during which he observes Cuban attitudes toward the revolutionary government and visits areas around revolution-controlled radio stations. After returning to Washington, he reports his findings to his supervisors at the CIA and offers several recommendations, including a suggestion that the Agency destroy the Cuban radio and television transmitters before or coincident with the invasion. Hunt's recommendation is based on his belief that, without radio and television to inform the country, Cuban leaders would be unable to rally mass support. (Hunt, pp. 36, 38)

**MAY 14, 1960:** The *New York Times* reports that a new commercial radio station will begin broadcasting soon from Swan Island. The station, the *Times* reports, plans to broadcast nothing of greater international import than waltzes, Latin American music, and commercials.

**MAY 17, 1960:** Radio Swan goes on the air on schedule. According to the CIA, the station's signal reaches not only its target area of Cuba, but the entire Caribbean as well. The station's programs are taped in studios in Miami, then routed through the Swan transmitter. (CIA, "Brief History of Radio Swan," Taylor Committee, Annex 2)

Bob Davis, the CIA station chief in Guatemala City, receives a message instructing him to build an airport. After getting Guatemalan permission, the agency contracts to have the airport built at Retalhuleu in 30 days for one million dollars. The airport is built in 90 days and ultimately costs $1.8 million. (Wyden, p. 37)

**MAY 19, 1960:** A small group of anti-Castro Cuban exiles, housed by the CIA in the motel Marie Antonet in Fort Lauderdale, are met by Manuel Artíme and two CIA officials, "Jimmy and Karl." Jimmy is identified as the chief of the operation and later as chief of the infiltration team. The team is subsequently transported to Ussepa Island off the Florida coast for training. The training is originally scheduled to last 15 days but extends into a month and a half. In early July, the Brigadistas, as they become known, are transferred by plane to camps in Guatemala. (Brigadista Diary p. 2–6)

**MAY 24, 1960:** CIA Director Allen Dulles updates the National Security Council on two semi-covert radio activities related to Cuba. He reports that "several well-known Cuban refugees [are] purchasing time for anti-Castro broadcasts from a short-wave station in Cuba." In addition, he announces that Radio Swan is now on the air for "test purposes. The station will go on the air quietly at first, will then attack [Dominican leader Rafael] Trujillo, and then later will begin to attack Castro." Radio Swan will be operated ostensibly by a commercial company. (NSC, "Discussion at the 445th Meeting of the National Security Council," May 24, 1960, 5/25/60)

**SUMMER 1960:** Howard Hunt visits operation headquarters in Coral Gables, Florida. There he meets an assistant to Phillips who is in charge of field propaganda work, and is dispensing CIA subsidies to several Cuban exile newspapers to allow subscriptions to Latin Americans to be sold at nominal cost and the anti-Castro word in countries where Fidel is regarded sympathetically.

Phillips decides that "a single station [is] not sufficient for the task" of transmitting adequate propaganda. He later writes that "[w]e soon created a second capability independent of Radio Swan and the exile political groups by having CIA agents buy space on existing radio stations around the perimeter of the Caribbean. These broadcasts were low key and not recognizable as anti-Castro. Only after D-Day would they become activist voices, to influence Cubans when they faced the decision of who would win and who would lose." Several stations with CIA ties, including Radio Cuba Independiente, La Voz de Cuba Libre, and Massachusetts-based WRUL, begin broadcasting anti-Castro messages. (Hunt, pp.46–47; Phillips, p. 122; Soley and Nichols, pp. 180–181)

**EARLY JULY, 1960:** Exile forces being trained on Ussepa Island are transferred to bases in Guatemala. They are taken to the Finca Helevetia owned by the Alejos brothers. There, this group of exiles is met by "Mr. Karl," the CIA official in charge of the training. Three Americans, Bill, Bob and Nick, are in charge of training exile members in radio communications.

The diary of an unidentified brigadista on a radio team describes a daily routine that beings at 6:45 a.m. with calisthenics and running. At 8:45, classes in radio and telegram communications are conducted; at noon lunch is held; classes resume at 2:00 p.m. and end at 6:00 p.m.; dinner at 7:00 p.m. and then a free evening to listen to the Voice of America or WRUL in New York, and to sneak a drink since alcohol is prohibited at the camp. (Brigadista Diary p. 8)

**JUL 21, 1960:** CIA headquarters sends a cable to Havana regarding an upcoming meeting between a Cuban volunteer agent and Raúl Castro. The cable states that "Possible removal top three leaders is receiving serious consideration at HQS," inquiring whether the Cuban agent is sufficiently motivated to risk arranging an accident for Raúl Castro and offering $10,000 after successful completion. After the agent agrees to carry out the task, the CIA cancels the assignment. (Wyden, p. 39)

**JUL 23, 1960:** CIA Director Dulles briefs Senator and presidential candidate John F. Kennedy at Hyannis Port on Cape Cod. The meeting lasts two-and-a-half hours and includes a description of the training of Cuban exiles for operations against the Castro government. (CIA Director Allen Dulles, *Memorandum for the President*, August 3, 1960)

**AUG 1960:** Richard Bissell meets with Colonel Sheffield Edwards, director of the CIA's Office of Security, and discusses with him ways to eliminate Fidel Castro. Edwards proposes that the job be done by assassins hand-picked by the American underworld, specifically syndicate interests who have been driven out of their Havana gambling casinos by the Castro regime. Bissell gives Edwards the go-ahead to proceed. Between August 1960 and April 1961, a series of plots to poison or shot Castro are pursued by the CIA with the help of the Mafia. The CIA's own internal report on these efforts states that these plots "were viewed by at least some of the participants as being merely one aspect of the over-all active effort to overthrow the regime that culminated in the Bay of Pigs." (CIA, Inspector General's Report on *Efforts to Assassinate Fidel Castro*, p. 3, 14)

—The *Miami Herald* considers publishing a story by David Kraslow about CIA training of Cuban exiles near Homestead, Florida. The story reports that the Justice and State Departments are unhappy about this violation of the Neutrality Act and are pressuring President Eisenhower to move all such CIA training operations. After meeting with Allen Dulles and being informed that publication would be most harmful to the national interest, the paper's editors decide not to print the story. (Wyden, pp. 45–46)

—The CIA hires a small New York public relations firm, Lem Jones Associates, Inc., to handle official announcements by the exile groups involved in the Cuba project. (Wyden, p. 117)

**AUG 18, 1960:** President Eisenhower approves a budget of $13 million for the covert anti-Castro operation, as well as the use of the Department of Defense personnel and equipment. However, it is specified at this time that no United States military personnel are to be used in combat. (Gleijeses, p. 10; Wyden, p. 30)

**AUG 28, 1960:** Cuba withdraws from the Seventh Consultative Meeting of the Ministers of the OAS after 19 governments vote against a Cuban proposal concerning the aggression by one American state against another. (*Informe Especial: 1960*)

**LATE SUMMER 1960:** The concept of the covert operation begins to shift from infiltrating teams to wage guerrilla warfare to an amphibious operation involving at least 1,500 men who would seize and defend an area by sea and air assault and establish a base for further operations. Minutes of the Special Group meetings in the fall of 1960 indicate a declining confidence in the effectiveness of guerrilla efforts alone to overthrow Castro. (Gleijeses, p. 10; Aguilar, p. 5)

**SEP 8, 1960**: Carlos Rodriguez Santana, a member of the anti-Castro forces being trained in Guatemala, dies in a training accident. He is the first casualty of the exile force. In his honor, the brigade assumes his assigned number — 2506 — as the name of the exile force.

**SEP 10, 1960:** The *New York Times* publishes a front-page story on Radio Swan. According to the *Times*, the station is owned and operated by the Gibraltar Steamship Company, with headquarters in New York. (NYT, 9/10/60)

**SEP 14, 1960:** A Cuban government radio commentary charges that the United States is pirating long-wave frequencies belonging to Cuba and calls Radio Swan's broadcasts a new aggression of imperialistic North America. (NYT, 9/15/60)

**SEP 26, 1960:** During an address before the United Nations General Assembly, Fidel Castro charges that the United States has taken over Swan Island and has set up a very powerful broadcasting station there, which it has placed at the disposal of war criminals. (NYT, 10/15/60)

**SEP 28, 1960:** The CIA attempts its first drop of weapons and supplies to the Cuban resistance. The air crew tries to drop an arms pack for a hundred men to an agent waiting on the ground. They miss the drop zone by seven miles and land the weapons on top of a dam where they are picked up by Castro's forces. The agent is caught and shot. The plane gets lost on the way to Guatemala and lands in Mexico, where it is impounded. (Thomas, p. 241; CIA, *Inspector General's Report on the Cuban Operation*, p. 1:98)

— On the same date, the CIA also attempts its first maritime supply mission. The pleasure cruiser "Metusa Time" delivers 300 pounds of cargo and picks up to exfiltrees. (CIA, *Inspector General's Survey of the Cuban Operation*, p. 1:110)

**OCT 7, 1960:** Raúl Roa, Cuba's Foreign Minister, denounces U.S. plans to invade Cuba, based on intelligence information obtained by Cuba's security services: "In the Finca Helvetia, located in the municipality of El Palmar, adjoining the departments of Retalhuleu and Quetzaltenango, acquired recently by Roberto Alejos, brother of the Guatemalan ambassador to the United States . . . numerous exiles and adventurers are receiving training under the command of North American military men. In August and September, more than a hundred airmen and American technical military personnel entered Guatemala. In the La Aurora airport bomber aircraft have been seen. The public rumor is that they serve a double mission to attack Cuba or to simulate a Cuban attack against Guatemala." (Molina, "Diario de Girón", p. 1–2)

— Senator John Kennedy, running for president, attacks the Eisenhower Administration for "permitting a communist menace . . . to arise only ninety miles from the shores of the United States." (Gleijeses, p. 24)

**OCT 14, 1960:** The United States issues a false fact sheet at the United Nations in response to Castro's accusations before the General Assembly. The paper addresses the issue of Radio Swan:

> There is a private commercial broadcasting station on the [Swan] islands, operated by the Gibraltar Steamship Company. The United States Government understands that this station carries programs in Spanish which are heard in Cuba, and that some of its broadcast time has been purchased by Cuban political refugees. (NYT, 10/15/60)

**OCT 16 and 21, 1960:** Kennedy again attacks Eisenhower's Cuba policy: "If you can't stand up to Castro, how can you be expected to stand up to Khrushchev?" And five days later: "We must attempt to strengthen the non-Batista democratic anti-Castro forces in exile, and in Cuba itself, who offer eventual hope of overthrowing Castro. Thus far these fighters for freedom have had virtually no support from our government."

Richard Nixon, running for president and fully aware of the anti-Castro activities taking place and being planned, attacks Kennedy's position on Cuba as irresponsible and reckless. Nixon argues that if the United States were to back the Cuban exiles, it would be condemned in the United Nations and would not accomplish our objective. "It would be an open invitation for Mr. Khrushchev . . . to come into Latin America and to engage us in what would be a civil war and possibly even worse than that." Nixon proposes a quarantine of Cuba. (Gleijeses, pp. 24–25; Wyden, pp. 67–68)

**OCT 24, 1960:** The Cuban Council of Ministers decrees the nationalization of another 166 U.S. businesses as a response to the aggressive measures of the U.S. against Cuba. (*Informe Especial: 1960*)

**OCT 30, 1960:** Guatemalan newspaper *La Hora* publishes a story disclosing that the CIA has built a heavily guarded $1 million base near Retalhuleu to train Cuban counterrevolutionaries for landing in Cuba. (Wyden, p. 46)

**OCT 31, 1960:** A cable from CIA Headquarters to a senior agency officer in Guatemala outlines a plan for amphibious invasion of Cuba by assault force of at least 1,500 men who will receive conventional military training. (CIA, *Classified Message*, October 31, 1960)

**NOV 1960:** President Eisenhower presses CIA Director Dulles about the lack of a Cuban government in exile. Dulles and Bissell assure him that the CIA is making progress. Eisenhower is skeptical. The President is quoted as remarking: "I'm going along with you boys, but I want to be sure the damned thing works." (Wyden, p. 68)

**NOV 4, 1960:** A CIA cable from Washington to the project officer in Guatemala directs a reduction in the guerrilla teams in training to 60 men and the introduction of conventional training for the remainder as an amphibious and airborne assault force. From this time on, the men become convinced of the importance of the landing operation and its superiority to any form of guerrilla action. (Aguilar, p. 6)

**NOV 8-9, 1960:** The CIA informs the Special Group of its plans, including the change in the conception of the operation from guerrilla infiltration to amphibious invasion. (Gleijeses, p. 11)

**NOV 13, 1960:** Young officers revolt in Guatemala. A major grievance is the presence of the CIA-directed Cuban Expeditionary Force in Guatemala. President Ydígoras calls for U.S. aid in putting down the rebellion, and

Brigade planes strafe the rebels, helping to put down the rebellion. (Gleijeses, p. 16)

—Guatemalan "friends" of the Cuban revolution supply intelligence to the Castro government on the activities of Cuban exiles in Guatemala. A six-page intelligence report records the build-up of exile forces over the previous summer and fall, the type of aircraft being used, and location of the training bases. (*Informacion sobre la contrarrevolucion Cubana en Guatemala*, 2/24/61)

**NOV 18, 1960:** CIA Director Dulles and Deputy Director for Plans Bissell visit President-elect Kennedy in Palm Beach and brief him on the plan to overthrow Castro. (Allen W. Dulles, *Memorandum for General Maxwell Taylor*, 6/1/61)

**NOV 19, 1960:** The *Nation* magazine prints an editorial entitled "Are We Training Cuban Guerrillas?" Following a query from a reader, the *New York Times* instructs its Central America correspondent, Paul P. Kennedy, to look into the story of CIA training of Cuban exiles in Guatemala. (Wyden, p. 46)

**NOV 29, 1960:** President Eisenhower meets with key aides from the State, Treasury, and Defense Departments, the CIA, and the White House. He expresses his displeasure with the general situation: "Are we being sufficiently imaginative and bold, subject to not letting our hand appear; and . . . are we doing the things we are doing, effectively?" Acting Secretary of State Dillon voices the department's concern that the operation is no longer secret but is known all over Latin America and has been discussed in U.N. circles. President Eisenhower states he thinks that "we should be prepared to take more chances and be more aggressive." (*Memorandum of Meeting with the President*, Tuesday, November 29, 1960, 12/5/60)

**DEC 6, 1960:** President Eisenhower meets with President-elect Kennedy to discuss the anti-Castro Cuban operation currently being planned. (Gleijeses, p. 26)

**DEC 8, 1960:** The CIA Task Force presents the new paramilitary concept to the Special Group. The Special Group authorizes use of Special Forces to train the Strike Force, the use of an air strip at Puerto Cabezas, Nicaragua, and supply missions. (Taylor Board, First Meeting, 4/22/61; Gleijeses, p. 12)

At the meeting of the Special Group, Colonel Edward G. Lansdale, an expert in guerrilla warfare, shares his doubts that the Cuban people will rise up in the face of the landings. He quizzes Dulles about the political base and popularity of the operation. (Wyden, pp. 72–3)

A seven-week training program begins in Guatemala with approximately 575 to 600 troops. (Aguilar, p. 170)

**DEC 20, 1960:** Admiral Robert Dennison, the Commander in Chief of the Atlantic Command (CINCLANT), sends the CIA 119 questions about the CIA operation. His questions infer that planning has been wholly inadequate for the invasion. Only twelve are answered. (Wyden, p. 79)

**DEC 31, 1960:** In a speech, Fidel Castro denounces the "imperialist plan" to invade Cuba. He attempts to focus world attention on the "danger our country is running," and declares that Cuba will "mobilize the people and adopt such measures as can persuade the imperialists that it will not be a military cakewalk." Castro warns the United States that "if they want to invade us and destroy the resistance they will not succeed . . . because as long as a single man or woman with honor remains there will be resistance." Castro predicts that a few thousand paratroopers with some boats will take neither the capital nor any major cities and that they will need many more troops and that they will pay a heavier price than in the landings at Normandy or Okinawa. ("Playa Girón," Primer Tomo, 8–1)

—The CIA conducts an air-drop for a 15-man reception team in Cuba that had requested 1,500 pounds of material. In addition to the requested material, the CIA plane drops 800 pounds of beans, 800 pounds of rice, and 160 pounds of lard, material the Cuban team "had not asked for, did not need, and could not handle." The excessive drop is only one way in which the CIA endangers this team; the plane also remains in the vicinity too long, flies with its landing lights on, and drops propaganda materials on the property of a member of the team. (CIA, *Inspector General's Report on the Cuban Operation*, pp. 1:99–100)

**LATE 1960:** The CIA purchases two LCIs (landing craft, infantry) in Miami. Since these two ships can carry only 150 men, the CIA charters two small (1,500–2,000 ton) freighters from a Cuban ship owner named Garca who asks only that operating expenses be covered. The LCIs are armed and kept as command ships and also used for other operations such as the raid on the Santiago refinery. (Aguilar, p. 70)

—José San Román, who had served in the Cuban military under both Batista and Castro and who had been imprisoned under both regimes, becomes Brigade commander of the forces in training. Four battalions are formed under Alejandro del Valle (First), Hugo Sueiro (Second, Infantry), Erneido Oliva (Armored), and Roberto San Román (Heavy Gun Battalion). (Johnson, p. 57; Wyden, p. 51)

The CIA later reports that during this period the effectiveness of Radio Swan begins to diminish: Although great numbers of Cubans still listen to the station, its credibility and reputation suffers because programming only represents the narrow interests of the Cuban groups producing the various broadcasts. The program producers are using exaggeration in order to sensationalize their broadcasts. For example, one of the announcers stated that there were 3,000 Russians in a park in Santiago de Cuba when the residents had only to walk to the park to see that this was untrue. (*Taylor Report, Annex 2*: CIA, Brief History of Radio Swan)

## 1961

**JAN 1, 1961:** Recruitment of Cuban exiles for training in Guatemala is significantly increased. (*Taylor Board, First Meeting*, 4/22/61)

**JAN 3, 1961:** At 1:20 a.m., the Cuban Ministry of Foreign Relations in Havana sends a telegram to the Charge d'Affaires at the U.S. Embassy informing him that the total number of personnel at the U.S. Embassy and Consulate should not exceed eleven persons. Further, U.S. government personnel in excess of this number "must abandon the national territory" of Cuba within 48 hours of receipt of the telegram. (Cuban Ministry of Foreign Relations, "Embassy Telegram 2667," January 3, 1961)

President Eisenhower meets with advisers at 9:30 a.m. to discuss steps to take on Cuba, including breaking of diplomatic relations in response to Cuba's demand that U.S. official representation in Cuba be cut to 11 people. Turning to discussion of planned covert action against Cuba, Gordon Gray quotes an unidentified source as describing the Cuban exiles in training as the best army in Latin America, to which General Lemnitzer, chairman of the Joint Chiefs of Staff, agrees. Assistant Secretary of State Mann argues that support for Castro has declined from approximately 95 percent to about 25–33 percent.

During the meeting, President Eisenhower states that he would move against Castro before January 20 if he were provided a really good excuse by the Cubans. Failing that, he says, perhaps the United States "could think of manufacturing something that would be generally acceptable." (*Memorandum of Meeting with the President*, January 3, 1961, 1/9/61)

At 8:30 p.m. the U.S. Department of State sends a note to the Cuban Charge d'Affaires advising of the decision to break diplomatic relations between the two countries and requesting that the Government of Cuba withdraw all Cuban nationals employed in the Cuban Embassy in Washington as soon as possible. (Department of State, *Telegram From the Department of State to the Embassy in Cuba*, Text of Note Delivered 8:30 p.m. January 3 to Cuban Charge, 1/3/61)

—Later in the day, Fidel Castro announces that Cuba will go to the U.N. and "declare that if the United States believes it has the right to promote counterrevolution in Cuba, and believes it has the right to promote counterrevolution and reaction in Latin America, then Cuba has the right to encourage revolution in Latin America!" (*Informe Especial: 1961*)

**JAN 4, 1961:** Senior CIA officials prepare a memorandum "to outline the status of preparations for the conduct of amphibious/airborne and tactical air operations against the Government of Cuba and to set forth certain requirements for policy decisions which must be reached and implemented if these operations are to be carried out." The concept of the plan is as follows:

> [T]he initial mission of the invasion force will be to seize and defend a small area. . . . There will be no early attempt to break out of the lodgment for further offensive operations unless and until there is a general uprising against the Castro regime or overt military intervention by United States forces has taken place.
>
> It is expected that these operations will precipitate a general uprising throughout Cuba and cause the revolt of large segments of the Cuban Army and Militia. . . . If matters do not eventuate as predicted above, the lodgment . . . can be used as the site for establishment of a provisional government which can be recognized by the United States. . . . The way will

then be paved for United States military intervention aimed at pacification of Cuba, and this will result in the prompt overthrow of the Castro Government.

Air strikes are seen as a crucial component of the invasion: "It is considered crucial that the Cuban air force and naval vessels capable of opposing the landing be knocked out or neutralized before amphibious shipping makes its final run into the beach." (CIA, *Memorandum For: Chief WH/4, Policy Decisions Required for Conduct of Strike Operations Against Government of Cuba*, 1/4/61)

**JAN 6, 1961:** The State Department says it doubts newspaper reports that Castro is planning to let the Soviet Union establish missile bases in Cuba. (Johnson, p. 58)

**JAN 10, 1961:** The *New York Times* publishes a front page story entitled "U.S. Helps Train an Anti-Castro Force at Secret Guatemalan Air-Ground Base." Written by Paul Kennedy, the article reports that "Commando-like forces are being drilled in guerrilla warfare tactics by foreign personnel, mostly from the United States." (Wyden, p. 46)

**JAN 11, 1961:** Ambassador Willauer of the State Department and Tracy Barnes of CIA discuss with representatives of the Joint Staff the overall problem of effecting the overthrow of Castro. This is the first time the JCS at the working level is informed of the plan being developed in the CIA for an invasion by a Cuban exile force. As a result, a working committee including representatives of CIA, State, Defense, and the JCS is formed to coordinate future actions in pursuit of this objective. (JCS, *Chronology of JCS Participation in Bumpy Road*)

**JAN 16, 1961:** The Interdepartmental Working Group on Cuba meets to discuss a Defense Department memorandum entitled "Evaluation of Possible Military Courses of Action in Cuba." The memo outlines military actions to be used "in the event currently planned political and paramilitary operations are determined to be inadequate."

Three possible courses of action are outlined: unilateral action by the U.S. armed forces under a contingency plan already approved by the JCS; invasion by an overtly U.S.-trained and supported volunteer army; and invasion by a combination of both possible courses of action. The memo concludes that "courses of action a and c are the only courses of action which assure success." (Department of Defense, *Evaluation of Possible Military Courses of Action in Cuba (S)*, Staff Study Prepared in the Department of Defense, 1/16/96)

**JAN 16-18, 1961:** The United States prohibits its citizens from traveling to Cuba unless specifically authorized by the State Department. In Cuba, an American citizen, John Gentile, is sentenced to 30 years in prison for being part of a group that carried out sabotage and assassination attempts against Cuban leaders. (Molina, "Diario de Girón", pp. 20–21)

**JAN 18, 1961:** Ambassador Willauer reports to Under Secretary of State Merchant that "the Group, DOD, CIA, and ARA (to a limited extent)" have updated DOD on "current thinking on the program for Cuba," and "after concluding this [they] assumed that the December 6 plan (updated in light of developments since that time) *might* not succeed in the objective of over-throwing the Castro regime." Willauer concurs with DOD's "Evaluation of Possible Military Courses of Action in Cuba" (January 16, 1961) that any chance of success hinges on several "very important policy decisions that many of [them] feel must be taken immediately."

Willauer also states his own view that the plan "will probably get support from many Latin American countries of democratic inclination in direct proportion to the degree [the U.S. is] felt to be siding in the overthrow of Trujillo (of the Dominican Republic) and generally are 'on the side of the angels' in the entire problem of dictatorships vs. free governments in the hemisphere." Finally, Willauer informs Merchant that his committee "weighed without coming to a conclusion the advantages of rapid, effective action by direct war in terms of getting matters over with without a long buildup of world opinion, vs. the inevitability of such a buildup under any seven-month program." (Ambassador Willauer, *Memorandum to Under Secretary Merchant, The Suggested Program for Cuba Contained in the Memorandum to You Dated December 6, 1960. 1/18/61*)

**JAN 19, 1961:** President Eisenhower meets again with President-elect Kennedy and endorses the covert Cuban operation. Eisenhower makes it clear that the project is going very well and that it is the new administration's responsibility to do whatever is necessary to bring it to a successful conclusion. According to notes taken during the meeting, "Senator Kennedy asked the President's judgment as to the United States supporting the guerrilla operation in Cuba, even if this support involves the United States publicly. The President replied "Yes, as we cannot let the present government there go on." (The White House, Meeting in the Cabinet Room, 9:45 a.m., January 19, 1961)

**JAN 25, 1961:** President Kennedy meets with the Joint Chiefs of Staff at the White House to discuss invasion planning. According to a memorandum on the meeting, Gen. Lemnitzer tells the President that in light of the "shipment of heavy new military equipment from Czechoslovakia—30,000 tons or more—clandestine forces are not strong enough. [The United States] must increase the size of this force and this creates very difficult problems. What is required is a basic expansion of plans." (Gen. Goodpaster, *Memorandum of Conference with President Kennedy, Washington, January 23, 1961, 10:15 a.m.*, 1/27/61)

**JAN 27, 1961:** The Joint Chiefs of Staff send a memorandum to the Secretary of Defense expressing their increasing concern that Cuba will become permanently established as a part of the Communist Bloc—with disastrous consequences to the security of the Western Hemisphere. They also state their belief that the primary objective of the United States in Cuba should be the speedy overthrow of the Castro government. The Joint Chiefs argue that the current Political-Para-Military Plan does not assure the accomplishment of this objective and recommend that an overall U.S. plan of action for the overthrow of the Castro Government be developed by an Inter-Departmental Planning Group. (Joint Chiefs of Staff, *Memorandum for the Secretary of Defense, U.S. Plan of Action in Cuba*, 1/27/61)

—Sherman Kent, chairman of the CIA's Board of National Estimates, sends Allen Dulles a secret memorandum entitled "Is Time on Our Side in Cuba?," which concludes that Castro's position in Cuba is likely to grow stronger, rather than weaker, as time goes on. The board, which does not know of the invasion plans, argues against the view that the Cuban population is eager to stage an uprising against Castro: while Castro will probably continue to lose popular support, this loss is likely to be more than counterbalanced by the regime's effective controls over daily life in Cuba and by the increasing effectiveness of its security forces for maintaining control. (Wyden, p. 93)

**JAN 28, 1961:** Kennedy receives his first briefing as President on the Cuban operation in a meeting attended by Vice President Lyndon B. Johnson, Secretary of State Dean Rusk, Defense Secretary Robert McNamara, National Security Adviser McGeorge Bundy, CIA Director Dulles, Chairman of the Joint Chiefs of Staff General Lemnitzer, Assistant Secretaries Mann and Nitze, and Tracy Barnes of the CIA.

After hearing the Defense Department's assessment that no course of action currently authorized by the United States Government will be effective in overthrowing the Castro regime, and the State Department's view that any overt military action not authorized and supported by the OAS will have grave political dangers, President Kennedy authorizes:

> 1) A continuation and accentuation of current activities of the Central Intelligence Agency, including increased propaganda, increased political action and increased sabotage. Continued overflights for these purposes were specifically authorized; 2) The Defense Department, with CIA, will review proposals for active deployment of anti-Castro Cuban forces on Cuban territory, and the results of this analysis will be promptly reported to the President; 3) The Department of State will prepare a concrete proposal for action with other Latin American countries to isolate the Castro regime and to bring against it the judgment of the Organization of American States. (McGeorge Bundy, *Memorandum of Discussion on Cuba, Cabinet Room, January 28, 1961*, 1/28/61)

—Fidel Castro, in a talk in Santa Clara, analyzes the causes of counterrevolution in Las Villas mentioning "the infiltration of public posts, in the municipal and national administration, and even in the army and police forces, by elements that are truly adventurist, negative, and corrupt who link up with henchmen who flee immediately . . . and begin to parachute arms into Escambray." (*Informe Especial: 1961*)

**JAN 30, 1961:** C/WH/4 Jake Esterline attends a briefing given by Colonel Jack Hawkins and members of the [deleted] PM Section to Deputy Director of Central Intelligence, Admiral Wright, General Bull, and General Barnes in preparation for the January 32 briefing of designees of the Chairman of the JCS. The briefing, presented in a special CIA Bay of Pigs task force "war room," emphasizes that "the proposed strike could be conducted with no overt U.S. military support other than the provision of one LSD (landing ship dock)." It was also emphasized that the "estimate of the likelihood of success was very high in terms of staying in the initial objective area long enough and in sufficient control to permit introduction of a 'Provisional Government' and provide a rationale for the subsequent employment of overt military force, if desired." (R.D. Drain, *Memorandum for the Record*, 1/30/61)

**LATE JANUARY 1961:** Brigadier General David W. Gray, chief of the Joint Subsidiary Activities Division of the Joint Chiefs of Staff, receives orders from the JCS to form a committee with four other officers to study the CIA plan on behalf of the chiefs. After reviewing what will come to be known as the "Trinidad Plan," Gray's group concludes that the invading Brigade could last up to four days, given complete surprise and complete air supremacy. Success will depend on uprisings in Cuba. Gray estimates the chances of success at about 30–70, but no figures are used in the Gray committees report. At a meeting with the Joint Chiefs on January 31, Gray's report becomes an official JCS document. (Wyden, pp. 89–90)

—A revolt occurs among the Cuban exiles in training in Guatemala. Almost half of the more than 500 men in camp resign, including the entire second and third battalions. The commander, "Pepe" San Román, then resigns, but the CIA operative in charge of the base, known as "Frank," reinstates him. The CIA transfers 12 men considered to be troublemakers to the jungle of northern Guatemala and imprisons them until after the invasion is over. (Johnson, p. 61)

**FEB 1–5, 1961:** In another act of sabotage, a tobacco warehouse is burned down in Cuba; losses are estimated at 12 million pesos. Three bombs explode in Havana and one in Santa Clara. Three people are arrested for the Havana bombings. (Molina, "Diario de Girón", pp. 32–33)

**FEB 3, 1961:** The Joint Chiefs of Staff approve JCSM -57–61, the Military Evaluation of the CIA Para-Military Plan for Cuba, and forward it to Defense Secretary McNamara. The evaluation concludes that "since the Cuban Army is without experience in coordinated offensive action, the invasion force should be able to successfully resist the initial attacks" but "lacking a popular uprising or substantial follow-on forces, the Cuban Army could eventually reduce the beachhead." According to the JCS, "the operation as presently envisaged would not necessarily require overt U.S. intervention." At the same time, the evaluation cautions that:

It is obvious that ultimate success will depend upon political factors. It should be noted that assessment of the combat worth of assault forces is based upon second and third hand reports. For these reasons, an independent evaluation of the combat effectiveness of the invasion force and detailed analysis of logistics plans should be made by a team of Army, Naval, and Air Force officers.

Despite the shortcomings pointed out in the assessment, the Joint Chiefs of Staff consider that timely execution of this plan has a "fair" chance of ultimate success and, even if it does not achieve the full results desired, could contribute to the eventual overthrow of the Castro regime. (JCS, Chairman L.L. Lemnitzer, *Memorandum for the Secretary of Defense, Military Evaluation of the CIA Para-Military Plan, Cuba*, 2/3/61)

**FEB 4 and 6, 1961:** President Kennedy writes to National Security Adviser Bundy inquiring whether the sharp differences of opinion on the Cuban operation have been settled and two days later asks again whether the differences between the Departments of State and Defense and the CIA have been resolved. The President asks if it has been determined what is to be done about Cuba and stresses that, if there are continuing differences of opinion between the agencies, he would like them brought to his attention. (Gleijeses, pp. 20–21)

**FEB 7, 1961:** Officials of the Departments of State and Defense, the White House, and the CIA meet to discuss the "Agency Plan" and the "JCS evaluation." According to a memo on the meeting, "while the soundness of the plan itself [is] at no time questioned, a number of questions [are] raised." Specifically, the group discusses the ability of the strike force to reach the mountains from the landing site, the chances of a popular uprising in support of the invasion, the international political ramifications of the plan, and the need to introduce U.S. forces to ensure success.

The group reaches no consensus on what course of action to recommend to the President. White House Adviser Richard Goodwin points out that the President has "made it quite clear that if there were unresolved differences of opinion of the Cuban problem, the persons concerned should come to the President's office and in his presence orally set forth their arguments for his consideration and eventual decision." (Assistant Secretary of State Thomas Mann, *Memorandum for the Record, Meeting on Cuba*, 2/7/61)

**FEB 8, 1961:** In a memorandum to the President, McGeorge Bundy high-lights the difference of opinion on the Cuba operation between the State Department, and CIA and Defense:

> Defense and CIA now feel quite enthusiastic about the invasion from Guatemala. At worst, they think the invaders would get into the mountains, and at best they think they might get a full-fledged civil war in which we could then back the anti-Castro forces openly. The State Department takes a much cooler view, primarily because of its belief that the political consequences would be very grave both in the United Nations and in Latin America.

Bundy notes that he and Richard Goodwin "join in believing that there should certainly not be an invasion adventure without careful diplomatic soundings" that are likely to support the position of the State Department. (McGeorge Bundy, *Memorandum from the President's Special Assistant for National Security Affairs to President Kennedy*, 2/8/61)

—In an afternoon meeting of President Kennedy and his top advisers, Richard Bissell of the CIA reports the assessment of the JCS: that the CIA plan for landing the brigade has a fair chance of success. Success is defined as an ability to survive, hold ground, and attract growing support from Cubans. At worst, the invaders should be able to fight their way to the Escambray and go into guerrilla action. After the State Department representatives point out the grave effects such an operation could have on the U.S. position in Latin America without careful and successful diplomatic preparation, President Kennedy presses for alternatives to a full-fledged invasion supported by U.S. planes, ships and supplies. A memorandum of conversation written by McGeorge Bundy records Kennedy's question: "Could not such a force be landed gradually and quietly and make its first major military efforts from the mountains—then taking shape as a Cuban force within Cuba, not as an invasion force sent by the Yankees?" Kennedy authorizes creation of a small junta of anti-Castro leaders to give the Brigade forces some political purpose. (McGeorge Bundy, *Memorandum of Meeting with President Kennedy, White House, Washington, February 8, 1961*, 2/8/61)

**FEB 8–16, 1961:** Internal resistance leader Lino Fernández leads an MRR squad into Yaguajay, to a camp once used by Camilo Cienfuegos during the revolution. Over the next week, the camp is marked for a air drop of supplies, and peasant recruits begin to sign up. Instead of the scheduled airdrop, however, the resistance force is surrounded by 16,000 government troops and police; Fernández and 500 of his men are captured on and around February 16th and taken to the Santa Clara jail.

**FEB 9, 1961:** Admiral Dennison, Commander-in-Chief, Atlantic Command, meets with the President and asks him if the Navy needs to prepare for any possible bail-out operations. The President responds definitely no, stating that if anything went wrong the force would fade into the hinterland. (Aguilar, p. 164)

**FEB 11, 1961:** In a memorandum to the President, Arthur Schlesinger argues that the "drastic decision" to enact the plan being promoted within the government only makes sense "if one excludes everything but Cuba." Taken in the context of "the hemisphere and the rest of the world, the arguments *against* this decision begin to gain force." He points out that there is no way to disguise U.S. complicity in the plan and "at one stroke, it would dissipate all the extraordinary good will which has been rising toward the new Administration through the world." (Arthur Schlesinger, Jr., "Memorandum from the President's Special Assistant to President Kennedy," 2/11/61)

The CIA's Board of National Estimates sends the Director a memorandum outlining probable international reactions to various U.S. actions against the Castro regime. The Board argues that the Soviet Bloc "would regard Castro's downfall as a substantial political defeat and would respond vigorously to any major U.S. move." While that response would be primarily political, in the event of a prolonged military struggle, the Bloc would seek to continue or increase military aid to the Castro regime. However, the Board "believe[s] that the Bloc would avoid a direct military confrontation with U.S. forces."

The Board also reports that most governments in Latin America would "at least privately approve of unobtrusive U.S. support for an opposition move against Castro . . ." However, reaction would ultimately depend on whether the United States is perceived to be "assisting the Cubans themselves to settle their own destinies," or as "imposing a new regime." As for "reactions elsewhere in the Free World," the Board believes "it would remind many people of the Soviet intervention in Hungary." (CIA, *Memorandum for the Director*, By Abbot Smith, Acting Chairman, Board of National Estimates, 2/11/96)

The CIA launches an attempt to infiltrate a team from Brigade 2506 into Cuba. The ship almost capsizes in heavy seas. The men swim ashore practically naked, without weapons, money, or radio equipment. They are the first of the Brigade infiltration teams to land in Cuba. (Johnson, p. 59)

**FEB 12, 1961:** The Voice of America announces it will broadcast a series of anti-Castro radio programs, beginning with a documentary "The Anatomy of a Broken Promise" which reviews Castro's pledges to hold elections and how these pledges were broken one by one. (NYT, 2/13/61)

**MID-FEBRUARY 1961:** Tony Varona, Antonio Maceo, and another member of the Frente arrive in the training camp in Guatemala. Varona, the coordinator and principal official of the Frente speaks to the Brigade and says that the Brigade headquarters cannot make decisions without first consulting the civilian structure in Miami. The following day, Varona expresses confidence in San Román's leadership. Brigade members greet this statement with catcalls and shouts of derision. (Johnson, pp. 62–63)

**FEB 14, 1961:** Adolph Berle writes a memo to Secretary Rusk on a decision making meeting on the Cuba operation. "We arranged leadership for the camps," he states. He also highlights a CIA paper on the dangers of aborting the operation. "It suggests that dismantling the Cuban operation may mean explosions in three or four countries in Central America. If it is accurate, we should be prepared for the consequences of dismantling." (*Cuba*, 2/14/61)

**FEB 15, 1961:** Thomas Mann, the assistant secretary for Inter-American affairs, writes a memo to Rusk opposing the invasion. Mann notes that the CIA's original plan is based on the assumption that the invasion will inspire a popular uprising which is unlikely to take place. "It therefore appears possible, even probable, that we would be faced with . . . a) abandoning the brigade to its fate, which would cost us dearly in prestige and respect or b) attempting execution of the plan to move the brigade into the mountains as guerrillas, which would pose a prolonged problem of air drops or supplies or c) overt U.S. military intervention."

Mann argues that international law, the inability to hide the hand of the United States, and the fact that Castroism would be more useful to the United States as a model of socio-economic failure, rather than as a martyr—or victor—against U.S. intervention all are reasons to abandon the operation. "I therefore conclude it would not be in the national interest to proceed unilaterally to put this plan into execution." (Mann, *The March 1960 Plan*, 2/15/61)

**FEB 17, 1961:** President Kennedy meets with representatives from the State Department, CIA, and Joint Chiefs of Staff, and following a discussion of planning and preparations for the invasion indicates that he would be in favor of a more moderate approach, such as mass infiltration. The President urges an examination of all possible alternatives. Since the meeting does not result in a decision, the military plan for a D-Day of March 5 is postponed. (Gleijeses, p. 22; Aguilar, p. 65)

Richard Bissell responds to the Mann argument with a comprehensive opinion paper arguing for the invasion. He addresses the "disposal" problem if the mission is aborted: Brigade "members will be angry, disillusioned and aggressive with the inevitable result that they will provide honey for the press bees and the U.S. will have to face the resulting indignities and embarrassments." Bissell concludes by arguing that this is the last opportunity for the U.S. to bring down Castro without overt U.S. military intervention or a full embargo:

> The Cuban paramilitary force, if used, has a good chance of overthrowing Castro or at the very least causing a damaging civil war without requiring the U.S. to commit itself to overt action against Cuba. Whatever embarrassment the alleged (though deniable) U.S. support may cause, it may well be considerably less than that resulting from the continuation of the Castro regime or from the more drastic and more attributable actions necessary to accomplish the result at a later date." (*Cuba*, 2/17/61)

**FEB 18, 1961:** McGeorge Bundy passes on both the Bissell and the Mann position papers to the President. "Bissell and Mann are the real antagonists at the staff level," Bundy writes in a cover memo. "Since I think you lean toward Mann's view, I have put Bissell on top."

Bundy's own position is that the United States should institute a trade embargo first, let internal opposition build for several months, and then launch "Bissell's battalion." At that point, he writes, "the color of civil war would be quite a bit stronger." (Bundy to JFK, 2/18/61)

**FEB 24–27, 1961:** A team of three officers from the Joint Staff examines and reports on the military effectiveness of the Cuban Expeditionary Force at its Guatemala base. The report includes the estimate that because of the visibility of activities at Retalhuleu in Guatemala and Puerto Cabezas, Nicaragua, the odds against surprise being achieved are about 85-to-15. The JCS air evaluation points out that if surprise is not achieved, the attack against Cuba will fail, adding that one Castro aircraft armed with .50 caliber machine guns could sink all or most of the invasion force. (Aguilar, p. 10)

**MAR 7, 1961:** Two Costa Rican deputies denounce the use of their country for training of exiled Cubans to invade Cuba. The deputies state that three fincas are being used for training and that the exiles have a boat, the *Don Fabio*, prepared to "leave for the Bay of Pigs, on the south coast of the province of Las Villas, in Cuba." (Molina, "Diario de Girón", pp. 70–72)

**MAR 8, 1961:** The Guatemalan Workers' Party (PGT) issues a denunciation of continued plans to invade Cuba. The Party reports that the Retalhuleu base is the site of a great movement of planes, "including daily flights between Guatemala and the Guantánamo naval base." The document adds that the port of Champerico has received 200 tons of bombs, explosives, and arms from an American ship that were taken immediately to the training bases in Retalhuleu and the Helvetia finca. (Molina, "Diario de Girón", pp. 72–73)

Internal resistance members set fire to a gas station in Cueto, Oriente, vandalize 12 delivery trucks at the nationalized Coca-Cola plant and set off an explosive device at the Antonio Guiteras electricity company. (*Informe Especial: 1961*)

**MAR 10, 1961:** CIA Director Dulles, preparing to meet with President Kennedy, is briefed on the agency's efforts to create a provisional government of exile leaders. "At the covert instigation of the Agency," a memo for Dulles begins, "six leading figures of the Cuban opposition met in New York City." The purpose of the meeting was to agree on procedures for electing a revolutionary council, and to draw up a minimal political and economic program. (CIA, *Status of Efforts to Form a Provisional Government of Cuba*, 3/10/61)

—A study appearing the same day from the CIA's Board of National Estimates, however, is much less reassuring. Entitled "Is Time on Our Side in Cuba?," it argues: "To be sure, the regime's once overwhelming popular support has greatly diminished in recent months and various instances of guerrilla opposition, sabotage and economic dislocation have arisen to plague it. However, we see no signs that such developments portend any

serious threat to a regime which by now has established a formidable structure of control over the daily lives of the Cuban people." (Wyden, p. 99)

**MAR 11, 1961:** At a White House meeting between 10:05 a.m. and 12:15 p.m.,
Richard Bissell presents the CIA's "Proposed Operation Against Cuba" to
President Kennedy. The paper provides four alternative courses of action
involving the commitment of the paramilitary force being readied by the
United States. These include the course of action favored by the CIA—the
Trinidad Plan, which involves "an amphibious/airborne assault . . . to
seize a beachhead contiguous to terrain suitable for guerrilla operations,"
with a landing of the "provisional government . . . as soon as the beachhead
had been secured." The invading force is expected to repulse attacks by
Castro militia with substantial losses to the attacking forces followed by defections from the armed forces and widespread rebellion. If the actions are
unsuccessful in detonating a major revolt, the assault force would retreat to
the contiguous mountain area and continue operations as a powerful guerrilla force. The assault, combined with a diversionary landing, according to
the CIA plan, has the potential for administering a demoralizing shock that
could lead to the prompt overthrow of the Castro regime. If not, guerrilla
action could be continued on a sizable scale in favorable terrain.

The President rejects the Trinidad Plan as too spectacular, too much like a
World War II invasion. He prefers a quiet landing, preferably at night, with
no basis for American military intervention. No decision comes from the
March 11 meeting and the President states his view that "the best possible
plan . . . has not yet been presented, and new proposals are to be concerted
promptly."

The same day Bundy signs National Security Action Memorandum 31 noting
that "the President expects to authorize U.S. support for an appropriate
number of patriotic Cubans to return to their homeland." Kennedy wants a
plan to be prepared that would be less spectacular in execution and therefore
more plausible as an essentially Cuban operation. CIA officials, directed by
Bissell, scramble to come up with a new plan in fewer than three days. (CIA,
*Proposed Operation Against Cuba*, 11 March 1961, pp. 1–12; Wyden, pp. 99–
101; and Gleijeses, p. 34)

**MAR 12, 1961:** A Cuban exile sabotage team completes a successful operation against the Texaco refinery in Santiago del Cuba. (CIA, *Inspector General's Survey of the Cuban Operation*, 1:25).

**MAR 15, 1961:** On or around this date, Mafia operatives pass poison pills manufactured at the CIA's Technical Services Division to their main contact in Havana, Juan Orta Cordova, a functionary in Castro's office. Orta fails to put the pills in Castro's drink; instead he returns them to his contacts. (CIA, *Report on Plots to Assassinate Fidel Castro*, pp. 27,28.)

**MAR 14 and 15, 1961:** The CIA presents three alternative invasion scenarios to the Working Group of the Joint Staff. The Joint Chiefs of Staff review the plans and choose the alternative recommended by the Working Group—the Zapata Plan which involves a landing at the Bay of Pigs. They add, however, that none of the alternative concepts is considered as feasible and likely to accomplish the objective as the Trinidad Plan. (JCS, *Evaluation of the Military Aspects of Alternative Concepts, CIA Para-Military Plan, Cuba*, 3/15/61)

**MAR 16, 1961:** At 4:15 p.m., Dulles and Bissell present President Kennedy with three alternative plans for the Cuban operation. Kennedy has been briefed in advance on the proposals by his national security adviser, who reports that the CIA "has done a remarkable job of reframing the landing plan so as to make it unspectacular and quiet, and plausibly Cuban in its essentials."

The first option is a modification of the Trinidad Plan, the second targets an area on the northeast coast of Cuba, and the third is an invasion at the Zapata Peninsula on the Bay of Pigs. The President orders modifications of the Zapata Plan to make it appear like more of an inside guerrilla-type operation. (Notes of General Gray; Gleijeses p. 36)

—Cuban security forces announce that 420 "counterrevolutionaries" have been put out of action in the Escambray campaign—39 killed in combat and 381 taken prisoner. Six of the rebel leaders are reportedly captured and some 80 members remain hidden in Escambray. (Molina, "Diario de Girón", pp. 80–81; *Informe Especial: 1961*)

**MAR 16, 1961:** Drawing on intelligence gathered in Cuba at the end of February, the CIA generates an information report that cites "diminishing popular support of the Castro government." The report estimates are that "fewer than 20 percent of the people" support Castro, and that "many Cubans think that it is possible that Castro will soon fall." It concludes that "approximately 75 to 80 percent of the militia units will defect when it becomes evident that the real fight against Castro has begun."

Bissell uses this and several similar intelligence reports to bolster his case that the invasion will spark a major uprising. (Richard Bissell, *Reflections of a Cold Warrior*, Yale University Press, 1996, pg. 180; CIA *Information Report, Diminishing Popular Support of the Castro Government*, 3/16/61)

**MAR 17, 1961:** The *New York Times* reports that in the coming weeks simultaneous invasions will take place at different points in Cuba. (*NYT*, 3/17/61)

**MAR 18, 1961:** Richard Bissell sends "Jim Noble," the last CIA station chief in Havana, to Miami to pull together the Cuban exile leadership into a unified body. The Cubans are summoned to the Skyways Motel where Noble's Spanish-speaking assistant Jim Carr tells them: "If you don't come out of this meeting with a committee, you just forget the whole fucking business, because we're through." Three days later, the exile groups announce the creation of the Consejo Revolucionario Cubano, replacing the FDR. Dr. José Miró Cardona is appointed coordinator. (Wyden, p. 116)

**MAR 18, 1961:** Leading officials of the internal opposition, including the military coordinators of the FDR, are detained while at a strategy meeting in Miramar. A number of them, including Humberto Sori Marin, Manuel Puig, and Rogelio Gonzalez Corso, are executed for treason a month later, in the midst of the Playa Girón invasion.

**MAR 22, 1961:** Cuban exile politicians reach an agreement and form a Revolutionary Council. Several days later, Tracy Barnes sends Arthur Schlesinger the first draft of a proposed Council Manifesto, which Schlesinger later describes as "so overwrought in tone and sterile in thought that it made one wonder what sort of people we were planning to send back to Havana." Barnes and Schlesinger recruit two Harvard academics, John Plank and William Barnes, to help redraft the document. (Schlesinger, *A Thousand Days*, p. 243.)

**MAR 24, 1961:** General Lemnitzer, Chairman of the Joint Chiefs of Staff, informs Admiral Dennison, (Commander-in Chief, Atlantic —CINCLANT) of the requirements for naval support for CIA Operation Crosspatch. One destroyer will escort the CEF ships until they are about three miles offshore.

A landing ship dock (LSD) will deliver landing craft (3 landing craft, utility— LCUs; and four landing craft, vehicle and personnel—LCVPs) to the transport area and U.S. naval air cover will be provided over the CEF ships from 6:00 a.m. on the day before the invasion (then scheduled for April 10, 1961). (*Rules of Engagement*, 3/24/61)

**MAR 27, 1961:** The CIA intensifies its propaganda campaign against Castro's government, directing the stations managers to inform Radio Swan's producers that their programs are terminated and replacing them with a new schedule that includes increased broadcasting hours. (Taylor Report, Annex 2: CIA, Brief History of Radio Swan)

**MAR 28, 1961:** Admiral Dennison proposes rules of engagement to General Lemnitzer including the provision that U.S. forces escorting the invasion force open fire if Cuban aircraft or ships reach a position to attack U.S. ships or attack the CEF ships. (*Rules of Engagement*, 3/28/61)

—In a discussion with the President, Arthur Schlesinger asks: "What do you think about this damned invasion?" Kennedy reportedly responds: "I think about it as little as possible." (Thomas, p. 251)

—U.S. overflights over Cuban airspace are suspended in preparation for the coming invasion. (CIA, *Inspector General's Survey of the Cuban Operation*, p. 2:26)

**MAR 29, 1961:** Arthur Schlesinger notes in his journal that "a final decision on the invasion will have to be made on April 4." He feels "the tide is flowing against the project." At a meeting in the Cabinet Room he finds the President growing steadily more skeptical. Kennedy asks Bissell: "Do you really have to have these air strikes?" Bissell says his group will work to insure maximum effectiveness for minimum noise from the air and reassures the President that Cubans on the island will join in a rising. (Schlesinger, *A Thousand Days*, p. 233,234)

**MAR 30, 1961:** Senator J. William Fulbright, chairman of the Senate Foreign Relations Committee, travels to Florida on Air Force One and hands President Kennedy a 3,766 word memorandum on the planned invasion. The memo describes the venture as ill-considered and that it will be impossible to conceal the U.S. hand. Fulbright also raises the issue of what to do if things go awry: "The prospect must also be faced that an invasion of Cuba by exiles would encounter formidable resistance which the exiles, by themselves, might not be able to overcome. The question would then arise of whether the United States would be willing to let the enterprise fail . . . or . . . would respond with progressive assistance as necessary to insure success. This would include ultimately the use of armed force; and if we came to that, even under the paper cover of legitimacy, we would have undone the work of thirty years in trying to live down earlier interventions." (Fulbright Memorandum, *Cuba Policy*, 3/29/61)

The CIA's *Current Intelligence Weekly Summary* continues to emphasize the strength of opposition to Castro within Cuba: Sabotage and organized resistance activities evidently are continuing to increase throughout Cuba despite a presumably steady gain in the strength of the government's instruments of repression. Accounts of attempted sabotage of industrial and agricultural installations are becoming increasingly frequent and anti-Castro terrorists are exploding bombs daily in Havana—twelve in a single day. (Wyden, p. 140)

**MAR 31, 1961:** Under Secretary of State Chester Bowles hands a memorandum to Secretary Rusk advising that a decision on the Cuba operation will be made at an April 4 meeting. Bowles considers the plan profoundly disturbing and a grave mistake. "[A]s the venture is now planned, the chances of success are not greater than one out of three. This makes it a highly risky operation. If it fails, Castro's strength and prestige will be greatly enhanced. If you agree that this operation would be a mistake, I suggest that you personally and privately communicate your views to the President. It is my guess that your voice will be decisive." Rusk files the memo away. (Schlesinger, *A Thousand Days*, p. 235; Wyden, pp. 120–121)

**EARLY APRIL 1961:** Rebel leader Manuel Artíme writes a "political testament," seeking to leave behind a statement if he is killed in the course of the planned invasion. "This struggle that we are undertaking," he writes, "may mark a new period in Cuban history; we do not seek to overthrow one more tyranny; we seek to extirpate the roots of an international monster that intends to absorb the free world." (Artíme, *Mi Testamento Politico*, undated)

—The State and Defense Departments and CIA reach a compromise on the air plan for the invasion. Limited air strikes will be made on D-2 (two days prior to the invasion) at the time of a diversionary landing of 160 men in eastern Cuba. These strikes are designed to seem like the actions of Cuban pilots defecting from the Cuban air force and thus supporting the fiction that air support for the invasion force is coming from within Cuba. The JCS does not favor the D-2 air strikes because of their indecisive nature and the danger of prematurely alarming the Castro force. The pre-invasion strikes are, however, included in the plan with the realization that the main reliance for the obstruction of the Castro air force must be placed on the D-Day strikes. (Aguilar, p. 16)

In a second attempt to assassinate Castro prior to the invasion, the CIA's mafia contacts pass poison pills and thousands of dollars to Tony Varona, a member of the anti-Castro Democratic Revolutionary Front. The head of WH/4, Jake Esterline, signs vouchers for the funds to be taken from the invasion budget. Varona claims to have an asset inside Cuba—a restaurant worker—who will have the opportunity to poison Castro. Cuban intelligence later reports that the closest Castro ever came to being assassinated is when poison pills hidden inside a icebox, and intended to be put in an ice cream cone, froze to the coils. (CIA, *Report on Plots to Assassinate Fidel Castro*, p. 32)

**EARLY and MID-APRIL 1961:** Anticipating an invasion, Fidel Castro begins preparations for Cuba's defense. He concentrates troops close to the most probable landing points throughout the island, particularly near access zones to the mountains—especially near Trinidad, where the Escambray guerrillas were eliminated in March. Also, expecting an attempt to destroy Cuba's air force, Cuban forces place out-of-service planes together in groups of three and disperses, camouflages, and surrounds with anti-aircraft batteries those planes that are in service.

**APR 3, 1961:** Dr. José Miró Cardona, head of the Cuban Revolutionary Council, meets with former U.S. Ambassador to Cuba Philip Bonsal, the State Department's Adolf Berle and Kennedy assistant Arthur Schlesinger. When propaganda to support the invasion is discussed, Miró Cardona complains that "Radio Swan is controlled by people who [are] not in my confidence." (Taylor Report, Memorandum of Meeting Twenty, 5/25/61)

**APR 4, 1961:** At a meeting at the State Department, President Kennedy polls a dozen advisers on whether to go ahead with the Bay of Pigs invasion. He has invited Senator Fulbright to voice his strong position against the operation.

After Fulbright outlines his objections, all vote in favor of moving ahead, with only Secretary of State Rusk remaining non-committal. After the meeting, the President takes Arthur Schlesinger aside and asks his opinion. After a rushed reply, Schlesinger returns to his office to draft a substantive memorandum outlining why the invasion is "a terrible idea." (Schlesinger, *A Thousand Days*, p. 236)

After a conference with the President, Secretary of Defense McNamara requests that the JCS reconsider the rules of engagement to insure that the U.S. will not become overtly engaged with Castro forces. (*Rules of Engagement*)

**APR 5, 1961:** Arthur Schlesinger sends President Kennedy a comprehensive memo laying out why the CIA invasion "seems to me to involve many hazards." He argues that the invasion force is not strong enough to topple Castro quickly and that the operation will turn into a "protracted civil conflict" that will lead to pressures to send in the Marines. The United States, he predicts, will be branded the aggressor; "Cuba will become our Hungary." The President reads the memorandum and tells Schlesinger, "You know, I've reserved the right to stop this thing up to twenty-four hours before the landing. In the meantime, I'm trying to make some sense out of it. We'll just have to see." (Schlesinger Memo, *Cuba*, 4/5/61; A Thousand Days, p. 240)

—At a meeting at the White House between the President, Secretary of Defense McNamara, General Lemnitzer, Dulles, Bissell, and General Cabell, it is agreed that the rules of engagement should definitely spell out the President's requirement that the operation be aborted if United States forces were required to protect the Brigade's ships from damage or capture. At this meeting the idea of fake defections and preliminary air strikes is discussed. The President indicates approval of the general idea but says everyone should consider further measures overnight and meet the following morning. (Pfeiffer, p. 100; and *Rules of Engagement*)

Edward Murrow, director of the United States Information Agency (USIA) hears from a *New York Times* reporter that operations are underway for a landing in Cuba, backed and planned by the CIA. The reporter indicates that the *Times* has a very full story which, however, they do not intend to print; he hopes to persuade USIA to authorize briefings of the press in Miami following the landing. Armed with this information, Murrow calls on the Director of Central Intelligence, who informs him that preparations are indeed underway, but does not give him details of the magnitude or the time of the landing. The Department of State agrees to provide policy guidance to the USIA beginning three days before the invasion, but this guidance is apparently not given and the USIA is caught unprepared. (Aguilar, p. 19)

—Cuba's Foreign Minister Raúl Roa calls the U.S. State Department's "White Paper" on Cuba "an undeclared declaration of war." He states that this document is almost identical to one circulated by the State Department in Latin America before the intervention in Guatemala. (*Informe Especial: 1961*)

**APR 6, 1961:** At the follow up to the April 5 meeting, the President questions CIA officials on whether a preliminary air strike would constitute an alarm to the Castro government that the invasion is underway. (Pfeiffer, p. 100)

**APR 6-7, 1961:** The Cuban Armed Forces Ministry announces that a vast counterrevolutionary plot organized from Guantánamo has been foiled. The Ministry states that a rebel group attempted to ambush an army and militia patrol in a place called "Los Montes de Pilabó" on February 25, resulting in the death of two militia members. In successive encounters revolutionary troops capture 107 rebels from a group known as the counterrevolutionary nucleus of Monte Rus. These arrests neutralize the internal counterrevolution in Oriente province according to the Ministry. (Molina, "Diario de Girón," pp. 109–110)

**APR 7, 1961:** The CIA sends a memo to General Gray, JCS Liaison Officer, modifying the naval support requirements to provide area coverage (instead of convoying the CEF ships) and to provide an extra day of air cover over the CEF ships. The invasion date is changed to April 17, 1961. (*Rules of Engagement*)

The Chairman, JCS, sends Admiral Dennison a memo with the revised rules of engagement, pointing out the necessity for avoiding any sign of U.S. participation. The destroyers are not to approach within 20 miles (instead of the previous three miles) of Cuban territory. U.S. naval units are not to open fire on Cuban ships or aircraft unless the CEF is attacked, and if U.S. forces intervene to protect CEF ships, the operation is automatically canceled. (*Rules of Engagement*)

—The *New York Times* runs a story by Tad Szulc entitled "Anti-Castro Units Trained to Fight at Florida Bases." The article overestimates the Brigade's strength at 5,000 to 6,000 men but discloses that training has been discontinued because the forces have reached the stage of adequate preparation. Near the end of the story, Szulc cites CBS as reporting unmistakable signs that invasion plans are in their final stages. Following discussions between President Kennedy and Times publisher Orvil E. Dryfoos, editors shrink the story from a four-column lead article on the front page to a one-column headline near the middle of page one. Even so, when Kennedy reads the story he exclaims that Castro doesn't need spies in the United States; all he has to do is read the newspaper. (NYT, 4/7/61; Wyden, pp. 153–154)

**APR 8, 11, 13, 1961:** Reconnaissance flights indicate that the Cubans have 36 combat aircraft. The number of aircraft taking part in the air strikes two days prior to the invasion and on the day of the invasion is increased from six to eight. (Aguilar, p. 128)

**APR 8, 1961:** Jacob Esterline and Jack Hawkins, the two CIA subcommanders most directly in charge of the invasion planning, go to Bissell's house in Northwest Washington, D.C. and inform him that they want to resign. Their primary concerns are changes that the White House has ordered in the operation making it far less likely to succeed; "by pruning away at the operation [the politicians] were making it technically impossible to win," they reportedly tell Bissell. Bissell asks them to stay on, arguing that the invasion will go forward with or without them. Reluctantly they agree to his request. (Wyden, p. 160; Thomas, p. 252)

**APR 10, 1961:** Richard Bissell briefs Attorney General Robert Kennedy on the operation. He rates the chance of success as two out of three and assures Kennedy that even in the worst case the invaders can turn guerrilla. "I hope you're right," the Attorney General responds. (Thomas, p. 253; Bissell, p 182.)

**APR 11, 1961:** The *New York Times* runs a leading article by James Reston on a sharp policy dispute in the administration about how far to go in helping the Cuban refugees overthrow the Castro government. (Wyden, p. 165)

**APR 12, 1961:** At a meeting attended by the President, the Secretary of State, the JCS, and other NSC officials, Richard Bissell presents a paper outlining the latest changes in the Zapata Operation. The paper includes a countdown to D-day which is now scheduled for April 17: D-7, Commence staging main force; D-6, First vessel sails from staging area; D -2, Diversionary landing in Oriente (night of D-3 to D-2); D-2, Limited air strikes; Two fake defector Brigade pilots in B-26s land in Florida to create the impression that the air strikes originate in Cuba; D-Day, Main landings—limited air strikes; Two B-26s and liaison plane land on seized airstrip; D-day to D+1, Vessels return night of D to D+1 to complete discharge of supplies; D+7, Diversionary landing in Pinar del Rio. President Kennedy does not give final approval to the plan at this meeting. However, he is informed that the decision cannot be delayed much longer as the no-go time for operations would be at noon, April 14. (Aguilar, p. 17)

At a press conference at the State Department, President Kennedy rules out, under any condition, an intervention in Cuba by the United States armed forces. (Johnson, p. 72)

—Theodore C. Sorensen, Kennedy's special counsel, who has not been informed about the Cuban operation, asks the President about the invasion. Kennedy cuts the conversation short: "I know everybody is grabbing their nuts on this," he graphically tells his aide. (Wyden, p. 165)

**APR 13, 1961:** Invasion Project Chief, Jake Esterline, sends an emergency cable to Puerto Cabezas, Nicaragua, requesting information on any change in the evaluation of the Cuban invasion force. In response, Colonel Jack Hawkins sends back a cable reporting "my confidence in the ability of this force to accomplish not only initial combat missions but also the ultimate objective of Castro's overthrow:

> These officers are young, vigorous, intelligent and motivated with a fanatical urge to begin battle for which most of them have been preparing in the rugged conditions of training camps for almost a year. . . . Without exception, they have utmost confidence in their ability to win. They say they know their own people and believe after they have inflicted one serious defeat upon opposing forces, the latter will melt away from Castro, who they have no wish to support. They say it is Cuban tradition to join a winner and they have supreme confidence they will win all engagements against the best Castro has to offer. I share their confidence." (*Memorandum for General Maxwell D. Taylor*, 4/26/61)

Bissell makes sure that Hawkin's cable is transmitted to the President who reads it on April 14; it helps convince Kennedy to go ahead with the invasion. (Wyden, pp. 168–169; Thomas, p. 253.)

—Adolph Berle and Arthur Schlesinger meet Dr. Miró Cardona at the Century Club in New York City. They tell him that the United States will not provide U.S. troops in support of the Brigade forces if problems develop on the beachhead. "Dr. Cardona displayed considerable resistance," Schlesinger reports back to the President. "If the Cuban movement against Castro failed . . . the United States would be held responsible." (Schlesinger, *Conversation with Dr. Miró Cardona*, 4/14/61)

**APR 14, 1961:** From the White House, President Kennedy calls Bissell and says the Saturday air strikes can go forward. He asks how many planes will participate and is told sixteen. "Well, I don't want it on that scale. I want it minimal." Bissell passes the order on for only eight planes to fly. "I believe the president did not realize that the air strike was an integral part of the operational plan he had approved," Bissell later writes in his memoirs. (Bissell, p. 183; Wyden, p. 170)

—Luis Somoza, the Nicaraguan dictator, comes to the dock to meet the Cuban forces about to launch the invasion: "Bring me a couple of hairs from Castro's beard," he reportedly tells them. (Johnson, p. 86)

**APR 15, 1961:** At dawn eight B-26 planes of the Cuban Expeditionary Force carry out air strikes at three sites to destroy the Castro air capability. Initial pilot reports indicate that 50 percent of Castro's offensive air was destroyed at Campo Libertad, 75 to 80 percent at San Antonio de los Baos, and five planes were destroyed at Santiago de Cuba. Subsequent photographic studies and interpretations indicate a greatly reduced estimate of the damage, amounting to five aircraft definitely destroyed and an indeterminable number of other planes suffering some damage. After the attacks, Castro orders his pilots to sleep under the wings of the planes, which are ready to take off immediately. (Aguilar, p. 18; Wyden, pp. 184–185)

—At 7:00 a.m., a bullet-ridden B-26 with Cuban markings lands at Miami International Airport. The Cuban pilot claims that he and three of his comrades have defected from Castro's air force in stolen planes. They claim to have carried out the attack against Castro's air fields and, after being hit by anti-aircraft fire and low on fuel, have flown to the United States. Reporters note that the plane's machine guns have evidently not been fired and that its nose is of solid metal while Castro's B-26s have plastic noses. Dr. Miró Cardona issues a statement from New York that the raids in Cuba were carried out by Cubans inside Cuba. On reading American wire service accounts of the defection, Fidel Castro comments that even Hollywood would not try to film such a story. (Johnson, pp. 90–91; Wyden, p. 185)

—Fidel Castro announces that, at 6:00 a.m., U.S.-made B-26 planes attacked simultaneously points in Ciudad Libertad, in Havana, San Antonio de los Baños, and Santiago de Cuba, in Oriente. "The Cuban delegation at the United Nations has received instructions to accuse directly the government of the United States as to blame for this aggression against Cuba." Castro announces that all militia and army units have been mobilized and placed on a state of alert. "If this air attack is the prelude to an invasion, the country is ready to struggle and will resist and destroy with an iron hand whatever force tries to land in our country." ("Playa Girón," Primer Tomo, 15–16)

—Nino Diaz leads a group of 160 men in the diversionary landing 30 miles east of Guantanamo. The landing is aborted. The reasons given are the failure to appear of a friendly reception party and the loss of three boats. The Cubans are ordered to land the following night (April 15/16). Again the 168 men do not land because of the breakdown of a reconnaissance boat and loss of time retrieving it, failure of a friendly landing party to appear, and heavy enemy activity in the area. The Diaz group is ordered to join the main invasion force, but they fail to arrive in time to participate. (*Sequence of Events*, 5/3/61)

—Cuba's Foreign Minister Dr. Raúl Roa, speaking before the United Nations General Assembly, accuses the United States of responsibility for the bombing attack on Havana, San Antonio, and Santiago. Cuba succeeds in getting the General Assembly to convene a special session of the First Commission (Political and Security Commission) of the Assembly to hear their charges against the U.S. At this meeting, Roa calls the bombing "undoubtedly the prologue to a large scale invasion, planned, organized, provisioned, armed, and financed by the government of the United States. . . . The Revolutionary Government of Cuba solemnly accuses the government of the United States, before the Political and Security Commission and before world public opinion of having resorted to the use of force to settle its differences with a member state of the organization."

In response, Adlai Stevenson, the U.S. representative to the U.N., states that there will be no intervention by the armed forces of the United States and that the United States will do everything in its power to assure that no American participates in any action against Cuba. Stevenson then presents photographs of the planes that landed in Florida claiming that their markings show them to be Cuban Air Force aircraft. He finishes stating that the "fundamental question is not between the U.S. and Cuba but among the Cubans themselves." (Pino Machado, "La Batalla de Girón," 5–10)

**APR 16, 1961:** The Airborne battalion moves from base camp in Guatemala to Puerto Cabezas, Nicaragua, during the night of April 15–16. At around noon, the President formally approves the landing plan and the word is passed to all commanders in the operation. Assault shipping moves on separate courses toward the objective area. The ships make their rendezvous at around 5:30 p.m. approximately 40 miles off the coast. They proceed in column and make rendezvous with U.S. Navy LSD (San Marcos) about 5,000 yards from Blue Beach. LCU and LCVP aboard the San Marcos are transferred to Cuban crews between 11:00 p.m. and 12:00 a.m. Radio Swan repeatedly broadcasts a message which Phillips and Hunt composed to give the appearance that the station is activating resistance groups in Cuba: "Alert! Alert! Look well at the rainbow. The fish will rise very soon. Chico is in the house. Visit him. The sky is blue. Place notice in the tree. The tree is green and brown. The letters arrived well. The letters are white. The fish will not take much time to rise. The fish is red." Hunt later writes that these were nonsense messages: "We couched it in terms that could, conceivably, confuse and misdirect Castro's G-2 . . . I remember thinking at the time of BBC's wartime broadcasts which used plain texts to communicate with resistance teams in Europe." (Johnson, p. 100; Hunt, p. 201)

—At about 9:30 p.m., McGeorge Bundy telephones General Cabell of the CIA to tell him that the dawn air strikes the following morning should not be launched until planes can conduct them from a strip within the beachhead. Bundy indicates that any further consultation with regard to this matter should be with the Secretary of State. General Cabell and Richard Bissell go to Secretary Rusk's office at about 10:15 p.m. Rusk tells them he has just been talking to the President on the phone and recommended that the Monday morning air strikes (D-Day) should be canceled and the President agreed.

Cabell and Bissell protest, arguing that the ships as well as the landings will be seriously endangered without the dawn strikes. The Secretary indicates there are policy considerations against air strikes before the beachhead airfield is in the hands of the landing force and completely operational and capable of supporting the raids. Rusk calls the President and tells him of the CIA's objections, then restates his own recommendation to cancel the strikes. The Secretary offers to let the CIA representatives talk to the President directly but they decline. "I don't think there's any point," Cabell tells Rusk. "I think I agree with that," Bissell also says. In his memoirs, Bissell writes that "I view this decision of Cabell's and mine as a major mistake. For the record, we should have spoken to the president and made as strong a case as possible on behalf of the operation and the welfare of the brigade." The order canceling the air strikes is dispatched to the departure field in Nicaragua, arriving when the pilots are in their cockpits ready for takeoff.

The Joint Chiefs of Staff learn of the cancellation at varying hours on the morning of April 17. Realizing the seriousness of the cancellation of air strikes, CIA officials try to offset the damage. They warn the invasion force of likely air attacks and the ships to expedite unloading and to withdraw from the beach by dawn. A continuous cover of two B-26s over the beach is laid on. At 4:30 a.m., General Cabell calls the Secretary of State at his home, reiterates the need to protect the shipping by providing air cover, and makes the request to the President by telephone. The President does not approve the request for air cover but authorizes early warning destroyers, provided they stay at least 30 miles from Cuban territory. (Bissell, p. 184; Wyden, pp. 198–201; Aguilar, pp. 20–21)

At the funeral of the victims of the April 15 attack Fidel Castro calls on "all units to make their way to their respective battalions . . . Let us face the enemy . . . with the conviction that to die for the country is to live, and to live in chains is to live in shame and disgrace." The leaders of the revolution take charge of their areas: Raúl Castro in Oriente province; Che Guevara in Pinar del Río, in the west; Juan Almeida in Santa Clara at the head of the Army of the Center; Ramiró Valdés responsible for Intelligence and Counterintelligence; Guillermo García in the tactical center of Managua, city of Havana. (Pino Machado, "La Batalla de Girón," p. 67)

On the afternoon of April 16, Commander Juan Almeida travels through the sector of the Bay of Pigs and visits the radio post of Punta Perdiz. He learns there that they have contact with the command post in Santa Clara but not with the Australia sugar mill where the closest concentration of troops is: Battalion 339 of the Cienfuegos militias. Unable to resolve the technical problems, he orders a company of the battalion situated the entire length of the bay to strengthen the defense. Almeida is informed that a band of 35 counterrevolutionaries has been spotted in the zone of Amarillas. He wonders why they have abandoned their wooded positions and embarked on this march south. The high command of the Cuban Armed Forces receives other reports of suspicious activities: movements of boats and signals in Baitiquirí, Baracoa Oriental, and Punta Alegre, Camaguey; a large and a small boat headed toward Santa Fe; four boats in the mouth of the Guajaibón River and two more to the right; three unknown boats six or seven miles out, seen from Havana; and black shadows in the sea at Punta Perdiz, Girón. (Pino Machado, "La Batalla de Girón," 67–68)

On the night of April 16, the Committees for the Defense of the Revolution are mobilized to detain those opposed to the revolution. In a few hours they detain thousands of individuals. (Pino Machado, "La Batalla de Girón," 67)

At 11:45 p.m., the head of the militia post of Playa Girón, Mariano Mustelier, sees a red light in the sea. Reaching the beach, he and a companion observe signals coming from a boat. Jumping in a jeep, they turn the lights on and off, thinking that it is a boat that has lost its way. A group of the invading forces fires at the jeep and puts out the lights. Mustelier fires back then returns to the militia post: "The North Americans have arrived." Mustelier orders the militia to retreat and to radio the announcement of the invasion to Santa Clara. They fail to get through. (Pino Machado, "La Batalla de Girón," 68–69)

**APR 17, 1961:** Aboard the Blagar, CIA agent Grayston Lynch (Gray) receives a message from Washington: "Castro still has operational aircraft. Expect you to be hit at dawn. Unload all troops and supplies and take ships to sea as soon as possible." On learning that the invading troops will meet resistance in the landing area due to failure to destroy all of the Cuban Air Force, the Blagar moves in close to shore and delivers gunfire support. Brigade troops commence landing at 1:00 a.m.

1:15 a.m. — The Brigade Commander, José Pérez San Román, goes ashore and begins unloading troops and supplies. Local militia discover the landing at once. Some shooting occurs, and the alarm is transmitted to troop and air headquarters throughout the island.

2:30 a.m. — Fidel Castro meets with key advisers to assess the incoming information. They examine the exceptional conditions of the Bay of Pigs: it is isolated from the rest of the island because of the Zapata swamp and only three roads link this area with the rest of the country. They conclude that this is the major attack that they have been expecting and that if there are others they will only be diversionary. Time is a critical factor. The invaders must be prevented from establishing a beachhead that will permit the U.S. to recognize a counterrevolutionary government on Cuban soil and intervene with arms to support it.

3:00 a.m. — Unloading of troops on the Caribe is completed. Unloading of troops from the Atlantico begins.

3:15 a.m. — Fidel Castro is awoken in Havana and told that the enemy is landing at Playa Larga and Playa Girón and that his platoons in the area are resisting. Castro alerts the forces in that section—a battalion of 900 men stationed at the Australia sugar mill on the road to Playa Larga and several platoons of armed militia.

Castro also mobilizes a battalion of militia in Matanzas Province, containing three mortar batteries and orders them to head toward Playa Larga while he dispatches three battalions from Las Villas Province to protect the other two major highways through the swamps. The air force gets orders to take off at dawn and attack the ships facing Playa Larga and Girón. After giving his orders, Castro leaves immediately for the Bay of Pigs. On arriving in the area, he is told that another landing has been detected in the province of Pinar del Rio. He hurries to Pinar del Rio only to find out that the report was false and no landing is taking place. (Johnson, pp. 109–110)

3:30 a.m. — Troops from the Atlantico come under fire.

3:35 a.m. — Castro orders Captain Osmany Cienfuegos to have all the battalions in his sector ready in trucks to leave for battle. A minute later he orders Militia Battalion 339, at the Australia sugar mill, to move toward the coast and the Matanzas School for Militia Leaders to be mobilized by emergency alarm. Advancing down the road from the Australia sugar mill to Playa Larga, prior to the official order, Militia Battalion 339 meets troops of the invading force and a firefight ensues. (Pino Machado, "La Batalla de Girón," 72–73)

3:44 a.m.—Radio Swan calls on the Cuban armed forces to revolt:

> Take up strategic positions that control roads and railroads! Make prisoners or shoot those who refuse to obey your orders! . . . All planes must stay on the ground. See that no Fidelist plane takes off. Destroy its radios. Destroy its tail. Break its instruments. Puncture its fuel tanks.

Throughout the day the station suggests the exile force is succeeding: "The invaders are advancing steadily on every front; Castro's forces are surrendering in droves."

It is reported, incorrectly, that Raul Castro has committed suicide. (Wyden, p. 208; Wise and Ross, p. 56; Penabaz, p. 48)

3:45 a.m.—Fidel Castro calls Battalion 1 of Special Forces of the Rebel Army, located in Cojímar, east of Havana, and orders Captain Aroldo Ferrer to send troops to the Marsh and await orders.

4:00 a.m.—Castro calls Captain Enrique Carreras at San Antonio base twenty miles west of Havana: "At this moment a landing is taking place at Playa Girón. But I want you to sink those ships! Don't let those ships go!" The pilots wait in their planes until 6:30 a.m., about 20 minutes prior to daylight, then take off. (Wyden, p. 251)

4:20 a.m.—In view of the Cuban response, the Brigade commander cancels the landing at Green Beach and puts this force ashore at Blue Beach.

Around 4:30 a.m. the main guidelines for the defending Cuban forces are established: with the order to wipe out immediately the invaders, they will attack from three directions—from the Australia sugar mill, from Covadonga and from Yaguaramas.

At 4:45 a.m. Castro calls the base at San Antonio de los Baños and gives the order to pilot Silva Tablada that two Sea Furies and one B-26 should take off at 5:20 a.m. to attack the boats in the Bay of Pigs and then return to Havana to report. At 5:10 a.m. he calls again: "You have to see if there are planes in the airport [at Girón]. If there are, shoot them, if not, give it to the boats in territorial waters. First objective: planes, second, boats and observe if there are movements of trucks near Girón." (Pino Machado, "La Batalla de Girón," 74–81)

The planes are ordered to take off at 5:00 a.m. and arrive over the target area 20 minutes later. Reaching the invasion area the pilots see seven or eight large boats and an indeterminate number of launches and landing craft. Captain Enrique Carreras Rojas, known by his comrades as "grandfather," launches the first attack. From a height of five to six thousand feet, he descends to fifteen hundred feet and fires four rockets at the "Houston," hitting it in the stern. The two other planes also fire rockets at the "Houston" and hit the target. The ship begins to zig-zag and turns around to reach the mouth of the bay and join the flotilla facing Playa Girón. (Pino Machado, "La Batalla de Girón," 83–84)

After returning to base for more fuel and ammunition, Carreras sets off again in his Sea-Fury for Playa Girón. The "Houston" lies "like a big mortally wounded fish," while the "Río Escondido" is about three miles to the south of the coast. He fires rockets that hit the "Río Escondido" dead center, and it goes up in flames. The "Río Escondido" goes down with 145 tons of munitions, 38,000 gallons of vehicle fuel and 3,000 gallons of aircraft fuel. Attacked by a B-26 with the colors, flag, and insignia of the Cuban armed forces, Carreras' Sea-Fury shoots it down. Another B-26 is shot down by a T-33 piloted by Captain Alvaro Prendes Quintana. ("Playa Girón," Primer Tomo, 91–111)

6:30 a.m. — Cuban air attacks on shipping and Blue Beach commence. Two hundred and seventy men land at Red Beach and immediately come under fire. The landing of the Second Battalion at Red Beach is slowed by motor trouble with the aluminum boats, the only landing craft available. The battalion can only use two out of nine boats for the 20-minute run from the Houston to the beach. The Fifth Battalion, which is to follow the Second, never gets ashore partly due to boat trouble and the lack of initiative of the Brigade Commander. Few supplies get ashore.

The Houston comes under air attack and is hit. It goes aground with about 180 men of the Fifth Battalion on the west side of Bahia de Cochinos—about five miles from the landing beach. During this air attack, machine gun fire damages the LCI Barbara J, disabling two of its engines. After cleaning up the Red Beach area, the troops of the Second Battalion push north about four miles but soon encounter militia forces which prevent them from reaching the southern exit of the road which they were to block.

6:40 a.m. — Friendly air support arrives.

7:30 a.m. — All vehicles and tanks are discharged from LCUs. After landing, the troops push out from the beach as planned. Parachutists of the First Battalion drop, seize the road center of San Blas ten miles northeast of Blue Beach, and establish outposts to the north and east to cover the routes of ingress into the beachhead. They are reinforced by the Third Battalion and a heavy weapons detachment.

8:25 a.m. — The Blagar shoots down a Cuban T-33. All troops are ashore at Blue Beach.

9:30 a.m. — The freighter Rio Escondido is sunk — by a direct rocket hit from a Sea Fury — with ten days reserves of ammunition on board, as well as food, hospital equipment and gasoline. All crew members are rescued and transferred to the Blagar. At Blue Beach, Rip Robertson shouts into his radio, "God Almighty, what was that? Fidel got the A-bomb?" "Naw," responds his CIA colleague Grayston Lynch, "that was the damned Rio Escondido that blew." (Wyden, p. 230)

10:00 a.m. — In the face of continuous air attacks, the contract skipper in charge of shipping radios CIA headquarters that if jet air coverage is not immediately available, the ships will put out to sea. Castro is told that the Matanzas cadet battalion has arrived along with the 225th Militia Battalion. He orders the cadet battalion south to take the town of Palpite. (Wyden, p. 257)

10:00 a.m. — Castro's Militia School Battalion takes the village of Pálpite. Informed by telephone, Fidel Castro replies: "We've won! We've won the war! We've sunk two ships and three launches and if they don't realize that they need to defend Pálpite then they've lost." He then gives the order to Fernández: "Advance and take Playa Larga. Wait for me in Australia (sugar mill)." (Pino Machado, "La Batalla de Girón," 94)

Meanwhile, the rest of the battalion of the Militia School continues toward the coast. At kilometer 21 they receive a prolonged and violent attack with bombs and artillery from two B-26s. At 11:00 a.m., two miles from Playa Larga, they enter into combat with the advance guard of the enemy forces. The planes continue to threaten. The invaders retire in the direction of the sea and set up positions on the beach. The battalion waits for nightfall to avoid the constant attacks of the planes. At 4:00 p.m. the B-26s return and attack with machine gun fire, rockets, bombs, and napalm. The militia battalion receives orders to advance toward Playa Larga. The invading force is dug in with its back to the sea in trenches and behind natural features. The militia has to advance without knowing where they will come into contact with the enemy. Huts set fire to by the invaders make the advancing militia a perfect target. As the militia begins its attack, four T-34 tanks of the Cuban Army appear to support the attack. Bazookas destroy the tracks and door of the first tank, rendering it useless. The second tank is damaged. The tanks are ordered to retreat. All night long the militia battalion fires mortars at the enemy positions. ("Playa Girón," Primer Tomo, 147–156)

At 10:30 a.m., the United Nations Political and Security Commission begins its planned debate on intervention in Cuba, Africa, and Korea. Roa accuses the United States of responsibility for the invasion of Cuba. Stevenson replies that these accusations are false and denies them categorically. What Roa is asking the U.N. to do, he says, is to protect the Castro regime against the natural anger of its own people. In his reply, Roa states that he has not come to the U.N. to ask support in defending Cuba against U.S. aggression but "to accuse the imperialist government of the United States before the conscience of the world." He informs the commission that Lázaro Cárdenas, former president of Mexico has arrived in Cuba that day to stand beside the Cuban people. (Pino Machado, "La Batalla de Girón," 12–20)

10:30 a.m.—Following the air attack which sunk the freighters, all ships in the landing area put out to sea with the order to rendezvous 50 miles off the coast. As ships withdraw, they continue to come under air attack. The freighters Atlantico and Caribe head south and do not stop until intercepted by U.S. Navy 110 and 218 miles respectively south of Cuba. The Caribe is never available for resupply operations while the fight on the beach lasts and the Atlantico does not get back to the rendezvous point until 4:45 p.m. on April 18.

3:30 p.m.—Based on a CIA request which has presidential approval, the JCS directs CINCLANT to establish a safe haven for CEF ships with U.S. naval air cover subject to the restrictions that no carrier ship operate closer than 50 miles from Cuban territory, no aircraft closer that 15 miles, and no more than four aircraft on station at one time. Commanders modify the rules of engagement of enemy aircraft to allow attacks if an unfriendly aircraft makes an aggressive move when headed towards a ship to be protected. (*Rules of Engagement*, p. 2)

Afternoon—Troops of the First and Third Battalions make contact with Castro forces and their outpost situated to the east is pushed back. Starting at about 5:00 p.m. and intermittently thereafter, San Blas comes under attack from forces coming down the road from the north. Radio communications within Blue Beach are nonexistent during the entire operation since the troops have to wade ashore and most of the portable radios get wet and never function thereafter. In the area north of Red Beach, fighting astride the road continues throughout the day, enemy tanks appear in mid-afternoon, and enemy artillery becomes active about 6:00 p.m. B-26 aircraft, rotated over the beachhead throughout the day, sink one gunboat, make strikes against Cuban ground troops at Red Beach, and inflict several hundred casualties, according to report. Four B-26s are lost to enemy T-33 action while the Castro air force loses two Sea Furies and two B-26s to anti-aircraft fire. (Aguilar, pp. 21–24)

At 7.15 p.m., the Cuban Revolutionary Council issues a press bulletin. The bulletin quotes a Council spokesman as predicting that before dawn the island of Cuba will rise up en masse in a coordinated wave of sabotage and rebellion which will sweep communism from our country. In another bulletin on D-Day the Revolutionary Council claims that "our information from Cuba indicates that much of the militia in the countryside has already defected from Castro." (Johnson, p. 129; CRC Bulletins No. 2 and 3, 4/17/61)

On the evening of D-Day the situation looks bad to the President in Washington. U.S. ships might have to be used. "I'd rather be an aggressor than a bum," he tells his brother Robert. (Wyden, pp. 264–265) (Aguilar, pp. 3–35; Johnson, pp. 103–139; Wyden, pp. 173–288)

10:00 p.m.—Castro assesses the situation for the night-time offensive with his advisors. As well as the main attack on Playa Larga, a battalion will advance parallel to the coast along the Soplillar road, take that village, and advance 30 kilometers to the east to be in the rearguard of the invading forces.

Battalion 111 will take that route and Battalion 144 will advance from Soplillar to Caleta del Rosario, a small hamlet on the coast between Playa Larga and Playa Girón, to cut off the retreat of invading troops at Playa Larga. (Pino Machado, "La Batalla de Girón," 106)

At the end of the first day of combat, the Brigade controls two of the three access roads and has the third within its line of fire. The Cuban Air Force has sunk two ships and a landing craft and damaged a ship and three barges. They have also brought down three B-26s and damaged two. A sixth plane crashes in the Nicaraguan mountains near Puerto Cabezas. The invading forces have shot down a Sea Fury and a B-26. A fourth road along the coast exists along which is advancing a reinforced battalion of the Cuban Armed Forces. (Pino Machado, "La Batalla de Girón," 107)

**APR 18, 1961:** Responding to the ease with which the T-33 aircraft is able to destroy the obsolete B-26, CIA leaders issue orders to bomb as many airfields as possible on the ground on the night of April 17-18 with fragmentation bombs. Three B-26s are launched for San Antonio de los Baos but fail to find the target.

3:00 a.m.—The troops north of Red Beach come under heavy attack in the early morning hours. Enemy tanks approach from the north and by 7:30 a.m. the situation is so difficult that the decision is made to move the force to Blue Beach.

4:00 a.m.—Artillery fire begins falling on the troops in the San Blas area and continues most of the day. Artillery fire and enemy pressure on the San Blas troops force a gradual contraction of their position around the town. They attempt a counterattack to the north in the afternoon, but it bogs down in the face of superior forces.

In the early hours of the morning, Fidel Castro receives information of an attack to the west of Havana. He returns to Havana and finds that the information is false. (Pino Machado, "La Batalla de Girón," 112-113)

4:40 a.m.—Castro orders forces from Battalion 180 or 144 to advance through Pálpite to reach Caleta de Rosario to cut the enemy in two. "Finally, Fidel says that Playa Larga must be taken without excuses." (Pino Machado, "La Batalla de Girón," 114-115)

At the air base of San Antonio, Captain Curbelos outlines the day's priorities to the pilots: bomb and fire on Playa Larga, destroy buildings in the hands of the enemy, and prevent the enemy from receiving reinforcements or war materials. "Today's mission will be to support our troops, to harass the enemy, and maintain domination of the air." (Pino Machado, "La Batalla de Girón," 116)

4:40 a.m. — Fidel Castro sends an eight-point order with step-by-step instructions for deploying the tanks. "Point eight is," Fidel says, "Playa Larga has to be taken *sin excusa*." (Wyden, p. 259)

7:00 a.m. — Radio Swan transmits the call to citizens of Havana to sabotage the electrical system by putting on all the lights in houses and connecting all electrical appliances at 7:45 a.m. (Pino Machado, "La Batalla de Girón," 117)

7:30 a.m. — The 2d Battalion at Red Beach reports that its position cannot be maintained without air support for more than 30 minutes. Movement to Blue Beach begins at 9:00 a.m. and is completed by 10:30 a.m. The Red Beach force has suffered about 20 casualties. After reaching Blue Beach, the retreating force has two-hours rest and gets additional ammunition and is ordered back to Red Beach to block the coast road against the forces they engaged in the Red Beach area. They encounter this force west of Blue Beach and heavy fighting ensues. It is not known what occurred, but it is assumed that the invaders succumbed to the superior numbers of Castro forces moving down from the south.

8:24 a.m. — Brigade commander reports that Blue Beach is under attack by 12 tanks and four jets, and requests supplies. Authority to use napalm is granted for use in the beachhead area.

10:10 a.m. — Red Beach is reported wiped out. José Ramón Fernández, Castro's principal troop commander, receives a call from Fidel to advance to Girón. (Wyden, p. 259–260)

10:30 a.m. — Cuban army troops take Playa Larga. Captain Fernández reports that the invading troops have moved toward Girón. "I am moving anti-aircraft and field artillery to Playa Larga to attack toward Girón. I expect to attack in daylight hours." Castro sends orders to Fernández to take Girón by 6:00 p.m. He also orders troops to advance on Girón from the east and to stay four kilometers from there. Fierce combat continues between Covadonga and San Blas. (Pino Machado, "La Batalla de Girón," 121–127)

At the United Nations, the Soviet delegate reads a letter from his country's prime minister to the President of the United States calling for "an end to the aggression against the Republic of Cuba" and reads a Soviet government declaration that "reserves the right—in the event that the intervention against Cuba does not end immediately—to take, jointly with other states, the necessary measures to lend assistance to the Republic of Cuba." At 10:00 p.m. Stevenson reads President Kennedy's reply to Soviet Premier Krushchev denying that the United States is intervening militarily in Cuba and claiming the right of the United States to protect the hemisphere from external aggression in the event of an intervention of outside forces. Stevenson goes on to claim that there is no evidence against the United States and that it is not true that the guerrillas have been brought by planes from the United States piloted by Americans. (Pino Machado, "La Batalla de Girón," 20–25)

12:00 p.m.—Blue Beach is reported under attack by MIG-15s and T-33s, out of tank ammunition, and almost out of small arms ammunition. President Kennedy receives a message from Soviet leader Nikita Khrushchev: "It is not a secret to anyone that the armed bands which invaded that country have been trained, equipped and armed in the United States of America. The planes which bomb Cuban cities belong to the United States of America, the bombs they drop have been made available by the American Government . . . As to the Soviet Union, there should be no misunderstanding of our position: we shall render the Cuban people and the Government all necessary assistance in beating back the armed attack on Cuba. We are sincerely interested in a relaxation of international tension, but if others aggravate it, we shall reply in full measure." Kennedy responds that the United States intends no military intervention in Cuba, but should an outside force intervene the United States will immediately honor its obligations under the inter-American system to protect this hemisphere against external aggression. (Johnson, pp. 151–152)

12:00 p.m.—National Security Advisor McGeorge Bundy reports to the President that the situation in Cuba is not good. "The Cuban armed forces are stronger, the popular response is weaker, and our tactical position is feebler than we had hoped. Tanks have done in one beachhead, and the position is precarious at the others." Bundy informs Kennedy that the CIA will press hard for further air help against a formidable enemy; he recommends that air support be provided because "in my own judgment, the right course now is to eliminate the Castro air force, by neutrally-painted U.S. planes if necessary, and then let the battle go its way." (Pfeiffer, Zapata report, Appendix F)

2:00 p.m. — With only about a third of the Cuban pilots at Puerto Cabezas willing to continue flying, Bissell, for the first time, authorizes American pilots to fly combat missions. Two CIA contract men, Peters and Seig, joined by Cuban pilots head for Cuba. Castro's troops mistake them for friendly aircraft and instead of dispersing they begin to cheer. The six Brigade planes swoop down, dropping napalm and regular bombs, firing rockets, inflicting what is claimed as 1,800 casualties and destroying seven tanks. (Wyden, pp. 235–236)

2:49 p.m. — The JCS directs CINCLANT to prepare unmarked naval planes for possible combat use following a call from Admiral Burke at the White House. This message makes clear that there is no intention of U.S. intervention. The aircraft are readied but permission is not given to use them.

4:00 p.m. — The Essex reports a long line of tanks and trucks approaching Blue Beach from the east. By the end of the day ammunition is very low throughout the beachhead. In spite of heavy fighting, casualties appear to be few among the invaders. At the end of the evening, CIA headquarters asks the Brigade commander, via the Blagar, if he wishes to be evacuated. He replies: "I will not be evacuated. We will fight to the end here if we have to." At the annual Congressional Reception, Robert Kennedy takes aside Senator Smathers of Florida and tells him, "The shit has hit the fan. The thing has turned sour in a way you wouldn't believe." (Wyden, p. 269)

In New York, Lem Jones issues another Revolutionary Council statement: Peasants, workers and militia are joining the freedom front and aiding the rapidly expanding area already liberated by the Revolutionary Command. The Cuban Revolutionary Council announces that the Cuban freedom fighters in the Matanzas area are being attacked by heavy Soviet tanks and MIG aircraft which have destroyed sizable amounts of medical supplies and equipment. (CRC, Bulletin No. 4, 4/18/61; Wyden, pp. 173–288; Johnson 140–153; Aguilar, pp. 3–35)

**APR 19, 1961:** At a meeting at the White House that begins just after midnight, the President, Vice President Johnson, McNamara and Rusk, all in white tie, with General Lemnitzer and Admiral Burke in dress uniform, hear a report on the status of the invasion force. Burke asks the President to "[l]et me take two jets and shoot down the enemy aircraft." The President says no, reminding Bissell and Burke that he has warned them over and over again that he would not commit U.S. forces to combat. Around 1:00 a.m., the President authorizes one hour of air cover from 6:30 to 7:30 a.m. for the invading brigades B-26s by six unmarked jets from the carrier Essex. The jets are not to seek air combat nor attack ground targets. By the morning of April 19, nine of the invading forces sixteen B-26s have been shot down and several of the remaining planes are in poor flying condition. The U.S. Navy Combat Air Patrol and the B-26s miss their rendezvous because the CIA and the Pentagon fail to realize a time-zone difference between Nicaragua and Cuba. Two B-26s are shot down and four Americans are lost.

—Later Radio Havana broadcasts communiqué No. 3: "The participation of the United States in the aggression against Cuba was dramatically proved this morning when our antiaircraft batteries brought down a U.S. military plane piloted by a U.S. airman who was bombing the civilian population and our infantry forces in the area of Australia Central." The radio says that papers found on the American pilots body identify him as Leo Francis Bell. (Wyden, pp. 277–278)

5:50 a.m. — A C-46 carrying 850 pounds of rockets and ammunition, maps, messages and communications equipment, lands on the Girón air strip. After dropping off equipment and picking up messages, maps, and a wounded pilot who had been shot down on D-Day, the plane flies back to Puerto Cabezas, Nicaragua.

6:00 a.m. — Cuban air strikes begin.

6:30 a.m. — The Blagar is due to arrive at Blue Beach escorting three LCUs with ammunition. During the night, however, the captain reports to CIA Headquarters that if low jet cover is not provided, he believes all ships will be lost. Prior to this time, he has requested a U.S. Navy destroyer. The CIA headquarters wire that a destroyer escort is not possible and the captain replies that if he cannot get a destroyer escort in and out of Blue Beach, his Cuban crew will mutiny. CIA Headquarters directs the ammunition ships to stop northern movement and to rendezvous some 60 miles south of the Cuban coast. Beyond an arrangement for another airdrop, no further effort is made to get in ammunition before the final surrender.

7:10 a.m. – 2:30 p.m. — Cuban forces close in on invasion force in Blue Beach sector with tanks and infantry in coordination with air attacks.

9:25 a.m. — Invasion brigade commander San Román reports that 2,000 militia are attacking Blue Beach from the east and west and that his forces need close air support immediately.

10:00 a.m. — Castro's troops enter San Blas and by 11:00 a.m. are approaching the last defenses blocking the road to Girón.

11:57 a.m. — JCS directs CINCLANT to send two destroyers to a position off Blue Beach to determine possibilities for evacuation.

1:12 p.m. — Based on a call from Admiral Burke from the White House, the JCS directs CINCLANT to have destroyers take CEF personnel off the beach and from the water to the limit of their capability.

2:00 p.m. — Landing force surrenders.

2:32 p.m. — Brigade Commander sends last message which is received by the Blagar and reads: "Am destroying all equipment and communications. I have nothing left to fight with. Am taking to the woods. I can't wait for you."

9:00 p.m. — The Revolutionary Council issues its sixth and final bulletin which claims that the recent landings in Cuba have been constantly and inaccurately described as an invasion. "It was, in fact, a landing of supplies and support for our patriots who have been fighting in Cuba for months. . . . [Today's action] allowed the major portion of our landing party to reach the Escambray mountains." (Johnson, p. 172; CRC Bulletin No. 6, 4/19/61)

Allen Dulles meets with former Vice President Richard Nixon and tells him: "Everything is lost. The Cuban invasion is a total failure."

**APR 20, 1961:** Fidel Castro speaks on television for four hours. He explains the reasons for the failure of the invasion: "Imperialism examines geography, analyzes the number of cannons, of planes, of tanks, the positions. The revolutionary examines the social composition of the population. The imperialists don't give a damn about how the population there thinks or feels." (Wyden, p. 295)

—At 7:46 p.m., on direction of the President to Admiral Burke, the JCS directs CINCLANT to take charge of CEF ships and personnel and get them safely to Vieques and to conduct destroyer patrols of Blue Beach tonight for possible evacuation of survivors. Some two dozen brigade members are eventually rescued. (*Rules of Engagement*, p. 4)

**APR 21, 1961:** At a press conference, President Kennedy accepts responsibility for the failed invasion: "There's an old saying that victory has a hundred fathers and defeat is an orphan." "What matters," he says, "is only one fact, I am the responsible officer of the government. " (Wyden, p. 305)

**APR 22, 1961:** President Kennedy charges General Maxwell D. Taylor, Attorney General Robert Kennedy, Admiral Arleigh Burke and Director of Central Intelligence Allen Dulles to study "our governmental practices and programs in the areas of military and paramilitary, guerrilla and anti-guerrilla activity which fell short of outright war with a view to strengthening our work in this area, with special attention to the lessons which can be learned from the recent events in Cuba." (Aguilar, p. 1)

Three days after the defeat of the exile brigade, Radio Swan is still giving cryptic battle orders. As it becomes clear that the invasion has failed, broadcasts state that some members of the brigade have escaped and joined resistance groups within Cuba. As the CIA later reports, the station then ceases to overtly promote insurrection and returns to a calm presentation of straight world news, avoiding all program content designed to incite the Cuban people. The producer of the consolidated program was instructed to present programs with a minimum of emotional content, but to continue the anti-Castro orientation through the selection of news items. (Wise and Ross, p. 356; Taylor Report, Annex 2: CIA, Brief History of Radio Swan)

**APR 23, 1961:** In a televised speech at the Popular University, Fidel Castro analyzes the reasons for the failure of the invasion: "We did not expect that they would send all their forces to one single point because even if that offered more immediate promise, nevertheless it risked a crushing and total defeat;

whereas sending their forces to a number of different points would never have had the characteristic of a crushing defeat, but of many small defeats . . . and they would have been able to maintain the fiction that these groups were still struggling." Castro goes on to state that information the Cuban government had received "that the last shipments of men and arms to Guatemala had arrived, that the enemy was moving, made us increase our vigilance . . . thinking that the moment of the enemy attack was close."

Castro explains that prior to the invasion, Cuban leaders had feared that one of the first things to happen in the case of an invasion would be the attempt to destroy Cuba's small air force. So "orders were given to disperse the planes . . . Two planes could not be together, and all the planes, absolutely, had to be dispersed over a large area." In the April 15 attack, he explains, in the attack on Ciudad Libertad no functioning aircraft were destroyed, only some that were out of service; in San Antonio they destroyed a transport plane and a combat plane; and in Santiago de Cuba, where the field was smaller and there was less possibility of dispersion, they destroyed another combat plane, a Cubana plane, and other civil aircraft.

Following these attacks, Castro continues, "We were alert: we had adopted the practice of sleeping in the afternoon and not sleeping at night; we were waiting . . . We calculated that this was not a harassment attack, because such an attack would have been carried out against industrial targets to try to cause damage; this was an attack . . . with a military objective of destroying our planes. So we concluded that the attack was only hours away. What we didn't know till now was why they didn't invade the same day; why they attacked two days later, which from a military view point was an error, because it put the world on a state of alert; we were already on a state of alert, but we reinforced these measures . . . we mobilized all the combat units."

Castro goes on to discuss the area in which the invasion took place: "We had considered, among the different landing points, that this zone [Bay of Pigs] was a possible landing point." This was an inhospitable area of impassable swamps where the people lived in wretched conditions prior to the revolution and no roads existed through the swamps. Since the revolution, Castro states, three roads across the swamps have been built, the coal miners now earn a decent living, and two hundred teachers were in the area at the time of the invasion carrying out the literacy campaign. "This gives an idea about the place that these people [the invading force and their backers] have chosen.

And it is important, because it shows the imperialist mentality, the opposite of the revolutionary mentality. The imperialist looks to geography, analyzes the number of cannon, planes, tanks, positions; the revolutionary looks to the social composition, that is the people. The imperialist doesn't give a damn about how the people think or feel, they don't care; the revolutionary thinks first of the people, and the population of the Zapata Swamp was entirely with us." (Pino Machado, "La Batalla de Girón," 445–470)

**APR 24, 1961:** National Security Advisor McGeorge Bundy writes a memorandum on the "administrative" causes of the Bay of Pigs disaster. Among the issues he lists are "secrecy" which made deliberation difficult, "too little time" for adequate consideration, the disposal issue, and "whether there can be such a thing as large-scale covert activity in a society like ours." Bundy's final conclusion, however, is that the CIA and the Kennedy White House

> managed to forget — or not to learn — the fundamental importance of success in this sort of effort. Limitations were accepted that should have been avoided, and hopes were indulged that should have been sternly put aside. Many of the lesser mistakes or failures listed above can be explained largely by the failure to recall this basic rule . . . .Success is what succeeds. (Bundy, *Some Preliminary Administrative Lessons of the Cuban Expedition*, 4/24/61)

**APR 26, 1961:** In a four-hour television appearance with more than 1,000 of the captured members of the invading forces, Fidel Castro tells the prisoners: "to execute you, which all our people would agree with, would only shrink our great victory." (*Informe Especial: 1961*)

**APR 29, 1961:** President Kennedy, Robert McNamara and Admiral Burke review a contingency plan on U.S. troop deployment to Cuba. The plan calls for an invasion force of 60,000 men and estimates that "complete control of the island could be obtained within eight days, although it was recognized that guerrilla forces would continue to operate" Two days later, McNamara advises the Joint Chiefs that they should be prepared to implement this plan, but that it "should not be interpreted as an indication that U.S. military action against Cuba is probable." (McNamara, *Cuban Contingency Plan*, 5/1/61)

**MAY 1961:** Responding to a public offer by Fidel Castro to exchange the Bay of Pigs prisoners for farm machinery, President Kennedy begins making phone calls to form the Tractors for Freedom Committee. The Committee, made up of Milton Eisenhower, Walter Reuther, Joe Dodge, and chaired by Eleanor Roosevelt, is privately to attempt to raise the needed money to make the exchange for the prisoners. (Paterson, p. 139)

**MAY 2, 1961:** Manuel Artíme Buesa, one of the leaders of Brigade 2506, is captured near the Covadonga sugar mill in the Zapata swamp with 21 other members of the exile force. (*Informe Especial: 1961*)

**MAY 5, 1961:** President Kennedy presides over a NSC meeting. Significant time is spent discussing post-Bay of Pigs policy. The NSC agrees that "U.S. policy toward Cuba should aim at the downfall of Castro . . . that the United States should not undertake military intervention in Cuba now, but should do nothing that would foreclose the possibility of military intervention in the future." The NSC also discusses a full U.S. trade embargo, organization of a multilateral trade embargo, and relations with the Cuban exiles. (483rd Meeting of NSC, *Record of Action*, 5/5/61)

**MAY 8, 1961:** Arthur Schlesinger sends a memorandum to the Political War-fare Subcommittee of the Cuban Task Force outlining the need to redefine the Cuba issue so as to garner national and international support for U.S. policy. He recommends a widespread public relations strategy targeting Europe, Asia, Africa, and the United States. (Schlesinger, Memorandum, 5/8/61)

**MAY 11, 1961:** The Taylor Committee in its initial report concludes that "a paramilitary operation of the magnitude of ZAPATA . . . exceeded the or-ganizational capacity of the CIA . . . and should have been transferred to the Department of Defense about November 1960. If the transfer of the operation was not approved, it should have been canceled." (Taylor Report, Appendix D, Study of the Anti-Castro Invasion (Zapata)

**MAY 20, 1961:** The Tractors for Freedom Committee sends a telegram to Fidel Castro announcing its intention to raise funds for the release of the prisoners. It reads, "We make this proposal not as a response to a demand for political ransom, but out of common humanity." (Eisenhower, p. 275)

**MAY 22, 1961:** The Committee, made up of Eisenhower, Walter Reuther, Joe Dodge, and Eleanor Roosevelt, are briefed at a Washington hotel by White House aide Richard Goodwin on the extent of the government's involvement. They are assured that Treasury will arrange tax exemption on gifts; the government will arrange transportation for the prisoners, and that their efforts have the full approval of the government. (Eisenhower, p. 277)

A representative team of ten prisoners arrives at 1:00 a.m. and repeats Castro's offer to trade the 1,214 prisoners for 500 "bulldozers." The Committee gives the prisoners a letter for Castro stating that they would raise funds for 500 agricultural tractors on the condition that they receive a list of the prisoners for verification. (Eisenhower, pp. 277-278)

**MAY 24, 1961:** President Kennedy issues a statement that calls upon citizens to contribute funds but adds that "the United States government has not been and cannot be a party to these negotiations." He adds that the government is "putting forward neither obstacles nor assistance to this wholly private effort." (Eisenhower, pg. 281)

**JUN 13, 1961:** General Taylor submits to President Kennedy the report of the Board of Inquiry. The Board's report summarizes the proximate cause of the failure of the invasion as a shortage of ammunition resulting from poor ammunition discipline by the invading forces, the loss of the freighters Rio Escondido and Houston, and the fact that all other ships in the landing area put to sea following the sinking of the freighters and so much of the supplies were not available while the fighting lasted. The Board finds that the causes of the ammunition shortage lay deeper in the plans and organization of this operation and the attitude toward it on the part of government officials.

Failure to destroy Castro's air force was due to restraints placed on the anti-Castro air force to protect the covert character of the operation. So only the B-26 was used as a combat aircraft because it had been widely distributed to foreign countries but it proved no match for the Cuban T-33. Prelanding strikes could only be flown from non-U.S. controlled airfields under the guise of coming from Cuban strips. It was not possible to use non-Cuban bases within easy reach of Cuba and the B-26s required nine hours to turn around for a second mission from Nicaragua. Prohibitions were placed on the use of American contract pilots and there were restrictions on the use of ammunitions, notably napalm. Finally, the Board finds the cancellation of air strikes at dawn on D-Day to be the most serious reason for the failure of the operation since it eliminated the last favorable opportunity to destroy the Castro air force on the ground. (Aguilar, pp. 1-2, 36-38)

The Taylor Board of Inquiry concludes that: "A paramilitary operation of the magnitude of Zapata could not be prepared and conducted in such a way that all U.S. support of it and connection with it could be plausibly disclaimed. . . . By about November 1960, the impossibility of running Zapata as a covert operation under CIA should have been recognized and the situation reviewed. If a reorientation of the operation had not been possible, the project should have been abandoned. However, the Board ends its assessment of the failure of the Bay of Pigs invasion with the conclusion that the preparations and execution of paramilitary operations such as Zapata are a form of Cold War action in which the country must be prepared to engage. If it does so, it must engage in it with a maximum chance of success. Such operations should be planned and executed by a governmental mechanism capable of bringing into play, in addition to military and covert techniques, all other forces, political, economic, ideological, and intelligence, which can contribute to its success." (Aguilar, pp. 40–43)

**JUN 25–30, 1961:** Following weeks of negotiations and political attacks against Kennedy for being willing to trade agricultural equipment for the release of the Cuban prisoners captured in the abortive invasion, the deal falls through and the private group, the Tractors for Freedom Committee (set up to deny plausibly official involvement in the exchange) is dissolved. (Johnson, pp. 244–245)

**JULY 8, 1961:** The CIA disseminates a new covert plan to overthrow Castro. The plan is critiqued in a memo from Arthur Schlesinger to Richard Goodwin, who is serving as head of the Cuba Task Force. Schlesinger argues that the plan will "invest our resources in the people least capable of generating broad support within Cuba." He recommends that "you stop this paper in its present form and demand that it be recast to make political sense." (Schlesinger, *Cuban Covert Plan*, 7/8/61)

**AUG 22, 1961:** Richard Goodwin sends a memo to President Kennedy following a secret meeting with Che Guevara in Uruguay. Goodwin advocates enhanced economic sabotage and covert operations, stepped up propaganda, and quiet military pressure. He also suggests continuing the "below ground dialogue" he has started with Che, and a conscious effort not to appear obsessed with Castro:

"Pay little public attention to Cuba. Do not allow them to appear as the victims of U.S. aggression. Do not create the impression we are obsessed with

Castro—an impression that only strengthens Castro's hand in Cuba and encourages anti-American and leftist forces in other countries to rally around the Cuban flag." (Goodwin, *Memorandum for the President*, 8/22/61)

**OCT 1961:** Lyman Kirkpatrick completes the "Inspector General's Survey of the Cuban Operation," a 150-page report on the Bay of Pigs Invasion. The report is highly critical of almost every aspect of the Agency's involvement with the failed invasion. In particular, it faults the CIA for poor planning and intelligence, misinforming the president, and mistreatment of its Cuban "assets." Among Kirkpatrick's key conclusions:

> The Central Intelligence Agency, after starting to build up the resistance and guerrilla forces inside Cuba, drastically converted the project into what rapidly became an overt military operation. The Agency failed to recognize that when the project advanced beyond the stage of plausible denial it was going beyond the area of Agency responsibility as well as Agency capability.

> The Agency became so wrapped up in the military operation that it failed to appraise the chances of success realistically. Furthermore, it failed to keep the national policymakers adequately and realistically informed of the conditions considered essential for success. . . . (CIA, *Inspector General's Survey of the Cuban Operation*, p. 143)

**NOV 1, 1961:** Richard Goodwin sends a memo to President Kennedy supporting the concept of a "command operation" on Cuba, commanded by Attorney General Robert Kennedy. The reorganization of the "all-out attack on the Cuban problem, Goodwin writes, sets the stage for the decision to launch a new, multifaceted, set of anti-Castro activities, code-named Operation Mongoose. "The beauty of such an operation over the next few months is that we cannot lose. If the best happens we will unseat Castro. If not, then at least we will emerge with a stronger underground, better propaganda and a far clearer idea of the dimensions of the problems which affect us." (Goodwin, Memorandum, 11/1/61)

**NOV 4, 1961:** A major new covert action program aimed at overthrowing the Cuban government is developed during a meeting at the White House. The new program, Operation Mongoose, is to be run by counterinsurgency specialist Edward G. Lansdale. A high-level inter-agency group, the Special Group-Augmented (SGA), is created with the sole purpose of overseeing Operation Mongoose. A memorandum formally establishing Mongoose is signed by President Kennedy on November 30. *(The Cuba Project, 3/2/62)*

**NOV 21, 1961:** Lyman Kirkpatrick provides a copy of the "Inspector General's Survey of the Cuban Operation" to incoming DCI John McCone. In a cover memo, Kirkpatrick characterizes the report as "fair" although "highly critical." He notes that "unfortunately, there has been a tendency in the Agency to gloss over CIA's inadequacies and to attempt to fix all of the blame for the failure of the invasion upon other elements of the Government, rather than to recognize the Agency's weaknesses reflected in this report." CIA officials later criticize the inspector general for providing the report to McCone before giving it to outgoing DCI Allen Dulles. (Memorandum for Mr. McCone, 11/20/61)

**NOV 24, 1961:** Copies of Lyman Kirkpatrick's "Inspector General's Survey of the Cuban Operation" are distributed to DCI Allen Dulles, Deputy Director General C.P. Cabell, Deputy Director of Plans Richard Bissell, Colonel J.C. King, and Jacob Esterline.

**NOV 28, 1961:** CIA Deputy Director Gen. C.P. Cabell calls Lyman Kirkpatrick to order that his report be restricted to a "need-to-know" basis, and not distributed beyond the six CIA officials who have already received it without explicit permission from the director. (Cabell Memo, 11/28/61)

**NOV 30, 1961:** A White House directive is distributed to key officials including Rusk, McCone, McNamara and others establishing a new top-secret operation "to help Cuba overthrow the Communist regime." (Untitled Memo, 11/30/61)

**DEC 1, 1961:** Guidelines are drafted for Operation Mongoose which state that "high authority"—a reference to the President—has determined "that higher priority be given to Cuba," and that General Edward Lansdale, a counter-insurgency specialist, has been designated "Chief of Operations." Lansdale is tasked to develop a program to spark an uprising within Cuba. (Draft Guidelines, 12/1/61)

**DEC 15, 1961:** CIA deputy director C.P. Cabell, furious over Kirkpatrick's report on the Bay of Pigs Invasion, drafts a memorandum entitled "The Inspector General's Survey of the Cuban Operation." In his memorandum he warns that "in unfriendly hands, it can become a weapon unjustifiably to attack the entire mission, organization, and functioning of the Agency." (CIA, *Inspector General's Survey of the Cuban Operation*, vol. 1)

## 1962

**JAN 18, 1962:** CIA Deputy Director of Plans, Richard Bissell, assisted by Tracy Barnes, completes a comprehensive rebuttal to the Kirkpatrick report. Entitled "An Analysis of the Cuban Operation," the 147-page response argues that "a large majority of the conclusions reached in the Survey are misleading or wrong." Key to the failure of the operation, the Analysis states, was the "crucial defeat in the air." But the CIA was not responsible for Castro's small airforce being able to attack the brigade, Bissell writes, putting the blame on Kennedy's decision to cancel airstrikes at the last minute. Defeat in the air "was directly and unambiguously attributable to a long series of Washington policy decisions."

In a lengthy set of conclusions, Bissell blames the defeat on political compromises made to preserve plausible denial of a clandestine operation that could not reasonably be kept covert. In a section titled "Lessons for the Future" he writes:

> What are the lessons for the future to be drawn from this unhappy experience? Perhaps the main one is that the U.S. should not support an operation such as this involving the use of force without having also made the decision to use whatever force is needed to achieve success. If the political decisions necessary to facilitate the effective use of force on an adequate scale, up to and possibly including the overt commitment of U.S. military forces, are too difficult to make, then the operation should be called off unless the odds in favor of success within the politically imposed restrictions are very great. (Bissell, *Analysis of the Cuban Operation*, pp. 25,26.)

**JUN 19, 1962:** At the urging of Attorney General Robert Kennedy, the Cuban Families Committee asks attorney James B. Donovan to represent them in their efforts to secure the release of the Bay of Pigs prisoners. The Committee is made up of parents, brothers and wives of prisoners taken during the invasion seeking their release. (James B. Donovan, "Chronology—'The Bay of Pigs,'" James B. Donovan Papers)

**JUL 3, 1962:** James B. Donovan meets with Robert Kennedy and is assured that his efforts to secure the release of the Bay of Pigs prisoners is in the national interest and that any negotiation with Castro would not be in violation of the Logan Act. (James B. Donovan, "Chronology— 'The Bay of Pigs,'" James B. Donovan Papers)

**AUG 31, 1962:** James B. Donovan meets for four hours with Castro in the Presidential Palace and details his proposal of medicine and baby foods but no cash or tractors.

**SEP 1, 1962:** Talks continue and Castro responds that the Cuban government has accepted the following proposals: payment of $2,925,000 in cash for 60 prisoners released April 14, 1962; and payments of indemnification of $25,000,000 worth of foods and medicines for the rest of the Brigade. Castro says the Cuban government will prepare a list of products needed by Cuba. (James B. Donovan, "Chronology—'The Bay of Pigs,'")

**OCT 10, 1962:** On his third trip to Havana, Donovan presents Castro with a memo of agreement stating that Castro will receive drugs at wholesale prices, baby food, banking arrangements to guarantee payment and an "act of faith delivery of 20 percent of goods before any prisoners are released. Castro objects to the offer on the grounds that, among other things, he wants an additional 35 percent taken off the drug prices and more than 20 percent payment before release. (Cuban Families Committee, *Memorandum of Agreement*, Havana, Cuba, October 1962)

**DEC 7–8, 1962:** Robert Kennedy meets with the Pharmaceutical Association and members of the baby food industry to discuss the need for voluntary contributions. He emphasizes the "U.S. responsibility for the prisoners, their courage, the non-strategic value of drugs," and "assure[s] them that [the] sight of returning prisoners would silence criticism." (James B. Donovan, "Chronology—'The Bay of Pigs,'" James B. Donovan Papers)

**DEC 21, 1962:** James Donovan and Fidel Castro sign an agreement in which the Cuban Families Committee "agrees that it will . . . supply the Government [Cuba] with medical and pharmaceutical supplies . . . before July 1st, 1963", and in return "every effort humanly possible will be made [by both parties] to effect the exchange of the prisoners upon delivery of the first shipment."

For its part, "the Government states its intention that the materials supplied under the agreement satisfy the indemnity fixed by the Revolutionary Tribunals which passed judgment, upon the happening of the Bay of Pigs." (Fidel Castro and James B. Donovan, *Memorandum of Agreement*, 12/21/62)

**DEC 23-24, 1962:** Castro releases the Brigade prisoners to the United States and they arrive at Holmstead Air force base in Florida. He also allows 1,000 relatives of the prisoners to leave by ship, the *African Pilot*, "as a Christmas bonus." Twenty-three United States citizens remain in prison in Cuba. Castro says that, after 80 percent of shipments of $53 million in food and medicine arrives, he will examine each case individually. (James B. Donovan, "Chronology—'The Bay of Pigs,'" James B. Donovan Papers)

# —Source Key

*Editor's Note*: This chronology is based on hundreds of recently declassified CIA, State Department and Pentagon documents, as well as Cuban, Cuban exile, and U.S. sources. Citations to selected sources are:

Aguilar = Operation ZAPATA: *The Ultrasensitive Report and Testimony of the Board of Inquiry on the Bay of Pigs, Introduction by Luis Aguilar*, Aletheia Books, 1981.

Bissell = Richard Bissell, *Reflections of a Cold Warrior*, Princeton: Yale University Press, 1996.

Blight = James G. Blight and Peter Kornbluh, *Politics of Illusion: The Bay of Pigs Invasion Reexamined*, Boulder, Co: Lynne Rienner Publisher, 1998.

Eisenhower = Milton Eisenhower. *The Wine is Bitter: The US and Latin America*. New York: Doubleday and Co., Inc., 1963.

Garthoff = Garthoff, Raymond L. *Reflections on the Cuban Missile Crisis*. 2nd ed. Washington, D.C.: The Brookings Institution, 1989.

Gleijeses = Piero Gleijeses. "Ships in the Night: The CIA, the White House and the Bay of Pigs." *Journal of Latin American Studies*, Feb. 1995, pp. 1–42.

Hunt = Howard Hunt. *Give Us This Day*. New Rochelle, NY: Arlington House, 1973.

*Informe Especial: 1960 and 1961* = Centro de Estudios Sobre America. "Crísis de Octubre: Cronología." *Informe Especial*, 1960 and 1961.

Johnson = Haynes Johnson. *The Bay of Pigs: The Leaders' Story of Brigade 2506*. New York: W. W. Norton and Co., 1964.

Molina, "Diario de Girón" = Gabriel Molina, "Diario de Girón," Editora Politica, *La Habana*, 1983.

NYT = *New York Times*

Penabaz = Manuel Penabaz. "We Were Betrayed: A Veteran of the Cuban

Invasion Speaks Out." *U.S. News and World Report*, Jan. 14, 1963, pp. 46–49.

Jack Pfeiffer = Jack Pfeiffer. The Taylor Committee Investigation of the Bay of Pigs. November 9, 1984.

Phillips = David Atlee Phillips. *The Night Watch*. New York: BAllentine, 1977.

Paterson = Thomas Paterson, *Contesting Castro*, Oxford University Press, Oxford, 1994

Pino Machado, "La Batalla de Girón" = Quintín Pino Machado, "La Batalla de Girón: Razones de una Victoria," Editorial de Ciencias Sociales, *La Habana*, 1983.

"Playa Girón," Primer Tomo = "Playa Girón: Derrota del imperialismo," first of four volumes, Ediciones R, *La Habana*, 1961.

Ranelagh = John Ranelagh. *The Agency: The Rise and Decline of the CIA*. New York: Simon and Schuster, 1987.

*Rules of Engagement* = U.S. Navy. *Memorandum for Record. Rules of Engagement Operations Bumpy Road.* pp. 1–4. Annex 29 of Taylor Committee documents, n.d.

Schlesinger = Arthur M. Schlesinger, Jr. *A Thousand Days: John F. Kennedy and the White House.* Boston: Houghton Mifflin, 1965.

*Sequence of Events*, 5/3/61 = CIA. *Sequence of Events (D-2 to D+2) and Organization and Operation of Command Post.* Annex 22 of Taylor Committee documents, 3 May 1961, pp. 1–11 and maps.

Soley and Nichols = Lawrence C. Soley and John S. Nichols. *Clandestine Radio Broadcasting: A Study of Revolutionary and Counterrevolutionary Electronic Communication.* New York: Praeger, 1987.

Szulc = Tad Szulc. *Fidel: A Critical Portrait.* New York: Avon Books, 1986.

Taylor Board, First Meeting, 4/22/61 = First Meeting of General Maxwell Taylor's Board of Inquiry on Cuban Operations Conducted by CIA. 1400–1800 hours, 22 April 1961, Quarters Eye.

Taylor Report = General Maxwell B. Taylor, *Paramilitary Study Group Report*, June 13, 1961.

Thomas = Evan Thomas. *The Very Best Men: The Early Years of the CIA*. New York: Simon and Schuster, 1995.

Wise and Ross = David Wise and Thomas B. Ross. *The Invisible Government*. New York: Random House, 1964.

Wyden = Peter Wyden. *Bay of Pigs: The Untold Story*. New York: Simon and Schuster, 1979.

# —Acknowledgments

This book is the result of a major historical project on the U.S. invasion of Cuba initiated, encouraged and supported by Kimberly Stanton and the John D. and Catherine T. MacArthur Foundation. My profound appreciation and respect goes to her and Kennette Benedict and Adele Simmons of MacArthur, as well as to Smith Bagley, Janet Shenk, Steve Cobble, and Jeanne Mattison of the Arca Foundation for the ideas, imagination, and resources provided to the Archive's Cuba Documentation Project. I also thank Andrea Panaritis and the board of the Christopher Reynolds Foundation for their positive encouragement and important support.

Brown University's James Blight and his critical oral history collaborator, janet Lang, provided the intellectual leadership and organizational framework for the Bay of Pigs work. I am also grateful for the sage advice and wisdom of Professor Philip Brenner who has been, since the beginning of time, a mentor, friend, and respected colleague.

The appreciation of the Archive's Cuba Documentation Project also extends to our Cuban, and Cuban-American, colleagues: the historians, analysts, diplomats, and participants who have supported the concept of comparing memories and records of this controversial history, as seen so differently from each side of the Florida straits. We look forward to a time when the Cuban equivalent of these documents can be declassified and examined—to advance an historical and mutual understanding between two nations.

The National Security Archive is an extraordinarily talented, thoughtful, and gracious group of professionals. Legal counsel Kate Martin used her vast powers of persuasion to convince the CIA that, after thirty-seven years, the time to declassify the Kirkpatrick report had come. James Woodard, a gifted Goliath of a researcher/writer, tirelessly handled the editing, proofreading and computer work necessary to transform a top secret document into a readable book. Special credit goes also to Master of the Web John Martinez for his on-line magic, and to Robin Rone for her indexing skills; and to Duncan Levin for his sharp eyes, as well as to Sue Bechtel, Mary Burroughs, Kristin Altoff, Will Ferroggiaro, Kate Doyle, and Malcolm Byrne for the ideas, support and patience they lend to the Cuba project every day. To Tom Blanton go the accolades for making the Archive a dynamic, effective, and always challenging player in the debate over U.S. foreign policy.

The CIA, the most controversial agency in the making and implementation of that policy, deserves credit for finally declassifying the Inspector General's report. A number of Agency officials—Steve White, Brian Latell, Michael Warner and Lee Strickland—as well as other members of the CIA's Historical Review Program, are to be commended for their efforts to overcome the institutional pathology of secrecy that has kept much of the CIA's fifty-year history of covert operations hidden from public view. A special thanks is due to Jacob Esterline and Jack Hawkins for sharing their acute memories of this historical event.

For their role in making these documents available for public viewing, thanks goes to Andre Schiffrin and his capable staff at the New Press, including Jessica Blatt, Grace Farrell, and Madeleine Gruen. The commitment of The New Press to public interest publishing provides an unparalleled service to disseminating information of this kind.

Finally, I want to extend my gratitude to my Uncle Sol, Aunt Betty, and my cousin Martin for constant support (and last minute copy editing), and to my parents, Hy and Joyce, and sisters Jane and Kathe and Grandmother Eve for their avid interest in this work. My very special appreciation goes to Cathy A. Silverstein, who has contributed so much to the positive energy and peace-of-mind necessary for completing this project. And, of course, a loving acknowledgment to the one and only Gabriel Kornbluh who makes every day a day to remember.

Peter Kornbluh
June 10, 1998

# —Index

26 July Movement, 68, 106, 118, 267

Acheson, Dean, 2

Action Movement for Recovery. See MAR

Air strikes, 38, 41, 53, 56–57, 126–127, 129, 138–39, 145, 150, 167–68, 225–28, 263–64, 282, 296–98, 304–10. See also covert operations: air

American forces in combat, 98–99; 31–18

Analysis of the Cuban Operation (Bissell rebuttal), 13–14, 134–76, 244–48, 250, 257, 328–29. See also Inspector General's Survey of the Cuban Operation

Arbenz, Jacobo, 8

Armas, Castillo, 152

Artime Buesa, Manuel Francisco, 67–68, 90, 132, 171, 222, 268, 272, 297

assassination, 8–10, 16, 264–65, 294, 298. See also CIA-Mafia plot to assassinate Castro

Barbara J (boat), 56, 84–88, 230–32, 311

Barnes, C. Tracy, 2, 13, 15, 248, 252, 256, 295

Bay of Pigs invasion, 1, 38–40, 303–19; aftermath, 99–102, 145–49, 320–30; and arrests, 52, 323; and assassination, 8–10, 264–65; as overt operation, 142–44; Blue Beach force, 39–41, 98, 305, 309–10, 316; budget, 105, 109; command structure, 42–47, 134–35, 179–214; consequences of cancellation, 55; errors in judgement, 135–37; failure or, 405, 11–12, 54–56, 99–102, 137–45, 240–42, 265–66, 320–30; Green Beach force, 39, 309; guerrilla warfare, 51–53, 116–26, 129, 260–61; overview, 24–41; Red Beach force, 39–40, 310, 315; security, 95–98; strategy for, 16–17, 47–58, 149–53

Bender, Frank, 70–72

Bender Group, 70–71

Berger, Sandy, 17

Bissell, Richard, 1, 2, 4, 6–10, 13–15, 239, 248, 252, 261–66, 267, 274, 278, 288, 291, 294–95, 299, 301, 305–29; and assassination of Castro, 8–10, 264–65. See Also Analysis of the Cuban Operation; Bay of Pigs invasion (aftermath)

Blagar (boat), 84, 87–88

Brigade 2506, 2, 4, 38–41, 136, 140, 175, 177–78, 221, 275, 280, 289–90, 319, 330; and capture, 323; release of, 330. See also Bay of Pigs invasion

Bundy, McGeorge, 5, 14, 50, 156, 184, 287–88, 291, 305–10, 316

Cabell, Pierre Charles, 9, 15, 35, 239, 256, 299, 305–15

Carrillo Hernandez, Justo Asencio, 67, 132, 171

Castro Ruz, Fidel, 1, 3, 5–7, 270, 275, 279, 304–30; as assassination target, 8–10, 16, 264–65, 298; meeting with James Donovan, 328–30; meeting with Richard Nixon, 267; U.S. attitude toward, 6–8, 110–15, 258–59, 267, 289. See also Castro regime

Castro Ruz, Raul, 9, 224, 273, 307

Castro regime: analysis of, 110–15, 119; proposed actions against, 112–14, 258–61, 267–68, 289

CIA-Mafia plot to assassinate Castro, 8–10, 265, 294. See also assassination; Castro Ruz, Fidel

covert operations, 15–17, 116–132, 148–49, 259; air, 78–82, 125, 138–40, 225–28, 279; maritime, 31, 82–89, 228–32, 275; training, 88, 90–95, 232–34

CRC, 142, 144, 148, 156, 215, 217, 220–21, 295. See also political opposition

Cuba: and Soviet Union, 4; and U.S. diplomatic relations, 280–81, 283; assessment of, 16, 110–15, 258–61; overflights, 37–41

Cuba Task Force. See WH/4
Cuban Freedom Fund campaign, 32–33
Cuban Missile Crisis, 4, 16
Cuban Revolutionary Council. See CRC

Davies, Albert, 209
Department of Defense. See DOD
Department of State. See DOS
DOD, 28, 141, 143, 179, 274, 283
Donovan, James, 328–30
DOS, 27, 141, 144, 146, 179, 266
Drain, Richard, 208
Draper, Theodore, 2
Droller, Gerard, 212
Dulles, Allen, 4, 11, 15, 151, 231, 255–56, 267, 269–70, 273, 278, 284, 292, 299

Edwards, Sheffield, 9, 265, 274
Egan, Frank, 210–11
Eisenhower, Dwight D., 2, 23–24, 35, 154, 267, 269–70, 274, 280–81, 283–84
Elena Eduardo, Martin, 72
Esterline, Jacob, 6–8, 10, 156, 207, 238, 258–66, 268, 285–86, 298, 301–320
executive branch. See Kennedy administration

FRD, 27–29, 31, 33–34, 42, 66–75, 91, 118, 215–24, 268–69, 295. See also political opposition
Frente Revoluionario Democratico. See FRD

Goodwin, Richard, 3, 325–27
Gray, David W., 155–57, 286
Guatemala, 2, 215, 271; training bases, 97, 227, 233, 259, 268, 277–80, 286, 290. See also military training
Guevara, Ernesto ("Che"), 3, 8, 315–27

Hawkins, Jack, 2, 6, 8, 16–17, 156, 210, 238, 258–66, 301
Hunt, E. Howard, 212–13, 270–72

INRA, 68
Inspector General's Survey of the Cuban Operation, 1, 2, 6, 10–13, 15, 17, 23–132, 241–56; 320–330. See also Bay of Pigs invasion (aftermath); Analysis of the Cuban Invasion

JCS, 53, 56, 113, 144, 149, 157, 286–87, 294
Joint Chiefs of Staff; See JCS

Kennedy administration, 16, 50, 139–40, 144–46, 155, 261–63, 285, 287, 291. See also Bay of Pigs invasion (aftermath)
Kennedy, John F., 1–3, 13, 16, 50, 155, 261–63, 273–74, 276, 278, 283–85, 287, 291–93, 296–97, 305–30
Kennedy, Robert, 9, 16, 151, 301, 315
King, J.C., 7, 9, 239, 264–65, 267–69
Kirkpatrick report. See Inspector General's Survey of the Cuban Operation
Kirkpatrick, Lyman, 1, 11, 15, 237, 239–50, 256, 320–30. See also Bay of Pigs invasion (aftermath)

Lynch, Grayston, 4, 309

Maceo Mackle, Antonio Jaime, 72, 132, 290
Mafia, 8–9, 265, 294. See also CIA-Mafia plot to assassinate Castro
Mallard, John, 208
MAR, 71
McCone, John, 11, 13, 15, 237, 239, 248, 253, 324–26
Miami, 58–63, 96, 107, 216–17. See also WH/4 (Miami operating base)
Military training, 29–30, 32, 34–35, 90–95, 186, 268–69; in the U.S., 34–35, 274, 277–79, 301. See also Guatemala (training bases)
Miro Cardona, José, 72, 129, 132, 156, 171, 217, 220, 222–23, 298, 303
Montecristi Movement, 67, 106
Movement to Recover the Revolution. See MRR
MRR, 68, 268, 271, 288–89

National Agrarian Reform Institute. See INRA
Nixon, Richard M., 7, 261, 267, 276–77

Operation Mongoose, 16, 326–27
Operation Trinidad, 157, 259–62, 286,
    293–94
Operation Zapata, 6, 11, 14, 157–66, 294–
    95, 302; adequacy of, 167–68; and
    political opposition, 215–224; Cuban
    support for, 169–73; organization, 179–
    214. See also Operation Trinidad; Bay
    of Pigs invasion

Phillips, David A., 210, 270–71, 273
photography, 168–69
plausible deniability, 13, 17, 47, 55–56, 99,
    138, 141, 143, 147–48, 265–66. See also
    Bay of Pigs invasion (aftermath)
political opposition, 103–106, 118, 132,
    215–24, 295. See also CRC; FRD
Program of Covert Action Against the Cas-
    tro Regime (CIA paper), 24, 103–109,
    269–70
propaganda, 27–28, 31, 38, 104, 107–108,
    269, 290. See also Radio Swan

Radio Swan, 27–28, 31–32, 37–38, 104,
    107, 131, 271, 273, 275–76, 280, 296,
    305, 320. See also Swan Island; propa-
    ganda
Ray Rivero, Manuel Antonio, 71, 132, 171–
    72, 223
Reichardt, Bernard, 212
Reynolds, Robert, 213
Rubio Padilla, Juan, 71
Rusk, Dean, 155, 261–62, 297, 305–27

sabotage, 172–73, 269, 286, 292–93, 297
Sanchez Arango, Aureliano, 68–69, 218
Scapa, Jacob, 211–12

Schlesinger, Arthur, 3–5, 184, 289, 295–96,
    299
Sea Gull (boat), 89
Seehafer, Ralph, 209–10
Special Group, 48–49, 157–58, 175, 195,
    227, 278. See also NSC
Sparks, Ernest, 211
Stanulis, Edward, 207
Stevenson, Adlai, 3, 305
Swan Island, 27–28, 31–32, 38, 269–71. See
    also Radio Swan

Taylor Board, 10, 237, 242, 250, 253–54
Taylor, Maxwell, 10, 137, 151, 179, 237, 242,
    249
Tejana (boat), 84
Toomey, Philip, 210

United Nations, 2–3, 276–77, 304–305
Urrutia y Lleo, Manuel, 171

Vandervoort, B.H., 213
Varona Loredo, Manuel Antonio, 67–69,
    71, 132, 219, 290, 298

Wasp (boat), 84
WH/4, 6, 8–9, 25, 27, 29–30, 36, 154–58,
    227, 238, 258–66, 268; and Havana
    station, 63–64; and strike force con-
    cept, 29–32; and sabotage, 36–37; bud-
    get, 24, 27; Development Projects
    Division, 27, 43–44, 75, 78–81, 227–28;
    intelligence support, 63–66, 187–88;
    Miami operating base, 58–63, 188–93,
    250–51; organization, 42–44; 179–214;
    paramilitary unit, 60–65; plan of opera-
    tions, 30–31
Wyden, Peter, 4

# —About the
# National Security Archive

**Peter Kornbluh** directs the Cuba Documentation Project at the National Security Archive. In 1996, he filed the Freedom of Information Act request that resulted in the declassification of the CIA's Inspector General's report on the Bay of Pigs. He is the author of many articles on U.S. policy toward Cuba, and coeditor of several books on U.S.-Cuban relations, including *The Cuban Missile Crisis, 1962*, and *Politics of Illusion: The Bay of Pigs Invasion Reexamined*. Since 1990, he has taught at Columbia University's School of International and Public Affairs.

**The National Security Archive** is a public interest research library located at George Washington University in Washington D.C. Founded in 1985, the Archive now holds "the largest collection of contemporary declassified national security information outside the U.S. government," according to the *Christian Science Monitor*. A project of the Fund for Peace, the Archive serves scholars, journalists, Congress, and citizens by obtaining and disseminating internal U.S. government records that are indispensible for informed public debate. The Archive has become "a 'Nexis' of national security," according to the *Washington Journalism Review*. "A state-of-the-art index to history."